Traversing
the Inner Seas

Traversing the Inner Seas

Contacts and Continuity in and around Scotland, the Hebrides, and the North of Ireland

Christian Cooijmans
Editor

Alan Macniven
John R Baldwin
Associate Editors

The Scottish Society for Northern Studies
Edinburgh 2017

Published in Scotland by
The Scottish Society for Northern Studies
c/o Scandinavian Studies, School of Literatures, Languages and Cultures,
University of Edinburgh
50 George Square, Edinburgh EH8 9LH

www.ssns.org.uk

ISBN 978-1-5272-0584-0

The Scottish Society for Northern Studies gratefully acknowledges grants towards
the publication of this volume from:

The Strathmartine Trust   The Marc Fitch Fund

Front Cover
Left: Iona Abbey (mango-two-friendly, Shutterstock.com)
Centre: Ben More from the Sound of Mull (Christian Cooijmans)
Right: Dun Carloway, Isle of Lewis (Christy Nicholas, Shutterstock.com)

Back Cover and Spine
Scotia Regnum (detail) – William Hole, 1607
(Reproduced with the permission of the National Library of Scotland)

Cover Design: Christian Cooijmans

Printed by Shetland Times
Gremista, Lerwick, Shetland, ZE1 0PX

CONTENTS

CONTRIBUTORS

Jamie Barnes (University of Glasgow)

Jamie Barnes is a PhD Candidate in archaeology at the University of Glasgow. His doctoral research centres on the Viking Age carved stones of the British Isles, with hogbacks and hammerhead crosses being his primary focus. Other research interests include the Viking Age in the Eastern Baltic Sea region, the Archaeology of Scotland, Insular art, Early Christian archaeology, and Pictish carved stones. For the latter, he has authored several statement of significance reports.

Christian Cooijmans (University of Edinburgh, Editor)

Christian Cooijmans is a PhD Candidate in Scandinavian Studies at the University of Edinburgh, from which he also holds an MSc in Medieval History. His current research focuses on the reach and repercussions of early Scandinavian movement across the Carolingian Empire. Besides all things Viking, Christian's academic interests include the digital humanities, as well as premodern historiography, palaeography, and manuscript studies. He currently also serves as a committee member for the Scottish Society for Northern Studies.

Clare Downham (University of Liverpool)

Clare Downham is a Senior Lecturer in Irish Studies at the University of Liverpool. Her research focuses on links between Britain and Ireland between the years AD 800 and AD 1200. Her first book, *Vikings Kings in Britain and Ireland*, was published in 2007, and her latest monograph, *Medieval Ireland, AD 400-1500*, is forthcoming with Cambridge University Press.

Nicholas Evans (University of Hull)

Dr Nicholas Evans is currently a Teaching Fellow at the University of Hull, having taught and researched at universities in Ireland and Scotland, and having undertaken a PhD on the Irish chronicles at the University of Glasgow. His research interests are medieval identities, perceptions of the past, and the political, social, and ideological development of societies in Britain and Ireland, with a particular focus on the written sources. He has published *The Present and the Past in Medieval Irish Chronicles* (2010) and *A Historical Introduction to the Northern Picts* (2014).

Ryan Foster (University of Edinburgh)

Ryan Foster worked as a geography teacher, before going on to complete an MA in Lake District Studies from Lancaster University. His thesis investigated whether the place-name element *-thwaite* in the Lake District was evidence of a Viking *landnám*. In 2013, he was awarded the Northern Scholars Scholarship for a PhD in Scandinavian Studies at the University of Edinburgh, where his research involves the study of Old Norse shieling names during the Viking Age.

Ian Peter Grohse (Volda University College)

Ian Peter Grohse is an Associate Professor of Medieval History at Volda University College, Norway. He received his PhD (2014) from the Norwegian University of Science and Technology in Trondheim and his MA (2009) from the Humboldt-Universität zu Berlin. Grohse's research focuses on Northern Europe in the central and late Middle Ages. Beyond his published works on Norwegian-Scottish relations, he has recently addressed matters of royal minority ('Fra Småbarns Munn – Myte og Propaganda', *Historisk Tidsskrift*, forthcoming) and anti-foreign movements in the late-medieval Realm of Norway (e.g. 'Nativism in Late Medieval Norway', *Scandinavian Journal of History*, forthcoming).

Mark A Hall (Perth & Kinross Culture Trust)

Mark A Hall works as a museum archaeologist, currently for Perth & Kinross Culture Trust and presently on secondment in the Outer Hebrides working on the Udal Project. His interest in medieval material culture focuses on early medieval – mainly Pictish – sculpture, the cult of saints, and gaming and reception studies (especially cinematic portrayals of the medieval past). He has published several articles and books, including *Playtime in Pictland: The Material Culture of Gaming in Early Medieval Scotland*, 'Board Games in Boat Burials: Play in the Performance of Migration and Viking Age Mortuary Practice', '"Pennies from Heaven": Money and Ritual in Medieval Europe', *The Lewis Chessmen: New Perspectives* (with David Caldwell), and 'The Meigle Stones: A Biographical Overview'. He is active on several committees and working groups, including the Scottish Strategic Archaeology Committee.

John Holliday (An Iodhlann, Tiree)

Dr John Holliday trained as a cell biologist before switching to medicine. He has worked for the Pintupi people in the western deserts of Australia and was then the GP on Tiree for thirty years. As well as collecting the place-names of the island, he has an interest in the social history of the community. He has written *Tiree: War amongst the Barley and the Brine* with Mike Hughes (2012), 'A Name without a Place, a Place without a Name: The Isleborg Puzzle (again)' (*West Highland Notes and Queries* 4:2, 2016), and *Longships on the Sand* (2016). He is currently working on a geographical history of the island.

Arne Kruse (University of Edinburgh)

Dr Arne Kruse is Senior Lecturer in Scandinavian Studies at the University of Edinburgh. His research and publications focus on coastal place-names in Scandinavia, medieval Scandinavian names in Scotland, and the more recent Scandinavian names of North America. His studies are typically interdisciplinary in nature, using place-names alongside history and archaeology to sketch patterns of distribution and widen our perception of the relationship between Scandinavian settlers and other languages and cultures.

Alan Macniven (University of Edinburgh)

Dr Alan Macniven is Senior Lecturer and Head of Scandinavian Studies at the University of Edinburgh, where he is responsible for a range of courses on the languages, literatures, and cultures of modern and medieval Scandinavia, including Old Norse and Viking Studies. His research to date has focused on Scandinavian place-names in Scotland and their value as indicators of cultural change. Alan's recent monograph, *The Vikings in Islay: The Place of Names in Hebridean Settlement History*, was shortlisted for the Saltire Society's Research Book of the Year award in 2016. The follow-up, *Scotland's Viking Namescapes*, is scheduled for release in 2018.

Alexandra Sanmark (University of the Highlands and Islands)

Alexandra Sanmark is Reader in Medieval Archaeology at the Centre for Nordic Studies, University of the Highlands and Islands. Her PhD thesis, from University College London, focused on the Christianisation of Scandinavia. More recently, she has been researching Viking-Age assembly sites as part of *The Assembly Project*, funded by HERA. The results of this project will be published in her forthcoming book, *Viking Law and Order: Places and Rituals of Assembly in the Medieval North*, published by Edinburgh University Press.

PREFACE

The title of this volume, for which we can thank its editor, Christian Cooijmans, is clearly descriptive of its content. But it also serves as an invitation to reflect on the various other journeys – in time, space, and outlook – that have led to its publication. First and foremost, it is brought to you at a point where the publisher, the Scottish Society for Northern Studies, prepares to celebrate fifty years of learned activity. Although the significance of this span may not be immediately apparent to younger readers, this is a journey whose relative brevity in historical terms belies some pretty fundamental changes in the practice and dissemination of academic research. Founded in Edinburgh in 1968, the Society is dedicated to the idiosyncrasies and interplay of the cultures of the North – broadly defined as Scotland and Scandinavia along with their diasporas and close neighbours. Over the past five decades, these themes have been pursued diligently on a number of fronts. Through regular day-conferences and workshops held around the country, we have striven to promote new research offering fresh insight into the history, archaeology, ethnology, literature, and place-names of the northern world.

The Society's peer-reviewed, paper journal, *Northern Studies*, soon to reach its fiftieth issue, has been the main vessel for the broader dissemination of this work. In common with the wider academic community, however, we are also beginning to embrace the benefits of computer-mediated communication and the internet. As we hurtle ever onwards into the digital age, our annual newsletter for members has evolved through a brief phase and an e-mail circular into a suite of online outlets, including a growing social media profile and a website packed with digital resources. Anyone making the journey to www.ssns. org.uk will find our back-catalogue scanned, archived, and available at no cost and very little effort beyond a few swipes or clicks and perhaps a short wait for the files to download.

Whilst moving boldly into this digital future, Northern Studies is nevertheless reluctant to cut all ties with the world of physical publishing. For the time being, we remain convinced by the tangible benefits of the printed word, and for the foreseeable future – and the ire, no doubt, of tablet manufacturers – committed to the production of physical books. With this goal in mind, our ongoing mission to create and share knowledge will also continue to prioritise our steadily growing body of monographs. These edited volumes of individually authored chapters and articles are developed, as a rule, from the high-point of the Society's calendar, our extended residential conferences. From the very beginning, the Society's residentials have sought to spotlight the heritage of as broad a sweep of the country as possible. In so doing, they have taken the membership to a range of locations from Castlebay to Forres, from Lerwick to Newton Stewart, and even, on occasion, across the border or the North Channel. Wherever possible, close collaboration with local groups has been secured to help deliver a more holistic experience of local culture and traditions. Through careful planning, expertly guided tours of local heritage landscapes and collections are dove-tailed with public addresses, recitals, and performances of poetry, music, and song to foster the congenial and stimulating milieu within which both lectures and wider discussions can flourish. By the time Northern Studies' residential conferences have run their course, the seeds of the ideas presented have not only been planted, but grown and blossomed.

Over the past five years, the Society has hosted three hugely successful residentials. With scores of speakers from a dozen different countries addressing audiences reaching into three figures, these have been truly cosmopolitan affairs. I have been fortunate enough to participate in all of them as both organiser and speaker. In 2012, we visited the Isle of Islay for four enlightening days of presentations on themes easily justifying the strapline *From Gall to Gael and Gallowglas*. Although based in Ionad Chaluim Chille Ìle (The Columba Centre), with its sweeping vistas across Loch Indaal, sessions were also held in the majestic Round Church in Bowmore, the conference suite at Ardbeg Distillery, and the impressive medieval-modern fusion of Ballygrant Community Hall. Visits to the high-cross at Kildalton, the churchyard at Kilchoman, the *Carragh Bhàn* traditionally thought to mark the burial of Manx king Godred Crovan, and the MacDonald residences on Eileann Mòr in Loch Finlaggan and at Dunyvaig were balanced with a traditional Ceilidh in Ballygrant, and a more formal whisky-tasting session at Ardbeg.

In 2014, the destination was Northern Ireland, this time for five days devoted to the *Hinterlands of the North Irish Sea*. The conference was co-hosted by Geography and Environmental Sciences at the University of Ulster. Although based at the University's Coleraine and Magee campuses, sessions in the Bushmills Community Centre, where we received a warm welcome from the Bushmills Historical Society, along with a number of venues in Port Stewart and Port Rush, provided a thorough introduction to the 'Triangle Town' area. In addition to the pristine streets and city walls of Legenderry (!), our excursions covered Ballycastle Bay, Bonamargy, and Fairhead. Visits to the late medieval and prehistoric fortifications of Dunluce and Dunseverick were brought to life by scholars involved in their excavation and conservation, as was our final trip to Belfast City airport via the stunning Antrim Coast and Carrickfergus Castle.

In 2015, another five-day residential saw the Society relocate to the isles of Coll and Tiree. Based at An Cridhe on Coll, which provided both conference facilities and accommodation, the weather remained unseasonably fine throughout, allowing us to strike out temporarily to Tiree. Although limited to one day, this expedition was particularly fruitful, taking in a session at the Community Hall, An Talla, with access to the historical centre, An Iodhlann, and visits to the Hynish Centre and Ballephuill Bay. Back on Coll, time at An Cridhe was supplemented with sessions at the Hebridean Centre at Ballyhaugh (courtesy of Project Trust) and at Breachacha Castle, kindly hosted by the present custodians, the Maclean-Bristols. Guided tours of the island revealed the unadulterated beauty of the landscape, as well as the secret life of the corncrakes at the RSPB reserve near Arinagour.

The main connecting factor in all three of these events was undoubtedly the sea. Ever-present as a calming backdrop on our tours and sometimes during the lectures and talks themselves, it leant the proceedings a soothingly atmospheric quality. As someone who was responsible for the logistics of these conferences, it became clear to me at a relatively early stage that the root of that atmosphere was not the water *per se* but the relative difficulty of access it presented to the modern traveller, and the glorious isolation that comes along with it. However, when standing at the coast at Fair Head in County Antrim, or high on the hillside at Dùn Bhoraraic on Islay, or Ben Hogh on Coll, the intervisibility of these places with their neighbours was striking, and went a very long way to explaining their historical connections. Until the days of health and safety and vehicle licences curtailed less reliable forms of transport, the 'Inner Seas' between the Hebrides, Ireland,

and the Scottish mainland were far less of a barrier to communication than a fast-track towards it – a pre-modern superhighway for people, resources, and ideas. And it is for this feeling of interconnectedness and commonality of formative experience that we have decided to explore all three conferences in this single volume.

The ten papers included here are representative of the best given. They may come to you shorn of the cultural and social matrix from which they originally sprung to life, but they have been greatly expanded and improved with the help of double-blind peer review and subsequent reflection. Viking-themed topics dominate, which is only to be expected for an area comprising the western hub of *Scotia Scandinavica*. Between them, they also cover the full range of source materials and approaches which have come to be associated with Northern Studies, touching on history, archaeology, place-names, and more. Given the cross-disciplinary nature of most of the papers, however, the distinctions are not always especially clear-cut! To help you navigate this material, we have decided to group them into three sections, reflecting their geographical relationship with the area under discussion: Those which concentrate on a specific locality *along* the Inner Seas; those whose observations span a number of different locations *across* them; and those where a significant part of the discussion plays out in the lands *beyond*.

Focusing primarily on discrete locations along the Inner Seas, we have John Holliday, Alan Macniven, and Mark Hall. The volume opens with Holliday's presentation of the fruits of his life-long collection of place-names and folk culture in the Gaelic-speaking environment of Tiree. Despite the overwhelming Gaelic bias in recent material, his discovery of a widespread, and potentially blanket Old Norse substrate are thought-provoking to say the least. The idea of a complete Norse take-over even further south in the Hebrides is explored by Macniven in his overview of Scandinavian place-names in Islay. Contrary to previous assumptions, his work suggests that the Viking impact on Islay was as transformative as it had been in the Northern Isles. This opening section concludes with Hall's investigation of the origins and importance of board games in the region through to the high Middle Ages, including their use at Lordship centres like Finlaggan.

With perspectives linking multiple locations within the Hebrides, or exploring their connections with the North of Ireland, the Scottish mainland and beyond, we have Claire Downham, Ryan Foster, Nicholas Evans, and Alexandra Sanmark. Downham begins with a review of later insular accounts of Scandinavian activity in the west, including the Battle of Clontarf, arriving at surprising conclusions. Foster follows with an analysis of place-names in the Outer Isles building on the Old Norse generics *sætr* and *ærgi*. His combination of onomastics with physical geography points to distinct and contrasting agricultural associations, and the potential adoption of those encountered at *ærgi* sites from a preceding Celtic tradition. Evans then demonstrates how an innovative analysis of the Irish annals can be used to trace lines of transmission of news, and with it influence in general. This second section is brought to a close by Sanmark's presentation of the Scottish dimension of a major European survey of Scandinavian administrative centres, known in Old Norse as *þing* or 'assembly' sites, whose many findings include a checklist of key attributes by which hitherto unrecorded examples might be identified and verified.

The final section is devoted to the area beyond the Inner Sea, with contributions from Arne Kruse, Jamie Barnes, and Ian Peter Grohse. Kruse opens with an exciting new perspective on the origins of the medieval kingdom of Norway, or *Laithlind* as it appears in the Irish annals. Barnes then considers the provenance and cultural import of the so-called 'Hammerhead' crosses of the Viking Age, sculptures whose apparent cultural hybridity appears to blend pagan and Christian symbolism. The volume concludes with Grohse's investigation of the Viking-like raids of later-medieval Hebrideans on Orkney, pointing to a longstanding continuity of practice connecting the latter-day Gaels of the Long Island with their Scandinavian ancestors, and showing that old habits really do die hard.

So there you have it, three main themes, ten authors, and a multitude of insights. We hope you enjoy them. If you are not already a member of the Society, we also hope that they will inspire you to consider joining via the website, attending one of our residentials yourself, and contributing either directly or indirectly to the next edited volume.

Alan Macniven
Kinghorn

Acknowledgements

The editor would like to express his sincerest gratitude to the twelve anonymous peer-reviewers who donated their time and expertise to this volume, and to Alan Macniven and John Baldwin for their invaluable support throughout the publication process. Additional recognition goes to David Caldwell, Peder Gammeltoft, Arne Kruse, Sarah Thomas, Colin Grant, and Laura Keizer for their assorted aid and advice.

The publication of this volume has been made possible with the generous financial aid provided by Lt Cdr Tom Bell, the Strathmartine Trust, and the Marc Fitch Fund.

Christian Cooijmans
Edinburgh

Along
the Inner Seas

Longhouses Below the Waves: A Place-Name Analysis of the Norse Settlement of Tiree

John Holliday[1]

[Tiree] had a more ancient name, *Rioghachd bar fo thuin*, i.e. 'The kingdom whose summits are lower than the waves' [...] the lowest and flattest country perhaps in Scotland.[2]

Introduction

It has long been a received wisdom that the Norse share of township and farm names declines from almost 100% in Orkney to 33% in Islay.[3] From this analysis, dubbed the 'Ratio Approach' by Macniven, it may have been concluded that Tiree was more lightly and more briefly settled by the Norse than islands to the north and west, fitting in a geographically appropriate way somewhere on a scale between Lewis and Islay. But a new and more detailed analysis of the place-names of Tiree has suggested that a strong Scandinavian influence was felt on the island, an influence that possibly lasted into the fifteenth century.[4]

A Feast of Place-Names

Tiree has not detained the archaeologist long. A number of finds were made in the eighteenth century: two coin hoards dated to AD 970-80 were dug up near Iron Age forts and are now held in the British Museum;[5] a probable Norse gold armlet was found but is now lost; and a pagan Viking burial was discovered in Cornaigbeg.[6] In the only modern excavation on the island, MacKie found a Norse comb in the walls of the Iron Age broch Dùn Mòr Bhalla.[7]

In addition, Tiree has been handed only a minor part on the stage of the Norse literary canon. In the eleventh-century poem *Magnúsdrápa*, Bjǫrn *krepphendi* described one of the overseas expeditions of Magnús

---

1 I would like to thank, in particular, Dr Berit Sandnes and Professor Richard Cox for their help with this analysis.
2 *Old Statistical Account* x, 393.
3 Macniven 2007.
4 Holliday 2016a.
5 Graham-Campbell 2011, 255.
6 *Old Statistical Account* x, 402.
7 MacKie 1974, 143-44 and plate XIIIg.

berfœttr, king of Norway between 1093 and 1103. In it he wrote, '[...] rǫnn rauð Tyrvist innan teitr vargr í ben margri [...]' [In Tiree the happy wolf coloured his tooth red in many a wound], whilst listing an additional number of Norse island names along the west coast of Scotland, such as *Ljóðhús* ('Lewis') and *Ívist* ('North Uist').[8] This demonstrates that the skald's audience was familiar with the principal landmarks of the Norse expansion zone in the North Atlantic. As will be discussed later, the *Orkneyinga saga* also contains a reference to Tiree.

But if the evidence from the disciplines of archaeology and skaldic poetry is a thin gruel, the field of onomastics has given us a feast. 18 km long and 1 to 10 km wide, Tiree is a 'Goldilocks' island for the single researcher; not too big and not too small. It has a heterogeneous landscape and has been the most fertile of the Hebrides, with a population that reached 4,453 in 1831 during the kelp boom.[9]

In 1768, the fourth Duke commissioned James Turnbull to survey and map the post-medieval landscape of the island in exquisite detail in advance of the introduction of the crofting system, and the present Duke has inherited one of the best archives of estate records in Scotland. The strong oral traditions of the island also attracted fieldworkers from the School of Scottish Studies in Edinburgh between the 1950s and 1970s, and only Uist has more recorded material.[10]

The first surveyors of the Ordnance Survey (OS) paid a great deal of attention to Tiree, collecting 676 place-names at a density of 7.8 names/km². While less than that in many of the Northern Isles, this was more than any other substantial Hebridean island; Coll has a density of 4.6, whilst Skye has 2.1. Unlike the rest of the Hebrides, the whole of Tiree was mapped at the 25 inch scale because of its widespread cultivation. This work by the OS on Tiree rescued twenty-three names with Norse elements, names, such as Tràigh Thallasgair on Craignish, which would otherwise have become extinct.

A notable contributor to their fieldwork on the island was John Gregorson Campbell, who had been inducted as the Church of Scotland minister of Tiree and Coll in 1861. Campbell, a noted folklorist, comfortable with written and spoken Gaelic, seems to have been very

---

8   *Norsk-Islandske Skjaldedigtning*, 405, quoted in Jennings and Kruse 2009, 81.
9   *Argyll Estate Instructions*, xxix.
10   The Tiree recordings have all been digitised and catalogued. They are available on http://www.tobarandualchais.co.uk.

interested in the work of the Ordnance Survey, and was noted as an informant for 88% of the names recorded by them on the island. But because of (or possibly despite) Campbell's attention, the cartographers gaelicised Tiree's Scandinavian toponyms enthusiastically; Port Aoir became Port Daor and translated as 'Dear Port', whilst Cnoc Charrastaoin made it to the Name Book as 'Christian Knoll' before someone put a pen through the entry.[11] We must therefore treat the orthography of the Norse names collected by the OS on Tiree with some caution.

Over the last thirty years, the author has collected over 3,300 Tiree place-names, adding some 126 probable Scandinavian names to the 129 collected by the OS.[12] This allows us to study medieval settlement on Tiree in greater detail than earlier scholars. However, we must remember that the surviving forms of many Norse place-names in the oral tradition are likely to have changed considerably over 800 years of transmission by Gaelic speakers. We can demonstrate this with names that do have early recorded forms: e.g. Cowelche in 1541[13] > Co' Dhèis today, and Mannawallis in 1390[14] > Manal today. Names that are still widely used – Ruaig, Balabhaig, or Haoidhnis – vary little between respective sources. But some names were hanging by a very fragile thread, known only to one or two people. For example, the OS collected Loch Earblaig in 1878, but the forms Loch Eallabal and Loch na Buaile were collected by the author from the only two islanders who still knew a name for the place. These 'last gasp' names, 14% of the total, are highly likely to have drifted away from their original form. Most fieldwork on Tiree has been with islanders born in the 1920s and 30s, and it is noticeable how the place-name vocabulary of the island has shrunk in the last twenty years, something also noted by Cox on Lewis.[15]

TÌR AN EÒRNA: THE LAND OF BARLEY

As well as its sunshine and wind, Tiree is well known for its past fertility and its ring of shell sand beaches. The island's exceptional cropping, particularly its barley harvest, were noted by many writers.

---

11 *OS Name Book* 28, 59.
12 Holliday 2016a.
13 *Exchequer Rolls of Scotland* 17, 527.
14 *Acts of the Lords of the Isles*, 29.
15 Cox 2002, 14.

Walker reported in 1764 that two years previously a crop of barley was harvested thirty-five days after sowing:

> Tirey has always been remarkable among the western Islands for its Fertility and the Goodness of its Crops [...] Of the 30,720 Acres which the island is supposed to contain, there appears, by the nearest Guess, to be fully two thirds or 20,000 Acres cultivated, which is a much larger Proportion than is to be found in any of the Islands.[16]

In 1541, Tiree was taxed at 686 bolls of bere, while Coll paid only 150.[17] There are eleven probable Norse enclosure names ending in -gerði, 'fence, field', or -geiri, 'a triangular piece of land', on Tiree,[18] compared to three in Carloway.[19]

Independent farming units on Tiree need access to four agricultural zones: the shore for seaweed collection, machair for winter grazing, in-bye land for arable and settlement, and sliabh for summer grazing, as well as peat and turf cutting. At least fifteen shieling place-names have survived on Tiree, and despite the island's small size it appears that a form of transhumance was practised. Gaelic (ScG) Àirigh Fhionnlaigh, 'the shieling of Finlay', in Caolas, is one of a number of Tiree shieling names less than a kilometre from the site of the closest mapped post-medieval settlement. In Assynt and on Fair Isle, many shielings have also been identified close to their parent settlement, although this does not appear to fit the standard transhumance model.[20] These may be examples of 'home shielings' in tathfolds just outside the head dyke.[21] Thirteen Tiree shieling names were coined with the ScG àirigh, one, on the remote slopes of Beinn Haoidhnis, with the Old Norse (ON) *sætr*,

---

16   McKay 1980, 181.
17   Dodgshon 1998, 68.
18   Àigeir, Boidhegeir, Cròinigeir, Croisgeir, Fòirneigeir, Gèisgeir, Groidegear, Hùnasgeir, Innisgeir, Òinegeir, and Sodhaigeir (see Holliday 2016a).
19   Cox 2002, 173, 268, 380.
20   Macgregor 1986, 98.
21   See Tait 2012, 303; Dodgshon 2015, 135.

whilst two were possibly coined with the ScG to ON loanword *ærgi*.[22] There has long been a debate as to why settlers in parts of the Norse expansion zone loaned *ærgi* alongside, or in place of, *sætr*, and it may be that further study of the Tiree material could help to shed light on this subject.[23]

The lack of a substantive harbour was regarded as a problem in the early modern period.

> [...] all the boats in Tiree, great and small, are hauled up high and dry [...] from the end of November to the end of March. During this time, the island is nearly locked up from all intercourse with other countries [...].[24]

However, eight small inlets with names ending in ON -*bryggja* ('landing place'), an uncommon generic in the rest of the Hebrides, survive.[25] It is plausible that Tiree's location on the sea lanes to the south, as well as the island's rich harvests of barley, made it a crucial part of Scandinavian naval and trading routes.

TIREE BEFORE THE NORSE

Tiree is likely to have been on the frontier of the kingdom of Dál Riata, with Picts inhabiting regions to the north and west. An annalist, writing several centuries *post factum*, described a visit to Tiree by Saint Comgall in 565. There, the saint encountered a 'Pictish' raiding party ('multi de Pictonibus').[26] Although the language of the early church on Tiree must have been Gaelic, we cannot assume that it was the only language spoken on Tiree before the arrival of the Norse, as the

---

22   From the Scottish Gaelic *àirigh*: Àirigh a' Mheannain, 'the shieling of the young goat'; Àirigh Fhionnlaigh, 'the shieling of Finlay'; An Àirigh Bhòidheach, 'the beautiful shieling' (two of); Corrairigh, 'the pointed shieling' (twice); Àirigh Fhearchair, 'the shieling of Farquhar'; Àirigh an Fhraoich, 'the shieling of the heather'; Àirigh Mhonaidh, 'the shieling of the moor'; Àirigh Fhearchair, 'the shieling of Farquhar'; Bothag na h-Àirigh, 'the bothy of the shieling'; An Àirigh, 'the shieling'; Àirigh na h-Aon Oidhche, 'shieling of the one night'. From the Old Norse *sætr*: Siadar. From the Gaelic to Old Norse loanword *áirge*: Caltronsairigh and possibly Hyring (see Holliday 2016a, 121).
23   Fellows-Jensen 1980, 64-74; Grant 2003, 128-39.
24   *New Statistical Account*, 217.
25   Borabrig, Cròdhabrig, Dusbrig, Eibrig, Ìbrig, Lìbrig (twice), and Sgràbraig.
26   *Vitae Sanctorum Hiberniae* 2, 11; Reeves 1854, 235.

dominance of the *Scotti* may have represented elite change as much as widespread migration, and the Picts made significant military advances in the 740s.[27]

The principal feature of pre-Norse culture on Tiree was its strong ecclesiastical presence. Later accounts of the saints' lives present Brendan as leading the way with the establishment of a church in 541, followed by Comgall of Bangor with a monastery.[28] The more contemporaneous *Vita S. Columbae* recorded both Columba and Findchán setting up monasteries on the island.[29] Of these the Columban Magh Luinge was recorded as still functioning in 774.[30] Insofar as the islands have currently been identified, Tiree is mentioned by Adomnán in five passages (I:19, I:36, II:15, II:39, and III:8), compared to Mull in three (I:22, I:41, and II:22), Skye in two (I:33 and II:26), Coll in two (I:41 and I:22), and Islay in one (II:23).[31] Three possible *annaid*-names, perhaps representing early church sites, have survived on Tiree: Annahynich (1509) in Hynish, Tauberbafanit (1654) in Sandaig, and Cnoc na h-Annaide (ScG, 'the hillock of the *annaid*') in Caolas.[32] The latter is surrounded by a cluster of ecclesiastical place-names, suggesting a substantial religious centre. Four Norse headland names – navigational and therefore often thought to be early – reference churches.[33] And Tiree, despite the difficulties of sculpting the local gneiss, has twelve examples of early medieval Christian sculpture at six sites, compared to nineteen carvings at twelve sites on Islay, nine carvings at six sites on Colonsay, six carvings at five sites on Mull, and none whatsoever on Coll.[34]

Tiree has six surviving chapel names in *cill* with intact dedications to saints from the sixth to the eighth century: Cill Brìghde, Cill Choinnich, Cill Fhinnein (twice), Cill Moluag, and Cill Tunnain. Four of these six names have no surviving structures, but have been stitched into the landscape of the island by its oral tradition. It is now accepted that some *cill*-names were coined in the late medieval period, and that

---

27   Downham 2015, 190.
28   Reeves 1854, 236.
29   *Life of Columba*, 279, 423.
30   U775.1: 'and Conall of Mag Luinge [...] died', in *Annals of Ulster*, 229.
31   *Life of Columba*; MacDonald 2010, 219-36.x
32   See Márkus 2012, 521; Holliday 2016a, 58.
33   Three of *Circnis* and one of *Crisnis*. See Holliday 2016a, 306, 318.
34   Fisher 2001, 123-25, 136-40.

dating them is therefore problematic.[35] Given the evidence of a strong influence of the early Church on the pre-Norse landscape, however, some Tiree *cill*-names are surely good candidates to be regarded as early medieval in origin. This is another area that could benefit from further research.

NORSE SETTLEMENT

As elsewhere in the Hebrides, accepted pre-Norse place-names are thin on the Tiree ground. Watson's reconstruction of the pre-Celtic name of the island itself, *Heth*, is the only undisputed toponym in this category.[36] By virtue of their onomastic obscurity and topographical significance, Cadruim (a striking rock complex with cup markings) and Taelk (an Iron Age fort site) may also have been coined in the Pictish Iron Age. Of the three Tiree monastic names recorded in the early Gaelic literature (Artchain, Bledach, and Magh Luinge), it is significant that none have reliably survived to modern times, although the location of one, Teampall Phàraig on the Kenavara headland, is still visible.

One compelling piece of evidence for the disruptive nature of Scandinavian settlement is the apparent lack of any Gaelic or pre-Norse place-names incorporated into the Norse names of Tiree as *ex nomine* onomastic units.[37] The usual understanding of a disruptive settlement process is the (violent) displacement of one language group by another. However, a community's internal dislocation within Tiree has also caused a substantial loss of traditional knowledge of the landscape in recent times. This was demonstrated by fieldwork in two townships. Balephetrish was cleared of its inhabitants in the nineteenth century to create a large farm that was recrofted in 1922. Fieldwork along a two-mile length of coastline added only two names to those collected by the Ordnance Survey. In Sandaig, eighty-two names were added to a similar length of shore. The indigenous — but resettled — population of Balephetrish had considerably less knowledge of their 'new' shoreline than the undisplaced crofters of Sandaig. It may be warranted to say, therefore, that we do not have to assume that the entire population of

---

35   Butter 2007, 214; Márkus 2012, 537.
36   Watson 1993 [1926], 85 (e.g. *Ethicam terram* in *Life of Columba* I:19 – see Broderick 2013, 12).
37   Kruse 2005, 161.

the island had been led away in chains to account for the scarcity of pre-Norse place-names.

It is plausible that the unlocated castle of Isleborgh was in fact the Castel Loch Hyrbol shown on Blaeu's 1654 map on ScG Loch an Eilein, 'loch of the island', in Heylipol. Its name may derive from ON *íla* 'well or spring' + ON *borg* 'fort'. This fits in with one reconstruction of the well-documented but complex development of the township name Hilibol.[38]

THE SEQUENCE OF NORSE SETTLEMENT

A map of proposed primary Norse farms on Tiree has been reconstructed using well-known criteria: a simplex, unqualified form, topographical nature, relation to a neighbouring secondary settlement, early appearance in rentals, and survival as a settlement name to the present day. Because of the 'four zones' needed by an independent farming unit, later settlement of Tiree was achieved by subdividing the island into smaller 'slices' or triangles. Names in *bólstaðr* in the Norse expansion zone are regarded as secondary settlements, and it may be the case that names containing *ból* play a similar role on Tiree.[39] Figure 1 shows a model of Norse primary and secondary settlement.

On Shetland, secondary Norse settlement was on less-favoured ground, away from the coast.[40] This does not seem to have been the case on Tiree; secondary settlements developed as sizeable and independent units, often eventually worth more than their 'mother' estates. For example, the 1541 Crown Rental valued Gott (presumed primary) as two merklands and Kirkapol (presumed secondary) as six.[41] This implies that later Scandinavian settlements were carved out by powerful new arrivals, equal to the early settlers. This is plausible, considering Tiree was on the route of ninth and tenth-century Viking expeditions heading towards the Irish Sea. This is quite unlike secondary settlement of the more isolated Iceland.

---

38   Holliday 2016b, 5-9.
39   Gammeltoft 2001.
40   Ibid., 202
41   Johnston 1991, 81, 84.

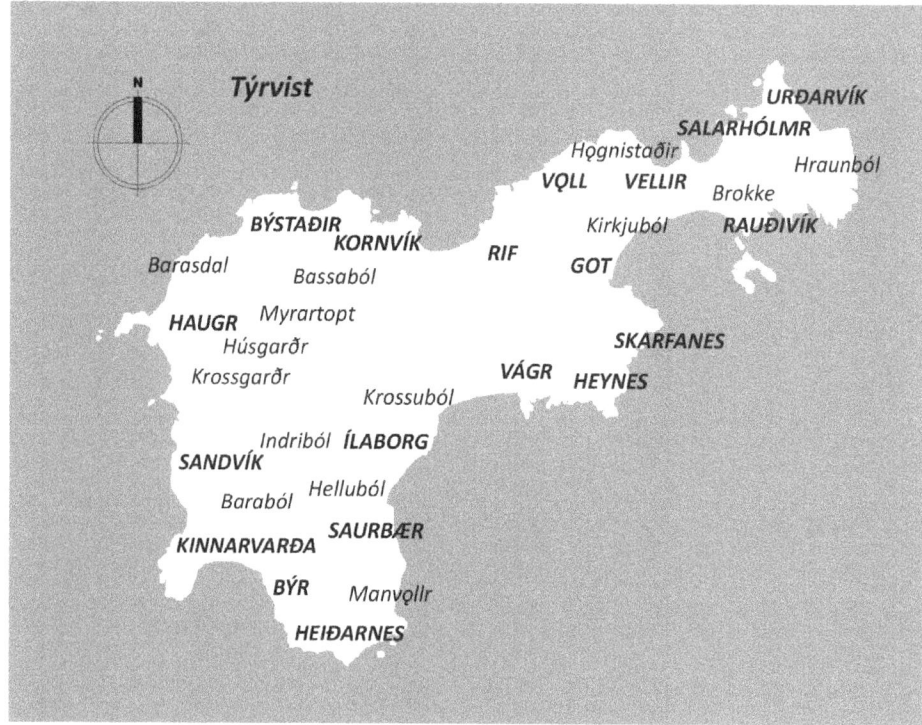

Figure 1: Norse primary (capitals) and secondary (lower case) settlements on Tiree.

'PEAK VIKING'

A key question is the intensity of Scandinavian settlement on Tiree during the period of 'peak Viking'. The 1509 Crown Rental lists thirty-one farming townships, twenty-two of which (71%) are Norse in origin.[42] In addition, four of the nine townships with Gaelic names today have Norse settlement or enclosure names within their boundaries. For example, Caolas contains the farm name Raonabol and the enclosure name Àigeir. All parts of the island appear to have been settled to some degree.

Detailed fieldwork is also available from Carloway on Lewis[43] and the island of Barra.[44] Carloway has 250 Norse names from a non-habitative

---

42   *Exchequer Rolls of Scotland* 13, 216-17.
43   Cox 2002.
44   Stahl 1999.

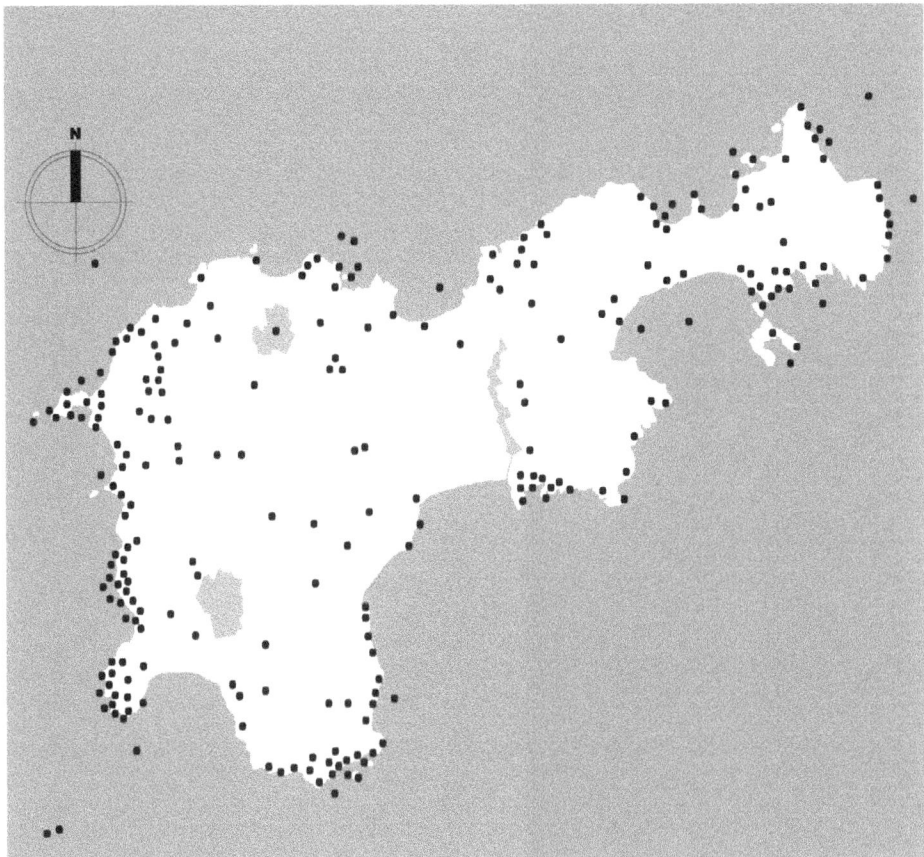

Figure 2: The distribution of probable Norse place-names on Tiree.

onomasticon of 3,806,[45] Tiree has 255 from 2,350, and Barra 196 from 2,627.[46] A glance at the first edition OS map shows how strongly the major landscape features of Tiree (and, to some extent, Barra) have been gaelicised, with an absence of stream, hill, and lake names ending in -gro (ON *gróf*), -val (ON *fjall*), and -vat (ON *vatn*). This is not necessarily because of Tiree's low-set geomorphology; the summit of Heastaval on Lewis is only 91 m, lower than Beinn Haoidhnis on Tiree at 141 m. This landscape re-gaelicisation can be interpreted, instead, to have been the result of intense competition for resources between Tiree's tightly-

---

45   Cox 2002, 112.
46   Analysis by the author.

packed farming townships, leading to the renaming of hill grazings, beaches, and watercourses. For example, the island's highest hill is likely to have had a Norse navigational name in *fjall*, but was renamed to Beinn Haoidhnis and then subdivided into Beinn Mhanail and Beinn Bhaile Phuill. It is therefore reasonable to conclude that a visitor to the Norse Hebrides would have noticed relatively little difference in Scandinavian settlement intensity between the three islands.

THE DURATION OF NORSE SETTLEMENT

The *Orkneyinga saga* has well-recognised limitations as a historical source,[47] but the text and context of chapter sixty-six implies that the Norse language was understood in at least one important household on Tiree in 1135. The saga relates how Sveinn Ásleifarson was forced to seek sanctuary on the tiny island of Egilsay:

> Lét byskup Svein þar vera um jólin, en eptir þat sendi byskup hann til Suðreyja í Tyrvist til þess manns, er Holdboði hét ok var Hundason; var hann þar hǫfðingi mikill ok tók allvel við Sveinni. Dvalðisk hann þar um ventrinn ok var vel virðr af allri alþýðu.

> [The bishop let Svein stay there for the rest of the Christmas season, and afterwards sent him to Tiree in the Hebrides to a man called Holbodi Hundason, a great chieftain, who gave him a good welcome. He stayed there over the winter and everyone thought well of him.][48]

The place-name evidence on Tiree supports a lengthy transition from Norse to Gaelic language dominance. Many of the Norse names of Tiree appear to have been well-'curated' by subsequent Gaelic-speaking islanders. We can only admire the fidelity of transmission in so many of the Norse names, for example Grianatobht, Naomhaig, Tòrasdal, Roisgal, Sgairinis, Sgaracleit, and Sgibinis. Numerous Norse loan words made their way into the island's onomasticon, as in ScG Cachaileith nam Fidean ('gate of the spot uncovered at high-tide'), derived from ON *fit* ('meadow land on the banks of a firth'). Many probable Norse place-names acquired the Gaelic definite article, as in An Ciaraig. 298 Gaelic

---

47   See Jesch 2010, 153-73.
48   *Orkneyinga Saga, 155*; Translation from *History of the Earls of Orkney*, 127.

place-names on Tiree contain a Norse *ex nomine* onomastic unit, as in Bacanan Mòra Ghorraig ('the big dunes of *Gorraig*'). Several Norse place-names have not been lost but transferred; Creachasdal, likely to be a name in ON *dalr*, 'valley or area of ground', is now an islet name nearly 1 km offshore.

The modern Gaelic pronunciation of Tiriodh by islanders is quite different from its pronunciation by regional Gaels, a very unusual situation in the Hebrides. Local people pronounce *Tìr-eadh* ['t'i: ʲəɣ] with first syllable stress and a terminal velar fricative. This has been strongly influenced by the Norse form *Týr Vist* with its emphasis on the specific first element. Regional Gaels today often say *Tir-ì-dhe* [ˌt'i 'ri: ʲə] with second syllable stress, which ultimately derives from the pre-Norse Gaelic *Tìr Iath*, and its emphasis on the specific second element.[49]

It was Watson who first pointed out that the Gaelic name for someone from Tiree – *Tiristeach* – derives from the ON *Týrvist*.[50] This contains the Old Irish habitation name suffix *-ach* at the end of the Norse name for the island. This implies that Gaelic speakers on Tiree were using the Norse name to describe the island for a substantial period.

Translation names occur when a place-name is accurately translated from one language to another. These are generally rare and are most likely to develop during a period when a community is fully bilingual.[51] An example on Tiree may be Coirceal from ON *korki*, 'oats' (itself a loan from the ScG *coirce*),[52] with ON *hóll*, 'rounded hill', alias ScG Druim a' Choirce ('the ridge of the oats').[53]

A greater-than-expected number of Tiree Norse place-names have a terminal *-an* or *-ain*. Some of these might be Norse to Gaelic loan words that have taken the Gaelic plural, diminutive, or locational suffix *-an*. Na Tangan and Tràigh nan Gilean are taken to be examples of this type.[54] But another possibility is that some contain a post-nominal (or post-positional) bound definite marker: the suffix *-inn* (m.), or *-in* (f.), which is common in Orkney, involving 12% of the names.[55] Examples

---

49   Ailean Boyd, pers. comm.
50   Watson 1993 [1926], 85.
51   Sandnes 2010, 45.
52   Cleasby and Vigfusson 1874, 351.
53   Holliday 2016a, 181, 312.
54   Ibid., 174, 337.
55   Sandnes 2010, 321.

from Orkney include Ayrean from ON *ærgin* ('the shieling(s)'),[56] Croan from ON *króin* ('the enclosure'),[57] Hewin and Hewing from ON *haug(r) inn* ('the mound'),[58] and Fursan from ON *forsinn* ('the waterfall').[59]

There are thirteen possible examples of the post-nominal bound definite marker on Tiree, including:

- Poll Bhalainn < ON *vaðillinn*, 'the shallow water': Valen is a common place-name in Norway.
- An Cnòmhainn < ON *króin*, 'the small pen, corner': this occurs in Orkney and there is a Kroan in Norway.
- Creag a' Briundainn < ON *brennan*, 'the land cleared by burning': see Brendo and Brinhyan in Orkney.[60]
- Eilean Greodhlainn < ON *hlíðin* (f.), 'the slopes', with ON *grjót*, 'stone': there is a Grøliin in Norway.
- Hyring (twice) < ON *eyrrin*, 'the gravel bank' or ON *ærgin*, 'the shieling(s)': Øren is a common place-name in Norway, and Ayrean is found in Orkney.
- Manndalen. This form is first recorded in a Tiree rental of 1496, following the 1390 form Mannawallis, whilst the name was recorded as Manuel vel Mandalon in 1674: Manndalen is a very common place-name in Norway.

The suffix *-itt* after neuter nouns has not been found on Tiree, and also seems to be absent from the Orkney material. Case marking of the post-positional suffix, for example the dative plural *-um*, whilst present in Norway, was not found in the Orkney material.[61]

Other possible examples from the Hebrides are:

- Forsanan < ON *forsin*, 'the waterfall', on South Uist: Forsen being a very common name in Norway.
- Holman < ON *hólminn*, 'the islet', on Raasay: Holmen being a common name in Norway.[62]
- Clèithbhinn < ON *kleifin*, 'the cliff', on Raasay: Kleiven being quite a common name in Norway.[63]

56	Ibid., 160.
57	Ibid., 106.
58	Ibid., 121.
59	Ibid., 231.
60	Ibid., 101.
61	Berit Sandnes, pers. comm.
62	MacKay 2013, 52.
63	Ibid., 12.

- Am Ballan on Islay < ON *balinn*, 'the grassy bank': Balen being a common name in Norway.[64]

The earliest known place-name using the post-nominal bound definite marker was recorded in Norway in 1336. However, the construction could be earlier than this, as explained by Sandnes: 'The [post-nominal] article was traditionally seen as an innovation in the Middle Norwegian period (1350 – 1500) but the date is being pushed backwards in modern research'.[65]

It is possible that Norse loan-names preferentially attracted the Gaelic suffix *-an*, as seems to have happened with Gribun < Gnípan on Mull.[66] But the forms Greodhlainn, Hyring (twice), Briundainn, and Cnòmhainn phonologically support a derivation from *-in(n)* rather than *-an*. Only three of the Tiree examples were recorded prior to the present research, and more detailed fieldwork into the micro-toponyms of other Hebridean islands is urgently needed. The use of the post-nominal bound definite marker in the Hebrides must, therefore, remain speculative at this time, but, if correct, could push the date for the creation of Norse names on Tiree into the fourteenth century.

GAELIC RESETTLEMENT

The process whereby Norse hegemony over Tiree weakened, as the island came increasingly under the control of powerful Argyll chieftains, is still opaque. Gaelic township names such as Balnow – from Am Baile Nodha, 'the new township' – are first recorded on Tiree in the 1509 Crown Rentals. The Blaeu map of 1654, presumed to be based on a lost Pont MS dating from the period of 1583 to 1614, recorded a significant number of Gaelic settlement names on the island, for example Keulis from ScG An Caolas, 'the narrows'. Another toponym mapped by Blaeu is Kory Finmackoul ('the hollow of Finn mac Cumaill'). This name locates the hero of the Finn Cycle of Tales (the Fiannaigheacht) to a natural amphitheatre around a striking glacial erratic on the shore of Balephetrish, covered with Bronze Age cup markings. This shows a Gaelic cultural marker strongly embedded in the island's landscape by the sixteenth century.

---

64   Macniven 2006, 358.
65   Sandnes 2010, 321-22.
66   Alasdair Whyte, pers. comm.

Norse place-names are not evenly scattered over Tiree, varying from none at all within the modern township boundaries of Kenovay and Middleton, to 27% in Hough. This variation could have been caused by incomplete Norse settlement, leaving pockets of Gaelic-speakers. A more convincing explanation, however, is that it was produced by a Gaelic resettlement that began as a focused plantation. One agent for this may have been the Church, which became an important landholder on Tiree in the later medieval period. The Prioress of Iona, for example, held Scarinish.[67]

There is some historical evidence for language transitions in Scotland. Sandnes has summarised the Norse-Scots transition in Orkney. The first known Scots letter from Orkney is dated to 1438, and the Impignoration took place in 1468. Yet the last documented use of spoken Norse was in the 1750s.[68] Norse, therefore, remained a vigorous language of the Orcadian farming community for two to three hundred years after the language of the elite changed from Norse to Scots. On Tiree, another language transition had just come to an end. The Scots-speaking ninth Earl of Argyll took possession of Tiree in 1679. The fifth Duke lived in London and communicated extensively in English with his chamberlain on Tiree from 1771 until his death in 1806.[69] The 1872 Education Act made education compulsory in Scotland, and English the language of tuition for all schools. Yet the 1901 Census of Tiree recorded that 44% of the island's population were still monoglot Gaelic speakers. For almost 300 years most islanders on Tiree spoke a different language from their landlord.

It seems plausible, therefore, that Norse was the dominant, high-status language on Tiree for three hundred years from the mid-ninth until the mid-twelfth century, and was widely spoken for a further two to three hundred years until the fifteenth century.

THE ETHNOLOGY OF NORSE SETTLEMENT

MacDonald has remarked on the treatment of the Norse in Hebridean tradition.

> Mention of the establishment, or re-establishment, of Gaelic control in the Hebrides in the Middle Ages brings me to what

67   MacLean-Bristol 1995, 81.
68   Sandnes 2010, 30.
69   *Argyll Estate Instructions*, 1.

must be one of the most remarkable features of all in this whole question of Norse tradition: that is the almost total loss of awareness in modern Gaelic oral tradition that there was at any time a powerfully established Norse-speaking, or even bilingual Gaelic/Norse population in the Hebrides [...] the surviving stories would usually confine the role of the Norse to that of a raiding and plundering enemy who were usually defeated.[70]

This stands in stark contrast to the flourishing 'Viking' industries of Up Helly Aa in Shetland and the Jorvik Centre in York.

There are a number of stories in the oral traditions of Tiree and Coll about *Na Lochlannaich*. The best-known is ScG Cath nan Sguab, 'The Battle of the Sheaves', recorded by Gregorson Campbell.[71] This tradition is a retelling, in a Tiree context, of a fourteenth-century Irish Fingalian story about the defeat of the Norsemen.[72] Although a version has also been collected from Colonsay,[73] the story has especially taken root on Tiree, remaining widely known to the present day. The tale portrays a heroic Hebridean underdog casting out the Norse villains. This recreated folk history of Scandinavian Tiree, however, is at odds with the argument presented here. Abundant place-name evidence on Tiree strongly points to a transformational and possibly violent Norse campaign to take control of the island, an extensive and prosperous subsequent Scandinavian settlement (probably alongside a lower status Gaelic-speaking population), and a later loss of Norse military and political control. This was followed by an extended period, possibly over a number of centuries, during which Norse influence slowly waned and a late medieval Gaelic culture gradually reasserted itself on the island. We know from genetic studies in the Hebrides that many descendants of the Norwegian settler population remained on the west coast. This 'rewriting' of Norse settlement history by later Gaels might be an echo of an earlier indigenous resentment of Scandinavian dominance.

CONCLUSION

Tiree, situated on the southern end of the archipelago and presently classified, both geographically and politically, as one of the 'Inner

---

70   MacDonald 1984, 277
71   Campbell 1891.
72   See *Duanaire Finn*, 55, 162.
73   MacNeill and MacLean 1953, SA1953.120.9.

Hebrides', has long been regarded as lightly brushed by the Norse wand. Prolonged fieldwork, however, has shown that the Scandinavian influence on Tiree was intense, extensive, and durable. The island's assets were its rich harvests of barley, a strategically useful location, its range of beach landing points, and, later, its highly Christianised landscape. The presence of such a large number of Norse place-names apparently containing the post-nominal bound definite marker, supports the hypothesis that Norse language and culture persisted among parts of the island's population into the late medieval period. Gaelic resettlement appears to have been gradual and only locally disruptive. Further place-name research on other west coast islands is urgently needed to develop our understanding of Scandinavian influence on the *Suðreyar*.

BIBLIOGRAPHY

PRIMARY SOURCES

Acts of the Lords of the Isles 1336-1493, Munro J and Munro R W (eds), 1986, Edinburgh: Scottish History Society.

Adomnán's Life of Columba, Anderson A O and Anderson M O (eds and trans), 1961, London: Thomas Nelson and Sons Ltd.

Argyll Estate Instructions: Mull, Morvern, Tiree 1771-1805, Cregeen E R (ed), 1964, Edinburgh: Scottish History Society.

Blaeu Atlas of Scotland, 1654, National Library of Scotland, EMW.X.015.

Den Norsk-Islandske Skjaldedigtning, Jónsson F (ed), 1912, B, vol. i, Gyldendalske Boghandel: Copenhagen.

Duanaire Finn, The Book of the Lays of Fionn: Part I, MacNeill E (ed), 1908, London: David Nutt.

Exchequer Rolls of Scotland, Stuart J et al. (eds), 1878-1908, Edinburgh: H.M. General Register House.

New Statistical Account of Scotland, 1834-45, vol. vii, Edinburgh: Blackwood and Sons.

Old Statistical Account of Scotland, Sinclair J (ed), 1791-1799, vol. x, Edinburgh.

Ordnance Survey Name Book Argyll, 1868-78, vol. 28.

Orkneyinga Saga, Guðmundsson F (ed), 1965, Íslenzk Fornrit XXIV, Reykjavík: Hið Íslenzka Fornritafélag.

The Annals of Ulster to AD 1131, Mac Airt S and Mac Niocaill G (eds and trans), 1983, Dublin: Dublin Institute for Advanced Studies.

The Orkneyinga Saga: The History of the Earls of Orkney, Pálsson H and
   Edwards P (trans), 1978, London: Penguin.
Vitae Sanctorum Hiberniae, Plummer C (ed), 1910, vol. 2, Oxford: Clarendon
   Press.

SECONDARY SOURCES

Broderick, G 2013, 'Some Island Names in the Former "Kingdom of the Isles":
   A Reappraisal', *The Journal of Scottish Name Studies* 7, 1-28.
Butter, R 2007, '*Cill*-names and Saints in Argyll: A Way towards Understanding
   the Early Church in Dál Riata?', unpublished PhD thesis, University of
   Glasgow.
Campbell, J G 1891, *The Fians: Or, Stories, Poems and Traditions of Fionn and
   his Warrior Band*, Waifs and Strays of Celtic Tradition: Argyllshire Series 4,
   London: David Nutt.
Cleasby, R and G Vigfusson 1874, *An Icelandic-English Dictionary*, Oxford:
   Clarendon Press.
Cox, R A V 2002, *The Gaelic Place Names of Carloway, Isle of Lewis*, Dublin:
   Institute for Advanced Studies.
Dodgshon, R A 1998, *From Chiefs to Landlords*, Edinburgh: Edinburgh
   University Press.
Dodgshon, R A 2015, *No Stone Unturned*, Edinburgh: Edinburgh University
   Press.
Downham, C 2015, 'The Break-Up of Dál Riata and the Rise of the Gallgoídil',
   in H Clarke and R Johnson (eds), *The Vikings in Ireland and Beyond:
   Before and After the Battle of Clontarf*, Dublin: Four Courts, 189-205.
Fellows-Jensen, G 1980, 'Common Gaelic *Áirge*: Old Scandinavian *Ærgi* or
   Erg?', *Nomina* 4, 67-74.
Fisher, I 2001, *Early Medieval Sculpture in the West Highlands and Islands*,
   Edinburgh: RCAHMS and Soc. Ant. Scot.
Gammeltoft, P 2001, *The Place-Name Element* Bólstaðr *in the North Atlantic
   Area*, Copenhagen: CA Reitzels Forlag A/S.
Graham-Campbell, J 2011, *The Cuerdale Hoard and Related Viking-Age Silver
   and Gold from Britain and Ireland in the British Museum*, London: British
   Museum Press.
Grant, A 2003, 'Scandinavian Place-Names in Northern Britain', unpublished
   PhD thesis, Glasgow University.
Holliday, J 2016a, *Longships on the Sand: Scandinavian and Medieval
   Settlement on the Island of Tiree: A Place-Name Study*, Tiree: An Iodhlann
   Press.
Holliday, J 2016b, 'A Name without a Place, a Place without a Name: The
   Isleborg Puzzle (Again)', *West Highland Notes and Queries* 4:2, 5-11.

Jennings, A and A Kruse 2009, 'One Coast – Three Peoples: Names and Ethnicity in the Scottish West during the Early Viking period' in A Woolf (ed), *Scandinavian Scotland – Twenty Years After*, St Andrews: Committee for Dark Age Studies, 75-102.

Jesch, J 2010, '*Orkneyinga Saga*: A Work in Progress?', in J Quinn and E Lethbridge (eds), *Creating the Medieval Saga*, Odense: University Press of Southern Denmark, 153-73.

Johnston, A R 1991, 'Norse Settlement in the Inner Hebrides 800-1300, with Special Reference to the Islands of Mull, Coll and Tiree', unpublished PhD thesis, University of St Andrews.

Kruse, A 2005, 'Explorers, Raiders and Settlers: The Norse Impact upon Hebridean Place-Names', in P Gammeltoft, C Hough, and D Waugh (eds), *Cultural Contacts in the North Atlantic Region: the Evidence of Names*, Lerwick: NORNA, SPNS, and SNSBI, 141-56.

MacDonald, A 2010, 'Adomnán's *Vita Columbae* and the Early Churches of Tiree', in J Wooding (ed), *Adomnán of Iona: Theologian, Lawmaker, Peacemaker*, Dublin: Four Courts, 219–36.

MacDonald, D A 1984, 'The Vikings in Gaelic Oral Tradition', in A Fenton and H Pálsson (eds), *The Northern and Western Isles in the Viking World*, Edinburgh: John Donald, 265-79.

Macgregor, L J 1986, 'Norse Naming Elements in Shetland and Faroe: A Comparative Study', *Northern Studies* 23, 84-101.

MacKay, R 2013, *Gach Cùil is Cèal/Every Nook and Cranny – Place Names, Part I: Raasay, Rona, Fladda and Eilean Taighe,* Guildford: Grosvenor House.

MacKie, E W 1974, *Dun Mor Vaul: An Iron Age Broch on Tiree*, Glasgow: University of Glasgow Press.

MacLean-Bristol, N 1995, *Warriors and Priests: the History of Clan MacLean 1300-1570*, East Linton: Tuckwell Press.

MacNeill, B and MacLean, M 1953, Blàr eadar na Lochlannaich agus na Colbhasaich, Audio Recording SA1953.120.9, Edinburgh: School of Scottish Studies.

Macniven, A 2006, 'The Norse in Islay: A Settlement Historical Case-Study for Medieval Scandinavian Activity in Western Maritime Scotland', unpublished PhD thesis, University of Edinburgh.

Macniven, A 2007, 'Lies, Damn Lies, Statistics and the True Significance of Islay's Norse Place-Names', Scottish Place-Name Society, www.spns.org.uk, accessed 2 July 2016.

Márkus, G 2012, *The Place-Names of Bute*, Donington: Shaun Tyas.

McKay, M (ed) 1980, *The Rev. John Walker's report on the Hebrides of 1764 and 1771*, Edinburgh: John Donald.

Reeves, W 1854, 'The Island of Tiree', *Ulster Journal of Archaeology* 2, 233-44.

Sandnes, B 2010, *From Starafjall to Starling Hill: An Investigation of the Formation and Development of Old Norse Place-Names in Orkney*, Scottish Place-Name Society, http://www.spns.org.uk, accessed 16 October 2014.

Stahl, A 1999, 'Place-names of Barra in the Outer Hebrides', unpublished PhD thesis, University of Edinburgh.

Tait, I 2012, *Shetland Vernacular Buildings 1600-1900*, Lerwick: Shetland Times.

Watson, W 1993 [1926], *The Celtic Place Names of Scotland*, Edinburgh: Birlinn.

WHAT'S IN A NAME? THE HISTORICAL SIGNIFICANCE OF NORSE NAMING STRATEGIES IN THE ISLE OF ISLAY

ALAN MACNIVEN

Communities of Old Norse-speakers arriving in the Inner Hebrides during the Viking Age would have had two main choices when it came to naming their new environment. They could either adopt the names already in use by the native Celtic populations, or create new ones using their own language and naming traditions. Where examples of adopted and new material can be identified, comparative analysis offers a welcome opportunity to add narrative detail to an otherwise document-starved period of Hebridean history. This chapter will explore the specific evidence for Norse naming strategies in the Isle of Islay, and what this might reveal about Norse-native relations during the settlement era.

INTRODUCTION

On Friday the 2nd of July 1266, the Norwegian nobles Askatinus and Andreas appeared on behalf of Magnús IV (later re-styled VI) in the church of the brothers at Perth before Alexander III, King of Scots. Their task was to cement the fledgling peace between Norway and Scotland, which had taken root since the death of Magnús' father, Hákon, in Kirkwall on his return from the Battle of Largs some three years earlier. The deal was simple; if the Scots left Orkney and Shetland alone, and agreed to pay a lump sum and annuity in refined silver, the Norwegians would, in return, amicably and socially, concede, resign, and quitclaim for Magnús and his heirs, either as suitors or possessors forever the '[Isle of] Mann, with the other islands of the Sodors and all the other islands of the south and west part of the great Haffue'.[1] Interestingly, the treaty entered into on that day also entailed that any offences perpetrated between Magnus and Alexander, as well as their ancestors and their people, were to be wholly remitted.[2] Just how far back this particular clause was intended to stretch is, of course, debatable. But it serves as an important reminder that unpleasantries

---

1   *Agreement between Magnus IV. of Norway and Alexander III. of Scotland. A.D. 1266*, 211.
2   Ibid., 215.

had been a defining characteristic of Norse-native relations in this part of the world for centuries, from the havoc wreaked by Hákon and his placemen in the 1260s and 1230s, to the 'Devastation of all the islands of Britain by heathens' listed in the *Annals of Ulster* under AD 794.[3]

In the absence of more comprehensive historical records, there has been a tendency to assume that Hákon's later medieval enmity followed patterns of interaction established during the Viking Age. Victorian notions of the Vikings as restless adventurers, unfettered by the conventions of Christian morality, but hopelessly addicted to hit-and-run raids on defenceless coastal monasteries, may no longer play such a large part in that assumption. But with the heritage language of the Western Isles being Scottish Gaelic and not Scandinavian, there is still a lingering reluctance to accept that the area was ever seen as anything more than a waystation by opportunistic Viking warlords *en route* to richer pickings in and around the Irish Sea. The trope of 'seasonal exploitation' has been especially resilient, stressing that the majority of Scandinavian visitors to the Hebrides during the Viking Age were fundamentally transient, and concerned only with the fleeting extraction of resources as opposed to permanent settlement.[4] However, where the analysis of this period has been widened to include other sources of evidence, such as material culture and genetics, it soon becomes clear that the Norse impact on local culture was both deep-reaching and long-lasting. Recent additions to the archaeological, linguistic, and place-name evidence for Scandinavian activity in the formerly Pictish Outer Isles, for example, have revealed a level of cultural disjuncture in the ninth century that cannot be satisfactorily explained without the invasion and permanent settlement of large numbers of ethnic Scandinavians.[5]

Further south, on the other hand, where the lack of new archaeological material, or indeed of any substantial programmes of excavation, has been palpable, the historical narrative remains surprisingly underdeveloped. In the islands between Argyll and Ireland, the apparent survival of

---

3   *Early Sources of Scottish History*, 471-78; *Annals of Ulster*, 794.7: 'Uastatio
     omnium insolarum Britanniȩ a gentibus'. The contemporary nature of this
     account is confirmed by its inclusion in *The Chronicle of Ireland* (see Charles-
     Edwards 2006, 257).
4   Nicolaisen 2001, 122-24; 1969, 16-17, but cf. 1977–80, 112. See also Sveas
     Andersen 1991; Barrett 2008, 413.
5   Smith 2001; Kruse 2005; Jennings and Kruse 2005; 2009a; 2009b; Macniven 2013.

the native Gaelic language from the early Historic Era to the later Middle Ages continues to underpin a 'North vs South' divide in Scottish Viking Studies, predicated on the assumption that 'extirpation' in the North gave way to 'integration' in the South. As with previously held views on the Outer Isles, a narrow evidential focus and agenda-driven presumption of cultural continuity has seen the discussion stagnate. To help redress the epistemological imbalance here, this chapter will review what might have happened when Viking settlers came to the Inner Hebridean island of Islay, in the far south-west of the archipelago, through the lens of local place-names.

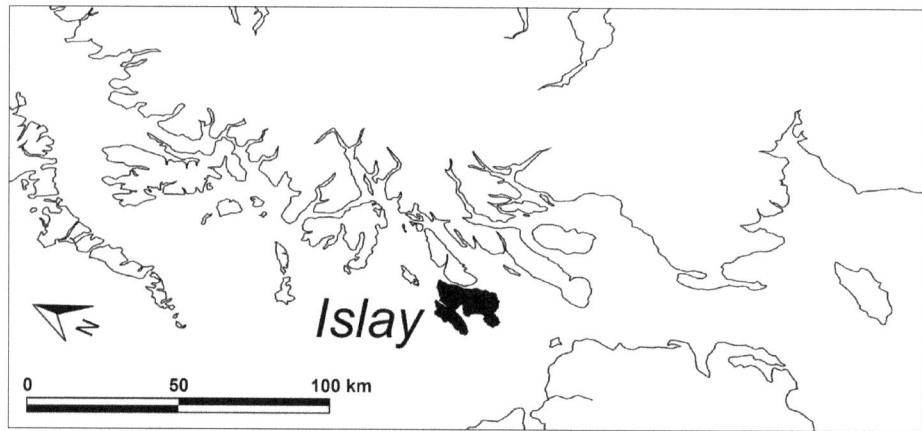

Figure 1: The Isle of Islay.

THE VIKINGS IN ISLAY

But what do we know about Islay and its Viking experience? Was it peaceful, predatory, piecemeal, or overpowering? Can we even be sure that the Vikings ever actually went there? If we were to rely on the documentary evidence alone, none of those questions could be answered with certainty. Between AD 740 and 1095, there are no contemporary references to the island itself, let alone the people or events which might otherwise have helped to define its cultural political identity.[6] There are several folk-tales suggesting early connections with Scandinavia. Peggy Earl notes one example deriving the island-name Islay from a mythical 'Danish' princess named Jula, and another recounting the slaying by Manx king Godred Crovan of a dragon on a hill at Imerchonart.[7] A third, well-known story remembers a battle between the 'Fenians' and the 'Danes' on a hillside called Sliabh a'Chatha (Gaelic for 'Battle Brae') near Gartmain on Loch Indaal.[8] But as all three tales can be read as simple literary tropes, it would perhaps be unwise to stress their value in historical research.

An alternative – if less reliable – way to cultivate the historical record is to begin with accounts of a later period and extrapolate backwards. Scandinavians are known to have been visiting Islay for a long time. These days, it seems, mainly to enjoy the opportunities for golf and malt whisky. In times gone by, however, the standard itinerary appears to have demanded a certain amount of bloodshed. By the time the Treaty of Perth was agreed in the late-thirteenth century, *Íl* or Islay is known to have been a named part of Christian Norway's cognitive geography for the best part of 200 years. Some forty years earlier, for example, the young King Hákon Hákonarson had been eager to assert himself in the Suðreys (Man and the Hebrides). The 1220s were a turbulent time in the Kingdom of the Isles, and the inability of Manx King Óláfr Guðrøðarson (Olaf 'the Black') to control its various warring factions provided Hákon with an irresistible window of opportunity.[9] The story is told in Sturla Þórðarson's near-contemporary biography, *Hákonar saga Hákonarson*.[10] Hákon's ploy was to install Hebridean warlord Óspakr Ögmundarson as king of the Hebrides, and provide

---

6   *The Annals of Ulster* record an earthquake in Islay under 740.3 – 'Terrimotus in Ili .ii. Id Aprilis'. The appearance of this episode in *The Chronicle of Ireland* confirms that it is roughly contemporary (see Charles-Edwards 2006, 212). The *Chronica Regum Manniae et Insularum* ('Chronicles of the Kings of Man and the Isles') tell us that Godred Crovan became king of Man and the Isles in 1079, and 'Regnauit aut<u>em</u> sedecim annis & mortuus <u>est</u> <u>in</u> insula que uocatur yle' [ruled for sixteen years before dying in the island which is called Islay] (*Chronica Regum Manniae et Insularum*: f.32v, f.33r-v). Other sources, including the *Annals of Inisfallen* under 1095.13, confirm that Godred was one of a great many victims of a plague that devastated Ireland and the surrounding area in that year.

7   *Tales of Islay*, 1, 18.

8   Canmore, NR36SW 10, accessed 30 May 2016.

9   See, for example, Costain-Russell 2015; Cowan 2015.

10   See, for example, *Hákonar Saga ins gamla*.

him with a fleet of eighty ships to oust Olaf. Given that Óspakr was also known as Uspak Hákon and Gille Escoib mac Dubgaill, and thought to be a grandson of Somerled MacGillebride,[11] it is clear that this was no random appointment, but a play on entrenched political divisions with underlying layers of dynastic entitlement and resentment. According to Sturla, 'Uspak' gathered his fleet in the Sound of Islay in 1230, in preparation for an attack on Bute. While in the Sound, he was joined by his brothers, Doggall and Dungadr (Dugald and Duncan), and their relative Sumarlidi (Somerled), whose generous display of hospitality towards the Norwegians included the provision of what is described in the saga as *vín sterkt*.[12] Although this phrase is invariably translated as 'strong wine', it is not beyond the bounds of possibility that what the Islesmen were, in fact, imbibing was an early form of *uisge beatha*, the Gaelic source-form for whisky, or the 'water of life'.[13] Whatever the case, the Norwegian contingent in Uspak's fleet are said to have been apprehensive of the drink on offer, not necessarily because of an innate sense of moderation, but to avoid being rendered insensible and duped. This turned out to be a wise move. Retaining both their sobriety and wits, the Norwegians quickly turned the situation to their advantage, dispatching the local troublemakers, including most of Uspak's relatives, without losing a man, and helping to precipitate a split in the Kingdom of the Isles in the process.

Uspak's expeditionary force is one of several Scandinavian fleets known to have visited Islay during the Christian Middle Ages. The list also includes Hákon's personal expedition through the Isles in 1263, in which he is said to have received the support of Angus of Islay, the chief of Clan Donald and progenitor of the later Lords of the Isles.[14] Prior to this, the island had also featured as a stop on Magnús *berfœttr* ('Bareleg') Óláfsson's psychotic trail of destruction in 1098, in which he sailed from Norway to Dublin to secure his overlordship of the area in the face of Scots expansion. According to Björn *krepphendi*'s ('Cripple Hand's') skaldic poem *Magnússdrápa*, around which Snorri Sturluson structured his early-thirteenth century *Magnúss saga berfœtts*, Magnús

---

11 Sellar 2000, 194, 202.
12 *Hákonar Saga ins gamla*, 102.
13 *Early Sources of Scottish History*, 475.
14 Ibid., 102-18.

is said to have caused smoke to be raised over Islay and devastated several others in a successful bid to assert himself:

§178	Vitt bar snjallr á slétta	[Warlike Magnús widely
	Sandey konungr randir.	Waste laid Sanday's grasslands.
	Rauk um Íl, þás jóku	Smoke rose up on Islay
	allvalds menn á brennur.	Isle as homesteads burned there.
	Sanntíri laut sunnar	South on [Kintyre] bloody
	Segga kind und eggjar.	Swords felled many Scotsmen.
	Sigrgœðir réð síðan	Manxmen many then by
	Snjallr Manvera falli.[15]	Magnús host were laid low.][16]

Given the known economic and political importance of Islay in the later Iron Age and Early Historic Era, it would be surprising if Hákon or Magnús were the only Scandinavian sea-kings to have coveted its gifts. The strategic value of Islay's location as a safe haven between the whirlpool of the Corryvreckann and the dangerous tidal currents of the North Channel should not be underestimated in this respect. While there are no surviving accounts of any earlier, pagan interaction, it is beyond doubt that Norwegian Vikings sailed very close to the island on their way to documented raids on the monasteries of Iona and Rathlin, or their ventures further south into Ireland and the Irish Sea.[17] Although not explicitly stated in the saga material or elsewhere, it is reasonable to assume that the island served as a pitstop for semi-fictional saga characters such as Ketill *flatnefr* ('Flatnose') Björnson and Harald *hárfagri* ('Fairhair') Halfdanarson on their voyages of the ninth century, establishing the prestigious itinerary later followed by the likes of Magnús and Uspak Hákon.

Whilst the military occupations of Islay in the late-eleventh and early-to-mid-thirteenth century were short-lived affairs, it is important to remember that they were the actions of centralised Norwegian kings. As eager as Magnús or Hákon may have been to be seen at the forefront of high profile naval campaigns, they were also keen to move on afterwards, delegating the process of consolidation to local underlings – a *modus operandi* unlikely to have been shared by the more hands-

---

15 *Magnúss saga Berfœtts*, 221.
16 Based on *Heimskringla*, 675-76.
17 Ó Corráin 1998a; 1998b; Downham 2007.

on warlords of the Viking Age. For pagan Scandinavian chieftains, the key to secular authority appears to have been the personal support of landed neighbours rather than divine anointment. In the better-understood Norse expansion into other parts of the North Atlantic, such as Iceland, it seems that establishing a strong local presence through extensive land-taking and the subsequent large-scale plantation of supporters was an important part of the colonisation process.[18] In those parts of Scotland's northern and western seaboard for which evidence is relatively abundant, invasion, colonisation, and cultural obliteration appear to have been the order of the day.[19]

Without closer consideration of the wider context, these kinds of development are difficult to reconcile with the apparent survival of the Gaelic language in Islay from the early Christian era to the present day. But with the island itself having completely disappeared from the documentary record for the duration of the Viking Age, it cannot simply be assumed that business continued as usual. Although Early Historic Islay is closely associated with the powerful *cenél nOengusso*, one of the leading families of Gaelic-speaking Dál Riata, the island's Viking Age hiatus saw all traces of this influence and even existence disappear. When Islay emerges once more into the light of history in the twelfth century, it is as the seat of the Argyll-derived MacSorley Kings of the Isles. Things had clearly changed in between. And where better to look to for the agents of that change than an influx of pagan Scandinavian settlers?

This is what seems to be suggested by the archaeological material. Although confirmed remains from Islay's Viking Age are limited to a selection of portable objects (Figure 2), it is worth noting that all of them are not only diagnostically Scandinavian, but of the high-status variety that point to the existence of a settled pagan elite.[20] With all of the artefacts having been found on or close to areas of fertile and easily worked arable land, it can also be assumed that the same Scandinavians controlled the local subsistence economy. In the absence of contemporary accounts, it is perhaps not immediately obvious what this tells us about the nature of the settlement process. With so much weight given to the idea of Celtic continuity in traditional histories of

18   Vésteinsson 1998.
19   Smith 2001; Jennings and Kruse 2005; 2009a; 2009b; Macniven 2013.
20   Macniven 2015, 61-63, 109-10.

the area, it might be tempting to imagine a small-scale elite takeover. However, the comparatively limited linguistic and genetic evidence points to something a bit more wide-ranging.[21] And considering the tens of thousands of Scandinavian pioneers, who together with their families, friends, servants, and slaves are known to have emigrated to the effective 'new world' of Iceland in the late-ninth and early-tenth centuries,[22] the most straightforward explanation is military subjugation followed by the settlement by large numbers of ethnic Scandinavians. Without the corroboration of more openly descriptive sources, or more comprehensive archaeological discoveries, the only realistic way of testing this theory lies in the closer scrutiny of the local names of places.

ISLAY PLACE-NAMES

At around 62,000 ha, Islay is the fifth-largest of Scotland's islands, around 25% smaller than Mull, in fourth place, but 15% larger than Mainland, Orkney, in sixth.[23] The population may have declined to 3,228 in the most recent census in 2011, from 3,457 in 2001, and a historic high of 15,772 in 1841.[24] But its richly varied landscape of machair, mountains, farmland, and freshwater bogs continues to support around 6,000 settlements, natural features, and other locations considered distinct enough to be recognised with an officially recorded name.[25] Whilst the percentage of names from Scots and standard English language backgrounds, which includes house numbers and public utilities, has now grown to around 40% of the total, the remaining 60% can be considered formally Gaelic in the sense that they have for centuries been used, preserved, and developed by the Gaelic-speaking community in accordance with the norms of local pronunciation and the demands of the Gaelic grammar system. However, there are many names for which this formal description does not sit well. For a number of writers, including Domhnall MacEacharna in his 1976 volume *The Lands of the Lordship: The Romance of Islay's Names*, their exotic character gives them an air of romance fully commensurate with the

---

21   For a comparative discussion of suggested models for Norse settlement in England and the Hebrides, see Macniven 2013.

22   Karlsson 2000, 11, 44-51.

23   Haswell-Smith 1996, 35, 74, 292.

24   Darling 1955, 83.

25   McWee 2001.

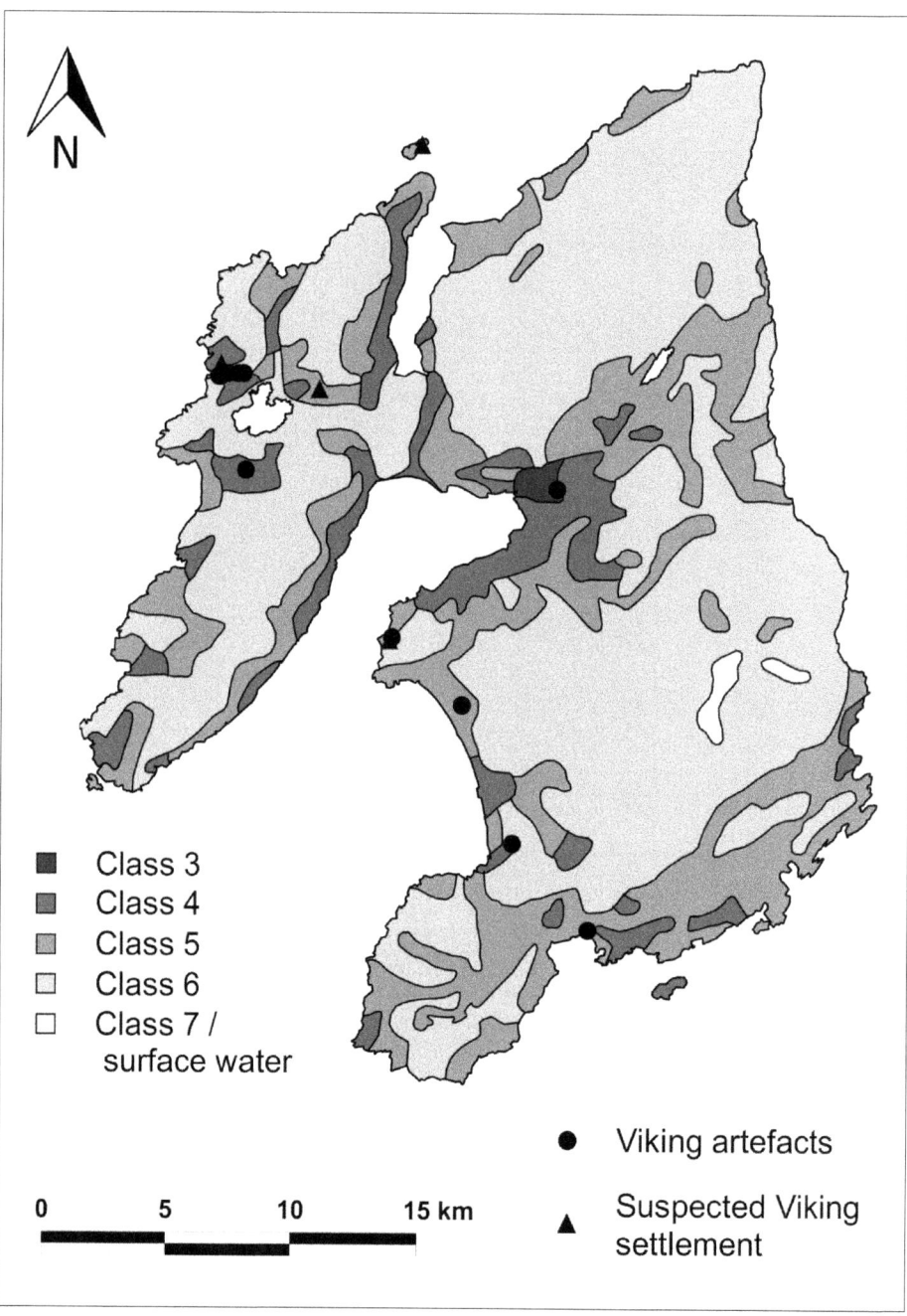

Figure 2: Viking Remains in Islay (adapted from Macniven 2015, 46, 62; Brown et al. 1982).

island's dramatic history.[26] Some of these names may sound Gaelic when spoken by the natives, and may even look Gaelic in their written forms, but make little sense when read as Gaelic word material. The hill known as Cnoc Crun na Maoil (NR 415 487, 162 m) and cultivated slope of Cnoc na Corra Mhaoil (NR 301 426), for example, in what is now the parish of Kildalton and Oa, could be understood as the 'Hill of the Crown of the Bare Rounded Hill' and the 'Knoll of the Great Top', respectively.[27] The hills of Beinn Tart a'Mhill (NR 210 569, 232 m) and Cnoc Garbh a'Mhill (NR 204 556, 120 m) in the Rinns peninsula would suggest the even more contrived 'Hill of the Thirsty Hill' and 'Hill of the Rough Hill'.[28]

Many other Islay place-names contain elements which might be understood in terms of their descriptive connotations, and in some cases are still productive in naming practices, but which *cannot* have been drawn from Goidelic word-stock. This list includes numerous naming elements such as *geodha* (m.), *gil* (f.), and *sgeir* (f.). The reason for all of this is quite simply that the material is not, ultimately, Gaelic in origin, but Old Norse – the language of the Vikings. Consequently, when viewed from a Scandinavian perspective, many Islay names take on new layers of meaning. The elements **Crun na Maoil* and **Corra Mhaoil* find easier derivation from ON **Grœnafjall*, 'Greenfell', or **Krúnafjall*, 'Crownfell', relating to the colour or shape of the hill, and **Kornavöllr*, 'Corn Field', pointing to agricultural activity. Similarly, the element **Tart a'Mhill* finds more convincing origins in Old Norse **Hjartafjall*, or 'Stag Mountain', with *hjarta* being the genitive plural form of *hjörtr* (m.), 'stag', and the transformation of initial /h/ into /t/ being a common feature of Gaelic adaptations of Old Norse place-names. The **Garbh a'Mhill* part of Cnoc Garbh a'Mhill makes more sense if it is seen as Old Norse **Skarfafjall*, from *skarfr* (m.), meaning 'cormorant', or possibly **Skarðafjall*, meaning 'Cleft Mountain', both indicative of the landscape and its qualities. Individual elements like *geodha*, *gil*, and *sgeir* can be explained as the Norse loan-words *gjá* (f.), 'chasm, rift in crags', *gil* (n.), 'deep narrow valley with river at the bottom', and *sker* (n.), 'skerry, rock', in Gaelic clothing.[29]

---

26   Maceacharna 1976.
27   Macniven 2015, 125, 137.
28   Ibid., 291-92, 341.
29   See, for example, Stewart 2004, 408-16; Gammeltoft 2004.

It should be stressed that these observations are hardly new. As far back as 1772, the Welsh traveller Thomas Pennant spent several days in Islay as a guest of the local gentry. What he learned there led him to observe that, 'There are more Danish or Norwegian names of places in this island than any other; almost all the present farms derive their titles from them, such as Persibus, Torridale, Torribolse and the like'.[30] This, however, is something of an exaggeration. At a generous estimate only around a fifth of Islay's modern place-name inventory contains any obviously Norse elements, either as survivors from the Viking Age or loan-words which have remained active in local naming practices in the years since. But it does beg the important question of how we know whether a name is Old Norse or Gaelic, and what, if anything, this might tell us about social interaction between the incoming Norsemen and the native Gaels

PHILOLOGY

In the late-nineteenth and early-twentieth centuries, there was a strong belief among language historians that all systematic changes in language could be reduced to a standardised series of discrete transformations. In Scotland, linguists including George Henderson, Alexander MacBain, and others went to great pains to map out the systematic changes by which modern Gaelic place-names might have evolved from Old Norse originals.[31] Their approach was straightforward; if a West Highland place-name was clearly not (Scots) English and could not reasonably be interpreted as Gaelic in its topographical context, they would then consider an Old Norse etymology. Then, as now, the identification of source languages was problematic. Despite the linguistic distance between the Goidelic and Germanic languages, the distinction between originally Gaelic or Old Norse material is not always clear. Take, for example, the three Islay examples of Corrary (NR 312 571, NR 324 455, NR 271 689), any or all of which could derive from either Old Norse *Káraærgi* ('Kári's Shieling') or Gaelic *Corr Àirigh* ('Shieling on the Round Hill').[32] Things get even more complicated with names like the now-lost Calumsary in the Rinns, which appears to contain both Old Norse and Gaelic elements – the originally Gaelic personal name Calum,

---

30 *A Tour in Scotland and Voyage to the Hebrides 1772*, 220-21.
31 Henderson 1910; MacBain 1922.
32 Macniven 2015, 201-2.

and either the Gaelic generic *àirigh* (f.) or its Old Norse counterpart *ærgi* (n.) – albeit in an Old Norse grammatical matrix demonstrated by the medial, genitive /s/.[33] Fortunately, the intervening century of place-name research has revealed a number of guiding principles that can help to establish the language background of individual names.

If the name in question comprises more than one element, the order of the elements can be diagnostic. In Gaelic, compound names tend to begin with a 'generic' element, describing the broad category of name, such as *baile* (m.), meaning 'township or farm', or *tigh* (m.), meaning 'house'. This is usually followed by the so-called 'specific' element, which adds distinguishing detail. In farm names, this might be the main crop grown, e.g. Ballygrant (NR 395 662) from Gaelic **Baile a'Ghràin*, 'Townland of the (Kiln-Dried) Corn',[34] a comment on its terrain or topography, e.g. Bailetarsin (NR 355 611) from **Baile Tarsuinn*, 'Township on the Slope', or Tigh nan Cnoc (NR 354 647), meaning 'House on the Hill',[35] or the name of the owner or tenant, e.g. Balole (NR 355 661) from **Baile Ola*, 'Ola's Township', or Tighcargaman (NR 363 495) from **Tigh Cargaman*, 'House of Cargaman'.[36] Compound Old Norse names, on the other hand, tend to consist of a specific element followed by a generic. Typical examples might include Cornabus (NR 334 464) from **Kornabólstaðr*, 'Corn Farm',[37] Sannaigmore (NR 237 707) from **Sandvík*, 'Sandy Bay', with the later addition of the Gaelic contrastive modifier *mòr* – meaning 'big' or 'greater' – presumably when the farm-district was sub-divided,[38] and Olistadh (NR 218 583) from **Óláfsstaðir*, 'Óláf's Steading'.[39] It will be noted that the written forms of the assumed Old Norse material are rather different from the standardised spelling of the same concepts. This can be explained in part as linguistic drift during centuries spent as oral artefacts in the alien language environment of the later medieval *Gàidhealtachd* before being crystallised in writing.

To get as close as possible to the original Scandinavian forms, the effects of the Gaelic grammar system have to be taken into account.

---

33   Ibid., 39, 309.
34   Ibid., 251-52.
35   Ibid., 195-96, 236-37.
36   Ibid., 252-53, 183.
37   Ibid., 163.
38   Ibid., 348-49.
39   Ibid., 344-45.

The impact of linguistic phenomena such as lenition, projection, back-formation, and prosthesis, which are common in Gaelic, can radically alter the appearance of a word and have to be reversed in the reconstruction of earlier forms. In Islay, the 'lenition' of a word-initial consonant appears to have transformed Old Norse *Torfnes* (NR 209 676: Turf Ness) into Gaelic Aird Thòrr-innis ('Headland of *Thòrrinnis*').[40] 'Projection' of the final consonant in a Gaelic definite article, such as *an*, would explain the development of Old Norse *Eyrabólstaðr* ('(Gravel) Bank Farm') into later *Nerabus* (NR 226 551) through a notional intermediate *AnEyrabólsaðr*.[41] 'Back-formation' of an assumed lenited initial consonant may have taken ON *Hánessker* to Eilean an Tannais-sgeir (NR 188 639),[42] whilst 'prosthesis' of a name with an extraneous /s/ or /k/ might see *Karlsstaðir* ('Karl's Farm') or *Haraldsstaðir* ('Harald's Farm') transformed into *Skerrols* (NR 351 638).[43] Additionally, because the fixed first-syllable-stress of Norse word material is unusual in Gaelic, where stress is more commonly delayed to a later syllable, it can also lead to unstressed elements in the middle and end of the name simply disappearing, further complicating attempted etymology, e.g. Thomas' derivation of Skerrols from an unnecessarily complex Old Norse *Skúrhólarstaðir*, 'Trench Hill Farm'.

Having taken numerous such transformations into account, Henderson was able to devise a complex series of charts showing how vowels and consonant clusters might have been adapted from Norse into Gaelic in initial, medial, and terminal positions.[44] There is no doubt that this linguistic 'ready-reckoner' is diagnostically helpful in many individual cases. But it would be wrong to imagine that it can be applied uniformly and successfully in all circumstances to the erstwhile Gaelic forms of West Highland place-names to reveal the 'factory-fresh' versions of originally Old Norse material. Steady progress in the theory and practice of place-name research in Scandinavia over the intervening century has helped to systematise the process, with the refinement of the 'historical-philological' approach to place-name etymology, in

---

40   Borgstrøm 1940, §80, 84; Oftedal 1956, 164-69; Thurneysen 1975, 74-89, 140-46; Cox 2002, 51-53; Stewart 2004, 405; Macniven 2015, 351-52.
41   Macniven 2015, 339-40.
42   Maceacharna 1976, 117 FN 17; Cox 2002, 64; Macniven 2015, 307.
43   *A Comparative and Etymological Table of the Names of Farms*; Macniven 2015, 232-33.
44   Henderson 1910, 342-57.

particular, stressing the value of interdisciplinary corroboration and the importance of real-world comparators.[45] One especially important observation is that the vocabulary, grammar, and syntax of a given Old Norse place-name will not always be perfectly aligned to those reconstructed from the standard language. Even where the component words are known to have been in use during the period when the names were coined, research has confirmed that the range of practical combinations is limited, that compounds can be formed with or without the use of standard Old Norse genitive markers, such as /-s/, /-ar/, /-u/, /-a/, or /-na/, and that it is quite possible to encounter plural forms where the singular might be expected, e.g. *staðir* instead of *staðr*.[46]

From a philological perspective, it is also important to stress that the earlier Scottish approach to this material does not deal with the effect of language contact. It simply takes the modern Gaelic spelling for a name – which might have drifted considerably over the years – and tries to approximate it, not to the dialect of Old Norse used locally when the names were created, but to the normalised forms of Old Norse devised by modern editors of the Icelandic sagas.[47] As a result, it leaves little room for the impact of dialectal variation or other linguistic anomalies on the eventual written forms of local place-names.

Marginalising the scope for localised developments in this way can complicate strict philological analyses. In Islay, this is demonstrated by recent treatment of to the so-called 'busses',[48] comprising the two dozen or so place-names still in use or preserved in old rentals and charters, which end in -*bus*, -*bolls*, -*pols* and -*pus*, or simplex *Bolsa* or *Bolsay*. Typical examples include Risa*bus* (NR 314 437) and Lura*bus* (NR 337 435) in the Oa, from Old Norse **Hrísabólstaðr*, 'Brushwood Farm', and **Leirabólstaðr*, 'Clay Soil Farm', and Persa*bus* (NR 417 690) in the north-east of the island, from **Prestabólstaðr*. 'Priest(s) Farm'.[49] Variant forms can be found in Gro*bolls* (NR338 598) from **Grábólstaðr* or **Gróubólstaðr*, referring to the perceived colour of the landscape (grey), or the female personal name *Gróa*,[50] Kep*pols*more (NR 383 661),

---

45   Rygh 1898, 4-8; Christensen and Kousgard Sørensen 1972, 119-60; Sandnes 2003, 109-11.

46   Macniven 2015, 39-41.

47   Pálsson 1996.

48   Macniven 2015, 71-74.

49   Ibid., 141-42, 172, 276-77.

50   Ibid., 212.

from **Kappa-, *Kjappa-, or *Keipabólstaðr*, after the male personal name or by-name Kappi, or pebbles, or goats, or rowlocks in reference to the profile of the local landscape.[51] Dùn Chollapus (NR 357 678), now a hill-name, appears to preserve a now-lost **Collapus*, most likely from an earlier **Kollabólstaðr*, 'Kolli's Farm'. Finally, we have the relatively transparent Bolsa (NR 386 775) and Bolsay (NR 227 571), both from simplex **Bólstaðr*, 'Farm'.[52] Although all of these endings are widely believed to have evolved from Old Norse *bólstaðr* (m.), meaning 'farm',[53] it has also been argued that they derive from a philologically convincing but otherwise unattested Old Norse *bólshagi*.[54] Accepting the possibility of local quirks, however, allows for an alternative explanation – that the attested endings have evolved from a misunderstanding of the morphemic boundaries in originally Old Norse *bólstaðr*, most probably towards the end of the island's Norse period, when active knowledge of the language among the settled population was rapidly disappearing in the face of encroaching Gaelic. Scrutiny of the written forms, along with local pronunciation, suggests that the element came to be tacitly understood as a combination of two lexically empty morphemes, **bóls* + **taðr*, with the terminal /s/ of **bóls* being mistaken for a common genitive marker. Following the later operation of the Gaelic grammar system, in a nominally bilingual environment, this would allow for the lenition of the intial /t/ in **taðr* to **aðr*, the loss of the terminal consonantal cluster due to syncope, and subsequent addition of the common Gaelic locative particle *aig*. Thus *bólstaðr* becomes terminal *-bussaig* or simply *-bus*, as can be seen from the local pronunciation of Robolls [ˈrɔːˌb̥ʉsig̊ʲ] and Persabus [ˈb̥ɛ̊ɾ̊səˌb̥ʌs].[55]

Although the exact mechanisms of this particular transformation are open to debate, it is important to note how unusually complex they appear to have been. Why the changes undergone by the other surviving Old Norse material seem to have been comparatively simple also requires an explanation. This can be found in the linguistic

---

51   Ibid., 267-68.
52   Ibid., 254-55
53   Gammeltoft 2001.
54   Cox 1994.
55   Macniven 2015, 71-72, 278, 276.

properties of names, and has important implications for how onomastic material can contribute to the historical narrative.

WHAT'S IN A NAME?

It is well-known that place-names most often originate in the standard word material available at the time of their creation. Technically speaking, this means that they are imbued with the same range of literal and abstract meaning implied by those words – allowing them to serve as shorthand for the series of interconnected observations and phenomena covering places, people, activities, and events. In practice, however, their successful operation requires only that they are distinct enough to function as unique address labels. As they need only be understood as a series of sounds to do so, they can remain effectively separate from standard word material, surviving the changes in grammar and fashion that might affect it over time, or even the replacement of the local language itself. Because of this, they also provide a convenient and resilient vehicle for the preservation through the ages of the actual words from which they were originally coined. It is for this reason that Old Norse name material has been able to survive in the Gaelic-speaking environment of Islay's recent past. And it follows that, by looking more closely at the context and format of that material, it should, in theory, be possible to comment on the relative status of Old Norse and Gaelic speakers on Islay, at the time or times when that the place-names were created.

Following a period of societal destabilisation in the Hebrides in the opening decades of the Viking Age, leading to a Norse takeover by the 840s, it seems that large numbers of ethnic Scandinavians made their way to the West Highlands and Islands.[56] Communities of Old Norse speakers arriving in Islay would have had two main choices when it came to naming their new environment – they could either adopt existing names or create new ones. These two over-arching strategies could be implemented in a number of different ways.[57] When it came to borrowing existing names, for example, a process technically known as onomastic transfer, adoption could have taken several forms. If settlers found themselves in a socially subordinate position to the native population, they are most likely to have learned and used the

---

56 See, for example, Macniven 2013.
57 Gammeltoft 2006.

established names of places – perhaps with minor adjustment for Old Norse pronunciation, known as 'phonological adaptation'. In these circumstances, any such adaptations would quickly have disappeared back into the dominant tradition, meaning they are unlikely to have left much trace. In Islay, the only definite example is preserved in the later medieval Icelandic sagas. The Latin *Ilea Insula* and Old Irish *Íl* used to name the island in pre-Norse texts including Adomnàn of Iona's *Life of St Columba*, the *Annals of Ulster*, and the *Chronicles of the Kings of Man and the Isles*,[58] can be found adopted in the thirteenth-century *Magnúss Saga Berfœtts* and *Hákonar saga Hákonarson* in the place-names *Íl* (Islay) and *Ílarsund* (Sound of Islay).[59] Contrary to what might be assumed, neither are likely to point to a low social status for the Norse settlers. Both can be satisfactorily explained as 'exploratory' names, adopted for basic utility without any clear need for deeper communication.[60]

Where the context of borrowing lacks meaningful communication, and names are not properly understood, phonological adaption can also be accompanied by lexical substitution – where the people doing the borrowing latch onto bits of the words that sound familiar, and tweak them to mirror those patterns, thereby making them easier to remember. To a monoglot speaker of modern English, for example, the Scottish Gaelic district name *Na h-Eileanan an Iar* ('The Western Isles') might be rationalised aurally as 'a nail in a jar'. Whilst the Islay namescape boasts several highly conspicuous examples of lexical substitution from Old Norse names being transferred into Gaelic, including Cnoc Crun na Mhaoil and the like, it is clearly significant that there are – as yet – no convincing examples of Gaelic names being adapted into Old Norse in this way.

NEW NAMES

The alternative to borrowing existing place-names would have been to create new ones. Clearly, a glut of genuinely new Norse names would suggest that the social standing of the incomers was elevated to the extent that they could simply ignore local tradition and establish their own. There appear to be many dozens of examples of this type of name

---

58   Broderick 2013, 11-12.
59   Gammeltoft 2007.
60   Kruse 2005.

in Islay, including settlements with habitative generics, such as Conisby (NR 62 619, from Old Norse **Konungsbýr*, 'King's Farm')[61] and Cragabus (NR 326 451, from **Krakabólstaðr*, 'Kraki's Farm'),[62] settlements with topographic generics, such as Proaig (NR 457 576, from **Breiðvik*, 'Broad Bay')[63] and Stremnish(more) (NR 311 408, from **Straumnes*, 'Headland of the Current'),[64] and the names of both major and minor natural features, such as Beinn Tart a'Mhill (as above) and Eas Forsa (NR 428677, from **Forsá*, 'Waterfall River') (Figure 3).[65] The distribution of this material across all parts of the island and all of its landforms suggests that the Old Norse speaking population and place-name 'user group' was not limited to marginal land or defensive enclaves.[66] Nor does it seem likely that they were confined to newly broken land. At only 62,000 ha, including extensive tracts of rugged upland and peat-bog, Islay was no continent of untapped agricultural potential. Besides which, it is clear that from the earliest available charters and rentals that many of the traditional farm-districts generally, and much of the best land within them specifically, were described by Old Norse place-names (See Figures 2 and 3).

It is, of course, possible that some of this ostensibly Old Norse material has in fact been adapted from pre-existing Gaelic names, or alternatively created long after the Viking Age by a linguistically Gaelic community using a selection of heritage loan-words from Old Norse. Take, for example, Crois Sgeir (NR199 614),[67] which could have originated in a later medieval Gaelic name, meaning 'The Skerry of/with the Cross', or an earlier Old Norse **Krossker*, meaning 'Cross Skerry', with or without any intended reference to any Christian ecclesiastical monuments. Ironically, it is precisely this difficult area in which we find the final, but perhaps most fruitful category of names in terms of commenting on Norse native relations: new names formed from existing name material with the addition of a new part, known as an epexegetic onomastic unit.[68] In Islay, there are numerous examples of

---

61   Macniven 2015, 301-2.
62   Ibid., 149-50.
63   Ibid., 174-75.
64   Ibid., 178-79.
65   Ibid., 257.
66   See Magnus Olsen's User Group Theory, e.g. Olsen 1934. Cf. Nieke 1984, 313.
67   Macniven 2015, 331.
68   Cox 1988-9.

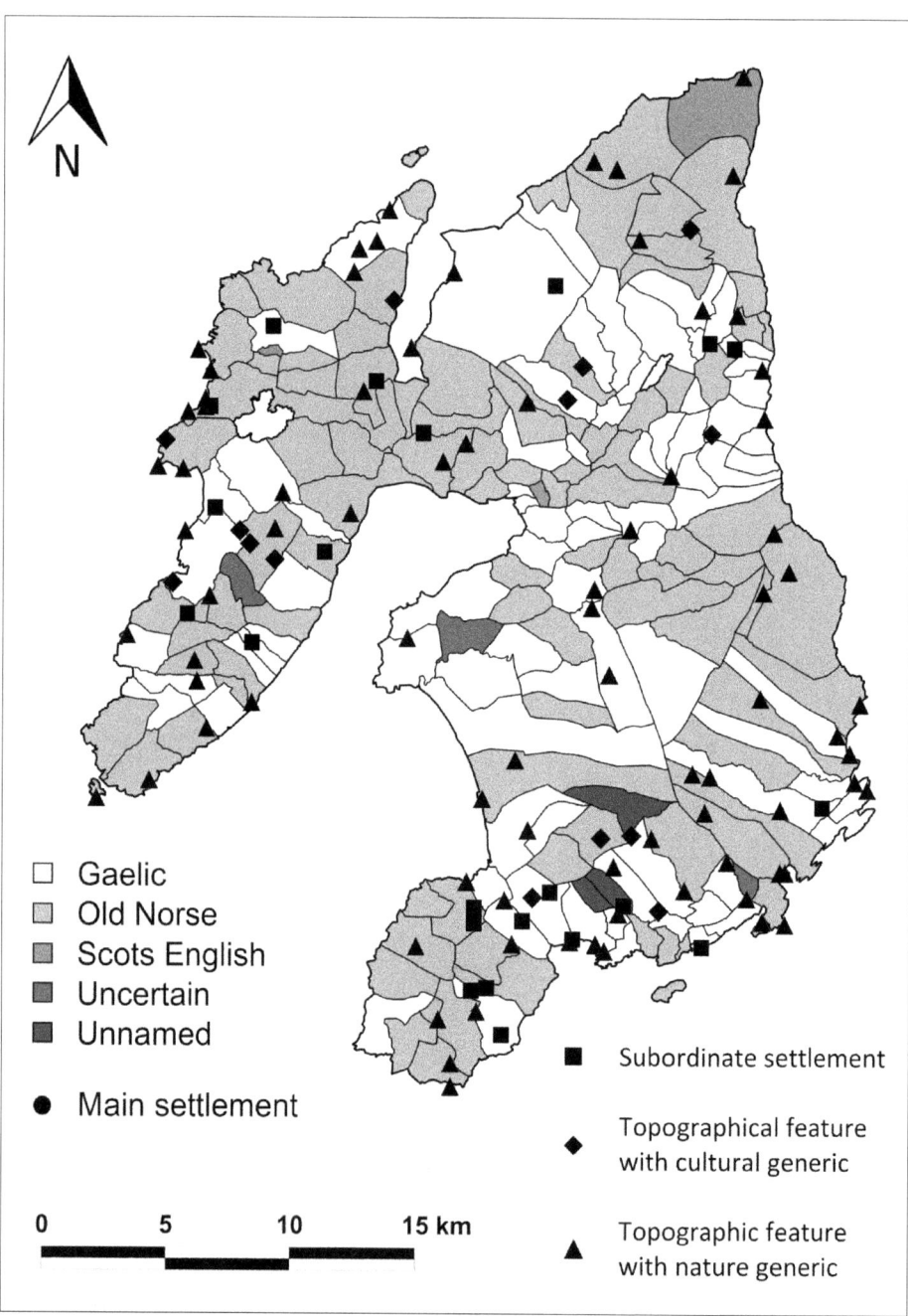

Figure 3: Distribution of likely Old Norse place-names in Islay (Adapted from Macniven 2015, 54).

this category, including Aird Thòrr-innis (NR 209 676, from Old Norse *Torfnes*, 'Turf Ness' or 'Peary Ness'),[69] Ben Cladville (NR 182 545, from *Glaðafjall*, 'Sunny Hill'),[70] Glean Egedale (NR 333 517, from *Eikadalr*, 'Oak Tree Valley'),[71] Loch Gruinart (NR 285 689, from *Grunnfjörðr*, 'Shallow Firth'),[72] Port Bhoraraic (NR 429 658, from *Borga(r)vík*, 'Fort Bay'),[73] and Eas Forsa (see above), to list but a few.

Until recently, names of this type were routinely described in settlement-historical studies as Gaelic-Norse 'Hybrids'.[74] Although the term is still occasionally used in historical overviews, it is important to stress that it is neither linguistically accurate, nor particularly helpful. Rather than reflecting some strange Norse-Gaelic creole or pidgin language, such as the heavily-accented Irish described as *gib gab* or *gic gac*, said to have been spoken by Norse merchants in tenth-century Ireland, these names are, in fact, formally Gaelic – albeit Gaelic names which have been created from pre-existing Norse material.[75] What their existence confirms is that the latter-day use of Gaelic in Islay supersedes a period when an important part of the settled population spoke Old Norse. With this in mind, it is important to ask just how many pre-Viking Age Gaelic names have survived in Islay. Apart from the name of the island itself, and possibly – although be no means certainly – a few others recorded in documents like the *Senchus fer nAlban*, with its assumed list of districts in Islay, the answer, surprisingly, is none that we can be sure about.[76]

DATING THE GAELIC MATERIAL

It was once argued that the relatively high concentration of the Gaelic generics *baile* (m., 'township, farm'), *cill* (f., 'chapel, church, graveyard'), and *sliabh* (m., 'hillside, slope, mountain') in the Inner Hebrides pointed to their productivity in Dalriadan times, before Gaelic had spread to the Scottish mainland, and long before the arrival of the

---

69   Macniven 2015, 351-52.
70   Ibid., 300-1.
71   Ibid., 154-55.
72   Ibid., 323-24.
73   Ibid., 273.
74   Maceacharna 1976, 82-3; Olson 1983, 134-76.
75   Schulze-Thulin 1996, 111; Downham 2015, 375.
76   Macniven 2015, 81-84.

Vikings.[77] The implication that a significant part of the local namescape had remained unchanged throughout the Middle Ages played a formative role in assumptions of cultural and population continuity, which remain stubbornly engrained. There are, however, good reasons to believe that distribution alone is not a particularly reliable guide to the antiquity of this material. In his investigation of the generic *baile* in nearby Ireland, Liam Price established that the word was used as a simple noun in Irish texts during the pre-Norse period. But it was also clear that its occurrence in place-names was uncommon until the later Middle Ages, when it is likely to have been developed to meet the needs of the ecclesiastical and secular authorities to describe a particular type of settlement, possibly with specific tax or rental status.[78] A similar study of *sliabh* names in the Rhinns of Galloway by Simon Taylor concluded that the concentration of the generic in south-west Scotland could also point to a later antecedence.[79] On Islay, it seems that the widespread distributions of both *baile* and *cill*-names are the results of administrative reforms by Oláfr Guðrøðarson of Man, Somerled MacGillebride, or his son Ranald, such as the introduction of written standards in bookkeeping, or the introduction of the parish system.[80] As can be seen in Figure 4, there is a central clustering of *baile* names around the Lordship centre on Eileann Mòr in Loch Finlaggan. It could be argued, for example, that this points to the apportionment or reclassification of a larger block of landholdings in fairly short order. Whilst the distribution of farm-districts with names based on Gaelic *cill* might appear to be more random, closer analysis of the hinterland of the *cill* farms in terms of their valuation in 'Old Extent' reveals it to be remarkably uniform, with each commanding an area worth approximately 6 quarters, 200 shillings, or 15 merks.[81] It can also be noted in this respect that, although only around 12% of Scotland's traditional parish names build on the element *cill*, it covers all of the Islay examples, including the early attested Kildalton, Killarow, Kilmeny, Kilchoman, and Kilnaughton.[82]

Figure 4: Distribution of Gaelic *baile* (LHS) and *cill* (RHS) in the farm-names

---

77 Nicolaisen 2001, 156-91
78 Price 1963. See also Flannagan 1978.
79 Taylor 2002.
80 Macniven 2015, 64-69.
81 Ibid., 94-98.
82 Ibid., 69.

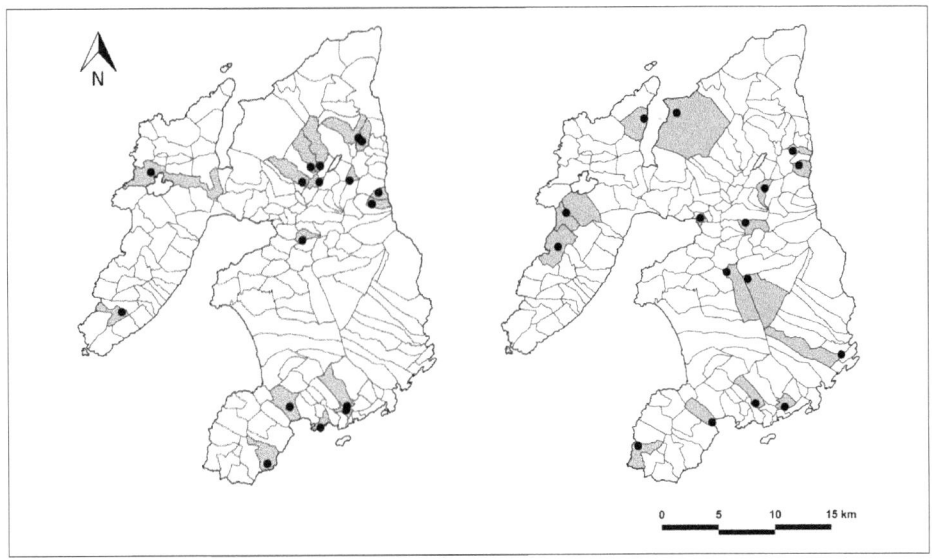

shown on Stephen MacDougall's 1749-51 *Map of the Island of Islay* (Adapted from Macniven 2015, 66, 68).

In establishing the age of individual Gaelic place-names in the Hebrides, progress has been made by focusing on aspects of grammar and syntax than distribution patterns. The investigation of syntax has been particularly informative, with names containing forms of the definite article in the medial position, such as Tighandrom (NR 373 461, from Gaelic **Tigh an Droma*, 'House on the Ridge') or Tigh nan Cnoc (NR 354 647, Gaelic for 'House on the Hill'),[83] likely to be later medieval developments. Those with the article in the initial position, such as An Lossit (NR 412 655, from **Losaid*, 'Kneading Trough'), are thought to be even younger.[84] In Islay, names of these types account for about a third of the total Gaelic name-pool, pointing to a significant redevelopment of the inventory in the relatively recent past, and allowing for the large-scale replacement of the island's Viking Age Scandinavian toponymy.

Of the remainder of Islay's Gaelic place-names, it is possible that some are ancient survivals. As with the exploratory names discussed earlier, however, this does not necessarily point to meaningful communication between Norse and native, simply their utility in the exploitation,

---

83   Macniven 2015, 236-37.
84   Watson 1904, xl-xli; Cox 2002, 111-24; Macniven 2015, 181-82, 273-74.

apportionment, and management of landed resources. A complicating factor in identifying any genuinely ancient material is the succession of onomastically rejuvenating waves of Gaelic-speaking immigration known to have swept over the island since the Viking Age. The most well-known of these are the mid-twelfth century arrival of Somerled MacGillebride from Argyll, the establishment of his sons as rulers of the Hebrides, and the subsequent period of cultural cross-fertilisation with the north of Ireland under the MacDonalds of Dunyvaig and the Glens. But attention should also be drawn to the arrival of the Cawdor Campbells in the seventeenth century, the innovations of the Shawfield Campbells in the eighteenth century, and the associated phases of population expansion, retraction, clearance, and settlement redistribution.[85] It would be surprising indeed if many of the Gaelic place-names recorded in conjunction with these developments are not neologisms, which have replaced by – or been adapted from – Norse precursors. One particularly clear example of this phenomenon is the appearance of the name *Ballemertine* in 1631 (now Ballimartin, NR 370 661, from Gaelic **Baile Mhartain*, 'Martin's Townland'), where it replaces the long-standing local name of *Stainepoll* (from Old Norse **Steinabólstaðr*, 'Stoney Farm' or possibly 'Stein's Farm').[86]

WHAT DOES ALL OF THIS MEAN?

Like Jurassic flies trapped in amber, place-names have the capacity to preserve linguistic data, even when their formative language milieu has undergone substantial change, decline, or death. In an area like Islay, where several languages are known to have been used as sequential *linguae francae* over the centuries, the extraction and classification of this data points to a shift from Gaelic to Old Norse and then back to Gaelic again, albeit of a different variety with strong evidence for an Old Norse substrate.[87] Closer analysis of the name material in its topographical, economic, and social contexts hints at the relative social status of the user groups of those languages. The survival of so many Old Norse names *in situ*, covering both settlements and natural features, indicates that long-standing native Gaelic traditions were cast aside by Norse settlers. It also suggests that the new traditions introduced by

---

85   Macniven 2015: 21-26. See also Caldwell 2008; Storrie 2011.
86   Ibid., 249-50.
87   Stewart 2004.

them gained enough acceptance to become implanted in the landscape and preserved locally until their original meanings had been forgotten. It would only have been at some point after this, when the shift from Old Norse to Gaelic was being driven to its inevitable conclusion by relentless waves of prestigious Gaelic-speaking immigrants, that the old names would have required topographical clarification through the addition of appropriately descriptive Gaelic language elements. Although the ratio of Old Norse to Gaelic names in Islay is relatively small in absolute terms, it is nevertheless of key significance that the Norse material is spread across the whole island, and not restricted to discrete parts of it.[88] With historical place-names most often coined by the neighbours of a site, and preserved most effectively by the wider community or 'user groups', it must be assumed that Old Norse became the main language of communication in Islay during the Viking Age. Its occurrence without any clear examples of ancient Gaelic names with Old Norse epexegetic onomastic units points not only to disjuncture in culture and probably also population at the beginning of the Norse period, but a gradual and largely peaceful transition at the other end of the early Middle Ages. From these observations alone, it seems reasonable to conclude that the assumed North-South divide in Scotland's Viking activity is more illusory than real – a reflex of changing circumstances in and around the Irish Sea, the far earlier re-alignment of the Inner Isles to inter-regional ethnic and political norms than their neighbours in the North, and subsequent radical changes in population distribution. And if this degree of change was possible in such a politically and strategically 'central' place as Islay, it is hard to believe that the same was not also true of the smaller islands nearby. Further research with this possibility in mind is likely to yield interesting results.[89]

BIBLIOGRAPHY

PRIMARY SOURCES

A Comparative and Etymological Table of the Names of Farms (or Townlands) in Lewis and Harris and Islay, Thomas F W L, s.a., National Museums Scotland Library, MS 574.

A Tour in Scotland and Voyage to the Hebrides 1772 by Thomas Pennant, Simmons A (ed), 1998, Edinburgh: Birlinn.

---

88   Macniven 2015, 20-22.
89   See, for example, Holliday 2016a; 2016b.

Agreement between Magnus IV. of Norway, King of Mann and the Islands, and the Most Serene King Alexander III. of Scotland. A.D. 1266, in *Monumenta de Insula Manniae or a Collection of National Documents Relating to the Isle of Man, Volume III*, Oliver J R (ed and trans), 1862, Douglas: The Manx Society, 210-17, https://books.google.co.uk/books?id=0R0tAAAAMAAJ, accessed 30 May 2016.

Annals of Ulster, Corpus of Electronic Texts, University College Cork, http://www.ucc.ie/celt/online/T100001A/, http://celt.ucc.ie/published/G100001A/, accessed 30 May 2016.

Annals of Inisfallen, Corpus of Electronic Texts, University College Cork, http://www.ucc.ie/celt/published/T100004/, http://celt.ucc.ie/published/G100004/, accessed 30 May 2016.

Chronica Regum Manniae et Insularum, Chronicles of the Kings of Man and the Isles, Broderick G (ed), 2004, Douglas: Manx National Heritage.

Early Sources of Scottish History, A.D. 500 to 1286, Volume Two, Anderson A O (ed and trans), 1922, Edinburgh: Oliver & Boyd, https://archive.org/stream/earlysourcesofsc02ande, accessed 30 May 2016.

Hákonar Saga ins gamla, in *Flateyjarbok: En samling af Norske Konge-Sagaermed Indskudte Mindre Fortællinger om Begivenheder i og Udenfor Norge Samt Annaler, III*, Vigfússon G and Unger C R (eds), 1868 Christiania: P T Mallings Forlasboghandel, 3-236.

Heimskringla: History of the Kings of Norway, Hollander L M (trans), 1964, Austin: University of Texas Press.

Magnúss saga Berfœtts, in *Heimskringla III*, Aðalbjarnarson B (ed), 1951, Íslenzk Fornrit XXVIII, Reykjavík: Hið Íslenzka Fornritafélag, 210-37.

Tales of Islay: Fact and Folklore, Earl P, s.a., Bowmore: Celtic House.

SECONDARY SOURCES

Barrett, J H 2008, 'The Norse in Scotland', in S Brink and N Price (eds) *The Viking World*. London: Routledge, 411-27.

Borgstrøm, C-H 1940, 'The Dialects of the Outer Hebrides', *Norsk Tidsskrift for Sprogvidenskap* I (sup. vol.), Oslo: Aschehoug.

Broderick G 2013, 'Some Island Names in the Former "Kingdom of the Isles": A Reappraisal', *The Journal of Scottish Name Studies* 7, 1-28.

Brown, C J, B M Shipley, and J J Bibby 1982, *Soil and Land Capability for Agriculture: South-Western Scotland. Handbook to Accompany the 1:250,000 Scale Soil and Land Capability for Agriculture Maps, Sheet 6*, Aberdeen: The Macaulay Institute for Soil Research.

Caldwell, D H 2008, *Islay: The Land of the Lordship*, Edinburgh: Birlinn.

Canmore, https://canmore.org.uk/, accessed 30 May 2016.

Charles-Edwards, T 2006, *The Chronicle of Ireland – Volume I: Introduction, Text*, Liverpool: Liverpool University Press.

Christensen, V and J Kousgård-Sørensen 1972, *Stednavneforskning 1*, Copenhagen: Universitetsforlaget i København.

Costain-Russell, R 2015, 'The Reigns of Guðrǫðr and Rǫgnvaldr, 1153-1229', in S Duffy and H Mytum (eds), *A New History of the Isle of Man. Volume III: The Medieval Period 1000-1406*, Liverpool: Liverpool University Press, 79-96.

Cowan, E J 2015, 'The Last Kings of Man, 1229-1265', in S Duffy and H Mytum (eds), *A New History of the Isle of Man. Volume III: The Medieval Period 1000-1406*, Liverpool: Liverpool University Press, 97-117.

Cox, R A V 1988-9, 'Questioning the Value and Validity of the Term 'Hybrid' in Hebridean Place-Name Study', *Nomina* 12, 1-9.

Cox, R A V 1994, 'Descendents of Norse Bólstaðr?: A Re-examination of the Lineage of Bost & Co.', in J R Baldwin (ed), *Peoples and Settlement in North-West Ross*, Edinburgh: Edinburgh University Press, 43-76.

Cox, R A V 2002, *The Gaelic Place-Names of Carloway, Lewis: Their Structure and Significance*, Dublin: Dublin Institute for Advanced Studies.

Darling, F F 1955, *West Highland Survey*, London: Oxford University Press.

Downham, C 2007, *Viking Kings of Britain and Ireland: The Dynasty of Ívarr to AD 1014*, Edinburgh: Dunedin Academic Press.

Downham, C 2015 'Coastal Communities and Diaspora Identities in Viking Age Ireland', in C Gerrard and G Thomas (eds), *Maritime Societies of the Viking and Medieval World*, Leeds, Maney Publishing, 369-83.

Flanagan, D 1978, *'Baile', Bulletin of the Ulster Place-Name Society* 1, 8-13.

Gammeltoft, P 2001, *The Place-Name Element Bólstaðr in the North Atlantic Area*, Copenhagen: Institut for Navneforskning, Det Humanistiske Fakultet, Københavns Universitet.

Gammeltoft, P 2004, 'Scandinavian-Gaelic Contacts: Can Place-Names and Place-Name Elements Be Used as a Source for Contact-Linguistic Research?', *Nowele* 44, 51-90.

Gammeltoft, P 2006, 'Scandinavian Influence on Hebridean Island Names', in P Gammeltoft and B Jørgensen (eds), *Names through the Looking-Glass. Festschrift in Honour of Gillian Fellows-Jensen, July 5th 2006*. Copenhagen: C. A. Reitzel, 53–84.

Gammeltoft, P 2007 'Scandinavian Naming-Systems in the Hebrides: A Way of Understanding how Scandinavians were in Contact with Gaels and Picts?', in B Ballin Smith et al. (eds), *West Over Sea: Studies in Scandinavian Sea-Borne Expansion and Settlement Before 1300*, Leiden: Brill, 479-95.

Haswell-Smith, H 1996, *The Scottish Islands*, Edinburgh: Canongate.

Henderson, G 1910, *The Norse Influence on Celtic Scotland*, Glasgow: J Maclehose and Sons.

Holliday, J 2016a, *Tiree Place-Names*, http://www.tireeplacenames.org/, accessed 30 May 2016.

Holliday, J 2016b, *Longships on the Sand: Scandinavian and Medieval Settlement on the Island of Tiree: A Place-Name Study.* Sarinish: An Iodhlann Press.

Jennings, A and A Kruse 2005, 'An Ethnic Enigma – Norse, Pict and Gael', in A Mortensen and S V Arge (eds), *Viking and Norse in the North Atlantic, Selected Papers from the Proceedings of the Fourteenth Viking Congress, 19–30 July 2001*, Tórshavn: Føroya Fróðskaparfelag, 251-63.

Jennings, A and A Kruse 2009a, 'One Coast – Three Peoples: Names and Ethnicity in the Scottish West during the Early Viking Period', in A Woolf (ed), *Scandinavian Scotland – Twenty Years After: The Proceedings of a Day Conference Held on 19 February 2007*, St Andrews: The Committee for Dark Age Studies, University of St Andrews, 75-102.

Jennings, A and A Kruse 2009b, 'From Dál Riata to the Gall-Ghàidheil', *Viking and Medieval Scandinavia* 5, 123-49.

Karlsson, G 2000, *Iceland's 1100 Years: History of a Marginal Society.* Reykjavík: Mál og Menning.

Kruse, A 2005, 'Explorers, Raiders and Settlers: The Norse Impact upon Hebridean Place-Names', in P Gammeltoft, C Hough, and D Waugh (eds), *Cultural Contacts in the North Atlantic Region: The Evidence of Names.* Lerwick: NORNA, SPNS, and SNSBI, 141-56.

MacBain, A 1922, *Place Names, Highlands & Islands of Scotland*, Stirling: Eneas Mackay, https://archive.org/details/cu31924028080533, accessed 30 May 2016.

Maceacherna, D 1976, *The Lands of the Lordship: The Romance of Islay's Names*, Port Charlotte: Argyll Reproductions.

Macniven, A 2013, 'Modelling Viking Migration to the Inner Hebrides', *Journal of North Atlantic Studies*, Special Volume 4, 3-18.

Macniven, A 2015, *The Vikings in Islay: The Place of Names in Hebridean Settlement History*, Edinburgh: John Donald.

McWee, R 2001, *The Islay Cultural Database*, Edinburgh: Private Publication.

Nicolaisen, W F H 1969, 'Norse Settlement in the Northern and Western Isles: Some Place Name Evidence', *Scottish Historical Review* 48, 6-17.

Nicolaisen, W F H 1977-80, 'Early Scandinavian Naming in the Northern and Western Isles', *Northern Scotland* 3, 105-21.

Nicolaisen, W F H 2001, *Scottish Place-Names: Their Study and Significance*, rev. edn, Edinburgh: John Donald.

Nieke, M 1984, 'Settlement Patterns in the Atlantic Province of Scotland in the 1st millennium AD: A Study of Argyll', unpublished PhD thesis, University of Glasgow.

Ó Corráin, D 1998a, 'The Vikings in Scotland and Ireland in the Ninth Century', *Chronicon* 2:3, 1-45.

Ó Corráin, D 1998b, 'Viking Ireland – Afterthoughts', in H B Clarke, M Ní Mhaonaigh et al. (eds), *Ireland and Scandinavia in the Early Viking Age*, Dublin: Four Courts, 421-52.

Oftedal, M 1956, *The Gaelic of Leurbost, Isle of Lewis*, Oslo: Aschehoug.

Olsen, M 1934, *Hvad Våre Stedsnavn Lærer Oss*. Oslo: Stenersen.

Olson, D 1983 'Norse Settlement in the Hebrides', unpublished Hovedoppgave (Master's) thesis. University of Oslo.

Pálsson, H 1996, 'Towards a Glossary of Norse Place Names in Lewis and Harris', *Scottish Gaelic Studies* 17, 314-24.

Price, L 1963, 'A Note on the Use of the Word *Baile* in Place-Names', *Celtica* VI, 119-26.

Rygh, O 1898, *Norske Gaardnavne: Forord og Inledning*, Kristiania: W.C. Fabritius & Sønners.

Sandnes, B 2003, 'Fra Starafjall til Starling Hill: Dannelse og Utvikiling av Norrønne Stedsnavne på Orknøyene', PhD thesis, Norges Teknisk-Naturvetenskapelige Universitet, Trondheim, http://www.spns.org.uk/ Starafjall.pdf (translated), accessed 30 May 2016.

Schulze-Thulin, B 1996, 'Old Norse in Ireland', in P S Ureland and I Clarkson (eds), *Language Contact across the North Atlantic: Proceedings of the Working Groups Held at University College, Galway (Ireland), 1992 and the University of Göteborg (Sweden), 1993*, Tübingen: Max Niemeyer Verlag, 83-113.

Sellar, W D H 2000 'Hebridean Sea Kings: The Successors of Somerled, 1164–1316', in E J Cowan and R A McDonald (eds), *Alba: Celtic Scotland in the Middle Ages*, East Linton: Tuckwell Press, 187-218.

Smith, B 2001, 'The Picts and the Martyrs, or did the Vikings Kill the Native Population of Orkney and Shetland?', *Northern Studies* 36, 7-32.

Stewart, T W 2004, 'Lexical Imposition: Old Norse Vocabulary in Scottish Gaelic', *Diachronica* 21:2, 393-420.

Storrie, M 2011, *Islay: Biography of an Island*, 3rd edn, Isle of Islay: The Oa Press.

Sveas Andersen, P 1991, 'Norse settlement in the Hebrides: What Happened to the Natives and What Happened to the Norse Immigrants?' in I Wood and N Lund (eds), *People and Places in Northern Europe, 500–1600: Essays in Honour of Peter Hayes Sawyer*, Woodbridge: Boydell, 131-47.

Taylor, S 2002, 'The Element "Sliabh" and the Rhinns of Galloway or Place-names and History: A Case Study', *History Scotland* 2:6, 49-52.

Thurneysen, R, D A Binchy et al. (eds) 1975, *Grammar of Old Irish*, Dublin: Dublin Institute for Advanced Studies.

Watson, W J 1904, *Place Names of Ross and Cromarty*, Inverness: Northern
  Counties Printing and Publishing.
Vésteinsson, O 1998, 'Patterns of Settlement in Iceland: A Study in Pre-
  History', *Saga Book* 25, 1-29.

Gaming Material Culture and Hybridity: Finlaggan and the Kingdom of the Isles at Play

Mark A Hall[1]

Introduction

A key objective of this chapter is to succinctly present the evidence for the playing of board and dice games in the Kingdom of the Isles, as an example of the region's social dynamics to set beside the better-known political dynamics, which several of the other chapters in this volume cover. One thing is certain in this regard, the politics on a day-to-day basis would have been informed by the dynamics of games play: its victories, its losses, its draws and its cheatings. The analysis offered is part of ongoing research on play in medieval Scotland in a European context.[2] The origin and initial development of board games was explored in a paper that examined the case to be made for the Roman introduction of board games into Britain and Ireland.[3] It is a fitting place to begin this investigation, both as a telling example of hybridity itself and as a root for the medieval hybridity that is the core of this chapter.

Roman Seeds in Celtic Soil

Both archaeological and linguistic bodies of evidence, as they currently stand, are fully amenable to the interpretation that board games were a Roman introduction to northern and western Europe, part of a cultural package – also including literacy and wine – which was fundamental to cross-frontier cultural interaction.[4] This paradigm is rooted in the ideas of Caillois and Dumazedier, both of whom argued for a culturally contextualised view of play.[5] Board games are not universal in provenance but, as far as their western history is concerned, appear to have a specific origin in and dissemination from mid-fourth millennium

---

1   I am grateful to Katherine Forsyth, Niall Sharples, David Caldwell, and Alan Macniven for their advice, support, and questions, as well as for the comments by an anonymous referee. All remaining errors are mine.
2   For example, Hall 2007; 2009; 2011; Hall and Forsyth 2011; Caldwell, Hall, and Wilkinson 2009; 2010.
3   Hall and Forsyth 2011.
4   Gelastin 2010, 64-88.
5   Caillois 2002 [1958]; Dumazedier 1968.

BC Egypt and the Fertile Crescent, spreading both east to India and west to the Mediterranean and thence to temperate Europe and north Africa. Cultural contacts with the Roman Empire were a key mechanism for board game diffusion; thus they entered the Germanic world, reaching far beyond the *limes* to Scandinavia. The process of dissemination was not a wholesale borrowing or slavish introduction but rather a creative indigenous response to stimulus in which board games were adapted to local cultural and social contexts. A clutch of board game equipment from first-century AD burials in south-east Britain are the key pieces of archaeological evidence and help to make the case for Celtic innovation upon Roman-introduced board games – paramount amongst them the Doctor's Grave, Stanway, Colchester (and its board laid in the grave for play).[6] In addition, similarly-dated equipment is evident from the Gambler's Grave, Knowth, Ireland,[7] and from slightly later dated sites in Scotland, notably Tarland and Scalloway.[8]

On the basis of the evidence from Stanway and Knowth, it can be suggested that board games reached Britain from newly-conquered Gaul at the very end of the first century BC. Gaming was then adopted by British elites of the south-east as part of a package of Continental and Roman culture (which also included wine-drinking, coinage, literacy, and burial with grave goods). Following the Roman conquest of the region in the mid-first century AD, the playing of Roman-style games became increasingly widespread, extending well beyond the imperial frontier from an early date. The gaming pieces from Tarland attest to their popularity amongst the Caledonian/Pictish elite. The Knowth evidence suggests that board-gaming reached Ireland either via direct Roman contact or through contact with indigenous elites in Britain. In the case of the latter, this could have occurred before the Roman conquest of Britain but certainly no later than a decade or two after that conquest and as part of a broader cultural package of interaction. The extent to which this was perceived as Roman, rather than British, is a moot point deserving further analysis.

HEBRIDEAN DICE

The gaming kit from Knowth includes three dice, and it is dice and their correlates and progenitors, 'astragali', which represent the earliest

---

6   Crummy 2007, 352-58; Schädler 2007, 359-74.
7   Eogan and Weekes 2012, 23-26.
8   Hall 2007, 6-7, 17-19; Wilson and Watson 1998, 174-75.

evidence we see in the Hebrides. They were used for the linked practices of gaming and divination/fortune-telling. The earliest forms of dice are the so-called parallelepiped variety. Such dice are generally numbered (with ring-and-dot motifs) on their four long faces, usually to represent three, four, five, and six (in varying orders), but not one and two. The shape of these dice may reflect the earlier tradition of lot forms, in which specific numbering was not marked but respective faces could be distinguished by differences in shape and colour. Casting sets of such lots was a form of fortune telling or divination. The dice were generally produced from the shafts of small long bones, typically the metapodials of sheep.[9] The appropriateness of using these bones may ultimately derive from the suitability of the animal in sacrifice, which would have authenticated the additional use of elements of the carcass for divination. Usually the ends of such bones are open, but even when they are solid and intact – as with some antler examples – they are not generally numbered. The limited quantity of end-numbered dice include an example from the Rock of Cashel in Ireland (with both ends numbered five) and two from Scotland: the Broch of Ayre, Orkney (where one of the ends is marked with a single dot within a double circle),[10] and Scalloway Broch, Shetland (where both ends are marked with four ring-and-dots).[11] These embellishments may be decorative or symbolic in a non-numerical way instead of representing additional dice values. This seems to be the case on a die from Bute, which has its ends decorated with a tri-lobed petal or leaf within a circle.[12] If the dice were being used as a set, the marking of the ends might distinguish a particular die from others in the same, or another, set. The Ayre and Bute examples are of a similar size to the Cashel example (whilst the Scalloway find is smaller).

Clarke catalogued twenty definite examples from Scotland – mainly from broch and wheelhouse sites in the Northern and Western Isles, with the exception of two from Caithness.[13] It has previously been suggested that the more recent excavation of five dice from Scalloway did little to challenge their suggested dating convention of the first

---

9   MacGregor 1985, 129.
10   Clarke 1970, 30, no. 7.
11   Smith and Wilson 1998, 174
12   Clarke 1970, 229, no. 1.
13   Ibid.

quarter of the first millennium AD.[14] However, closer analysis of the Scalloway dice suggests this to have been a hasty conclusion. In fact, their discovery pushes the dating range for such dice into the mid-first millennium AD. Four of them were recovered from the second phase. Although this phase is broadly dated between 100 BC and AD 500, the dice were stratigraphically linked to its terminus, suggesting a late-fifth century date. The fifth example originates from the start of phase three (AD 500-600), giving the whole group a tight dating and a hint of continuity in practice across a time of transition. The later dating of the Scalloway group also lends some support to the similar dating of the six dice from Dun Cuier, Barra.[15] Although several authors subsequently questioned the dating, it was reaffirmed following a re-evaluation of Barra's archaeology by the Sheffield University SEARCH project.[16] The gaming material at Dun Cuier also included at least one conical antler piece and a series of small stone discs.[17] Five of the dice were found in the ashy deposits around the central hearth, probably where they were made, and helped to conjure up, for the excavator Youngs, 'the long northern nights, with the central fire and perhaps a feeble fish oil lamp the only means of lighting the interior of the dun'.[18] Within the interior, use beside the fire makes sense. Their find spots may reflect divinatory rituals (with the dice deliberately placed about the hearth and left there, cf. Bornais comments below) rather than them simply being lost or abandoned during manufacture about the hearth. The dice from Foshigarry and Bac Mhic Connain, North Uist, could also date to the mid-first millennium AD, part of a range of objects indicating (non-exclusive) Irish contact across the Hebrides at this time.[19]

In 1984, Raftery noted that there were sixteen parallelepiped dice from Iron Age and early medieval Ireland – all of them bone accept for a single wooden example from Ballinderry Crannog.[20] Raftery suggested the Irish material comprised two groups, differentiated in size: one small and one large – the smaller examples being earlier in date (i.e. earlier part of the first millennium AD). The same pattern has also been

---

14   Hall 2007, 9.
15   Youngs 1956, 319-20, fig. 13.5-10.
16   Brannigan and Foster 2002, 101.
17   Youngs 1956, 320, 324, fig. 13.20.
18   Ibid, 304.
19   Hallén 1994, 225-26; Armit 1996, 180.
20   Raftery 1984, 247.

observed in the Scottish material.[21] More recently, both large and small examples have been excavated in Bornais, South Uist.[22] Notably, these examples date to the fifth and sixth centuries AD, consistent with the late date for the Scalloway example referred to above.

As to the uses of such dice, these could have included gambling games, controlling moves in board games (with or without gambling), and fortune telling or divination (none of these uses being mutually exclusive). The dice from the Knowth 'gamblers'-burial were interred alongside two sets of gaming pieces.[23] These applications might be accompanied by an intrinsic, emotional, or commemorative appeal to keep dice as heirlooms.[24]

THE NORSE-GAEL TRANSITION: FROM BORNAIS TO LEWIS

By the second half of the first millennium AD, we can see a range of gaming equipment held in common by Picts, Scots, and Irish, evidenced by archaeological finds and textual records. In his paper on Applecross during the late Pictish period, Mac Lean quotes from the Old Irish *Scela Cano meic Gartnain*, describing Cano's departure for Ireland with the people of Skye in AD 688:

> [...] a royal retinue sailing in currachs, complete with fifty well-armed warriors, fifty well-dressed ladies and fifty liveried gillies each with the silver leads of two greyhounds in his right hand, a musical instrument in his left hand and a board of a fidcheall game on his back, along with the gold and silver playing men.[25]

Fidcheall is the Irish name for a group of *tafl* games held in common across northern Europe, and known as 'hnefatafl' in Scandinavia. Potentially derived from the Roman game *Ludus Latrunculorum*, they were important in Scotland during the early medieval period, having been demonstrated by Ritchie to be an example of the cultural tradition common to Picts, Scots, and other Celtic peoples, representing a '[...] direct link between Ireland, Dalriada and northern Pictland, presumably

21 Smith and Wilson 1998, 174.
22 Sharples 2012.
23 Hall and Forsyth 2011, 1328-1330.
24 For new thinking on recognising heirlooms in the archaeological record, see Gilchrist 2013.
25 Mac Lean 1997, 174.

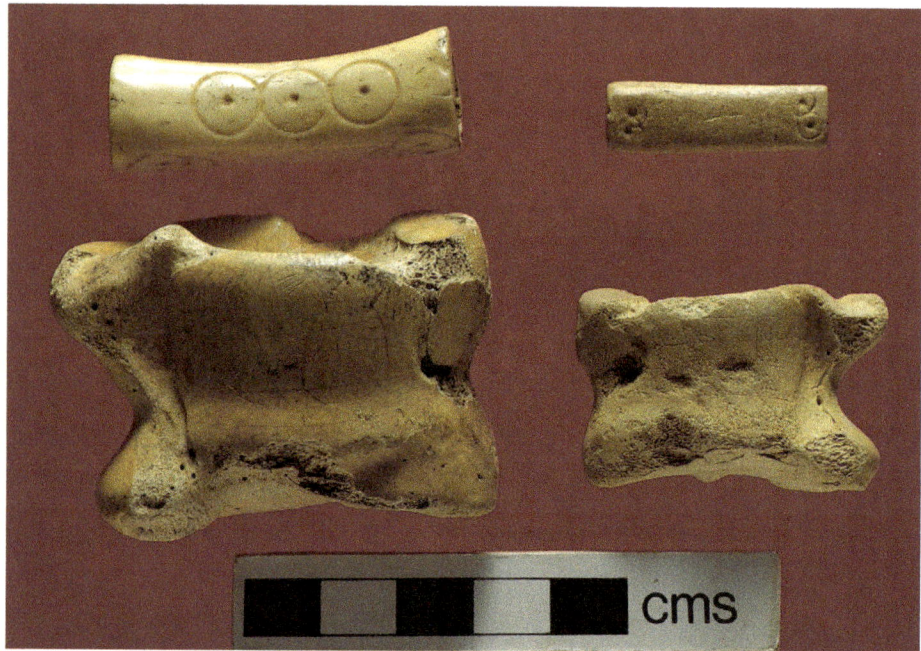

Figure 1: Parallelepiped dice and astragali from Bornais, South Uist (Copyright and courtesy Department of Archaeology, University of Cardiff).

through a common heritage'.[26]

From a Scandinavian perspective, perhaps the pivotal excavated site – spanning the fifth to fourteenth centuries – is Bornais, South Uist, which serves as a compelling window to a world that transitioned from Pictish to Norse to Gaelic. There are elements of gaming kits from all the excavated mounds of the settlement at Bornais. The late Iron Age or Pictish occupation of Mound 1 (approximately spanning the fifth to ninth centuries) substantially comprised a house, which was burnt down, rebuilt, and then completely dismantled during the mid-first millennium AD. The excavated gaming kit includes two parallelepiped dice, two astragali, a variety of ceramic and shell counters, and three pegged playing pieces (probably from a tafl game).[27] Previously, I have discussed the use of these and other astragali and parallelopiped dice for divination. The Mound 1 excavation report interprets the context of the finds – unburnt and placed in the burnt layer of the fire-consumed

26 Ritchie 1987, 62.
27 Sharples 2012, 84-87, 266-71, 281, fig. 182, nos. 1880, 2244, 2400.

wheel-house – as indicating an act of divination, perhaps to determine the propitiousness of reoccupying the house site, with the divination tools buried afterwards.[28] I have drawn comparisons to the unusual chequer-like design on one of the Bornais astragali, likening it to a pattern on a stone disc from Shetland.[29] Intriguingly, it is now suggested that the pattern on the Bornais piece may represent a recording of events, potentially associated with the divinatory use of the astragalus.[30] Although both astragali and parallelepiped dice gradually fell out of fashion, their divinatory and gaming functions endured in conventional cubic dice and other objects. From the Norse middens and centre of Mound 2a (in use between the late-tenth and fourteenth centuries), four such dice were recovered, three of them blanks (indicating on-site manufacture and associated with bone-making debris) and one numbered non-conventionally with opposing faces 1:6, 2:4 and 3:5.[31] Introduced in Roman times, the cubic shape was by far the commonest form of medieval die. In addition, several complete or fragmentary pieces of Scandinavian type were found, most notably cylindrical and piriform examples, particularly used in hnefatafl.[32]

In terms of gaming practice there seems to be no significant cultural barrier from Pictish to Norse to Gaelic; variations in the design of pieces do not mask the type of game in question, whilst discoveries of kits inside houses (in different room spaces), in middens, and in ancillary buildings suggest a wide social accessibility. This does not mean, however, that any social hierarchy within a community would not be partially reflected by gaming kits made of higher-quality and more expensive materials. Finds of some pieces within the central space of the wheelhouse are paralleled by gaming piece from the central area of another wheelhouse at Cnip, Lewis.[33] However, this material is stratigraphically dated to the first century AD, presenting an untenable date for a type of gaming piece most closely paralleled by wooden examples from twelfth-to-fourteenth-century Minsk and Novgorod.[34] Although their materials are different, the pieces are stylistically identical

---

28   Hall 2007, 21-25; Sharples 2012, 84, 263.
29   Hall 2007, 22-23.
30   Sharples 2012, 268.
31   Sharples forthcoming.
32   Ibid.
33   Armit 2006, table 2.3; Hunter 2006, 150.
34   Armit 2006, 221; Linder 1994, 175 (plate), 210 (plate); Rybina 2007, 355-56.

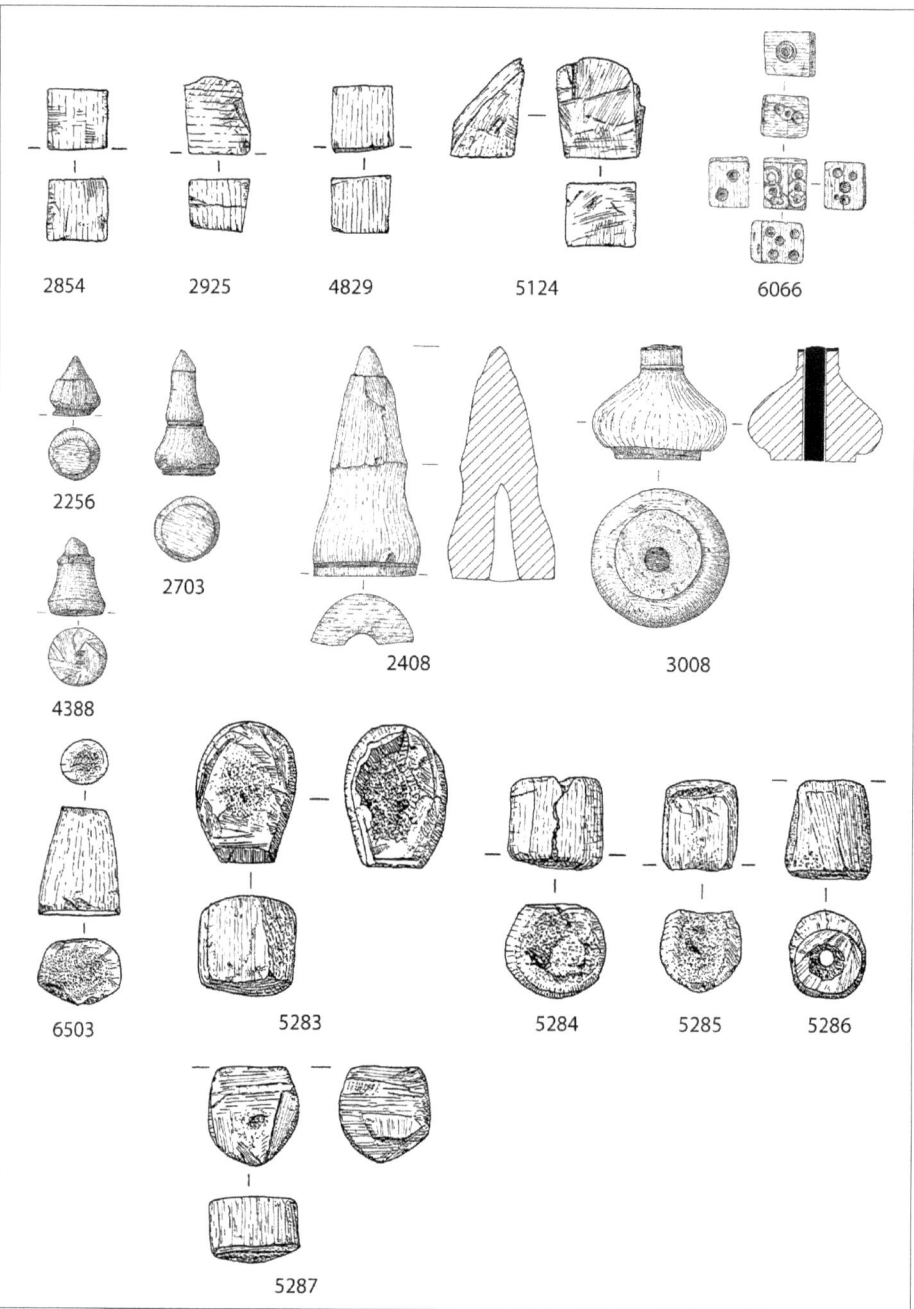

Figure 2: Norse period gaming pieces from Bornais, South Uist (Copyright and courtesy Department of Archaeology, University of Cardiff).

(if less accomplished or more worn in Cnip), sharing a Scandinavian background of Viking colonisation. As such, the Cnip piece is more likely to relate to local Norse evidence, including a Viking cemetery, and may have ended up in the wheelhouse area through disturbances in the stratigraphy of the sand that covered the site.[35]

The more limited quantities and range of material from other sites in the Uists – Udal,[36] Foshigarry and Bac Mhic Connain,[37] Sollas,[38] Machair Leathan,[39] and the Norse house of Drimore[40] – confirm this picture of board games as a staple social pursuit across cultural contexts. From the settlement complex at the Udal (especially Udal North) comes a range of medieval finds approximately spanning the ninth to thirteenth

Figure 3: A selction of the Norse and medieval gaming kit from the Udal North mound, North Uist (photograph by Mark A Hall for CnES Udal Archaeology Project).

35   Armit 1996, 197-201.
36   The Udal material has not been published but has been recently examined by the author with a view to full publication. For a general background, see Crawford 1986 and Ballin Smith 2012.
37   Hallén 1994.
38   Campbell 1991.
39   Beveridge 1911.
40   Maclaren 1974.

centuries, primarily made of bone and comparable to the material from Bornais, South Uist (see above), and Lödöse, Sweden (as yet unpublished but examined by the author). The most distinct piece from the Udal, in the context of the Isles, is a well-made but damaged bone disc, decorated with ring-and-dot and presumably used for the game of tables.

The late Iron Age sites at Foshigarry, Bac Mhic Connain, and Sollas (all in North Uist) provide the typical parallelepiped dice and pegged playing pieces, whilst Machair Leathan (South Uist) provides a decorated, domed bone piece echoing a Roman-style gaming piece. The Norse house at Drimore (South Uist) contributes a conical playing piece – the head of a pegged piece – like the other pieces just listed, used in a variant of hnefatafl/*fidcheall*. The Uig area of Lewis provides us with some key evidence for the continuity and changes to these games and their social stratification. The Lewis hoard of gaming pieces includes possible hnefatafl pieces, tablesmen, and, of course, a series of well-known chess pieces. Their late-twelfth to early-thirteenth-century dating makes them very early figurative chess pieces, possibly the earliest from the Isles, although they are mixed with abstract pieces equally suitable as chess or hnefatafl pawns. More singular abstract chess pieces are signalled by a chess knight from Rothesay Castle, Bute, which is in a style that predates figurative pieces. Rothesay Castle, however, is no earlier in date than the late-twelfth century (or, more likely, early-thirteenth); given that abstract pieces continued to be made and used after the introduction of figurative pieces, a thirteenth-century date for this find is not impossible. The example from Rothesay may well be contemporary with the Lewis pieces, possibly reflecting a different cultural influence: an Anglo-Norman one. There are similar abstract pieces in ivory and jet from Coldingham, Kirkwall, and Perth, dating as late as the fourteenth century.

The hoard of gaming pieces from Lewis is generally regarded as being of Norse origin. Its deliberate presence on Lewis and in the Hebrides is strongly indicative of the Norse-Gael transition. Documentary and literary corroboration for this is provided by a thirteenth-century supplicatory address to Islay's Lord, Aonghus Mór MacDomhnaill (d. 1296), seeking payment for a debt owed by his father, Donald, great grandson of Somerled (the progenitorial 'Lord of the Isles'). In his analysis of the poem, Bateman remarks on the manner in which the

Figure 4: A selection of the Lewis chessmen (Copyright and courtesy British Museum).

poet – who may have been Irish – refers to Aonghus' illustrious Norse ancestors, which went out of fashion as Clan Domhnaill and other Hebrideans came to assert a more exclusively Gaelic identity.[41] The first two verses (of a total of thirty-one) help to establish the cultural context to be explored here, and I quote them from the recent translation by Thomas Clancy:

Ceannaigh duan t'athar, a Aonghas,   [Purchase your father's poem, Aenghus

---

41   *Duanaire na Sracaire*, 53.

agad atá teach an ríogh:	the house of the king is yours,
As tú fréamha is bláth an bhile,	You are the tree's root and blossom:
Adéara cách dlighi a dhíol.	all say it's right that you buy it.
Agad do fhágaibh a láithreach,	To you he left his position,
leat gach lúireach, leat gach séad,	yours each mail shirt, each treasure,
a áit a luirg 's a chloidhmhe corra	His hats, his staves, his slender swords
duit 's a fhoirne donna dead.	Yours his brown ivory chess-sets.][42]

Although the poem describes Aenghus as king of Lewis, we cannot discount that this may be merely flattery, perhaps as part of the poet's aim to persuade Aenghus to do his kingly duty and settle his father's debts. Hence, the long listing of possessions he inherits from his father Donald (the eponym of Clan Donald) includes, of course, his ivory chess sets, or, more accurately, sets of playing pieces.[43] The poem, then, is an acknowledgement of the importance of chess and board games as an elite pursuit, an indication of their elite status, and an affirmation of their role in carrying social identity across familial generations (again raising the prospect of them being passed on as heirlooms).

This word picture of chess (or rather board games) as a key attribute of noble accomplishment and elite lifestyle echoes those found in other European texts describing skill at board games. Petrus Alfonsi, in his *Disciplina Clericalis* (c. 1100-1125), lists chess as one of the seven skills of a good knight, whilst in the chanson *Huon de Bordeaux* (c. 1200), the knight-hero (disguised as a minstrel) intones nine attributes, including unsurpassed skill at chess and tables.[44] For the elites of the North Sea world, *Orkneyinga Saga* lists board games as the first of nine key skills or attributes of a nobleman, featuring in a poem by Kali Kolsson before he is made Earl Rognavald.[45] The word being translated to 'chess' in both cases is *tafl*, which, although not literally meaning 'chess', certainly came to denote that game. Its literal meaning of 'table' (i.e. a board game) was applied to hnefatafl and its variants long before chess. The idea of playing of games as one of the marks of a great man became an aspect

---

42   *The Triumph Tree*, 288-91.
43   On the implication of sets and their colour, see Hall 2014a.
44   Eales 1986, 15; Vale 2001, 171; Murray 1913, 738.
45   *Orkneyinga Saga*, ch. 58; the same, alternative translation of this poem can be found in both Bibire 1988, 226, and *The Triumph Tree*, 190.

of the panegyric code found in Gaelic poetry,[46] although texts surviving from the seventeenth century onwards cite the games as tables (i.e. backgammon), dice, and cards.[47] These documents include verses such as:

Gu talla nam píos	[To the hall of cups
Far am faramaich' fion,	Where wine-quaffing makes din,
Far am falaichear mile crann	where a thousand bets are concealed
Bhiodh cruit is clarsach	A harp and a clarsach
'S mnà uchd-àille	and fair-bosomed women
An tùr nan tàileasg geàrr	in the tower of the short gaming boards' [tables]
Ruaig air dhisnean,	Dice being shaken
Foirm air thitibh	pieces on tables
'S òr a sios mar gheall,	and gold thrown down as stake,
Aig ogha Iarla Ile	In the hall of the grandson
Agus Chinn Tire,	of the Earl of Islay,
Rois is Innse Gall	of the Hebrides, Kintyre and Ross][48]

Dh'fhaighte an t'aras	[In your house could be counted
Ceòl nan clarsach,	music of the clarsach,
Fòirne air thàilisg,	a crowd at the gammon,
Mnà uch-àillte	fair-bosomed women
As crùin an geall mun cuairt	and crowns being waged all round][49]

Gu àras mo ruin	[To the hall of my love
'N cluinnte clàrsaochean ciùil,	Where harp's music was heard,
Iomairt thàilisg air chrùntaibh òir	Gambling at the gammon for crowns of gold][50]

46 Caldwell et al. 2009, 177, 180-81.
47 *Gair Nan Clarsach*, 100-5, 126-27; *An Lasair*, 67.
48 *Song to Dòmhnall Gorm Og MacDonald of Sleat*, written in the mid-seventheenth century by the vernacular poet Iain Lom. In *Gair Nan Clarsach*, 100-5, verses 8, 9, 12, 13.
49 *A Song to Lord Grant*, written c. 1640 by Seumas MacGriogair, in *Gair Nan Clarsach*, 122-27, verse 2.
50 *Let the Song Make its Way*, written c. 1695 by Iain Lom, to Dòmhnall a' Chogaidh, and in which 'gammon' is backgammon or tables. In *Gair Nan Clarsach*, 162-63, verse 3.

The implications and aspiration of the panegyric code were not universally accepted, however. Donald Monro's 1549 account of the Hebrides, containing a comment on the passing or decline of the Lordship of the Isles, still holds an echo of gaming as he states that Finlaggan councillors carried on 'albeit their Lord were at his hunting or at any other games'.[51] The account seems to be identifying such pursuits not with the strength of kings and nobles but their self-indulgence and lack of responsibility. This is both a rhetorical argument by Monro, aimed to fuel his retrospective 1540 reasoning, and a typical anti-gaming sentiment, representing a strand of moral, reforming zeal throughout the medieval period.

FINLAGGAN IN FOCUS: THE ISLES AT PLAY

Remaining on Islay, excavations at Finlaggan have given us some crucial evidence for the importance of gaming to the social identity of the medieval Lords of the Isles, as well as their retinues and households. To date, these excavations have not furnished any pieces of the quality of the Lewis gaming hoard, perhaps in part because such pieces may remain in the unexcavated areas of the site, notably its underwater middens. However, we must also take into account the peripatetic nature of the Lordship of the Isles, which would undoubtedly have seen the foremost pieces of gaming equipment moving around with their Lord as well as being much more carefully looked after. From evidence elsewhere, we know that the best-quality pieces were only discarded in exceptional circumstances, a good example being the Gloucester *tabulae* – or tables – set (discussed below). The bulk of the evidence from Finlaggan is more prosaic, indicating that such pastimes were not confined to the amusements of the elite but were much more widely enjoyed. By the end of the European medieval period, its various polities and cultural zones had their own ideas on which games were the most popular: usually chess, tables or nine men's morris. There was also a widespread social satire that depicted chess as the game of kings and nobles, tables as that of burgesses, and nine men's morris as that of the peasantry and urban poor.[52] The evidence from Finlaggan is broadly in line with this satire or parody, consisting of a graffiti gaming board,

---

51 Caldwell 2003, quoting *Monro's Western Isles of Scotland and Genealogies of the Clans*, 57.
52 Hall 2001.

Figure 5: Fragment of incised stone gaming board (alquerque) from Finlaggan, Islay (Copyright and courtesy NMS).

stone discs, and bone tablesmen. As such, they form an appropriate peg on which to hang an examination of the wider contexts of such material.

The graffiti board is the only fragment of a gaming board so far found at Finlaggan. The board design is scratched as a graffito on a mica-schist/schistose slate. It was found in the 1993 excavation season, in the fill of a beam slot that relates to the abandonment of building H. Its use as a gaming board presumably predates its use as a building slate, the graffito having possibly been scratched out to pass the time during construction work. The fragment of board design comprises two conjoined squares cut by horizontal, vertical, and diagonal lines. In the left hand square, the central crossing point for all the lines is marked by a somewhat broken circle, whilst a hint of something in the right hand square is evident. Although incomplete, its design suggests that the board was intended for the game 'alquerque', despite the fact that the aforementioned circle motifs do not normally occur on an alquerque board.[53] Incised or graffiti alquerque boards seem to have been quite rare in Britain until comparatively recently. Examples have been recorded from the cloisters of Norwich Cathedral, from Norwich Castle, and from St Mary's Church, Cavendish, Suffolk. From Scotland, numbers have increased significantly, with eighteen boards or fragments thereof known to this author. There are twelve examples from Inchmarnock (or thirteen if we include an unrecognised example from its assemblage of slates),[54] two examples from Castle Sween,[55] a fragment from Carrick Castle,[56] a fragment from Dundonald Castle,[57] a previously unrecognised example from Threave Castle, Galloway,[58] and an unfinished example from Ballumbie Church, Angus.[59] All of these boards are broadly dateable between the thirteenth and sixteenth centuries.

Although we can be reasonably certain that the Finlaggan fragment is an alquerque board, we can be less certain about what games were played on it. The Spanish Alfonso Codex of 1283, a gaming compendium compiled for King Alfonso X ('the Wise') of Leon and Castille, describes three variations of the game, using three, nine, or twelve pieces for each of two players. These appear to be identical to the game of merels (also known as morris or mill), but alquerque now tends to be separately classified.[60] Alquerque seems more accurately equated with games such as 'Fox and Geese'. The Spanish variant of this – 'Catch the Hare' – is also recorded in the Alfonso Codex as being played on the alquerque board.[61] That being said, the types of board used for nine men's morris and alquerque were, again according to the Alfonso Codex, different.[62] The gaming pieces used on each board – resembling abstract chess

---

53   For the game, see Murray 1952, fig. 27; Parlett 1999, fig. 151a.
54   Ritchie 2008, 119. The unrecognised example is IS61: Lowe 2008, 168-69.
55   Ewart and Triscott 1996, illus. 15.52, 16.52.
56   Ewart and Baker 1998, illus. 23.29.
57   Caldwell 2004, 101, illus. 49.
58   Good and Tabraham 1981, fig. 13, no. 201.
59   Hall unpublished; forthcoming, 6 and table 1, no. 2.
60   Parlett 1999; Murray 1952.
61   Parlett 1999, 187 and fig. 12.1.
62   Endrei and Zolnay 1986, pl. 28 [alquerque], pl. 50 [nine men's morris].

Figure 6: Two bone tablesmen from Finlaggan, Islay (Copyright and courtesy NMS).

pawns – do appear to have been identical, further widening the range of games that some of the Lewis hoard pieces could have been used for. Of course, it should come as no surprise to learn that boards and pieces were used as flexibly as possible, not least to minimise the amount of equipment needed when travelling. From the fourteenth century, triple game boards (combining chess, tables, and merels) were becoming increasingly popular in Europe. Although it would be easy to see the fragment of a gaming board from Finlaggan as a rather ephemeral, low status item, this need not have been the case. It could, for example, have been part of a kit used for teaching, possibly indicating that building H, with which it was associated, had a school function. Slates from numerous sites in the Isles and on the west coast indicate such a teaching function, most notably at the monasteries of Inchmarnock, off Bute, and Kilwinning, Ayrshire. A large number of boards from Inchmarnock include examples for hnefatafl, merels, and alquerque, whilst a smaller but still significant clutch, recently excavated at Kilwinning, comprises mainly unprovenanced finds from within the chapter house and cloister area, the latter location having the best light for such play within a monastery. At both Inchmarnock and Kilwinning, there are additional slates incised with pictures and practice letters, adding weight to their educational function. However, such slates do not appear to have been the sole preserve of ecclesiastical sites, as there are several secular sites in Ayrshire and Argyll that exhibit smaller quantities of the same range of material. This suggests that an element of learning, including literacy and games play, was being practiced within castle environments (though presumably using clerics as teachers). At Dundonald Castle, Ayrshire, excavations recovered fragments of a slate incised alquerque board, a daldos board, and two merels boards, one of them also incised for writing, with the probable phrase *in nomine* clearly visible.[63] At Carrick Castle, Argyll and Bute, the gaming kit excavated comprises a fragment of alquerque board, an incomplete daldos board, and a stone counter incised with a queen-like graffito (possibly a draughts piece or an improvised chess piece).[64] Also in Argyll and Bute, excavations at Castle Sween produced three fragments of alquerque boards and a stone disc with a graffito on each face.[65] Along with the much larger incised slate assemblages from Inchmarnock (discussed above) and from St Blane's monastery, Kingarth, Bute,[66] they are linked to a wider group of sites with similar slates from the western littoral of Britain, including St Patrick's Isle (castle and cathedral), Peel, Isle of Man,[67] and Tintagel Castle and Church, Cornwall,[68] demonstrating a ready access to slate as both a raw material and a reused or recycled one.

A great number of stone discs were excavated from Finlaggan, but the larger amongst these are unlikely to be gaming pieces, more likely serving as cooking or storage-pot lids, for example.[69] Even the more appropriately-sized discs are not automatically gaming pieces, as McLees observed when discussing the similar stone discs from Trondheim: 'it is possible that these stone discs represent finished items designed for some other function or that the majority were blanks destined to become perforated and perhaps decorated spindle whorls'.[70] Alternatively, the discs may have been components in some sort of rudimentary system of weights and measures, or tokens related to counting or tallying. A total of thirty-eight stone discs were excavated at Finlaggan

---

63   Caldwell 2004, fig. 49 and see 106, no. 86 and fig.47 for a stone gaming disc.
64   Ewart and Baker 1998, illus. 23.
65   Ewart and Triscott 1996. 542-54.
66   Anderson 1900.
67   Freke 2002a; 2002b; 2002c; Cubbon 2002; Trench-Jellicoe 2002.
68   Thorpe 1989; Nowakowski and Thomas 1990; 1992.
69   cf. Scalloway: Sharples 1998, 144-6, 180.
70   McLees 1990, 67.

– several on Council Island – and these are broken down into four size groupings: small (twenty-five examples), medium (six examples), large (five examples), and very large (two examples). Comparable but slightly larger collections of such discs were recovered from Jarlshof (Shetland), Hurly Hawkin (Angus), and Whithorn (Galloway).[71] Like the assemblage from Whithorn, Finlaggan has produced none of the more polished types identified in Henshall's scheme for the Hurly Hawkin material, most of them being roughly chipped discs. It is worth noting that much smaller quantities of discs (of stone and other materials) have been found throughout Britain and further afield, dating from the Neolithic to the post-medieval period.[72]

The small and medium pieces are most relevant here, the former being particularly compatible in size with the alquerque board fragment. Overall, such pieces have previously been accepted as gaming counters, and no obvious reason exists to suggest otherwise for Finlaggan.[73] Given its function as a high-status feasting site, one would expect evidence of corollary activities like gaming. There is a clear size compatibility between some of the Finlaggan discs and its gaming board but none of the material comes from what we might call a context of play. In other words, the contexts in which the pieces were found – including middens, gardening soil, and postholes – are all secondary in terms of gaming activity. They are indicative of loss and disposal of the material after their active use. Those that were misplaced would presumably be no great loss, and the ephemeral nature of the discs (and their use) certainly makes this likely. For an example of such gaming kit in an archaeological context of use rather than loss, we need only to look across the water to the Antrim coast. There, by the early-sixteenth century, the possessions of the MacDonald lordship included Dunluce Castle, where the excavation of a blacksmith's workshop has revealed something of the social spread of gaming. The workshop was situated at a central crossroads of the town of Dunluce, founded in 1608 (along with a manor house) to succeed the castle. In and around the smithy, a mixture of stone discs and a conical gaming piece were found (along with a cluster of clay pipe fragments), leading the smithy to be interpreted as a pivotal social space for the community to pass

---

71   Hamilton 1956; Henshall 1982; Nicholson 1997.
72   For a detailed listing, see Hall forthcoming.
73   Though Henshall 1982, 235, explores the possibility of rubbing or grinding tools.

the time.[74] The use of a smithy as a social gaming space acts as a counterpoint to those lordly gaming spaces implied in the Gaelic poetry cited above.

The final, key element of the Finlaggan gaming assemblage to be discussed is its three bone counters or playing pieces, all from fifteenth-century contexts; two from house floors and one from the cobbling of a path. All three pieces are readily identifiable as belonging to the tablesmen group of gaming pieces. Such pieces, along with dice, were used in the game of tables (although they would also have been suitable for draughts later on). Tables were a family of games, ultimately deriving from the Roman game of *tabula* and today surviving as backgammon.[75] Popular throughout the medieval period, their reputation is apparent from the numerous finds of pieces and boards (notable examples including the sets from Gloucester, England, and Mayenne, France),[76] as well as medieval depictions of the game (e.g. on the misericords in Manchester Cathedral and St George's Chapel, Windsor, both late-fifteenth century).[77]

The two smaller examples from Finlaggan were found together, one bearing zoomorphic decoration and the other geometric interlace. This decorative difference does not argue against a close association, as they may well represent opposing sides of the same set of pieces. Of course, we cannot rule out that the pieces represent two separate sets, with each side in each set being of similar design but distinguished in colour. Sets may also have been of mixed media; black-stained wooden discs, for example, could have been opposed by bone or ivory pieces rather than pale wooden ones.[78] By contrast, the third piece is about a third bigger than the other two pieces and more plainly decorated. Both types fit into recognised series.

The zoomorphic smaller piece bears a depiction of a prancing quadruped. Its head is turned backwards, its mouth is open to display a protruding tongue, and a short, single horn rises from its forehead. The whole beast pushes against the border of the disc, refusing to be confined by it. There are two close parallels to this; an antler tablesmen

---

74   Breen 2012, 159-60, fig. 6.23.
75   Murray 1952, 57-69; Parlett 1999, 58-87.
76   Watkins 1985, 41-69; Darvill 1988, 81-85; Grandet and Goret 2012.
77   Hall and Leahy 1996; Hall 2009.
78   Egan 1998, 294.

from Trondheim, Norway, is decorated with a prancing beast in a mid-twelfth-century Urness-Romanesque style but found in a late-thirteenth-to-fourteenth-century context.[79] The beast lacks a horn and has a long, pointed tail but otherwise has a strikingly similar pose. The second parallel is also a tablesmen, of walrus ivory, from the mid-twelfth century.[80] It boasts a greater sophistication of treatment than either the Trondheim or the Finlaggan piece.[81] Beckwith describes the beast as a dragon, but the clear lack of wings and single horn rising from the forehead surely indicates a unicorn. This is also a likely identification for the Finlaggan piece.

From Scotland, there is a small tally of figurative, bone gaming pieces: a crowned mermaid from Iona Abbey, a grotesque from Dalcross Castle, a rabbit or hare from the Bishop's Palace of Kirkwall, a centaur from Stonehaven, a horseman and rabbit from Urquhart Castle, and an eagle from Melrose Abbey.[82] None of these pieces originate from a secure archaeological context and have been conventionally dated, on artistic grounds, to the eleventh and twelfth century, consistent with the wider European Romanesque series of such pieces.[83] More recently, however, the pieces from Iona and Rhum have been dated to the fifteenth or sixteenth century, in line with the West Highland art tradition.[84] The vitality and prevalence of that tradition does not exclude the possibility of such gaming pieces. However, the figurative nature of all but two of them suggests that they do owe something to the earlier Romanesque tradition, indicating a potential strand of conservatism within West Highland culture.[85] This could have been fuelled by the generational transfer of such gaming pieces as heirlooms.

---

79 McLees 1990, fig. 26, 64-65, 204.
80 Beckwith 1972, cat. 159, illus. 256.
81 McLees 1990, 65, where he also notes that the backward looking animal motif is 'not uncommon in connection with Continental gaming discs [...] (see Goldschmidt 1975 [1926], various)'.
82 Society of Antiquaries of Scotland 1952-53, 204; 1871, 321; 1896-97, 80; Kluge-Pinsker 1991, cat. B60, B57, B56, B58, B55; Glenn 2003, 182-83; Caldwell 1982, 27; Beckwith 1972, cat. 110; Samson 1982, 475, fig. 6.92; Innis 1852, 297.
83 Mann 1977. These are all made of skeletal material, and the copper alloy exceptions from Ireland – including the four in Roe 1945, 766-69 – have recently been interpreted as weights, and are thus displayed in the 'Medieval Ireland 1150-1550' gallery of the National Museum of Ireland, Dublin.
84 Glenn 2003, 184-85.
85 Steer and Bannerman 1977, 186-87.

The smaller of the two interlace-decorated pieces from Finlaggan is much worn, but appears to be composed of two bands of interlace with pellets used to fill the gaps. As such, it resembles some of the interlace and pellet work on the Fife and Eglinton bone caskets.[86] As noted by Steer and Bannerman, although the 'combination of pellets and interlacing occurs on tenth-eleventh century Anglo-Scandinavian sculpture in northern England, Galloway and the Isle of Man and on earlier metalwork [...] plaitwork with interspersed pellets is found on the head of a cross of fifteenth century date at Kilfinan'.[87] The Fife and Eglinton caskets, as well as the importance of the casket as a motif in West Highland art, suggest a further possible relevance to this discussion. Such caskets would have had a number of storage uses, for '[...] letters, personal ornaments, keys etc.'[88] and, in addition, to hold gaming pieces. The Eglinton and Fife caskets certainly have the capacity for such storage. Caskets like these were common in medieval Europe, in a variety of materials: ivory, wood, leather and metal, as well as bone.[89] Found on a number of sites, fragments, particularly of bone, add to the number of surviving, complete examples. Most notably, these include fragments from Loughor Castle, Glamorgan, which have been interpreted as the remains of a box for storing gaming pieces (for chess and tables) found at the same site.[90] The possessions of Henry VIII included a large number of surviving, complete caskets, chests, and boxes, of which some were used to store chess and tables sets, as recorded in the inventory made following Henry's death.[91] Nothing resembling a chest or casket mount has been recovered from Finlaggan, although a latch from a casket lock was recovered from the same context as the two bone counters. The site also produced a small key, suitable for locking such a casket, as well as a copper-alloy corner strengthener, which could have been fitted to a casket corner

---

86   Callendar 1926; Glenn 2003, 186-91.
87   Steer and Bannerman 1977, 175-76.
88   Ibid., 176.
89   For examples, see Cherry 1982, 132-40.
90   Redknap 1993, 150-58.
91   *The Inventory of King Henry VIII*, e.g. nos. 3085, 3228, 3234, 3444, 11662; Haywood 1997, 8-15.

or purse (which could also be used for the keeping of gaming pieces).[92] The decorative repertoire and style of the Fife and Eglinton caskets has led to their late medieval attribution. However, the aforementioned gaming piece bears only pellet and interlace, and thus a slightly earlier date cannot be ruled out. A slightly larger fifteenth-to-sixteenth-century whalebone playing piece, decorated with a similar interlace pattern, was found in a cave on Rhum, and is on display in the National Museum of Scotland, Edinburgh.[93] Several pieces, now lost, were also found at St Andrews and Forfar Loch.[94] The only other bone tablesman exhibiting interlace known to this author is an example from a twelfth-century context at Ashagover Abbey, Lough Corrib, bearing (worn) simple zoomorphic interlace.[95] We should also note a wooden disc from Trondheim, carved with double-thread interlace and dated to the eleventh or early-twelfth century.[96]

The third bone disc is somewhat larger, its upper surface incised with two concentric circles just inside the rim and a central compass point within a small circle. It is thus very similar to the small group of tablesmen within the Lewis hoard.[97] Its condition is marred by a series of deep penetrating splits running across the upper surface. The simpler geometric style of decoration on this piece distinguishes it from the other two bone playing pieces, and, again, is consistent with a wider series of such items. These simpler forms of larger tablesmen come in a variety of materials – bone, stone, re-used pottery, and wood – with an assortment of ring and dot and/or concentric circle decorations. Examples include Perth High Street,[98] Urquhart Castle,[99] and Aberdeen.[100] These range in date from the twelfth to fifteenth century. Outside Scotland, the picture is similar, and a brief list could include Goltho (Lincolnshire),[101]

---

92   Full publication of this material is pending in Caldwell forthcoming, but see also
      Caldwell 2014, 237-39.
93   Glenn 2003, 185.
94   Hall 2007, 23-24; Munro 1882, 20-25, fig. 7; Hay-Fleming 1931, 197-98, fig. 15.
95   Roe 1945, 157, fig. 3.
96   McLees 1990, 72.
97   Stratford 1997, illus. 35.
98   MacGregor 2011, 101-02; Curteis et al. 2012, 283.
99   Samson 1982, 475, fig. 6.
100   MacGregor 1982, 182, illus. 104, where they are described as spindle whorls.
      They do, however, fit with this series as well, and the ambiguity between such
      spindle whorls and gaming pieces, alluded to above, is discussed by MacGregor
      1985, 137, 187; Hall & Leahy 1996, 235.
101   Beresford 1987, 191-2.

Loughor Castle (Glamorgan),[102] London,[103] York,[104] and Trondheim.[105] There are also variations: from Rothesay Castle, Bute – and on display in Bute Museum[106] – originates a bone tablesman, decorated with a floral motif within concentric circles, paralleled by wooden examples from Threave Castle and Perth.[107] Perhaps the implication is that there were standardised sets in circulation.

The single, larger tablesman from Finlaggan is ostensibly less accomplished than the two smaller pieces and perhaps supports the idea of board games being locally played across all social levels. The Lord of the Isles and his elite companions were peripatetic in their occupation of Finlaggan, and so it would have been for their prized sets of chess and tables. What was not peripatetic was the poorer quality material culture of the permanent occupants who cared for the site in the absence of their Lord. Nevertheless, chess pieces and pegged pieces are notably absent from the Finlaggan assemblage. We know from Aenghus Mór's poem that playing pieces for board games – presumably chess but also hnefatafl and its Irish correlate *fidcheall* – would have been familiar, whilst excavations at Kilellan Farm, Ardnave, demonstrate that pegged playing pieces were used on Islay as throughout the rest of the Isles.[108] The importance of high status gaming – tables, chess and *fidcheall/* hnefatafl in particular – undoubtedly continued at Finlaggan. Both here and across the Isles, the ruins of various halls underline the importance of feasting as part of the cultural dynamic and exercise of power of the region.[109] Combining the evidence for gaming and feasting, a mixture still alive in the seventeenth-century poems quoted above, allows us to observe how individual aspects of culture may be combined to produce fuller statements of identity. It is therefore appropriate to draw on some telling Irish evidence.

The twelfth-century Book of Leinster and the fourteenth-century Book of Leccan record the layouts and seating arrangements for royal

---

102   Redknap 1993, 150-58.
103   Egan 1998, 294.
104   Rogers 1993, 1405-06.
105   McLees 1990, 61-72; 195-211.
106   Hall 2014, 169.
107   Good and Tabraham 1981, 119, fig. 15.151; Curteis et al. 2012, 283.
108   Ritchie 2005, 146.
109   David Caldwell, pers. comm.

banquets at Tara.[110] The plans and texts equate rank with particular cuts of meat; highest ranks would get both the best cuts and sit closest to the king. This was a strictly hierarchical arrangement, upheld to reflect a deeper cosmic order, which would stave off chaos. The pig carcass was seen to produce seven better cuts and seven poorer cuts. The former included the shank or *colpthae*, and those entitled to it included druids, vassal lords, pipers or flutists, and *fidscheallaig* – expert players of board games. Sayers suggests that status may have been accorded to these *fidcheall* players because of an association with the king.[111] This association may have entailed coaching the king, playing against him, and being expected to win on his behalf in other matches. They were co-ranked with musicians, whilst being higher in rank than a range of craftsmen (including goldsmiths), charioteers, royal stewards, physicians, cooks, storytellers, jugglers, jesters, and farters (*braigetóiri*). The late-sixteenth-century poetry of Tadhg Dall Ó Huiginn includes a verse comparing Tara to the king's square on a *fidcheall* board.[112] This allegory recalls an eighth-century metaphor in the poetry of the Irish monk Blathmac, comparing God's layout of the stars in the heavens (with Christ as their king) to the layout of a *fidcheall* board, with Christ as the king piece.[113] The role of the board-game players, the *fidscheallaig*, was marked enough to give rise to a surname in the West Cork area: 'Feehilly' or 'Fehilly', anglicised versions of *Ó Fithcheallaigh*, meaning 'chess-player'.[114] This name starkly contrasts those used to denote dice-players or gamblers: *cearrach*, meaning 'dextrous player of games', 'gambler', 'dicer'. This term derives from *cearr* meaning 'wrong', 'awkward', 'unlucky', 'left or left-handed', and 'astray'.[115] The Book of Leinster and the Book of Leccan deploy a very distinctive symbolism to define social status, suited to a Gaelic milieu but by no means unique, particularly concerning board games. Across medieval Europe, chess represented a key element in the depiction of social hierarchy and relative status. The most well-known and explicit of these depictions is

---

110 McCormick 2002, fig. 4; Sayers 1990.
111 Sayers 1990, 95-96.
112 *A Bhfuil Aguinn Dár Chum Tadhg Dall Ó Huiginn*, 198-99.
113 *The Poems of Blathmac*, quatrain 192.
114 De Bhulbh 1997, 190-91. Originally, the name would have signified '*fidcheall* players', or more accurately, 'board-game players'.
115 Ibid.

Jacobus de Cessolis' *Liber de moribus hominum et officiis nobilium sive super ludo scachorum*, 'the book of the habits of people and the duties of nobles or about the game of chess', which equates social divisions to chess pieces. Thus, the king, queen, bishop, knight, and rook pieces represent the nobility, whilst the pawns designate eight categories of craftsmen, which were expected to show loyalty and not to exceed their station. These included untrustworthy types, which, like in the Irish evidence cited above, included gamblers.[116]

CONCLUSION

This brief tour of the evidence from Islay, as well as some of its neighbours in the Irish Sea/west coast cultural zone, has sought to demonstrate that the playing of board games was both prevalent and stratified throughout society. Present evidence demonstrates that board and dice games began to be manufactured, exchanged, acquired, played, and adapted in the Western Isles by the early first millennium AD. This phase represents one of the roots for the later flourishing of play in the Isles, which adds distinctive colour to the cultural hybridity that marks the early and late medieval centuries. Tracking game types and their development reveals a flux of entanglements and transformations that are pivotal to evolving cultural identities. The arrival of new peoples brought new games, often with similar roots – albeit grown in a different cultural soil – to those already played. Hence, Scandinavians arriving with hnefatafl would readily understand the *fidcheall* games being played by the indigenous dwellers of Pictish and Gaelic descent. Terminology for board games is fluid and generic, often carrying the broad meaning 'board-game': *fidcheall*, *tafl*, and *tables* all essentially designate a board for play. This is a flexible, functional terminology easily applied to a variety of games, in which names were not the sole determinants of the activity; the board, the pieces, the rules, and the players were all part of the equation that decided which game would be played. Thus, in later medieval texts (and presumably conversations), *fidcheall* and *tafl* were readily applicable as names or alternative names for new games, including chess. Specifics changed within broad cultural contexts, which meant identities could adapt and develop whilst not abandoning their roots; they could even develop a sense of rootedness,

---

116   Dalen-Oskam 2000, 67-68; Murray 1913, 537-558, 529-537.

helped by the permanence of play. Although the cultural and ethnic transitions that took place in the Isles between the ninth and fifteenth centuries were not determined by board games, board games were part of the Isles, an entangled network of sea, land, and people, as well as the objects they transported, abandoned, redefined, and preserved within that space.

All levels of society sought to play, but social elites staked out such play as their right and privilege, in part as an attempt to control freedom through access to free or leisure time. The combined evidence of historical sources and archaeology illuminates a long-lived tradition of gaming, particularly board games, available to all but particularly visible as an essential aspect of court and elite lifestyles in the west of Scotland. Placed in its European context, elite entitlement and ownership – in the face of widespread games play – proclaimed itself by the production of lavish boards and pieces, well beyond the pockets of all but royalty and nobility (and the later mercantile *nouveau riche*). Playing such games contributed to individual and group identities, often working in conjunction with other aspects of cultural behaviour, to create an identity that was partially identical yet partially competing with that of others. Recent work has shown that some of the deeper rhythms of late Iron Age life in the Western Isles, specifically the utilisation of human bone, continued during the new Scandinavian hegemony, and so it was with board games.[117]

BIBLIOGRAPHY

PRIMARY SOURCES

Duanaire na Sracaire: Songbook of the Pillagers, Anthology of Scottish Verse to 1600, Bateman M and McLeod W (eds), 2007, Edinburgh: Birlinn.

An Lasair: Anthology of 18th Century Scottish Gaelic Verse, Black R (ed), 2001, Edinburgh: Birlinn.

The Poems of Blathmac, son of Cú Brettan, Together with the Irish Gospel of Thomas and a Poem of the Virgin Mary, Carney J (ed), 1964, Dublin: Irish Text Society.

The Triumph Tree: Scotland's Earliest Poetry AD 550-1350, Clancy T O (ed and trans), 1998, Edinburgh: Canongate.

---

117   Shapland and Armit 2012.

A Bhfuil Aguinn Dár Chum Tadhg Dall Ó Huiginn (1550-1591) – The Poetry of Tadhg Dall Ó Huiginn, Knot E (ed), 1926, vols i-ii, Dublin: Irish Texts Society.

Monro's Western Isles of Scotland and Genealogies of the Clans, Munro R W (ed), 1961 [1549], Edinburgh: Oliver & Boyd.

Gair Nan Clarsach – The Harp's Cry: An Anthology of 17th Century Gaelic Poetry, Ó Baoill C (ed) and Bateman M (trans), 1998, Edinburgh: Birlinn.

Orkneyinga Saga: The History of the Earls of Orkney, Pálsson H and Edwards P (trans), 1978, London: Penguin.

The Inventory of King Henry VIII – Volume 1: Transcript, Starkey D (ed), 1999, London: Society of Antiquaries of London.

SECONDARY SOURCES

Anderson, J 1900, 'Description of a Collection of Objects Found in Excavations at St Blane's Church, Bute, Exhibited by the Marquis of Bute', *Proc. Soc. Antiq. Scot.* 34, 307-25.

Armit, I 1996, *The Archaeology of Skye and the Western Isles*, Edinburgh: Edinburgh University Press.

Armit, I 2006, *Anatomy of an Iron Age Roundhouse: The Cnip Wheelhouse Excavations, Lewis*, Edinburgh: Society of Antiquaries of Scotland.

Ballin Smith, B 2012, *The Udal: Iain Crawford's Excavations on the Machair 1963-1994*, Glasgow: The Udal Project and GUARD Archaeology.

Beckwith, J 1972, *Ivory Carvings in Early Medieval England*, London: Harvey Miller.

Beresford, G 1987, *Goltho: The Development of an Early Medieval Manor c. 850-1150*, London: English Heritage.

Beveridge, E 1999 [1911], *North Uist: Its Archaeology and Topography with Notes upon the Early History of the Outer Hebrides*, Edinburgh: Birlinn.

Bibire, P 1988, 'The Poetry of Earl Rognvald's Court', in B E Crawford (ed), *St Magnus Cathedral and Orkney's Twelfth-Century Renaissance*, Aberdeen: Mercat Press, 208-40.

Brannigan, K and P Foster 2002, *Barra and the Bishop's Isles: Living on the Margin*, Stroud: Tempus.

Breen, C 2012, *Dunluce Castle: History and Archaeology*, Dublin: Four Courts.

Caillois, R 2002 [1958], *Man, Play and Games*, M Barash (trans), Chicago: University of Illinois.

Caldwell, D 1982, *Angels, Nobles and Unicorns: Art and Patronage in Medieval Scotland*, Edinburgh: NMAS.

Caldwell, D 2003, 'Finlaggan, Islay – Stones and Inauguration Ceremonies', in R Welander, D J Breeze, and T O Clancy (eds), *The Stone of Destiny*, Edinburgh: Society of Antiquaries of Scotland, 61-76.

Caldwell, D 2004, 'Inscribed and Engraved Slates', *Scottish Archaeological Journal* 26:1-2, 107-10.

Caldwell, D 2014 'The Lordship of the Isles Identity Through Materiality', in R Oram (ed), *The Lordship of the Isles*, Leiden: Brill, 227-253.

Caldwell, D forthcoming, *Excavations at Finlaggan, Islay*.

Caldwell, D, M A Hall, and C Wilkinson 2009, 'The Lewis Hoard of Gaming Pieces: A Re-examination of their Context, Meanings, Discovery and Manufacture', *Medieval Archaeology* 53, 155-203.

Caldwell, D, M A Hall, and C Wilkinson 2010, *The Lewis Chessmen Unmasked*, Edinburgh: NMS Publishing.

Callander, J G 1926, 'A Casket of Cetacean Bone', *Proc. Soc. Antiq. Scot.* 9, 105-17.

Campbell, E 1991, 'Excavations of a Wheelhouse and Other Iron Age Structures on Sollas, North Uist, by R J C Atkinson in 1957', *Proc. Soc. Antiq. Scot.* 121, 117-73.

Cherry, J 1982, 'The Talbot Casket and Related Late Medieval Leather Caskets', *Archaeologia* 107, 131-40.

Clarke, D V 1970, 'Bone Dice and the Scottish Iron age', in *Proceedings of the Prehistoric Society* 36, 214-32.

Crawford, I A 1986, *The West Highlands and Islands: A View of 50 Centuries. The Udal (N. Uist) Evidence*, Cambridge: Great Auk Press.

Crummy, P 2007, 'The Gaming Board in CF47: The Remains as Found, Possible Reconstruction and Post-Depositional Movements', in P Crummy et al., *Stanway: An Élite Burial Site at Camulodunum*, London: Society for the Promotion of Roman Studies, 352-58.

Cubbon, A M 2002, 'Merels Boards', in D Freke (ed), *Excavations at St Patrick's Isle, Peel, Isle of Man 1982-88 Prehistoric, Viking, Medieval and Later*, Liverpool: Liverpool University Press, 276-81.

Curteis, A, C A Morris, and N Q Bogdan 2012, 'The Worked Wood', in N Q Bogdan et al. (eds), *Perth High Street Archaeological Excavations 1975-1977. Fascicule 2: The Ceramics, the Metalwork, and the Wood*, Perth: Tayside and Fife Archaeological Committee, 223-316.

Dalen-Oskam, K van 2000, 'The Flying Chess-set in the Roman van Walewein', in G H M Claassens and D F Johnson (eds), *King Arthur in the Medieval Low Countries*, Leuven: Leuven University Press, 59-68.

Darvill, T 1988, 'Excavations on the Site of the Early Norman Castle at Gloucester 1983-84', *Medieval Archaeology* 32, 1-49.

De Bhulbh, S 1997, *Sloinnte na h-Éireann/Irish Surnames*, Limerick: Comhar-Chumann Ide Naofa Teo.

Dumazedier, J 1968, 'Leisure', in D Sills (ed), *International Encyclopaedia of the Social Sciences*, New York: MacMillan, 248-53.

Eales, R 1986, 'The Game of Chess: An Aspect of Medieval Knightly Culture', in C Harper-Bill and R Harvey (eds), *The Ideals and Practice of Medieval Knighthood*, Woodbridge: Boydell, 12-34.

Egan, G 1998, *The Medieval Household: Daily Living c.1150-c.1450*, London: HMSO/Museum of London.

Endrei, W and L Zolnay 1986, *Fun and Games in Old Europe*, Budapest: Corvina.

Eogan, G and B Weekes 2012, 'Late Iron Age Burials', in G Eogan, *Excavations at Knowth 5: The Archaeology of Knowth in the First and Second Millennium AD*, Dublin: Royal Irish Academy, 13-44.

Ewart, G and F Baker 1998, 'Carrick Castle: Symbol and Source of Campbell Power in South Argyll from the 14th to the 17th century', *Proc. Soc. Antiq. Scot.* 128, 937-1016.

Ewart, G and J Triscott 1996, 'Archaeological Excavations at Castle Sween, Knapdale, Argyll and Bute 1989-1990', *Proc. Soc. Antiq. Scot.* 126, 517-57.

Freke, D 2002a, 'Slate Artefacts', in D Freke (ed), *Excavations at St Patrick's Isle, Peel, Isle of Man 1982-88 Prehistoric, Viking, Medieval and Later*, Liverpool: Liverpool University Press, 272-73.

Freke, D 2002b, 'Architectural Fragments', in D Freke (ed), *Excavations at St Patrick's Isle, Peel, Isle of Man 1982-88 Prehistoric, Viking, Medieval and Later*, Liverpool: Liverpool University Press, 291-92.

Freke, D 2002c, 'Miscellaneous Stone Artefacts', in D Freke (ed), *Excavations at St Patrick's Isle, Peel, Isle of Man 1982-88 Prehistoric, Viking, Medieval and Later*, Liverpool: Liverpool University Press, 293-304.

Galestin, M C 2010, 'Roman Artefacts beyond the Northern Frontier: Interpreting the Evidence from the Netherlands', *European Journal of Archaeology* 13.1, 64-88.

Gilchrist, R 2013, 'The Materiality of Medieval Heirlooms: From Biographical to Sacred Objects', in H P Hahn and H Weiss (eds), *Mobility, Meaning & Transformations of Things*, Oxford: Oxbow, 170-182.

Glenn, V 2003, *Romanesque and Gothic Decorative Metalwork and Ivory Carvings in the Museum of Scotland*, Edinburgh: NMS Publishing.

Goldschmidt, A 1975 [1926], *Die Elfenbeinskulpturen aus der Romanischen Zeit: XI.-XIII. Jahrhundert*, Berlin: Deutscher Verein für Kunstwissenschaft.

Good, G L and C J Tabraham 1981, 'Excavations at Threave Castle, Galloway 1974-78', *Medieval Archaeology* 25: 90-140.

Grandet, M and J-F Goret 2012, *Échecs et Trictrac Fabrication et Usages des Jeux de Tables au Moyen Âge*, Paris: Musee du Chateau de Mayenne.

Hall, M A 2001, 'Gaming-Board Badges', in H J E van Beuningen, A Koldeweij, and D Kicken (eds), *Heilig en Profaan 2: 1200 Laatmiddeleeuwse Insignes uit Openbare en Particuliere Collecties*, Cothen: Rotterdam Papers, 173-78.

Hall, M A 2007, *Playtime in Pictland: The Material Culture of Gaming in Early Medieval Scotland*, Rosemarkie: Groam House Museum.

Hall, M A 2009, 'Where the Abbot Carries Dice: Gaming-Board Misericords in Context', in E C Block (ed), *Profane Imagery in Marginal Arts of the Middle Ages*, Turnhout: Brepols, 63-81.

Hall, M A 2011, 'Playtime: The Material Culture of Gaming in Medieval Scotland', in T Cowan and L Henderson (eds), *A History of Everyday Life in Medieval Scotland 1000-1600*, Edinburgh: Edinburgh University Press, 145-68.

Hall, M A 2014a, '"To You He Left … His Brown Ivory Chessmen": Cultural Value in the Lewis hoard of Gaming Pieces', in D Caldwell and M A Hall (eds), *The Lewis Chessmen: New Perspectives*, Edinburgh: NMS Publishing/ SAS, 221-42.

Hall, M A 2014b, 'Board of the Kings: The Material Culture of Playtime in Scotland AD 1-1600', in M Teichert (ed), *Sport und Spiel bei den Germanen: Nordeuropa von der Römischen Kaiserzeit bis zum Mittelalter*, Boston: De Gruyter, 163-96.

Hall, M A 2016, 'Ecclesia Ludens: Board and Dice Games in a Scottish Monastic Context', *Proc. Soc. Antiq. Scot.* 145, 1-15.

Hall, M A forthcoming, 'Finlaggan at Play: The Gaming Equipment', in D Caldwell, *Excavations at Finlaggan* (title tbc).

Hall, M A unpublished, 'Incised Stone Gaming Board', in D W Hall and R Cachart, Ballumbie excavation report.

Hall, M A and K Forsyth 2011, 'Roman Rules? The Introduction of Board Games to Britain and Ireland', *Antiquity* 85:330, 1325-1338.

Hall, M A and K Leahy 1996, 'A Decorated Antler Disc from Scopwick, Lincolnshire', *Antiquaries Journal* 76, 234-37.

Hallén, Y 1994, 'The Use of Bone and Antler at Foshigarry and Bac Mhic Connain, Two Iron Age Sites on North Uist, Western Isles', *Proc. Soc. Antiq. Scot.* 124, 189-231.

Hamilton, J R C 1956, *Excavations at Jarlshof, Shetland*, Edinburgh: HMSO.

Hay-Fleming, D 1931, *St Andrews Cathedral Museum*, Edinburgh: Oliver & Boyd.

Haywood, M 1997, 'The Packing and Transportation of the Possessions of Henry VIII, with Particular Reference to the 1547 Inventory', *Costume* 31, 8-15.

Henshall, A 1982, 'The Finds', in D B Taylor (ed), 'Excavations at a Promontory Fort, Broch and Souterrain at Hurly Hawkin, Angus', *Proc. Soc. Antiq. Scot.* 112, 225-44.

Hunter, F 2006, 'Bone and Antler', in I Armit, *Anatomy of an Iron Age Roundhouse: The Cnip Wheelhouse Excavations, Lewis*, Edinburgh: Society of Antiquaries of Scotland, 136-51.

Innis, C 1852, 'Antiquities and Works of Art Exhibited', *Archaeological Journal* 9, 297.

Kluge-Pinsker, A 1991, *Schachspiel und Trictrac: Zeugnisse Mittelalterlicher Spielfreude in Salischer Zeit*, Sigmaringen: Thorbecke.

Linder, I M 1994, *Schach: Schachfiguren im Wandel der Zeit*, Moscow: H.G.S.

Mac Lean, D 1997, 'Maelrubai, Applecross and the Late Pictish Contribution West of Druimalban', in D Henry (ed), *The Worm, the Germ and the Thorn: Pictish and Related Studies Presented to Isabel Henderson*, Balgavie: Pinkfoot Press, 173-87.

MacGregor, A 1982, 'Bone, Antler and Ivory Objects', in J C Murray (ed), *Excavations in the Medieval Burgh of Aberdeen 1973-81*, Edinburgh: Society of Antiquaries of Scotland, 180-82.

MacGregor, A 1985, *Bone, Antler, Ivory and Horn: The Technology of Skeletal Material Since the Roman Period,* London: Croom Helm.

MacGregor, A 2011, 'The Worked Bone', in N Q Bogdan et al. (eds), *Perth High Street Archaeological Excavations 1975-1977. Fascicule 4: Living and Working in a Medieval Burgh – Environmental Remains and Miscellaneous Finds*, Perth: Tayside and Fife Archaeological Committee, 97-116.

Maclaren, A 1974, 'A Norse House on Drimore Machair, South Uist', *Glasgow Archaeological Journal* 3, 9-18.

Mann, V B 1977, 'Romanesque Ivory Tablesmen', unpublished PhD thesis, New York University.

McLees, C 1990, *Games People Played: Gaming pieces, Boards and Dice in the Medieval Town of Trondheim*, Trondheim: University of Trondheim.

McCormick, F 2002, 'The Distribution of Meat in a Hierarchical Society: The Irish evidence', in P Miracle and M Milner (eds), *Consuming Passions and Patterns of Consumption*, Cambridge: McDonald Institute, 25-31.

Munro, R 1882, *Ancient Scottish Lake Dwellings or Crannogs*, Edinburgh: David Douglas.

Murray, H J R 1913, *A History of Chess*, Oxford: Oxford University Press.

Murray, H J R 1952, *A History of Board Games Other Than Chess*, Oxford: Oxford University Press.

Nicholson, A 1997, 'The Stone Artefacts', in P Hill, *Whithorn and St Ninian: Excavation of a Monastic Town 1984-91*, Stroud: Alan Sutton, 447-49.

Nowakowski, J and C Thomas 1990, *Excavations at Tintagel Parish Churchyard, Cornwall, Spring 1990: Interim Report*, Truro: Cornwall Archaeology Unit.

Nowakowski, J and C Thomas 1992, *Grave News from Tintagel*, Truro: Cornwall Archaeology Unit.

Parlett, D 1999, *Oxford History of Board Games*, Oxford: Oxford University Press.

Raftery, B 1984, *La Tène in Ireland: Problems of Origin and Chronology*, Marburg: Vorgeschichtlichen Seminars Marburg.

Redknap, M 1993, 'The Bone Gaming Pieces', in J M Lewis, 'Excavations at Loughor Castle, West Glamorgan 1969-73', *Archaeologica Cambrensis* 142 (1992-93), 99-181.

Ritchie, A 1987, 'The Picto-Scottish Interface in Material Culture', in A Small (ed), *The Picts: A New Look at Old Problems*, Dundee: Dundee University, 59-67.

Ritchie, A 2005, *Kilellan Farm, Ardnave, Islay: Excavations of a Prehistoric to Early Medieval Site by Colin Burgess and Others 1954-1976*, Edinburgh: Society of Antiquaries of Scotland.

Ritchie, A 2008, 'Gaming Boards', in C Lowe (ed), *Inchmarnock: An Early Historic Island Monastery and its Archaeological Landscape,* Edinburgh: Society of Antiquaries of Scotland, 116-27.

Roe, H M 1945, 'Medieval Bronze Gaming Piece from Laoighis', *Journal of the Royal Society of Antiquaries of Ireland* 75, 756-59.

Rogers, W 1993, *Anglian and Other Finds from Fishergate*, York: Council for British Archaeology.

Rybina, E A 2007, 'Chess Pieces and Game Boards', in M Brisbane and J Hather (eds), *Wood Use in Medieval Novgorod*, Oxbow: Oxbow Books, 354-59.

Samson, R 1982, 'Finds from Urquhart Castle in the National Museum Edinburgh', *Proc. Soc. Antiq. Scot.* 112, 465-76.

Sayers, W 1990, 'A Cut Above: Ration and Station in an Irish King's Hall', in *Food and Foodways: Explorations in the History and Culture of Human Nourishment* 4:2, 89-110.

Schädler, U 2007, 'The Doctor's Game: New Light on the History of Ancient Board Games', in P Crummy et al., *Stanway: An Élite Burial Site at Camulodunum*, London: Society for the Promotion of Roman Studies, 359-74.

Shapland, F and I Armit 2012, 'The Useful Dead: Bodies as Objects in Iron Age and Norse Atlantic Scotland', *European Journal of Archaeology* 15:1, 98-116.

Sharples, N M (ed) 1998, *Scalloway, A Broch, Late Iron Age Settlement and Medieval Cemetery in Shetland*, Oxford: Oxbow Books.

Sharples, N M (ed) 2012, *A Late Iron Age Farmstead in the Outer Hebrides: Excavations at Mound 1, Bornais, South Uist*, Oxford: Oxbow Books.

Sharples, N M (ed) forthcoming, *The Norse Settlement of the Outer Hebrides: Excavations at Mounds 2 and 2A, Bornais, South Uist*, Oxford: Oxbow Books.

Smith, A N and G Wilson 1998, 'Dice', in N M Sharples (ed), *Scalloway, A Broch, Late Iron Age Settlement and Medieval Cemetery in Shetland*, Oxford: Oxbow Books, 174.

Society of Antiquaries of Scotland 1871, 'Donations to the Museum and Library', *Proc. Soc. Antiq. Scot* 7, 321.

Society of Antiquaries of Scotland 1896-97, 'Donations to the Museum and Library' *Proc. Soc. Antiq. Scot.* 31, 80.

Society of Antiquaries of Scotland 1952-53, 'Donations to and Purchases for the Museum', *Proc. Soc. Antiq. Scot.* 87, 201-9.

Steer, K A and J W M Bannerman 1977, *Late Medieval Monumental Sculpture in the West Highlands*, Edinburgh: RCAHMS/HMSO.

Stratford, N 1997, *The Lewis Chessmen and the Enigma of the Hoard*, London: British Museum Press.

Thorpe, C 1989, 'Incised Pictorial Slates from Tintagel', in C Thomas (ed), *Cornish Studies* 16, 69-78.

Trench-Jellicoe, R 2002, 'Early Christian and Viking Age Sculptured Monuments', in D Freke (ed), *Excavations at St Patrick's Isle, Peel, Isle of Man 1982-88 Prehistoric, Viking, Medieval and Later*, Liverpool: Liverpool University Press, 282-90.

Vale, M 2001, *The Princely Court, Medieval Courts and Culture in NW Europe*, Oxford: Oxford University Press.

Watkins, M 1985, *Gloucester, the Normans and Domesday: Exhibition Catalogue and Guide,* Gloucester: Gloucester Museum.

Wilson, G and P Watson 1998, 'Conical Gaming Pieces', in N M Sharples (ed), *Scalloway, A Broch, Late Iron Age Settlement and Medieval Cemetery in Shetland*, Oxford: Oxbow Books, 174-75.

Youngs, A 1956, 'Excavations at Dun Cuier, Isle of Barra, Outer Hebrides', *Proc. Soc. Antiq. Scot.* 89, 290-328.

Across
the Inner Seas

Scottish Affairs and the Political Context of *Cogadh Gaedhel re Gallaibh*

Clare Downham[1]

The Battle of Clontarf is one of the most famous conflicts in Irish history. It was fought between the forces of Brian Boru, over-king of Ireland and his allies (including the *mormaer* of Mar in Alba), and the forces of viking Dublin, Leinster and their allies (including men from Orkney and the Hebrides) on Good Friday 1014. The scale of the battle was noted by chroniclers in Britain, Ireland and the Continent.[2] Nevertheless, the saga narrative *Cogadh Gaedhel re Gallaibh* or 'The War of the Irish and the Foreigners', which was composed long after the event, has been very influential in shaping historical interpretations of the conflict. One under-researched aspect of *Cogadh* is the portrayal of Scottish affairs. In this chapter I seek to demonstrate the significance of northern Britain in the narrative, and to interpret the political context in which it was written.

Despite its historical significance *Cogadh Gaedhel re Gallaibh* survives in only three manuscripts. The earliest copy survives in the famous Book of Leinster (Dublin, Trinity College, MS 1339 [H.2.18]), compiled in the second half of the twelfth century. *Cogadh* is the last text in this manuscript, whose loss of final leaves means that only the first 29 sections of narrative are preserved. The recension found in the Book of Leinster (siglum 'L') differs from that found in two later manuscripts. The second manuscript containing *Cogadh* is Dublin, Trinity College, MS 1319 [H.2.17] (siglum 'D').[3] This two-volume manuscript contains texts of various ages and sizes. The section containing *Cogadh* was written down in the late-fourteenth or early-fifteenth century. It is lacunose with leaves missing from both the beginning and the end of the narrative. The only complete version of *Cogadh* is a transcript on

---

1   I should like to thank Denis Casey, Nick Evans, Rosemary Power, and Máire Ní Mhaonaigh for reading and commenting on drafts of this chapter.

2   *Ademari Cabannensis Chronicon*, iii, 54-55, 172-73; *Mariani Scotti Chronicon*, 1014; *Annals of Clonmacnoise*, 1007 [=1014]; *Annals of the Four Masters*, 1013 [=1014]; *Annals of Inisfallen*, 1014; *Annals of Loch Cé*, 1014; *Annals of Ulster*, 1014; *Chronicon Scotorum*, 1014; *Brenhinedd y Saesson*, 1013 [=1014]; *Brut y Tywysogyon: Peniarth MS. 20*, 1014; *Brut y Tywysogyon: Red Book of Hergest*, [1014].

3   Arnott and Gwynn 1921, 351-97.

paper made by the famous Irish scribe Mícheál Ó Cléirigh (Brussels, Bibliothèque Nationale, MS 2569-2572, fos 103–34r, siglum 'B'). His transcript was made from an earlier copy he made in March 1628 of the now lost 'Book of Cu Connacht O'Daly'. *Cogadh* is the longest narrative in the Brussels manuscript, which mainly comprises Irish historical poems and genealogies.[4] The 'B' and 'D' versions of *Cogadh* are more closely related to each other than 'L'. James Henthorn Todd made an edition and translation of the text for the Rolls Series, published in 1867, which drew on all three manuscripts. Denis Casey has pointed out, however, that Todd probably did not use the Brussels manuscript directly, but relied instead on a copy made for him by Eugene O'Curry, which is now TCD MS 1408.[5] Todd divided the narrative of *Cogadh* into 121 sections and his section numbers will be used in this chapter. Nevertheless, a more accurate edition of the Book of Leinster text has been provided by Anne O'Sullivan, published in 1983.[6]

In terms of content, the narrative of *Cogadh* can be divided as follows: sections 1-3 provide an overview of the time frame covered by the narrative from the 790s until the reign of Brian Boru, during which time Ireland suffered depredations from Vikings. Sections 4-35 contain a terse narrative of Viking attacks throughout Ireland until the early tenth century. Apart from sections 37-39, the narrative from section 36 adopts a more florid narrative style, dramatically slowing the chronological pace of the narrative. Sections 40-60 deal with events focused on Munster and the struggle between Brian's family and the Vikings in the late tenth century, whilst sections 61-88 narrate the glorious deeds of Brian's reign until the eve of the battle of Clontarf. The remainder of the narrative focuses on events at Clontarf, which are described in vivid detail. The last three sections of the narrative (119-21) describe the aftermath of the battle. Despite the stylistic and narrative contrast between sections 4-35 and sections 40-121 of *Cogadh*, Scottish affairs can be seen to have a significant place throughout the narrative.

SCOTTISH AFFAIRS IN THE EARLIER SECTIONS OF *COGADH GAEDHEL RE GALLAIBH*

The narration of Scottish affairs in *Cogadh* can be compared to the Irish chronicles that the author(s) drew on to provide a historical

4   Gheyn 1907, 46-48.
5   Denis Casey, pers. comm.
6   *Book of Leinster*, v, 1319-25.

backbone to the narrative. Chronology and historical accuracy are often subordinate to the propagandist purpose of *Cogadh*, which was to promote the interests of the descendants of Brian Boru. This is particularly true of the sections detailing Scottish affairs. The earlier sections (4-35) of *Cogadh* promote the notion that there was a long history of antagonism between Vikings and the kings of Alba. The first example of this is found in section twelve of the narrative, which describes a battle between a Viking fleet from Ireland and the rulers of Dál Riata. The Book of Leinster recension preserves the fullest account:

> **CGG(L)§12** Tancatar iar sain cóic longa & tri fichit co Dublind Atha Cl*iath*, & ra hindrit Lagin co Margi leo. & Mag mBreg. Tucsat Dál Riatai cath don longissein Uair ra chuatar lám chlá rá Herend fathúaid ar milliud Lagen & Breg. Ra marb*ad* sin chathsin Eoganán m*ac* Oengusa rí Dáil R*iatai*.

> [There came after that three score and five ships to Dublin of Áth Cliath, and Leinster was plundered by them to [Sliab] Mairge and Mag Breg.[7] Dál Riata gave battle to this fleet; for they went, with the left hand to Ireland northwards after the plundering of Leinster and Brega. Eóganán, son of Óengus, king of Dál Riata was killed in that battle.][8]

This battle corresponds to the one described in the *Annals of Ulster* for the year 839, during which Eoganán son of Oengus and many of the men of Fortriu were killed.[9] It holds an important place in Scottish historiography. *Cogadh* claims that this fleet travelled from Dublin, although this is not mentioned in Irish chronicles.

Comparison between the text of *Cogadh* and Irish chronicles suggests that annals from 841 and 839 were conflated to create this account. The first part of the account in *Cogadh* appears to correspond to that in the now lost *Chronicle of Ireland* for the year 841. This text underpins surviving accounts in the *Annals of Ulster* and *Chronicum Scotorum*:

---

7   In B and D manuscripts of CGG the variant reading 'fargi' (sea) is given,
     but plundering from Dublin to the sea does not make sense. Sliab Mairge
     (Slievemargy, Co. Laois) lay towards the western border of Leinster with Osraige
     and lies within the same county as Sliab Bladma (Slieve Bloom, Co. Laois). Mag
     mBreg (the plain of Brega) lay in Uí Néill territory.

8   *Book of Leinster*, v, 1321; cf. *Cogadh*, 12-13, 226 *(*§12).

9   *Annals of Ulster*, 839.

AU 841.4 Longport oc Duiblinn as-rorta Laig*in* 7 Oi Neill etir tuatha 7 cealla *co* rice Sliabh Bledhma.

CS 841.2 Longport og Duibhlinn, as ar loitedh Laighin ocus H. Neill eidir tuathaibh ocus cellaib co Sliab Bladma.[10]

[A longphort at Dublin from which the Leinstermen and the Uí Néill were plundered, both peoples and churches, as far as Sliab Bladma.][11]

Based on Irish chronicle records, 841 has been regarded as the year during which the Viking camp at Dublin was founded, although recent discoveries of Viking burials around the margins of what was once the *dubh linn* – or 'black pool' – have indicated that there may have been earlier Viking activity in the region.[12] The second part of the account in *Cogadh* corresponds to the *Annals of Ulster* for the year 839:

AU 839.9 Bellum re genntib f*or* firu F*o*rtrenn in quo ceci*derunt* Euganan m. Oengusa 7 Bran m. Oengussa 7 Ẹd m. Boanta 7 alii pene innumerabiles ceciderunt.

[The heathens won a battle against the men of Fortriu and Eóganán son of Óengus, Bran son of Óengus, Áed son of Boanta, and others almost innumerable fell there.]

There is no suggestion in the Irish chronicles that the Vikings who attacked northern Britain in 839 came from Ireland. It is chronologically impossible that the raiders who attacked Leinster and Southern Uí Néill territory from Dublin in 841 then went on to fight a battle in northern Britain in 839. Perhaps the author of *Cogadh* conflated his annalistic sources to bring Dublin Vikings into conflict with the ancestors of the royal line of Alba, creating a narrative of historical antagonism between them. As Nick Evans has pointed out, both Áed and Eóganán are listed as kings in *Duan Albanach*, with which the author of *Cogadh* may have been familiar.[13]

---

10   The same record is found in the *Annals of Clonmacnoise*, 838 [=841], and the *Annals of the Four Masters*, 840 [=841].
11   *Chronicle of Ireland*, 841.4.
12   Simpson 2005, 32-54.
13   Nick Evans pers. comm. See also Jackson 1957.

The next event of Scottish interest in *Cogadh Gaedhel re Gallaibh* describes a battle between Vikings from Ireland and Causantín mac Cináeda (Constantine son of Kenneth).[14]

> **CGG(L)§25** Ra hindarbait da*no* Dubgenti a Her*ind* ar sain. & dochuatar i nAlbain. & ro brisisset cath for feraib Albain. du i tor*chair* Constantin m*ac* Cinaeda ardri Alban & sochaide mor malle riss. Is andsain na maid in talam fo feraib Alban.

> [The Black gentiles after this were driven out of Erinn and went to Alba, where they gained a battle over the men of Alba in which were slain Causantín son of Cináed, high king of Alba, and a great multitude with him. It was then that the earth burst open under the men of Alba.][15]

The chronology in this section is distorted. *Cogadh* places the death of Causantín after the battle of Strangford Lough, even though the battle was fought in 877 and the king died in 876.[16] Again, it is Vikings from Ireland who are seen to cause trouble in Alba, but the linkage between the events is anachronistic. The author of *Cogadh* may have deliberately conflated two accounts in the *Annals of Ulster*:

> **AU875.3** Cong*ressio* Pictorum fri Dubghallu 7 strages magna Pictorum facta est

> [An encounter between the Picts and the Dark foreigners and a great slaughter was made of the Picts.]

> **AU877.5** Belliolum occ Loch Cuan eit*ir* Finngenti 7 Dubgennti in quo Alban*n*, dux na nDubgenti, cecidit.

> [A skirmish at Loch Cúan between the Fair heathens and the Dark heathens, in which Hálfdann, leader of the Dark heathens, fell.]

A further hint that the author of *Cogadh* rewrote rather than copied information drawn from earlier sources may be the inclusion of the term

---

14   *Cogadh*, 26-27, 232 (§25).
15   Manuscript B removes the clause 'in which fell Constantine [...] and a great multitude with him', thus removing an anachronism from the text. *Cogadh*, 26, no. 7.
16   *Annals of Ulster*, 877; Dumville 2000, 81.

'Alba'. As David Dumville has noted, 'Alba' is used in Irish chronicles to describe 'Britain' before AD 900, but after that date the term is used to describe the northern British polity ruled by the descendants of Cináed mac Ailpín (Kenneth Mac Alpin).[17] Causantín's death is recorded briefly in the *Annals of Ulster* and *Chronicum Scotorum* in the year 876 where he is called *rex Pictorum* ('king of the Picts'). Irish chronicles do not record Causantín's death at the hands of Vikings, but this information can be found in the 'X' group of Latin lists of kings of Alba. King-lists 'D' and 'I' add the location of the battle as *Merdo fatha* or *Inverdufatha*, which has been identified with Inverdovat, Fife. The reconstruction of the text of the *Chronicle of the Kings of Alba*, suggested by David Dumville and endorsed by Alex Woolf, indicates that Causantín may have died by Viking hands at Atholl.[18] The claim in *Cogadh* that an earthquake swallowed the men of Alba may owe more to literature than to history, although its inclusion is not easy to explain.[19]

A little later in *Cogadh* (section 27), it is stated that Vikings left Ireland and went to Alba under the leadership of Sigtryggr son of Ívarr. This report is not found in the Book of Leinster version of the text, but appears only in the two later manuscripts:

CGG(D/B)§27 fo fhacsat gaill Erind, ocus lottar in Albain im Sitriuc mac Imar.

[The foreigners left Erinn and went to Alba under Sigtryggr son of Ívarr.][20]

At this juncture, the Book of Leinster states 'Mór tra d'ulc daronsat Gaill i nHer*ind* sin bl*iadain*sin' [great evil did the foreigners bring into Ireland in this year]. This report appears to correspond with the *Annals of Ulster* record of events for 893:

---

17 Dumville 1996.
18 Anderson 1980, 267, 274, 283, 288, 290; Dumville 2000, 81; Woolf 2007, 111-12. Causantín's death is also described in the 'Prophecy of Berchán' but Vikings are not identified as his nemesis: *Prophecy of Berchan*, 43, 85.
19 1 Samuel: 14:15; Numbers 16: 30-34. Cf. Bray 1992, 116.
20 *Cogadh*, 28-29. The reference to Sigtryggr son of Ívarr fits with the theme of section 27 relating to the deeds of the sons of Ívarr in Ireland. The departure of Sigtryggr is followed neatly by the arrival of Rǫgnvaldr grandson of Ívarr described in the opening of section 28. It may therefore have been part of the original composition of *Cogadh Gaedhel re Gallaibh* but omitted from the Book of Leinster copy.

AU 893.4 Mescbaidh mór *for* Gallaibh Atho Cliath co n-dechadu*r* i n-esriuth, indala rand dibh la m. nImair, ind rann n-aile la Sichfrith nIerll.

[A major dissension among the foreigners of Áth Cliath, so that they dispersed, one section of them with the son of Ívarr, the other with Jarl Sigfrøðr.]

The same event is reported in the *Annals of Inisfallen* (893): 'Genti do dul a Herind isin blia*dain* so' [Gentiles went from Ireland in this year]. In neither of the Irish records is Alba identified as a destination of the departing Vikings.[21] It must have seemed pertinent to the author (or interpolator) of *Cogadh Gaedhel re Gallaibh* to mention this point. It fits with other references to Alba in *Cogadh*, which stress the difficulties caused by Vikings from Ireland in northern Britain.

The next event in *Cogadh* to relate to Alba is the record of the death of two Viking leaders, Rǫgnvaldr and Óttarr. The event is related briefly in the Book of Leinster account: 'Rachuatar i nAlbain iar tain. Et tucsat fir Alban cath dóib. & ra marb*ad* and .i. Ragnall & Oittir' [They went into Alba after that, and the men of Alba gave battle to them and they were killed there, that is Rǫgnvaldr and Óttarr].[22] The account in the later manuscripts gives more detail, linking their death to a battle against Causantín mac Áeda (Constantine II) of Alba:

CGG(D)§29 Ro innarbait iarsin tra asin Mumain, ocus dacuatar in nAlbain, ocus tucsat cath [do] Constantin mac Aeda .i. do rig Alban, ocus ro marbait aroen and, .i. Ragnall ocus Otir, ocus ár a muntiri leo.

[They were afterwards banished from Munster and went into Alba; and they gave battle to Causantín, son of Áed, that is to the king of Alba, and both were killed therein, that is, Rǫgnvaldr and Óttarr, and their retinue was slaughtered with them.][23]

This conflict can be identified with the battle of Corbridge fought in 918. The event is described in the *Annals of Ulster*, the *Annals of*

---

21 *Annals of Ulster*, 892 [=893].
22 *Book of Leinster*, v, 1325.
23 It should be noted that this sentence at the end of section 29 follows an interpolation in *Cogadh* and should follow on from the end of section 28 of that text. *Cogadh*, 34-35.

the Four Masters, the *Chronicle of the Kings of Alba*, and, less reliably, in the *Fragmentary Annals of Ireland*.[24] The first three accounts are given as an appendix to this chapter. Despite heavy casualties on the Vikings' side, Rǫgnvaldr went on to rule York from 918 until his death in 921. Therefore, Causantín did not dispatch him on this occasion. The record of *Cogadh* may have deliberately twisted facts to present this well-known Scottish king as an effective opponent of Vikings. This portrayal suited the anti-Scandinavian sentiments of *Cogadh*.[25] The fact that Causantín would later ally with Vikings of Dublin at the battle of Brunanburh goes unmentioned. Viking relations with Alba are presented in *Cogadh* as uniformly antagonistic, and links between Vikings in Ireland and Scotland are emphasised.[26]

SCOTTISH AFFAIRS IN THE LATER SECTIONS OF *COGADH GAEDHEL RE GALLAIBH*

From section 36 of *Cogadh,* the narrative style is more florid and the chronological pace of the narrative slows to focus on the deeds of the Dál Cais and their most famous son, Brian Boru. One of the claims made about Brian is that, at the height of his power, he was able to levy a royal tribute from Saxons and Britons, specifically from Lennox and Argyll.[27] These were territories that may have lain outside the kingdom of Alba in 1014.[28] Brian's tribute-gathering across the seas is not attested in chronicles. Brian's secretary famously assigned him the title *Imperator Scottorum* when entering his name into the Book of Armagh. Around the same time that Brian exhibits this imperial title, Rǫgnvaldr, king of Man and the Isles, died in Munster in 1005, although sadly no political context is given to interpret whether Rǫgnvaldr was a vassal, ally,

---

24   *Annals of Ulster*, 917 [=918]; *Annals of the Four Masters*, 916 [=918]; *Fragmentary Annals of Ireland*, 180-83 (§459).
25   *Cogadh*, lxxxv, 35.
26   In the tract labelled *On the Fomorians and Lochlanns*, included in Leabhar Mór na nGenealach and compiled by Dubhaltach Mac Fhirbisigh (Duald MacFirbis), the death of Rǫgnvaldr and Óttarr is attributed to Áed Finnliath of the Southern Uí Néill. As Aed died in 879, this is chronologically impossible. *Leabhar Mór na nGenealach*, iii, 44-51.
27   *Cogadh*, 134-37 (§78).
28   Neville 2005, 14. It is possible that Lennox was part of the kingdom of Strathclyde or Galloway during this period, although little is known of the contemporary political history of the region. *Cogadh*, 134-37 (§87).

or enemy of Brian.[29] It is interesting that *Cogadh* avoids proclaiming Brian's supremacy over all the *Scotti* of Alba, despite indicating that he wielded influence over the western seaboard of northern Britain.[30]

Cogadh's description of Vikings continually refers to their moral depravity. However, particular censure is reserved for Vikings from Argyll and the Northern and Western Isles who came to fight at Clontarf. These men were a common enemy of both Alba and Munster:

> Comtinol sloig buirb, barbarda, dicheillid, dochisc, dochomaind, do gallaibh Insi Orc, ocus Insi Cat, a Manaind ocus a Sci, ocus a Leodus; a Cind tiri ocus hAirer Goedel.

> [An assembled army of ignorant, barbarous, stupid, wild, anti-social foreigners of Orkney and Shetland, from Man and from Skye, and from Lewis, from Kintyre and Argyll.][31]

Cogadh therefore focuses on the common enemies of Alba and Munster living on the fringes of northern Britain. The saga also gives significant attention to the contingent from Alba which fought alongside Munster at the Battle of Clontarf. The battle is said to open with single combat between two men; Domnall mac Eimín, *mormaer* of Alba, and Plait, son of the king of Lochlann:

> Ro comraicetar ardus and sin, Domnall mac Emin, mormaer Alban, o Briain, ocus Plait mac ri Lochland, tren milid gall; ar na rád do

---

29 *Annals of Inisfallen*, 1004 [=1005]; *Chronicon Scotorum*, [1005]. Rǫgnvaldr may have been the grandson of Haraldr king of Limerick who died in 940. Colmán Etchingham has drawn attention to the record of Brian as 'ardrí Gaidhel Érenn ocus Gall ocus Bretan' in the *Annals of Ulster* for 1014, suggesting that Brian regarded himself as heir to Anglesey as well as the Isles owing to the campaigns of Manx kings on the island. The reference to Lennox in *Cogadh* may prompt consideration of whether the Britons whom Brian held claim to rule were in northern Britain as well as/rather than Wales. Etchingham, 2001, 180.

30 Denis Casey has pointed out (pers. comm.) that the men of Lennox were said to have descended from Conall Corc of Cashel of the Eóganachta of Munster. The author of *Cogadh* may have been tapping into a genealogical tradition in order to link the kingship of Munster with Lennox. See *Corpus Genealogiarum Hiberniae*, 358 (LL 318b42); *Athdioghluim Dana*, i, 173-74 and ii, 102-3; cf. *Triumph Tree*, 258-59.

31 *Cogadh*, 150-53 (§87).

Plait in adaich remi, ni rabi i nErind fer bad incomlaind do, do gab immoro, Domnall mac Emin do laim é fachetoir, ocus ba cuimnech cechtar de, ar maitin. Is arsin tanic Plait a cath na lureach amach, ocus asbert fo thri faras Domnall? id est Cait ita Domnall? Ro recair Domnall ocus asbert, sund, a sniding ar se. Ro comraicsetar iarsun, ocus ro gab cach ic airllech araile dib, ocus i trocair cechtar reraile, ocus is amlaid ro tuitset ocus claidium cechtar de tre cridi araile, ocus folt cechtar de i ndurnd a cele. Ocus ro be sin a cet comlond na dessi sin.

[First then were drawn up there, Domnall, son of Emin, mormaer of Alba, on Brian's side, and Plait, son of the king of Norway, brave soldier of the foreigners; because Plait was saying the night before that there was not a man in Ireland who was able to fight him. Domnall, the son of Emin immediately took him up, and each of them remembered this in the morning. Then Plait came forward from the battalion of the men in armour, and said three times 'Faras Domnall?' that is 'Where is Domnall?' Domnall answered and said 'Here you wretch' said he. They fought then, and each of them endeavoured to slaughter the other; and they fell by each other, and the way they fell was, with the sword of each through the heart of the other; and the hair of each in the fist of the other. And the combat of that pair was the first.][32]

The story of the noble from Alba is given top billing and described in dramatic terms, each warrior dying with his sword through the heart of the other. Domnall mac Eimín meic Cainnig, *mormaer* of Marr in Alba, is the last of the fallen leaders named on Brian's side in the battle in the *Annals of Ulster, Annals of the Four Masters*, and the *Annals of Loch Cé*. In the *Annals of Boyle*, he is simply identified as a *mormaer* in Alba, and *Chronicum Scotorum* identifies him by name only.[33] Curiously, the *Annals of Inisfallen*, which is a Munster-based account, makes no mention of Domnall. It is unknown whether other leaders from Alba fought alongside Domnall in 1014, as the chronicles focus on the leaders who fell rather than those who fought and survived.

---

32   Ibid., 174-77 (§100).
33   *Annals of Clonmacnoise*, 1007 [=1014] call him 'Donnell mᶜEvin mᶜCaynich earle of Dombarr in Scottland'.

The meaning of the term *mormaer* has been debated and variously translated as 'great steward', 'sea-steward' from Gaelic, or 'earl' from its rendering in Latin as *comes*.[34] A key towards the understanding of the word in *Cogadh* may be a reference elsewhere in the narrative to Osli mac Dubcenn (grandson of the last king of Limerick) as *mormaer da maeraib*. This implies that, to the author of *Cogadh*, *mormaer* was placed in a hierarchy above lesser *maer* and may have overseen territories on behalf of the king.[35] I have suggested elsewhere that Domnall may have fought for his own interests, perhaps in opposition to the earl of Orkney, rather than being a delegate of the king of Alba at Clontarf.[36] It did, however, suit the author of *Cogadh* to exaggerate Domnall's significance in the battle, promoting a theme of common interests between Alba and Munster.[37]

Domnall mac Eimín made his first appearance in *Cogadh* shortly before the duel that felled him. Brian sends Domnall as a messenger to his son Murchad, to instruct him not to take an advanced position on the battlefield but to fall back in line with the other troops.[38] Murchad refuses, saying that he will never yield his position although there would be many false heroes that day who would. Domnall replies that he would never give way, and the author confirms that Domnall's promise would be fulfilled. This earlier passage did not yet identify Domnall as a *mormaer* of Alba, but it shows him to be a trusted messenger of Brian who fulfils his duty and stands by his word. The passage builds dramatic tension as the reader is prepared for the tale of Domnall's heroism that is predicted.[39]

Thomas DuBois has noted an overwhelming focus on Irish affairs in *Cogadh Gaedhel re Gallaibh*, remarking that 'the narrative follows

---

34 Duffy 2013, 150.
35 Ibid., 151, 172; *Cogadh*, 146-47 (§84). Seán Duffy has argued that Domnall was an ally or a vassal of Brian.
36 Downham 2007, 157.
37 The links between Scotland and Ireland shortly before the battle of Clontarf are demonstrated in the year before the conflict took place. In 1013 the army of Mide, led by the provincial overking Mael Sechnaill, attacked lands north of Dublin, but his forces were defeated by Sitric of Dublin and his Leinster allies. The fallen included 'int Albanach', whose name indicates links with Alba: *Annals of Inisfallen*, 1013; *Cogadh*, 148-49 (§84).
38 *Cogadh*, 170-71 (§97).
39 Duald MacFirbis indicated in the seventeenth century that Domnall was a member of the MacLeod clan of Harris. *Leabhar Mór na nGenealach*, ii, 51, 717 (§775.2, 1365.2).

characters only during their time in Ireland, providing no details of where they go or what they do when they leave the island'.[40] The inclusion of northern British affairs appears to be the exception that proves the rule. This may in part reflect the perception of Alba as an integral part of the Gaelic world, but it may also reflect the political circumstances in which *Cogadh* was composed. I would argue that the presentation of past events was deliberately twisted to show the common interest shared by Brian's family and leaders in Alba to keep the Vikings of the Isles in check.

THE DATE OF *COGADH GAEDHEL RE GALLAIBH*

The date of *Cogadh Gaedhel re Gallaibh* is significant to understanding relations between Ireland and Scotland at the time it was composed. On linguistic and stylistic grounds, the saga was composed in the late eleventh or early twelfth century.[41] More specific origins have been posited based on historical evidence. Anthony Candon and Máire Ní Mhaonaigh have identified Muirchertach Ua Briain, the great-grandson of Brian Boru, as the most likely patron of the saga.[42] Muirchertach was the most successful of Brian's descendants and he appears to have based aspects of his public image on the career of his great-grandfather.[43] This includes the gift of gold placed on the Altar of Armagh in 1103, perhaps in imitation of his great-grandfather's gift in 1005.[44] Muirchertach also rebuilt the fortress of Kincora in 1096, which Brian had constructed in 1012.[45] Muirchertach's reign witnessed a flurry of artistic production, and so the creation of a new history of Brian Boru might fit well with this context.[46] Ní Mhaonaigh has suggested a date range for the creation of *Cogadh* after the alliance between Muirchertach and Magnús Berfœttr ('Barelegs') king of Norway collapsed in 1103 and before Muirchertach was struck down with an illness that led to a temporary loss of power in 1114.[47]

More recently, Seán Duffy has assigned a late-eleventh-century date to the text.[48] This earlier dating is based on the positive representation

40   DuBois 2011.
41   For a summary of scholarship on this matter, Casey 2013, 142-45.
42   Candon 1988; Ní Mhaonaigh 1995.
43   Ní Mhaonaigh 1995, 368-74.
44   *Annals of Ulster*, 1005, 1103.
45   *Annals of the Four Masters*, 1096; *Annals of Inisfallen*, 1012.
46   Gem 2006; Ó Carragáin 2010.
47   *Annals of Inisfallen*, 1114; Ní Mhaonaigh 1995.
48   Duffy 2013, 198, 242.

of Donnchad son of Brian Boru in *Cogadh*. It was at Donnchad's behest that Tadc, grandfather of Muirchertach Ua Briain, was killed in 1023. It would seem unlikely that Muirchertach would have been a patron to a positive representation of Donnchad, so Duffy posits an earlier date of composition when the descendants of Donnchad were in exile from Munster. Nevertheless, Denis Casey has suggested that the pro-Donnchad material was added in the early twelfth century, and I would support that argument.[49]

The first difficulty with accepting the pro-Donnchad material as criteria for re-dating *Cogadh* is that it survives only in one late witness – the sole complete version of *Cogadh*. Working out the textual history from one late manuscript is fraught with difficulty. The text transcribed by Mícheál Ó Cléirigh may diverge from the original narrative composed at least half a millennium before. Where witnesses of *Cogadh* can be compared, a number of interpolations have been identified. This includes material showing a bias towards Bréifne interpolated in manuscript 'D'.[50] The importance of *Cogadh* in the Middle Ages led later authors to influence the text. The material that presents a pro-Donnchad stance sits at the very end of *Cogadh* and may have been added on to an earlier version. It sits rather awkwardly as a post-climactic narrative. The story of the Battle of Clontarf closes with a list of the fatalities of the battle and reference to the fulfilment of Brian's will. However, the last three sections of *Cogadh* (119-121) create a new narrative, relating how Donnchad son of Brian overcomes three challenges to his new-found authority.[51] The post-Clontarf narrative has a self-contained character that could have been devised separately and then added to *Cogadh*.

---

49   Casey 2013, 157.
50   Ní Mhaonaigh 1992.
51   *Cogadh*, 210-17. First it is reported that Donnchad had the oxen of Dublin slaughtered; a request came from King Sigtryggr of Dublin to leave nineteen of the oxen for each one that they took, but Donnchad refused. It is then reported that the Dál Cais carried their injured from the battlefield but were faced by a revolt from the men of South Munster (Desmond) who demanded hostages. Donnchad refused and his men prepared themselves for battle with such bravery (including stuffing moss into their wounds so they could fight) that leaders of Desmond declined to oppose them. After that, the king of Ossory demanded hostages, but the wounded warriors of the Dál Cais became angry and ordered that stakes be set up so that they might be tied upright in order to fight. This prompted the men of Ossory to decline battle and one hundred and fifty of Donnchad's men died of frustrated anger.

The tone of final sections of *Cogadh* is in contrast to previous references to Donnchad in the saga which, as Casey notes, are generally negative or ambivalent.[52] The lack of reference to Donnchad's half-brother Tadc in *Cogadh* does not discredit his son Muirchertach as a possible patron of the text.[53] If pro-Donnchad material was added to the narrative of *Cogadh*, then there is a possibility that some pro-Tadc or anti-Donnchad sentiments were edited out at the same time; Casey discusses one possible instance where this has occurred.[54] In sum, the re-dating of *Cogadh* based on pro-Donnchad material found at the very end of the text is insecure. Compared with other parts of the text, the ill-fitting and contrary nature of this material lends weight to the suggestion that it was added to the main narrative. The contextual argument for composition of *Cogadh* in the reign of Muirchertach Ua Briain, espoused by Candon and Ní Mhaonaigh, remains strong.[55] It is therefore to the reign of this king that one might look to interpret why Scottish affairs are given such prominence in the narrative of *Cogadh Gaedhel re Gallaibh*.

THE DESCENDANTS OF BRIAN AND LINKS ACROSS THE IRISH SEA

Throughout the *Cogadh Gaedhel re Gallaibh*, historical distortions are made with an eye to bolstering the position of Brian Boru's descendants. This propagandist slant is obvious in some areas, including the uniformly negative view of Vikings and the celebration of Brian's victories over them. Brian won a high position of influence over the Viking ports of Limerick, Waterford and Dublin during his career.[56] It has been pointed by Donnchadh Ó Corráin and others that the narrative of *Cogadh* helped to justify the domination of these ports by Brian's descendants.[57] Seán Duffy has also highlighted that Irish intervention in the Viking towns drew Uí Bhriain into a wider web of Irish Sea politics.[58]

---

52   Casey 2013, 145-49, 152, n.46.
53   Ibid., 145.
54   Ibid., 151. Cf. *Cogadh* 200 (§113); *Annals of Loch Cé*, 1014.
55   This also fits with Casey's suggestion that a version of *Cogadh* was produced for Brian Gleanna Maidhir. Casey 2013.
56   *Annals of Inisfallen*, 977, 984, 999.
57   Ó Corráin, 1978, 31-32.
58   Duffy 1992, 93-94.

Cogadh's interest in northern British affairs may reflect the ambitions of Brian's descendants in the kingdom of the Isles and Galloway. Brian's son Donnchad formed an alliance with Echmarcach son of Ragnall (Rǫgnvaldr), who was intermittently king of Dublin as well as king of the Isles and part of Galloway.[59] In 1072, Donnchad's nephew Toirrdelbach took control of Dublin and two grandsons of Brian were killed on the Isle of Man in the following year, perhaps attempting to assert control over the Isles.[60] After Toirrdelbach's death in 1086, his son Muirchertach ua Briain held ambitions that ranged across Ireland and across the eastern seaways.[61] His attempts to dominate the kingdom of the Isles and Dublin were initially thwarted by Gofraid mac Arailt (Guðrøðr Haraldsson, better known as 'Godred Crovan') who died in 1095. The Isles may have then fallen under the control of Domnall mac Taidc, nephew of Muirchertach.[62] When Magnús berfœttr, king of Norway, arrived in the Irish Sea in 1098 he asserted direct control over Man.[63]

Muirchertach sought to regain influence in the eastern seaways through the betrothal of his daughters, one to Sigurðr son of Magnús in 1102 and another to the Cambro-Norman baron Arnulf de Montgomery. With Sigurðr in mind, it is interesting to note that one of the key combatants at Clontarf according to *Cogadh*, is 'Plait, son of the king of Norway', but he does not appear in chronicle records. This figure may have been invented to reflect relations with Norway at the time when *Cogadh* was written. Magnús posed a threat to Muirchertach's interests in the Hebrides, but the marriage alliance which was planned to offset this threat was short lived.[64] When Magnús met a violent death in Ulster in 1103, his young son immediately departed for Norway, leaving Muirchertach's daughter behind. [65]

---

59   Ibid., 97; Casey 2013, 157.
60   *Annals of Ulster*, 1073.
61   For a summary of his career, see Candon 1988.
62   Duffy 1992, 105, 109. Duffy has pointed out that the *Banshenchas* identify Tadc as the husband of a daughter of Echmarcach mac Ragnaill, which may have supported his claim to rule Man.
63   Candon 1988, 404; Duffy 1992, 109.
64   *Cronica regum Mannie et Insularum*, fos 34v-35r; *William of Malmesbury, Gesta Regum Anglorum* i, 571; *Ecclesiastical History of Orderic Vitalis* v, 218-19, 222-23; *Annals of Ulster*, 1098; *Annals of the Four Masters*, 1098; *Orkneyinga Saga*, §§39-43; *Heimskringla*, trans. Laing, §§9-12, 25-27, ed. Aðalbjarnarson, §§8-11, 23-25; *Ágrip af Nóregskonungasögum*, §§50-51; *Morkinskinna* trans. Andersson and Gade, §§58-59; eds. Jakobsson and Guðjónsson, §§61, 63.
65   Candon 1988, 407, 411-12.

Contemporary attitudes in Munster towards Alba and the Kingdom of the Isles are hinted at in the *Annals of Inisfallen*. This chronicle was compiled during Muirchertach's reign in Munster and has been linked with the church of Emly.[66] In its records relating to Scotland, the chronicle includes obits of kings of Alba, but unlike the *Annals of Ulster*, Book of Leinster, *Annals of Tigernach*, and *Chronicum Scotorum*, it does not record the obits of 'kings' of Moray. Could it be that rulers in Munster were more sympathetic to, and simply more interested in, the royal line of Alba compared to that of Moray?[67] It may be telling, given Uí Bhriain ambitions in the Isles, that while the *Annals of the Four Masters*, *Annals of Tigernach*, and *Chronicum Scotorum* record Magnús as 'king of Norway and the Isles' at his death in 1103, the *Annals of Inisfallen* do not acknowledge Magnús's title in the Hebrides, but merely record him as 'king of the foreigners'.[68]

The interest in Scottish affairs in *Cogadh Gaedhel re Gallaibh* fits the political context of the reign of Muirchertach ua Briain. In 1103 that Muirchertach Ua Briain received a camel as a gift from King Edgar of Alba in 1105.[69] This implies a political effort to cultivate good relations. The leaders of Alba and Munster held common interests in the political stability of the Hebrides and Man. In 1111-14, Domnall mac Taidc, the nephew of Muirchertach Ua Briain, was established (or re-established) as King of Man and the Isles, although Munster domination would collapse thereafter.[70] The Isles may have served as a conduit for information about Clontarf that appeared in the work of thirteenth and fourteenth-century Icelandic writers, including *Njáls Saga*, *Orkneyinga Saga*, and *Þórsteins saga Síðu-Hallsonar*. Various authors have discussed the theory of a 'Brjáns saga', which was composed in one of the Viking towns of Ireland and then exported overseas.[71] Nevertheless, a copy

---

66   Grabowski and Dumville 1984, 3-107.
67   Duffy 2000.
68   *Annals of Inisfallen*, 1103.
69   Ibid., 1105. It should be noted that one of the few 'foreigners' praised for bravery in *Cogadh* is Plait, son of the king of Norway. This may reflect on the alliance that Muirchertach had built with Sigurðr son of the king of Norway. According to *Morkinskinna*, Sigurðr later returned to Ireland and exacted tribute. This deed (which would have taken place before 1130) is not attested in Irish chronicles. *Morkinskinna*, trans. Andersson and Gade, §70; *Morkinskinna*, eds Jakobsson and Guðjónsson, §77.
70   Duffy 1992, 115-16.
71   For discussion of a hypothetical Gaelic-Scandinavian Brjáns saga, see Ó Corráin 1998, 447-52; Hudson, 2002; Duffy 2013, 231.

of *Cogadh* or a verbal account based on it may have made its way north in the twelfth or thirteenth century. Skalds or ambassadors visiting Alba, the Isles, or Ireland may have brought information about Clontarf to Iceland.[72]

Three arguments emerge from this analysis. The first is that Scottish affairs have a significance in *Cogadh Gaedhel re Gallaibh* that deserves further investigation. The second is that these references show a consistent outlook throughout the narrative, that is, both in the terse opening sections and in the more extended saga dealing with Brian's reign. Finally, it is argued that northern British affairs may have been woven through *Cogadh* with an eye to promoting Uí Bhriain rule in the Isles in the early twelfth century. Its positive portrayal of Uí Bhriain's historical links with Alba reflected the political links that were cultivated between Muirchertach and Edgar. One is left to envisage the ceremonial arrival of Edgar's camel at the court of the Munster king in 1105, imagine the reaction of the courtiers, and to ponder whether a copy of *Cogadh Gaedhel re Gallaibh* was sent to Scotland by way of return in a diplomatic gift-exchange.

APPENDIX: THREE RECORDS OF THE BATTLE OF CORBRIDGE

AU918.4 Gaill Locha Da Caech do dergiu Erenn, .i. Ragnall rí Dubgall, & na da iarla, .i. Ottir & Graggabai & sagaith dóoib iar sin co firu Alban. Fir Alban dono ara cenn-somh co comairnechtar for bru Tine la Saxanu Tuaiscirt. Do-gensat in genti cethrai catha dibh, .i. cath la Gothbrith ua n-Imair; cath lasna da iarla; cath lasna h-óc-tigerna. Cath dano la Raghnall i n-eroloch nad-acadur fir Alban. Roinis re feraibh Alban forsna tri catha ad-conncadur co rolsat ár n-dimar dina genntibh im Ottir & im Graggabai. Raghnall dono do-fuabairt iar suidhiu i l-lorg fer n-Alban coro la ar dibh acht nad-farcbath ri na mor-móer di suidibh. Nox prelium dirimit.

[The foreigners of Waterford i.e. Rǫgnvaldr, king of the dark foreigners, and the two jarls, Óttarr and Gragabai, forsook Ireland and proceeded afterwards against the men of Alba. The men of Alba, moreover, moved against them and they met on the bank of the Tyne in northern Saxonland. The heathens formed themselves into four battalions: a battalion with Guðrøðr grandson of Ívarr, a

---

72 Rosemary Power has recently suggested a thirteenth-century context for the transfer of stories (pers. comm.).

battalion with the two jarls, and a battalion with the young lords. There was also a battalion in ambush with Rǫgnvaldr, which the men of Alba did not see. The men of Alba routed the three battalions which they saw, and made a very great slaughter of the heathens, including Óttarr and Gragabai. Rǫgnvaldr, however, then attacked in the rear of the men of Alba, and made a slaughter of them, although none of their kings or mormaers was cut off. Nightfall caused the battle to be broken off.]

AFM916[=918] Oitir & na Goill do dhul o Loch Dá Chaoch i n-Albain, & Constantin, mac Aedha do thabhairt catha dóibh, & Oitir do mharbhadh co n-ár Gall immaille friss.

[Óttarr and the foreigners went from Waterford to Alba; and Causantín, the son of Aed, gave them battle, and Óttarr was slain, with a slaughter of the foreigners along with him.]

CKA bellu*m* Tine more factu*m* est i*n* xuiii a*n*no *inter* Co*n*stantínu*m* et Regnall et Scotti habueru*nt* uíctoría*m*.

[The battle of Tynemoor was fought in the eighteenth year between Causantín and Rǫgnvaldr and the Scots won the victory.]

BIBLIOGRAPHY

PRIMARY SOURCES

Ademari Cabannensis Chronicon, Bourgain P et al. (eds), 1999, vol. iii, Turnhout: Brepols.

Ágrip af Nóregskonungasogum: A Twelfth Century Synoptic History of the Kings of Norway, Driscoll M J (ed), 2008, 2nd edn, London: Viking Society for Northern Research.

Annals of Clonmacnoise, Murphy D (ed), 1896, Dublin: Royal Society of Antiquaries.

Annála Ríoghachta Éireann. Annals of the Kingdom of Ireland by the Four Masters, O'Donovan J (ed and trans), 1848-51, 7 vols, Dublin: Royal Irish Academy.

Annals of Inisfallen, Mac Airt S (ed and trans), 1944, Dublin: Dublin Institute for Advanced Studies.

Annals of Loch Cé, Hennessy W (ed and trans), 1871, London: Rolls Series.

Annals of Ulster, Mac Airt S and Mac Niocaill G (eds and trans), 1983, Dublin: Dublin Institute for Advanced Studies.

Athdioghluim Dana, McKenna L (ed and trans), 1939-40, 2 vols, London: Irish Texts Society.

The Book of Leinster, Formerly Lebar na Núachongbála, Best R I et al. (ed and trans), 1954-83, 6 vols, Dublin: Dublin Institute for Advanced Studies.

Brenhinedd y Saesson, Jones T (ed and trans), 1971, Cardiff: University of Wales Press.

Brut y Tywysogyon: Peniarth MS. 20 Version, Jones T (ed and trans), 1952, Cardiff: University of Wales Press.

Brut y Tywysogyon: Red Book of Hergest Version, Jones T (ed and trans), 1973, Cardiff: University of Wales Press.

The Chronicle of Ireland, Charles-Edwards T (trans), 2006, 2 vols, Liverpool: Liverpool University Press.

Chronicon Scotorum, Hennessy W (ed and trans), 1866, London: Rolls Series.

Cogadh Gaedhel re Gallaibh: The War of the Gaedhil with the Gaill, Todd J H (ed and trans), 1967, London: Rolls Series.

Corpus Genealogiarum Hiberniae, O'Brien M A (ed), 1976, Dublin: Dublin Institute for Advanced Studies.

Cronica regum Mannie et Insularum, Broderick G (ed and trans), 1995, 2nd edn, Douglas: Manx National Heritage.

The Ecclesiastical History of Orderic Vitalis, Chibnall M (ed and trans), 1968-80, 6 vols, Oxford: Oxford University Press.

Fragmentary Annals of Ireland, Radnor J N (ed and trans), 1978, Dublin: Dublin Institute for Advanced Studies.

Heimskringla: Sagas of the Norse Kings, Laing S (trans), 1961, London: Dent.

Heimskringla, Aðalbjarnarson B (ed), 1951, 3 vols, Reykjavík: Íslenzk Fornrit.

Leabhar Mór na nGenealach: The Great Book of Genealogies, Ó Muraíle N (ed and trans), 2003-04, 5 vols, Dublin: De Búrca.

Mariani Scotti Chronicon, in *MGH SS V*, Waitz G (ed), 1884, Hanover: Hahn, 481–562.

Morkinskinna, Jakobsson Á and Guðjónsson Þ I (eds), 2011, 2 vols, Reykjavík: Íslenzk Fornrit.

Morkinskinna: The Earliest Icelandic Chronicle of the Norwegian Kings, Andersson T M and Gade K E (trans), 2000, Ithaca, NY: Cornell University Press.

Orkneyinga Saga, Guðmundsson F (ed), 1965, Reykjavík: Íslenzk Fornrit.

Orkneyinga Saga: The History of the Earls of Orkney, Pálsson H and Edwards P (trans), 1981, Harmondsworth: Penguin.

Prophecy of Berchan: Irish and Scottish High-Kings of the Early Middle Ages, Hudson B (ed and trans), 1996, Westport, CN: Greenwood.

Triumph Tree: Scotland's Earliest Poetry, Clancy T (trans), 1998, Edinburgh: Canongate.

William of Malmesbury, Gesta Regum Anglorum, Mynors R A B et al. (eds and trans), 1998–99, 2 vols, Oxford: Oxford University Press.

SECONDARY SOURCES

Anderson, M O 1980, *Kings and Kingship in Early Scotland*, rev. edn, Edinburgh: Scottish Academic Press.

Arnott, T K and E J Gwynn 1921, *Catalogue of the Irish Manuscripts in the Library of Trinity College Dublin*, Dublin: Hodges Figgis.

Bray, Dorothy Ann 1992, *A List of Motifs in the Lives of the Early Irish Saints*, Helsinki: Academia Scientiarum Fennica.

Candon, Anthony 1988, 'Muirchertach Ua Briain, Politics and Naval Activity in the Irish Sea, 1075–1119', in G Mac Niocaill and P F Wallace (eds), *Keimelia: Studies in Medieval Archaeology and History in Memory of Tom Delaney*, Galway: Galway University Press, 397- 415.

Casey, Denis 2013, 'A Reconsideration of the Authorship and Transmission of *Cogadh Gaédhel re Gallaibh*', *Proceedings of the Royal Irish Academy* 113C, 139-61.

Downham, Clare 2007, *Viking Kings of Britain and Ireland*, Edinburgh: Dunedin Academic Press.

DuBois, Thomas A 2011, 'Juxtaposing *Cogadh Gáedel re Gallaib* with *Orkneyinga Saga*', *Oral Tradition* 26:2, 267-96.

Duffy, Seán 1992 'Irishmen and Islesmen in the Kingdoms of Dublin and Man, 1052-1171', *Ériu* 43, 93-133.

Duffy, Seán 2000, 'Ireland and Scotland 1014–1169: Contacts and Caveats', in A Smyth (ed), *Seanchas: Studies in Early and Medieval Irish Archaeology, History and Literature in Honour of Francis J. Byrne,* Dublin: Four Courts, 348-56.

Duffy, Seán 2013, *Brian Boru and the Battle of Clontarf*, Dublin: Gill and Macmillan.

Dumville, David N 1996, 'Ireland and Britain in *Tain Bó Fráich*', *Études Celtiques* 32, 175-87.

Dumville, David N 2000, 'The Chronicle of the Kings of Alba', in Simon Taylor (ed), *Kings, Clerics and Chronicles in Scotland, 500-1297: Essays in Honour of Marjorie Ogilvie Anderson*, Dublin: Four Courts, 73-86.

Etchingham, C 2001, 'North Wales, Ireland and the Isles: The Insular Viking Zone', *Peritia* 15, 145-87.

Gem, R 2006, 'St Flannan's Oratory at Killaloe: A Romanesque Building of *c.*1100 and the Patronage of King Muirchertach Ua Briain', in D Bracken and D Ó Riain-Raedel (eds), *Ireland and Europe in the Twelfth Century: Reform and Renewal*, Dublin: Four Courts, 74-105.

Gheyn, J van den 1907, *Catalogue des Manuscrits de la Bibliothèque Royale de Belgique*, vol. vii, Brussels: H. Lamertin.

Grabowski, Kathryn and David Dumville 1984, *Chronicles and Annals of Medieval Ireland and Wales: The Clonmacnoise Group of Texts*, Woodbridge: Boydell.

Hudson, Ben 2002, 'Brjáns Saga', *Medium Aevum* 71:2, 241-68.

Jackson, Kenneth 1957, 'The Duan Albanach', *Scottish Historical Review* 36, 125-37.

Neville, Cynthia J 2005, *Native Lordship in Medieval Scotland: The Earldoms of Strathearn and Lennox, c. 1140-1365*, Dublin: Four Courts.

Ní Mhaonaigh, Máire 1992, 'Breifne Bias in *Cogad Gáedel re Gallaib*', *Ériu* 43, 135-58.

Ní Mhaonaigh, Máire 1995, 'Cogadh Gáedel re Gallaib: Some Dating Considerations', *Peritia* 9, 354-77.

Ó Carragáin, Tomás 2010, 'Rebuilding the "City of Angels": Muirchertach Ua Briain and Glendalough, ca. 1096-1111', in J Sheehan et al. (eds), *The Viking Age in Ireland and the West: Proceedings of the Fifteenth Viking Congress*, Dublin: Four Courts, 258-70.

Ó Corráin, Donnchadh 1978, 'Nationality and Kingship in Pre-Norman Ireland', in T W Moody (ed), *Historical Studies XI: Nationality and the Pursuit of National Independence, Papers read before the Conference held at Trinity College, Dublin, 6-31 May 1975,* Belfast: Appletree, 1-35.

Ó Corráin, Donnchadh 1998, 'Viking Ireland; Afterthoughts', in H B Clarke et al. (eds), *Ireland and Scandinavia in the Early Viking Age*, Dublin: Four Courts, 421-52.

Simpson, Linzi 2005, 'Viking Warrior Burials in Dublin: Is this the *Longphort?*' in S Duffy (ed), *Medieval Dublin VI*, Dublin: Four Courts, 11-62.

Woolf, Alex 2007, *From Pictland to Alba 789-1070*, Edinburgh: Edinburgh University Press.

The Use of the Scandinavian Place-Name Elements -*Sætr* and -*Ærgi* in Skye and the Outer Hebrides: A Site and Situation Study

Ryan Foster

Introduction

The violence of Viking raids is well documented in contemporary chronicles and annals. What is absent, on the whole, from the historical record is the settlement of people who spoke Old Norse (ON) in the British Isles. The distribution of Norse place-names seems to show a widespread Scandinavian settlement in parts of northern Scotland, the Northern Isles, and the Hebrides.[1] Scandinavian settlement in the Outer Hebrides has been confirmed by the archaeological excavation of settlements at Barvas[2] and Bostadh[3] on the Isle of Lewis, Udal on North Uist,[4] and Drimore,[5] Bornish,[6] and Cille Pheader[7] on South Uist.

The Scandinavian settlement in the Hebrides was substantial and durable enough to allow the coining of the term *innsi gall* ('Isles of the Foreigners') in the Irish annals. This settlement also seems to have developed into some form of regional polity,[8] as seen by the appearance at different times of *toiseach* ('chieftain'),[9] *Ladgmainn* ('lawman'),[10] and *ri* ('king') of the *Innsi Gall*.[11] The development of a social hierarchy may also be reflected by the use of place-names, with primary settlements surrounded by subordinate farming units.[12] The different elements within the farm would have their own individual names such as *þveit*-clearing and *sætr*-shieling.[13] Farm-name generics such as *bær/býr* ('farm'), *staðir*

---

1   Oftadal 2009; Fraser 1974, 19.
2   Armit 1996.
3   Neighbour and Burgess 1997.
4   Crawford and Switsur 1977.
5   MacLaren 1974.
6   Sharples 2005.
7   Parker Pearson et al. 2004.
8   Sharples and Smith 2009, 109; Clancy 2008, 26; Woolf 2007, 298-300.
9   *Annals of the Four Masters*, 851 [=853]. Woolf suggests this may be a later interpolation. See Woolf 2007, 299-300.
10 *Ladgmainn* in *Annals of the Four Masters*, 960 [=962], and *Lagmannaibh na n-Innsedh* in Ibid., 972 [=974].
11 *Annals of Ulster*, 988 [=989].
12 Olson 1983, 33-34; Brink 1999, 425.
13 Crawford 1995, 8; Øye 2004, 96; 2005, 361; 2009, 102.

('place/farm'), *bólstaðr* ('farm'), as well as *sætr* ('shieling'), are found in many areas of Scandinavian settlement, although variation in the distribution pattern of each element exists.[14] The fact that the same generics were being used to coin farm names in Scandinavia and abroad seems to suggest that overseas settlement included the importation and implementation of a farming economy from Scandinavia, rather than just a takeover of pre-existing settlements.[15]

This 'farming economy' was centred on the available arable land, as well as how less fertile land, around this primary area, was used to supplement the resource base and facilitate its intensive, but sustainable, exploitation.[16] Within this system, the farm and shieling were integral and indivisible parts of what Ditlev Mahler referred to as a 'decentralised farming economy'.[17] The area within the farm boundary was called – in ON – the *innan garðs* ('within the fence/infield') of arable, meadows, and enclosed pastures, and the *utan garðs* ('outside the fence') of outfield grazing and shielings.[18] This systematic use of shielings, or *sætr*, has a long history in Norway, and involves the movement of livestock some distance from the home farm between late spring and autumn.[19] The shieling system kept cattle away from the cereal crop and hay meadows in the *innan garðs*, and increased the potential grazing land available.[20] The cattle returned to the home farm in autumn and brought nutrients with them from the surrounding area, in the form of manure, to fertilise the infields.[21]

There is regional variation in the terminology used to denote a shieling in Norway.[22] However, other than the use of *sel* in Iceland, *sætr* seems to have been the only ON shieling name exported to areas of Scandinavian settlement. On the basis of onomastic and archaeological evidence, possible shieling sites have been suggested in many areas of Scandinavian settlement around the Atlantic Ocean, including the

---

14   Sandnes 2006, 241; Kruse 2007, 10.
15   Mahler 1995, 487.
16   Ibid., 488.
17   Ibid., 487.
18   Øye 2003, 10; 2004, 96.
19   Magnus 1986; Bjørgo 1986; Prescott 1999, 219.
20   Adderley and Simpson 2005, 714; Segertröm and Emanuelsson 2002, 181.
21   Pedersen 1999, 50; Zimmermann 1999, 315.
22   Beito 1949, 11-237; Reinton 1969, 24.

British Isles,[23] the Faroe Islands,[24] Iceland,[25] and Greenland.[26] The question I wish to examine is: why did ON speakers adopt a Gaelic term, *ærgi,* to denote a shieling when they had brought with them a corresponding ON term in *sætr?*

LOCATION OF THE STUDY

The Outer Hebrides, also called the Western Isles and the Long Island, are located in the far north-west of the British Isles and consist of a 210 km-long archipelago, stretching from Lewis in the north to Mingulay and Berneray in the south (Figure 1). The Minch separates the Outer Hebrides from the mainland, spanning 38 km at its narrowest. The Little Minch divides the islands of the Outer Hebrides from Skye, situated closer to the mainland, along with the Small Isles to the south (Canna, Rhum, Muck, and Eigg).

GEOLOGY

The Outer Hebrides are geologically uniform, formed from metasedimentary rock, principally Lewisian gneiss. This uniformity is broken by a small outcropping of Torridon sandstone found around Stornoway on Lewis, and intrusive felsic igneous rock, mainly granites, forming the bedrock of Harris and the southern portion of Lewis. In comparison, Skye and the Small Isles are formed from extrusive mafic lavas, mainly basalt, with bands of sedimentary rock along the north-eastern and southern coast of Skye and granite in central Skye and western Rhum.

TOPOGRAPHY AND DRIFT GEOLOGY

Quaternary glaciation eroded the gneiss of northern Lewis into an extensive erosion platform, which, on deglaciation, was covered by hummocky moraine to a depth of up to 6 m.[27] The gentle slopes and thick layer of till on Lewis restrict drainage and promote peat growth, leading to extensive blanket peat deposits.[28]

---

23   Pearsall 1961; Whyte 1985; Fellows-Jensen 1980.
24   Dahl 1970; Mahler 1991; 1995; 2007.
25   Hitzler 1979; Hastrup 1989; Sveinbjarnadóttir 1991.
26   Albrethsen and Keller 1986.
27   Hall 1995, 5; Boyd and Boyd 1990, 67.
28   Hudson et al. 1982, 19; Boyd and Boyd 1990, 67.

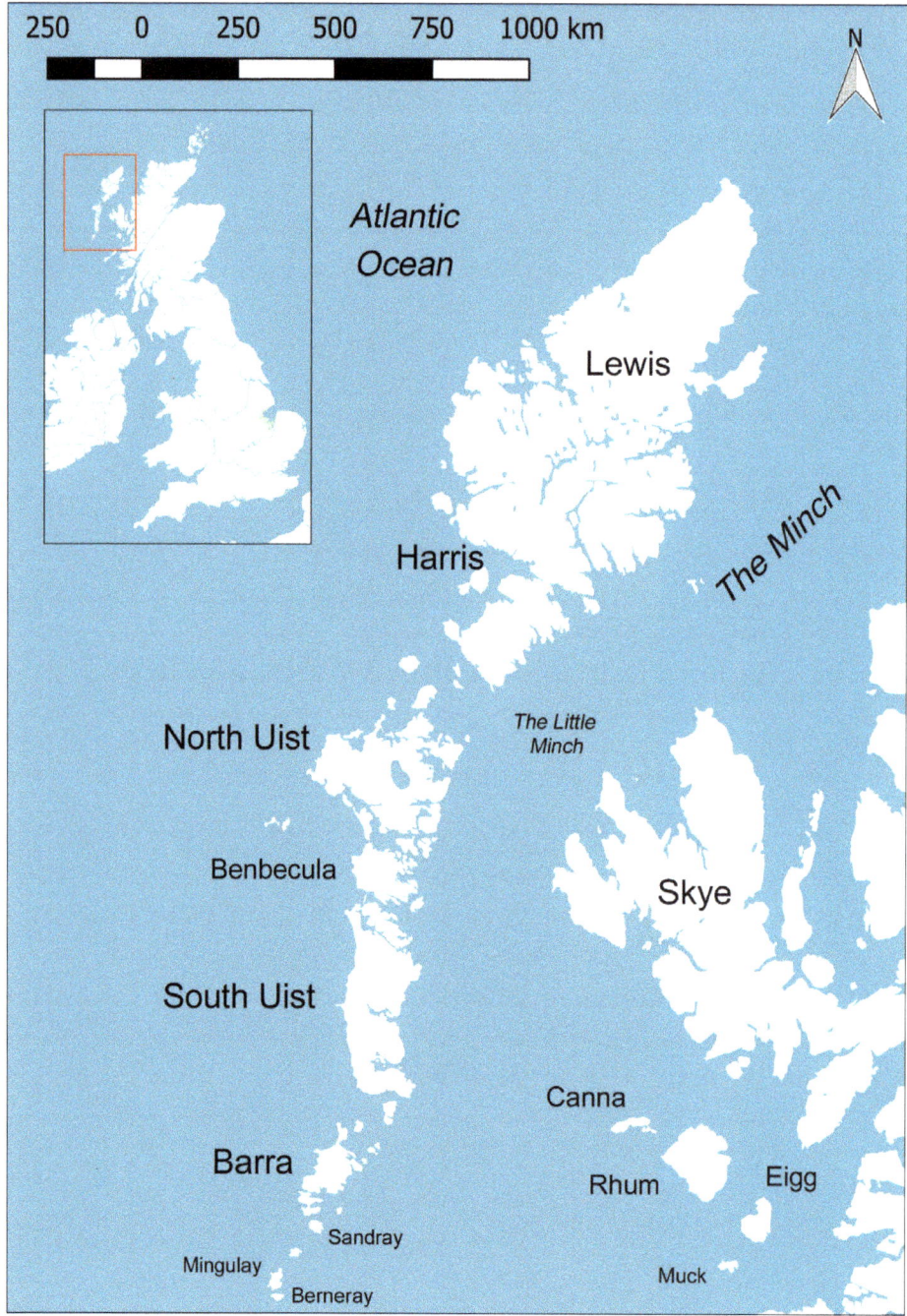

Figure 1: The Outer Hebrides, Isle of Skye, and the Small Isles.

The Uists, also formed from gneiss, are similarly low-lying, mainly below 100 m above sea level (ASL). South Uist, and to a lesser extent North Uist, have a tripartite division in drift geology.[29] This consists of an eastern, more mountainous coast covered by peat, a band of calcareous sand – called machair – running down the west coast, and an intermediate zone between the two, where peat has become mixed with windblown calcareous sand from the machair, known as the 'blacklands'.[30] The term machair, after the Gaelic for 'fertile plain', is a local term for calcareous soil now predominantly used as dune pasture, but formerly utilised for arable cultivation.[31] Being relatively productive, the machair was the core area for Neolithic and Viking Age settlement on the Uists.[32] Brayshay reported a similar situation on Barra, with the same three main types of soil association found on South Uist.[33]

Glaciation on the granites of south-western Lewis, Harris, and parts of Barra created a knock and lochan landscape.[34] Weathering and erosion of the granite formed a shallow acidic colluvium of little agricultural potential, but with some pockets of more fertile soils from fluvioglacial deposition.[35]

Quarternary glaciation on Skye, in comparison, led to the formation of glacial troughs. Its soils are relatively infertile, though more fertile soils developed on thicker glacial deposits or along fluvioglacial gravels in valleys and bays.[36] Where drainage was poor, peat formation was initiated, but where drainage was better, brown forest soils and humus-iron podzols formed. As a result of the cool climate, brown forest soils are oligotrophic rather than eutrophic; these are slightly acid, with medium to low base cation saturation and are considered moderately fertile.[37]

CLIMATE

The warmest average temperature of 12.9°C occurs in July and August, whilst the temperature in the coldest months of January and February

---

29   Brayshay et al. 2000, 361.
30   Owen et al. 1996, 128.
31   Gilbertson et al. 1996, 72, 119.
32   Owen et al. 1996, 128; Armit 1996, 164; Parker Pearson 2012, 12.
33   Brayshay 1992, 99-103.
34   Peacock 1984; Gordon 1993.
35   Boyd and Boyd 1990, 70; Peacock 1984; Gordon 1993.
36   Armit 1996, 24.
37   Fitzpatrick 1964, 48; Brayshay 1992, 102-3.

reaches an average of 4.1°C, with only a 0.7°C difference in the average annual maximum temperature between Stornoway in the north of the Long Island and Barra in the south. Skye has similar temperatures to Stornoway, although the higher mountains give a greater temperature range. Overall, the Outer Hebrides have one of the lowest temperature ranges in Britain, at 8.8°C.[38]

Wind is one of the defining characteristics of the climate, with a mean winter speed of 10 m/s, and 5 m/s in summer.[39] The wind brings rain, and the annual rainfall varies from around 1000 mm in parts of Lewis, 1193.5 mm on South Uist, to 2400 mm on the high ground of Harris, whilst the higher mountains of Skye can receive over 3000 mm of rain per year.[40]

DISTRIBUTION OF SHIELING NAMES

There are eighty-four Viking shieling names in total: fifty-four *sætr* and thirty *ærgi* names in the study area. Overall, *sætr* and *ærgi* have a complementary distribution (Figure 2). Whereas *sætr* names are found almost exclusively on Lewis and predominate in northern Skye, *ærgi* names are concentrated in North and South Uist. There are only three locations where both *sætr* and *ærgi* names can be found together: the southern coast of Harris, the north-west coast of North Uist, and a single topographical *ærgi* name, Cnoc an Tiongalairidh (NB1937), which is found among the *sætr* names on north-west Lewis.[41]

The distribution of *sætr* names is as follows: thirty-one on Lewis,[42]

---

38   Angus 1991, 30.
39   Gloyne 1968; Hudson et al. 1982.
40   Met Office 2016.
41   Cox 2002, 220.
42   Where possible, all shieling name spellings follow the first-edition OS maps (1:10,560). Barashader (NB450417), Borghaster (NB211412), Caiashader (NB553607), Carashader (NB100329), Cearsiadair (NB341201), Cnoc Eirdshader (NB203425), Cnoc Ghuirshadair (NB510329), Cnoc Iorshader (NB094368), Corriseadair (NB321194), Cuidhsiadar (NB546582), Earshader (NB164339), Eorshader (NB386181), Eorshader (NB163370), Gearraidh Eileaster (NB224380), Geidhshader (NB114314), Giurshadir (NB415345), Grimashadar (NB407257), Thámarshader (NB391255), Hashader Mòr (NB393249), Horshader (NB242431), Laimishader (NB183424), Linsiadar (NB210319), Seisiadar (NB553341), Sgeir Cuidshader (NB270497), Siadar (NB387542), Siader (NB194388), Sulaisiadar (NB536351), Tigh Thaisader (NB459397), Tom Shader (NB333497), Ungashader (NB125297).

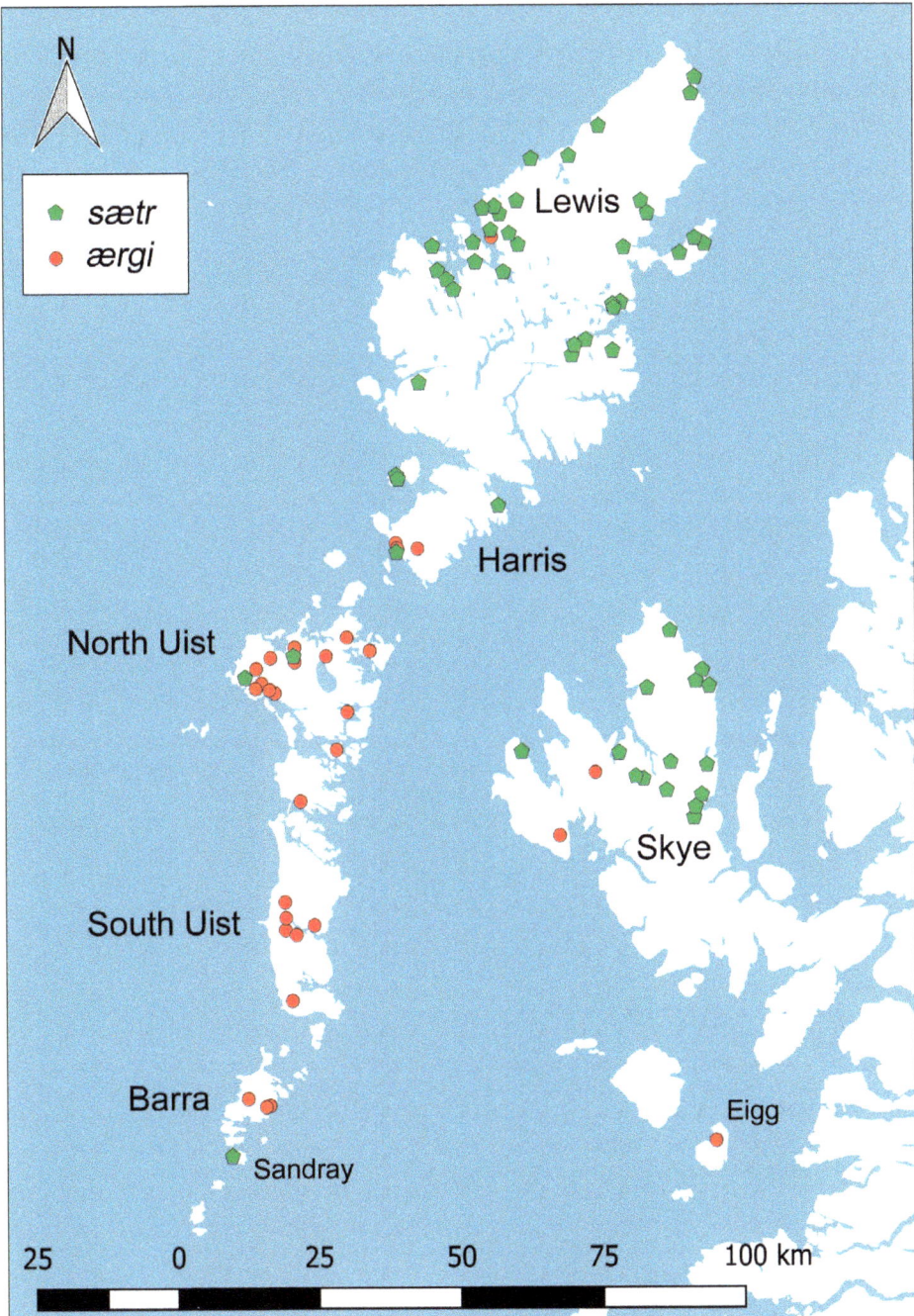

Figure 2: The distribution of the ON *sætr* and *ærgi* shieling names.

fifteen on Skye,[43] three on Harris,[44] two each on Taransay[45] and North Uist,[46] and a single site on the western most tip of Sandray.[47] The distribution of *ærgi* names, by contrast, is represented by only a single instance on Lewis,[48] three on Harris,[49] two on Skye,[50] twelve on North Uist,[51] six on South Uist,[52] three on Barra,[53] and one each on Benbecula,[54] Grimsay,[55] and Eigg.[56]

The *sætr* names have a predominantly coastal distribution, on average 802 m inland, it is only on Skye that *sætr* names are found in more inland locations, with an average distance of 1206 m from the sea. This may be due to the more varied mountainous conditions, creating pockets of pasture land to be exploited, although no *sætr* names have survived in the higher Cuillin range or any part of southern Skye.

Despite their coastal location, the majority of *sætr* names are protected from the prevailing south-westerly wind by being either located on the east coast or sheltered in bays or by other islands. These locations would be protected from the strongest wind and waves and are therefore less likely to be at risk from destructive gales or spray on vegetation, while at the same time benefiting from the ameliorating effect of the sea, especially in winter.[57]

---

43   Annishader (NG437509), Armishader (NG501501), Ben Roishader (NG391484), Culeshader (NG473416), Dun Gershader (NG489451), Ellishader (NG499654), Flashader NG348531), Herishader (NG513629), Marishader NG490638), Sheader (NG407632), Sheader (NG184544), Sheader (NG452723), Shullishadder (NG477434), Uigshader (NG378490), Uigshader (NG429464).
44   Kyles Sheader (NF996883), Drinisiader (NG173945), and Loch Uiseadair (NB055152).
45   Sheader (NB004007) and Vatasater (NB007001).
46   Loch Brinishader (NF720699) and Loch Eisiadair (NF806728).
47   Sheader (NL631919).
48   Cnoc an Tiongalairidh (NB1937).
49   Greanary (NF995898), Reisary (NG031886), Loch Ìosal Vassary (NF997889).
50   Heisary Burn (NG307502), Soarary (NG239404).
51   Bogarh Aulasary (NF809720), Buile Risary (NF766729), Corary (NF740713), Dusary Mill (NF765670), Honary (NF900752), Horisary (NF761677), Loch Aulasary (NF937728), Loch Sandary (NF810743), Loch Sandary (NF737681), Loch Vausary (NF747690), Maari (NF861724), Obisary (NF891631).
52   Altisary (NF805287), Ben Corary (NF756282), Loch Hoxary (NF756303), Loch Vaccasary (NF758329), Trossary (NF757167), Unasary (NF772274).
53   Ersary (NL704996), Gunnary (NF671011), Skallary (NL 697994).
54   Gunisary (NF798492).
55   Loch Hornary (NF868571).
56   Corrairigh (NM476883).
57   Weaver et al. 1996, 148; Brayshay et al. 2000, 361.

The distribution of *ærgi* names on North and South Uist is predominantly coastal, though they are on average 1493 m inland; on average, this is 691 m further inland than *sætr* names. The location on the relatively flat western coast of the Uists is more open to south-westerly winds.[58] At a distance of over 1 km inland, salt spray will be reduced, improving grazing quality of the land, whilst still being close enough to still receive blown sand, which can mix with the peat to form the moderately fertile blackland soils.[59] These soils run north to south, between the fertile machair of the western coast and the infertile peats of the east coast; the majority of *ærgi* names are located along this central band of soil in the Uists.

There are only two possible *ærgi* names on Skye: Heisary Burn (NG307502) and Soarary (NG239404). The former now only relates to a topographical feature, whilst the latter is the highest *ærgi* name in the study area, at 200 m ASL, with a specific element which may refer to a shieling for sheep (ON *sauðr* (m.)).[60] Soarary may well be atypical, not only being located at a higher altitude, but specifically referring to sheep, whereas *ærgi* by its definition relates to cattle. This may represent a location where sheep milking, in particular, was practised, as in Iceland and the Faroe Islands.[61]

It must be remembered that we may only be looking at a fraction of the original number of shieling names. More marginal sites may have been abandoned and forgotten, or the generic element may have been replaced over time.[62] The language shift to Gaelic, which occurred after the Viking Age, made it more likely that the generic element *sætr* would be replaced through a lack of comprehension. The formation of epexegetic 'ex-nomine units', such as Airigh Shader (NB315177) and Airigh Horshader (NB242431) on Lewis – which effectively mean 'the shieling [Gaelic *àirigh*] of the shieling [ON *sætr*]' – highlight how the element *sætr* had lost its lexical meaning to the inhabitants once Gaelic gained dominance.[63]

At the same time, *ærgi* as a cognate of the Gaelic *àirigh*, is more likely to have been translated back into Gaelic. Simplex *ærgi* name

---

58   Brayshay et al. 2000, 361.
59   Parker Pearson and Smith 2012, 3, 7.
60   MacBain 1922, 173; Forbes 1923, 77.
61   Bergsåker 1978, 87-94; Thorsteinsson 2008, 83.
62   Cox 2002, 123.
63   Cox 1988-89, 3.

survive in England,[64] Shetland,[65] Orkney,[66] and the Faroe Islands.[67] This contrasts to a complete absence of simplex *ærgi* names in the Outer Hebrides and throughout Scotland as a whole. It is therefore likely that some *ærgi*, especially simplex names, were adopted by Gaelic speakers who understood the meaning of the name and either converted it to a simplex Gaelic *àirigh* name, or gave it a Gaelic-specific element. Either way, they rendered the ON name *ærgi* unrecognisable.

DEFINITIONS

The term *sætr* (n.) refers to 'sit' or 'seat', and is a cognate of the Norse place-name element *setr* (n.).[68] The two terms refer to pastoral activity; both initially had the meaning of a shieling, and are now virtually indistinguishable from each other in the British Isles.[69] The suggestion has been made that, during an early initial expansion of farming in Norway, *setr* was originally used to denote a shieling.[70] Many of these later developed into permanent farms, which necessitated the need to differentiate them from shielings proper, leading to the use of *sætr*.[71] In the rest of this chapter, I will refer to *sætr* with the specific meaning of a summer pasture, as both generics originally had the meaning of a shieling and are now difficult to separate.[72]

The headword *erg* (n.) is used by Cleasby and Vigfusson for *ærgi,* and its meaning is provided as: a Gaelic word, 'answering to the Scot. *shiel* or *shieling*'.[73] Fellows-Jensen has argued that this use of the headword is due to mistranslation into Danish of an Icelandic version of *Orkneyinga saga*.[74] The definition of *ærgi* is vague and similar to *sætr*, whilst not providing any clues as to why *ærgi* was adopted. *Ærgi* is believed to have been adopted from the Scottish-Gaelic *àirigh* (f.). Edward Dwelly and Alexander MacBain agree the definitions of the Gaelic *àirigh* to be either 'a summer residence for herdsman and cattle' or a 'hill pasture'.[75]

64 Fellows-Jensen 1977-78, 20.
65 Jacobsen 1936, 177; Stewart 1987, 26.
66 Marwick 1952, 227; Grant 2003, 169.
67 Jakobsen 1936, 208; Matras 1956, 52-53.
68 Nicolaisen 2001, 118.
69 Crawford 1987, 102-3; Nicolaisen 2001, 118.
70 Fellows-Jensen 1984, 161.
71 Ibid.; Crawford 1987, 108; Nicolaisen 2001, 118.
72 Cleasby and Vigfusson 1874, 525, 619.
73 Ibid., 133.
74 Fellows-Jensen 1980, 68; 2002, 9.
75 Dwelly 1973, 20; MacBain 1911, 10.

The definition of the Gaelic *àirigh* is too similar to that of ON *sætr* to fully explain its adoption, unless *ærgi* just replaced the *sætr* as the term for a shieling.[76] The use of both elements in Cumbria would suggest that this was not the case.[77] However, MacBain links the Gaelic term with the early Irish *áirge/áirghe*, (pl. *-righe* and *-rgheadha)* as 'a place where cows are', 'a dairy', or 'a herd of cattle'.[78] Likewise, Patrick Dinneen gives the meaning of Irish *áirge* (f.) to be: 'herd of cattle', 'pasture', 'herdsman's hut', or 'milk herd'.[79] The definition of Irish *áirge* would seem to have more of an emphasis on dairying, as opposed to the Scottish Gaelic *àirigh*, which stresses the summer pasture; it is this that I would suggest to be important.

POSSIBLE REASONS FOR THE DISTRIBUTION

Richard Cox found *àirigh* to be one of only six Gaelic loanwords from ON in western Lewis; there are ninety ON loanwords in the local Gaelic by comparison.[80] The place-name evidence in the Outer Hebrides during the Viking Age is overwhelmingly ON.[81] The only exceptions seemingly consist of some of the major island names, such as Skye (*Scia* in Andomnàn), Lewis, and the Uists.[82] Why was *àirigh* adopted when incoming ON-speaking settlers brought with them a lexicon of place-names, which they coined for newly-founded settlement and with which they renamed many existing ones?

Do surviving *ærgi* names in the Outer Hebrides represent pre-Viking Age Gaelic settlements taken over by incoming Scandinavian settlers? Richard Cox has argued that Gaelic was spoken in Lewis prior to the arrival of Scandinavian settlers and that some Gaelic place-names are pre-Norse.[83] The exact linguistic situation at the start of the Viking Age is unknown, as documentary sources are non-existent for the Outer Hebrides at this time. Bannerman suggests that, in the sixth century AD, the northern limit of Gaelic Dál Riata could be found at Coll and

---

76   Kruse 2007.
77   Fellows-Jensen 1983, 43.
78   MacBain 1911, 10.
79   Dinneen 1970, 24.
80   Cox 1991, 486.
81   Henderson 1910, 185; MacBain 1922, 70; Watson 1926, 38-39; Small 1968, 5;
      Fraser 1974, 19; 1978, 4, 19-20; Fellows-Jensen 1984, 152-53; Stahl 1999, 365;
      Kruse 2004, 104; 2005, 158; Jennings and Kruse 2005, 251; Gammeltoft 2006, 65.
82   Kruse 2005, 141-42; Gammeltoft 2007, 487.
83   Cox 1991, 488; 2002, 118.

Tiree, and Ardnamurchan on the mainland.[84] The inferences were that people north of this line were likely to be Pictish, and therefore possibly speakers of P-Celtic or a Brythonic dialect, compared to the Q-Celtic speakers of Dál Riata.[85] If the inhabitants were Pictish, it is unlikely for *ærgi* names to represent pre-Viking *àirigh* sites.

The argument for Gaelic being widely spoken in the Outer Hebrides during the pre-Viking period is rejected by Kruse, who points out that there is a lack of Gaelic terms incorporated into ON ex-nomine units.[86] Ian Fraser's study of place-names on Lewis noted that Norse names were more coastal, whilst Gaelic names had a more inland distribution, and concluded the Gaelic names on Lewis are, on the whole, post-Norse and relatively late.[87] Whatever the pre-Viking linguistic situation was, Nicolaisen has suggested that the Western Isles were a 'nameless landscape' in the eyes of the incoming Scandinavian settlers, making it unlikely for *ærgi* names to have simply been the product of Viking appropriation of pre-existing Gaelic farming units.[88]

Eric Cregeen suggested that Gaelic *eary* place-names, found in the Isle of Man, were the result of early Norse settlers being outnumbered by native Gaelic-speaking women. As the women would have worked at the shieling, they would have named the workplace by giving it a Gaelic name.[89] The gender division of work in Old Norse society would seem to give credence to this suggestion, with dairy work being a female role.[90] However, as Gillian Fellows-Jensen has pointed out, although this is a reasonable suggestion, it does not explain the export of the name to areas that had few or no Gaelic-speakers, such as the Northern Isles and Cumbria.[91]

It is unusual, then, to find *ærgi* (n.), a Gaelic loanword used to describe a minor settlement such as a shieling, during the period of Scandinavian dominance over the Outer Hebrides. Thomason and Kaufman define borrowing as 'the incorporation of foreign features into a group's native language by speakers of that language: the native

---

84   Bannerman 1974, 28.
85   Foster, 1996, 19; Kruse 2005, 149.
86   See Kruse 2004, 160-62; Jennings and Kruse 2005, 30.
87   Fraser 1978, 15, 19.
88   Nicolaisen 1979-80, 110. See also Fraser 1978, 19.
89   Cregeen, cited in Megaw 1978, 339.
90   Jochens 1995, 122; Myrdal 2008, 64, 70.
91   Fellows-Jensen 1983, 43.

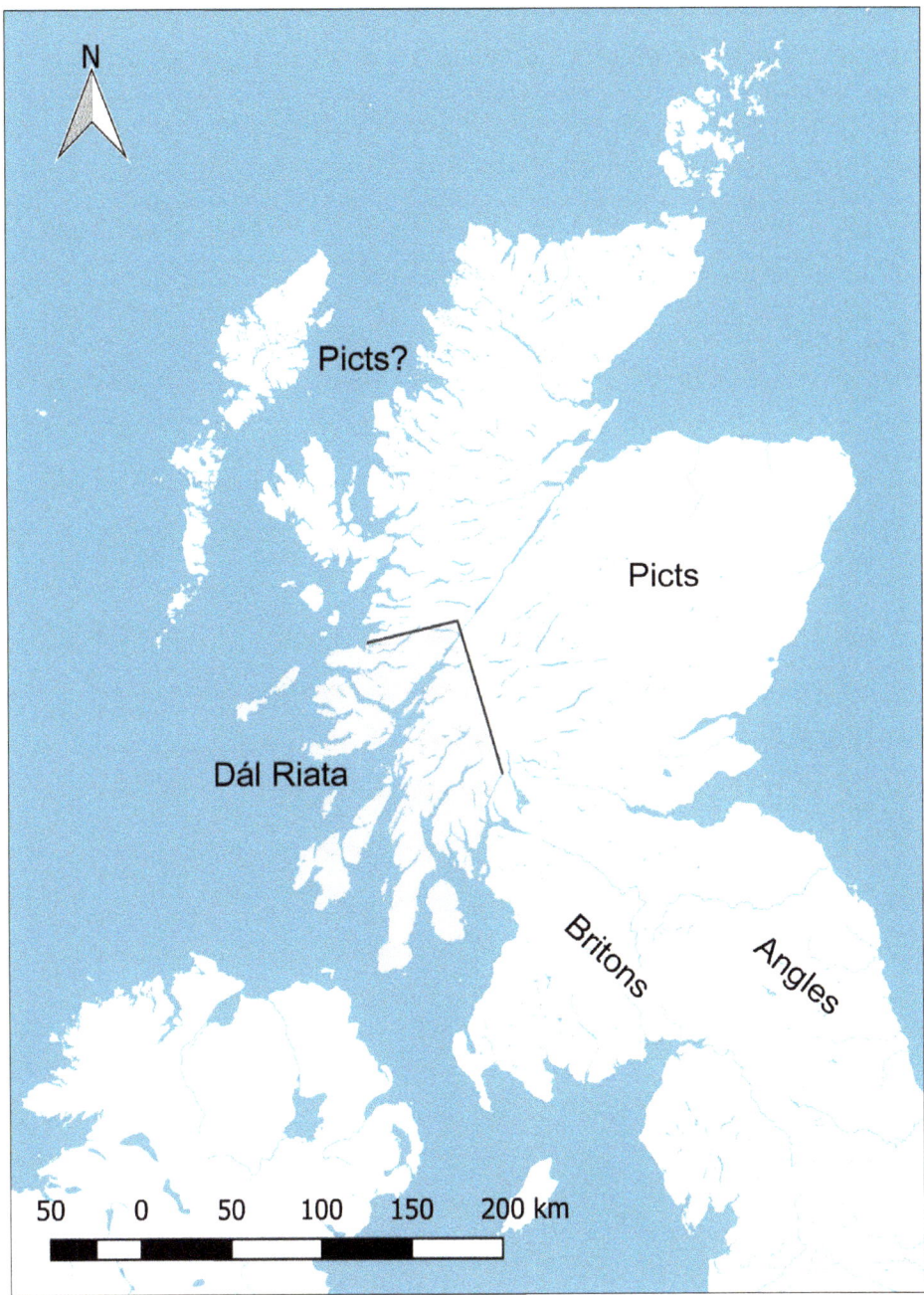

Figure 3: The distribution of linguistic groupings in northern Britain, mid-seventh century (after McNeill and MacQueen 2000).

language is maintained but changed by the addition of the incorporated features'.[92] Britta Schultz Thulin noted forty Gaelic nouns in ON,[93] but 160 ON nouns in Irish,[94] a similar dominance of ON loans as Richard Cox had found in western Lewis. Such uneven borrowing might be a result of the unequal status of the respective languages.[95]

Odlin suggests that 'larger numbers, greater prestige and more political power' are a major influence on the direction of lexical borrowing.[96] In this situation, the ON *sætr* should have been used to describe a shieling, as no reason existed to adopt *ærgi* from the subordinate Gaelic. One possible explanation is that the loanword was needed to designate new things or concepts that ON-speakers encountered in the colonies.[97] Alternatively, both terms were used, but each was retained with a specialised meaning.[98] Either way, this suggests a specialised use of both *sætr* and *ærgi* in the Hebrides. This may be related to the physical characteristics of the settlement, or, as Gillian Fellows-Jensen put it: 'there must have been Something characteristic about the location or the function of the *ærgi* in the Scottish colonies that led Viking settlers there to refer to it by the Gaelic term rather than by a Scandinavian word such as *sætr* or *sel*'.[99]

Theoretical Considerations

The basic premise of my study of settlement location is that human decision-making is rational at the time a settlement is founded. This means that the site chosen will be the optimum position within that locality for a particular type of settlement, according to a set of criteria upheld by those founding it.[100] The needs of an individual would influence the set of criteria used, and may be split into those elements needed for survival, such as water, food, and shelter, but also taking into account any cultural, social, or personal aspects.[101] This means

92   Thomason and Kaufman 1991, 37.
93   Schulte-Thulin 1992, 65-79.
94   Schulte-Thulin 1996, 83.
95   Weinreich 1968, 59; Antilla 1989, 155; Odlin 1989, 13; Thomason and Kaufman 1991, 44; Thomason 2001, 66; Myers-Scotton 2002, 31.
96   Odlin 1989, 13.
97   Weinreich 1968, 54, 56; Antilla 1989, 155.
98   Weinreich 1968, 55.
99   Fellows-Jensen 1985, 73-74.
100   Wood 1978, 258.
101   Nunn 2009, 316; Gold 1980, 21.

that a site may be optimal in one society or culture's view, but not in another, depending on the criteria used and priority given to individual criteria. Particular cultures may have considered a specific location or environment to be marginal, depending on their preferences and needs, or, as Brian Roberts suggests: 'Settlement forms and patterns are a product of interactions between the natural environment and all aspects of society. Ultimately forms and patterns are a product of choices made by individuals and societies'.[102]

A site will therefore harbour clues on the criteria used for its selection; the choice of one site over another should highlight favourable locational factors for that particular settlement.[103] By conducting a study of the locational factors of a generic element, the motivation and needs of those who initially founded such settlements may be discernible. As both generic elements are concerned with cattle farming, it is possible that a common characteristic exists for the location chosen for each place-name element, which made it more suitable for a type of cattle farming.

METHOD

I have conducted a survey of shieling names in the Outer Hebrides and Skye, using the first edition Ordnance Survey (OS) maps (1:10,560). Although the information on the maps was collected several hundred years after the Viking settlers first arrived, it represents the first comprehensive survey of place-names that has a uniform coverage and scale.

Once the survey was completed, I used modern OS maps to complete a topographical survey of the characteristic features found at each site, and the British Geological Survey for the geology data.[104] Data on soil, modern vegetation, and supplementary information on the geology was gathered from soil maps by Scotland's Soils.[105] This information was then collated and compared to highlight any differences in settlement location.

---

102   Gratten 1998, 16; Edwards and Whittington 1998, 61; Roberts 1982, 3.
103   Amedeo and Golledge 1975, 291.
104   British Geological Survey 2016.
105   Scotland's Soils 2016.

RESULTS

ALTITUDE

Increasing altitude has several effects on climate, including increase in wind speed, increased cloud cover, precipitation, lower temperatures, and a longer winter, which shortens the growing season.[106] Nagy and Grabherr report a drop of three species for every 200 m of elevation (1-2°C drop in temperature), and, as a consequence, the range of food plants available for livestock would also decrease.[107]

	-ærgi names	*-sætr* names
Below 50 m	69%	60%
Below 100m	92%	86%

Figure 4: Altitude of Viking shieling names.

The majority of both *sætr* and *ærgi* names are found below 100 m ASL (Figure 4). The difference in height is so marginal that there would be virtually no discrepancy in temperature as a result of altitude.

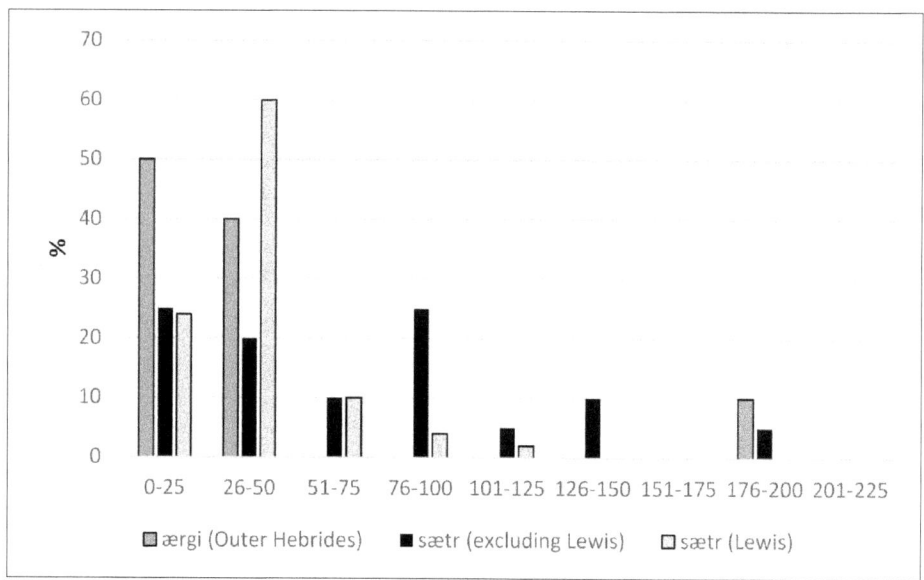

Figure 5: The altitude of *sætr* and *ærgi* names.

---

106   Nagy and Grabherr 2009; Larcher et al. 2010
107   Nagy and Grabherr 2009

Altitudinally, there is no real difference between *sætr* and *ærgi* names; 94% of *ærgi* names are below 150 m ASL, whilst 98% of *sætr* names are as well; even on the more mountainous Skye, 87% of *sætr* names are below 150 m ASL. When comparing Lewis and the Uists, both composed of gneiss, 97% of *sætr* names on Lewis and 100% of the *ærgi* names on the Uists are below 100 m ASL. Altitude is therefore not a deciding factor in the choice to use *sætr* and *ærgi* place-name elements in the Outer Hebrides.

ASPECT

The aspect of a settlement governs the amount of direct light a site gets, and the time of day it receives direct light, if at all. This has an effect on air and soil temperature, which can affect growth rates and soil water availability during parts of the year, due to the difference in potential evapotranspiration rates.

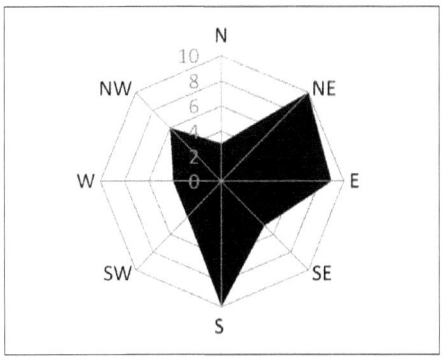

Figure 6: Aspect of *sætr* sites.　　Figure 7: Aspect of *ærgi* sites.

There is a marked difference in aspect between the two generics. Although *sætr* names share a preference with *ærgi* names for a southern aspect, *sætr* also exhibit an east to north-easterly aspect. In the Northern Hemisphere, a southern aspect will receive higher concentrations of direct sunlight over a longer period than other aspects, promoting a longer growing season. The temperature in spring will rise faster on a southern slope, allowing vegetation to grow at an earlier date. However, higher temperatures may lead to water stress in summer when precipitation decreases.

A north-easterly aspect in a temperate Northern Hemisphere climate will have a lower surface temperature and wetter environment, which has been found to have a higher herbage mass.[108] This, in turn, may affect soil nitrogen transformation, with higher nitrogen found on northern-facing slopes, which is a key preference in fodder selection in beef cattle.[109]

DRIFT GEOLOGY

With reference to the soil types in Figure 8, with 57% of *ærgi* names being found on or near peaty soils on the Uists, it would seem they were situated on poorer soils than *sætr* names, with 52%. This is misleading, as the majority of *ærgi* names are situated on the transition from machair to peat soil in the blacklands, where the addition of wind-blown calcareous sand improves the peat, leading to the growth of mesotrophic grassland for grazing.[110]

More *sætr* names are found near alluvial soils (6% compared to 3%), which is unusual, as alluvial soils are today considered fertile. This may be due to the low level of rainfall on the Uists, restricting the size of rivers and their ability to form flood plains. Skye and the southern half of Lewis, however, get higher rainfall and consequently have larger streams and some rivers. Although alluvial soils are today used for arable, these would provide rich tall herb communities for hay making before modern drainage.[111]

Brown forest soils are considered one of the more fertile soils in Scotland and are more commonly found close to *ærgi* names (20%) compared to *sætr* names (14%).[112] Also, 20% of *ærgi* names and 11% of *sætr* names are close to humus-iron podzols, which, although naturally acidic and nutrient deficient, are able to be improved.[113] In total, 43% of *ærgi* names are found on soil types that are considered fertile or improvable, although these types of soils only account for 32% of those found at *sætr* sites.

---

108 Sigua et al. 2011, 67; Nadal-Romero et al. 2014, 1713.
109 Hishi et al. 2014, 343; Plymale et al. 1987; Berry et al. 2002, 448.
110 Dodgshon 1988, 140; Parker Pearson 2012, 14.
111 Emanuelsson and Segerström 1998, 80; Hughes and Huntely 1988, 94.
112 James Hutton Institute 2016.
113 Ibid.

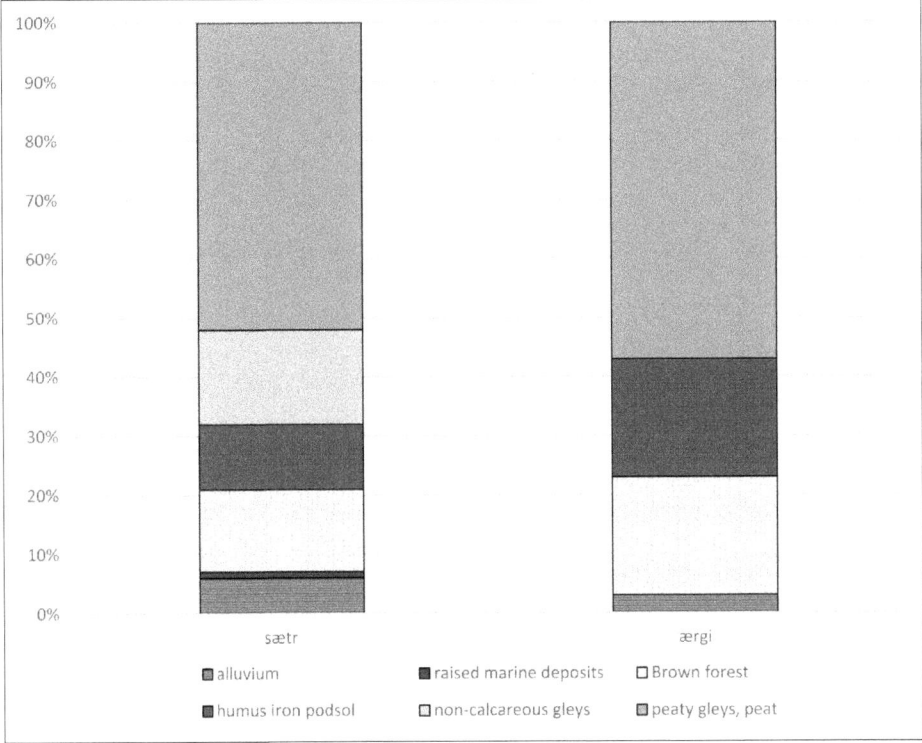

Figure 8: Soil types found at *sætr* and *ærgi* names.

Non-calcareous gleyed soils account for 16% of those found at *sætr* sites; these soils are restricted to grazing land, are poorly drained, and require careful management if they are not to be damaged by livestock. The 52% of *sætr* names close to the various types of peaty soil are likely only to be used as rough grazing, as the limited area of calcareous machair on Lewis and Skye do not allow large areas of mixed soil to be formed, which does happen on the blacklands of the Uists.

When comparing the *ærgi* names on the Uists to the *sætr* names on Lewis, soil fertility seems to have been a deciding factor for the use of shieling names. Even when looking at *ærgi* names outside of the Uists, over 50% are on soils that are considered good to moderately fertile, compared to between 32% and 35% of *sætr* names. This would lead to better quality pasture at *ærgi* sites, and would suggest soil fertility had some influence on the generic used to name a shieling location.

DISCUSSION

The complimentary distribution pattern of *sætr* and *ærgi* names on Skye and the Outer Hebrides is unlikely to be accounted for by using a chronology of generic elements as proposed by Marwick and Nicolaisen.[114] The colonisation of the Uists, in this scenario, must have been later than that of Lewis and Skye, after *sætr* was replaced by *ærgi*. This would mean that *airigh* must either have been encountered during the colonisation of the Uists, or else brought back from travels further south. As suggested earlier, later Scandinavian settlement in Cumbria (c. AD 902), for which both *sætr* and *ærgi* were still active as place-name elements,[115] would suggest that a simple chronology of settlement names, with *sætr* being replaced by *ærgi*, was not the case.

Alan Macniven has raised the possibility that the complimentary distribution of *sætr* and *ærgi* might be connected to the MacSorley Lordship of the Isles in the twelfth century.[116] Certainly, Lewis and Skye were part of the Kingdom of Man in AD 1156, whereas the Uists, Small Isles, Mull, Islay, Jura, and Arran belonged to Somerled's dominion (Figure 9). Under the Gaelic MacSorleys, it is possible that the use of the place-name element *àirigh* may have been spread or led to the preferential retention of *ærgi* names as a cognate to the Gaelic *àirigh*. The distribution of *ærgi* names along the Sutherland coast and in Caithness, as well as aforementioned Cumbria, would suggest that this is not the only reason for the distribution pattern.

An alternative suggestion may be that a higher population on the more environmentally favourable Uists made any indigenous language more resilient. Some or all of the *ærgi* names on the Uists may represent pre-existing *àirigh* names that were appropriated by incoming Scandinavians. If this was the case, it may have been here that the word was first adopted. There is, however, no evidence to prove that the Uists were Gaelic-speaking. Even if they were, Alan Macniven's study of the place-names of Islay, an island closer to the Dál Riata heartland and known to be Gaelic-speaking prior to the Viking Age, would seem to show extensive Scandinavian settlement, including the formation of *sætr* names (which are absent from South Uist).[117]

---

114   Marwick 1952, 227-51; Nicolaisen 2001, 87-94.
115   Fellows-Jensen 1985, 74; Oram 2000, 248.
116   Macniven 2006, 190-92.
117   Ibid., 192-93

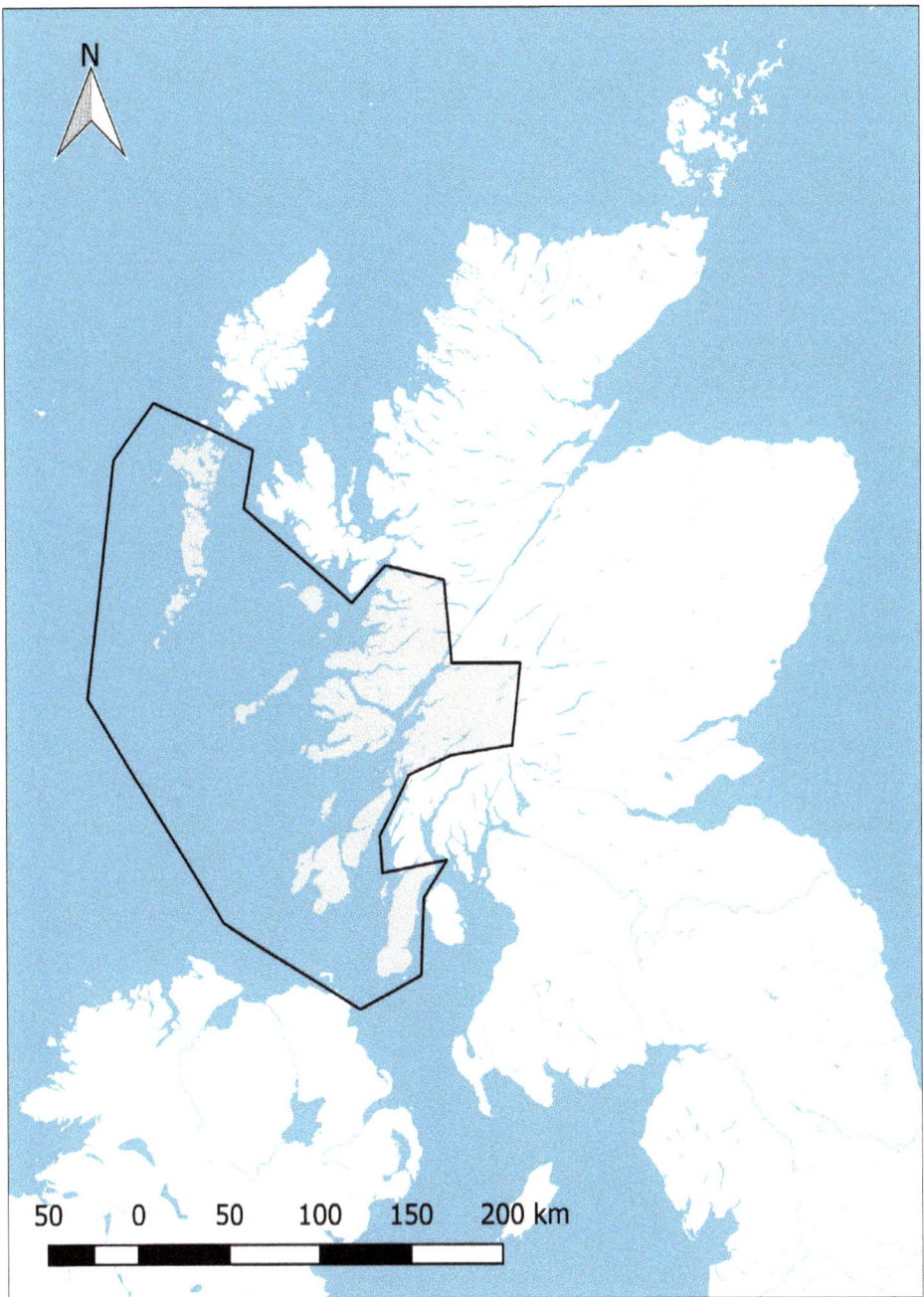

Figure 9: Area controlled by the MacSorley dynasty (after McNeill and MacQueen 2000).

A possibility therefore exists for the distribution pattern to reflect environmental constraints imposed on the farming economy during the Viking Age. The lower precipitation across much of Lewis is negated by the undulating topography, which, combined with the drift geology and low evapotranspiration, leads to waterlogging of the soil and extensive blanket peat formation. Like Skye, with its high level of precipitation, the soil moisture content is likely to be high, resulting in anaerobic soil conditions that promote the formation of peat. This, in turn, limited the extent of pasture and would therefore affect how Viking Age farmers used the land.

The waterlogging of the soil in Lewis and Skye leads to the formation of peat, peaty gleys, and podzols. In turn, these lead to vegetation dominated by acid heather heath and bog. Hardy beef cattle and calves are able to exhibit weight gain regardless of vegetation and climate.[118] Dairy cattle have a higher demand for nutrient rich fodder;[119] this is to cover the extra energy requirement of producing milk.[120] Beef cattle select vegetation not just purely for energy intake, but for nitrogen content.[121] The north east to east aspect of *sætr* names further encourages a higher nitrogen content of the soil.[122]

The *ærgi* names of the Outer Hebrides, principally the Uists, are located at low levels, on south-facing slopes, and on soil that is locally fertile. The peaty soils of the Blacklands of the Uists, rather than promoting heather moor (as on Lewis), forms mesotrophic grassland due to the input of calcareous material from the machair.[123] The *sætr* names of Lewis and Skye are also low-lying, but are found on north-facing slopes and on less fertile soils. Bone assemblages from known Viking Age settlements seem to corroborate the environmental constraints on farming practices.

At Bornais in South Uist, fusion data showed that 20% of cattle died in the first year, and another 40% in the second year, with only a third of cattle surviving beyond their fourth year. When dental records were used for dating, over 50% of cattle were dead by their first year, a quarter

---

118   Berry et al. 2002, 451.
119   Sæther et al. 2006; Fraser et al. 2009, 368.
120   Hofstetter et al. 2011, 717.
121   Berry et al. 2002, 450.
122   Plymale et al. 1987.
123   Pankhurst and Mullin 1991; Kent et al. 1996; Weaver et al. 1996; Angus 1997; Brayshay et al. 2000.

having died within a month of being born. This has been suggested as evidence of a dairy strategy for cattle.[124] The bone assemblages on South Uist show an increase in the keeping of cattle compared to sheep from the pre-Viking Age. Whilst sheep were kept for one to two years and slaughtered after one shear, cattle show evidence from neonatal bones of a probable dairy economy. Mulville has suggested that:

> 1. Sheep were rarely brought to the settlement (except as culled animals) and may have been kept on the blacklands and/or the heather moor to the east of the island.
> 2. Cattle were kept close to the settlement to assist calving and establish milk, before neonatal animals were killed, and the cattle later removed to surrounding areas.[125]

What cannot be shown is whether male cattle predominate in neonatal assemblages, or whether male cattle and dry cows were treated differently to the milk herd, either being taken away earlier or even kept away from settlements in the machair.

The Scandinavian settlement at Bostadh on Lewis has few cattle dying young (7-10 months), which has been seen as evidence of meat production by Thoms, as cattle was kept over winter until they were at their prime for meat production.[126] Neonatal deaths account for only 7% of the total assemblage in Phase 1, which decreases with time throughout the phases until they represent less than 1% in Phase 4 (the Norse phase). Unlike on South Uist, these cattle do not show evidence of high neonatal deaths, and neonatal remains decrease in the assemblage over time. Thoms concluded that this does not suggest that a dairy economy was being practiced at Bostadh.[127] Improved husbandry practices are suggested by age-of-death evidence from the Norse period.[128] A lack of evidence does not rule out a dairy economy, as taphonomic losses may have been heavy due to the acidic conditions. The fact that cattle seem to have been kept until they were are at their prime for meat production, however, suggest that a different livestock management system was in use on Lewis during the Viking Age.[129]

---

124   Mulville 2005, 165.
125   Ibid., 167.
126   Thoms 2003, 221
127   Ibid., 221
128   Ibid.
129   Ibid., 221, 223

CONCLUSION

The distribution of *sætr* and *ærgi* names in the Outer Hebrides and Skye show a complimentary distribution. Rather than being a result of linguistic change, this distribution may have developed as a human response to environmental constraints. Altitudinally, there was no real difference in the location of each place-name element, as both were found mainly below 100 m ASL. The *ærgi* names of the Outer Hebrides are found on locally fertile soil, which allowed the growth of mesotrophic grassland, prime grazing land. The *sætr* names of Lewis and Skye, by contrast, are located on soils that are less fertile, but produce vegetation with a higher nitrogen content, which is better suited to beef production. The bone assemblages from Bostadh on Lewis and Bornais in South Uist, although not shieling sites, seem to show different farming strategies, with Bostadh concentrating more on beef production, whereas a dairy strategy was followed at Bornais. This would match Cleasby and Vigfusson's definition of *sætr* as a general pasture, whilst *ærgi*, as a dairy, seems to have the Irish definition *áirge*.[130]

It is possible that Scandinavian settlers encountered intensive dairy farms, *áirge,* either in the Scottish Isles or in Ireland. Their own corresponding term, *sætr*, may have had a much more general connotation of summer farm, which encompassed summer grazing for all types of cattle, including milk cows. Scandinavian settlers adopted *áirge* as a term for an intensive summer milking place, and the differentiation of grazing land to suit different pastoral regimes points to an overall intensification of farming during the Viking Age.

BIBLIOGRAPHY

PRIMARY SOURCES

Annála Ríoghachta Éireann. Annals of the Kingdom of Ireland by the Four Masters, O'Donovan J (ed and trans), 1848-51, 7 vols, Dublin: Royal Irish Academy.

Annals of Ulster, Mac Airt S and Mac Niocaill G (eds and trans), 1983, Dublin: Dublin Institute for Advanced Studies.

---

130   Cleasby and Vigfusson 1874, 525, 619.

SECONDARY SOURCES

Adderley, W P and I A Simpson 2005, 'Early-Norse Home-Field Productivity in the Faroe Islands', *Human Ecology* 33:5, 711-36.

Albrethsen, S E and C Keller 1986, 'The Use of *Sæter* in Norse Medieval Greenland', *Arctic Anthropology* 23:1-2, 91-107.

Amedeo, D and R G Golledge 1975, *An Introduction to Scientific Reasoning in Geography*. New York: Wiley.

Angus, I S 1991, 'Climate and Vegetation of the Outer Hebrides', in R J Pankhurst and J M Mullin (eds), *Flora of the Outer Hebrides*, London: Natural History Museum, 28-31.

Angus, S 1997, *The Outer Hebrides: The Shaping of the Islands*. Cambridge: White Horse Press.

Antilla, R 1989, *Historical and Comparative Linguistics*, 2nd edn, Philadelphia: John Benjamins.

Armit, I 1996, *The Archaeology of Skye and the Western Isles*, Edinburgh: Edinburgh University Press.

Bannerman, J W M 1974, *Studies in the History of Dalriada*, Edinburgh: Scottish Academic Press.

Beito, O 1949, *Norske Sæternamn*. Oslo: Aschehoug.

Bergsåker, J 1978, 'The Keeping and Milking of Sheep in the Old Subsistence Economy of Scandinavia, Iceland and Northern Europe', in J. Baldwin (ed), *Scandinavian Shetland: An Ongoing Tradition?*, Edinburgh: Scottish Society for Northern Studies, 85-96.

Berry, R, P L Jewell, F Sutter, P J Edwards, and M Kreuzer 2002, 'Selection, Intake and Excretion of Nutrients by Scottish Highland Suckler Beef Cows and Calves, and Brown Swiss Dairy Cows in Contrasting Alpine Grazing Systems', *Journal of Agricultural Science* 139, 437-53.

Bjørgo, T 1986, 'Mountain Archaeology: Preliminary Results from Nyset-Steggje', *Norwegian Archaeological Review* 19:2, 122-27.

Boyd, J M and I L Boyd 1990, *The Hebrides: A Natural History*, London: Collins.

Brayshay, B A 1992, 'Pollen Analysis and the Vegetational History of Barra and South Uist in the Outer Hebrides', unpublished PhD thesis, University of Sheffield.

Brayshay B A, D Gilbertson, M Kent, K J Edwards, P Wathern, and R E Weaver 2000. 'Surface Pollen-Vegetation Relationships on the Atlantic Seaboard: South Uist, Scotland', *Journal of Biogeography* 27:2, 359-78.

Brink, S 1999, 'Social Order in the Early Scandinavian Landscape', in C Fabech and J Ringtved (eds), *Settlement and Landscape: Proceedings of a Conference in Århus, Denmark, May 4-7 1998*, Aarhus: Aarhus University Press, 423-39.

British Geological Survey 2016, www.bgs.ac.uk/data/mapviewers/home.html, accessed 20 January 2016.

Clancy, T C 2008, 'The Gall-Ghàidheil and Galloway', *Journal of Scottish Name Studies* 2, 19-50.

Cleasby, R and G Vigfusson 1874, *An Icelandic-English Dictionary,* Oxford: Oxford University Press.

Cox, R A V 1988-89, 'Questioning the Value and Validity of the Term "Hybrid" in Hebridean Place-Name Study, *Nomina* 12, 1-10.

Cox, R A V 1991, 'Norse-Gaelic Contact in the West of Lewis: The Place-Name Evidence' in P S Ureland and G Broderick (eds), *Language Contact in the British Isles: Proceedings of the Eighth International Symposium on Language Contact in Europe, Douglas, Isle of Man, 1988.* Berlin: De Gruyter, 479-93.

Cox, R A V 2002, *The Gaelic Place-Names of Carloway, Isle of Lewis: Their Structure and Significance,* Dublin: Dublin Institute for Advanced Studies.

Crawford, B E 1987, *Scandinavian Scotland,* London: Leicester University Press.

Crawford, B E (ed) 1995, *Scandinavian Settlement in Northern Britain,* London: Leicester University Press.

Crawford, I and R Switsur 1977, 'Sandscaping and C14: The Udal, North Uist', *Antiquity* 51, 124-36.

Dahl, S 1970, 'The Norse Settlement of the Faroe Islands', *Medieval Archaeology* 14, 60-73.

Dinneen, P 1970, *An Irish-English Dictionary,* Dublin: Irish Texts Society.

Dodgshon, R A 1988, 'The Ecological Basis of Highland Peasant Farming: 1500-1800 A.D.' In H H Birks, H J B Birks, P E Kaland, and D Moe (eds), *The Cultural Landscape: Past, Present and Future,* Cambridge: Cambridge University Press, 139-52.

Dwelly, E 1973. *The Illustrated Gaelic Dictionary.* Edinburgh: Birlinn.

Edwards, K J and G Whittington 1998, 'Disturbance and Regeneration Phases in Pollen Diagrams and their Relevance to Concepts of Marginality', in C M Mills and G Coles (eds), *Life on the Edge: Human Settlement and Marginality,* Oxford: Oxbow, 61-66.

Emanuelsson, M and U Segerström 1998, 'Forest Grazing and Outland Exploitation during the Middle Ages in Dalarna, Central Sweden: A Study Based on Pollen Analysis', in H Andersson, L Ersgard, and E Svensson (eds), *Outland Use in Preindustrial Europe,* Lund: Institute of Archaeology, 80-94.

Fellows-Jensen, G 1977-78, 'A Gaelic-Scandinavian Loan-Word in English Place-Names (erg)', *Journal of the English Place-Name Society* 10, 18-25.

Fellows-Jensen, G 1980, 'Common Gaelic *Áirge,* Old Scandinavian *Ærgi* or *Erg*', *Nomina* 4, 67-74.

Fellows-Jensen, G 1983, 'Scandinavian Settlement in the Isle of Man and North West England: The Place Name Evidence', In C Fell, P Foote, J Graham-Campbell, and R Thomson (eds), *The Viking Age in the Isle of Man: Select Papers from the Ninth Viking Congress, Isle of Man, 4-14 July 1981*. London: Viking Society for Northern Research, 37-52.

Fellows-Jensen, G 1984, 'Viking Settlement in the Northern and Western Isles', in A Fenton and H Pálsson (eds), *The Northern and Western Isles in the Viking World*, Edinburgh: John Donald, 148-68.

Fellows-Jensen, G 1985, 'Scandinavian Settlement in Cumbria and Dumfrieshire: The Place-Name evidence', in J R Baldwin and I D Whyte (eds), *The Scandinavians in Cumbria*, Edinburgh: Scottish Society for Northern Studies, 65-82.

Fitzpatrick, E A 1964, 'The Soils of Scotland', in J H Burnett (ed), *The Vegetation of Scotland*, Edinburgh: Oliver & Boyd, 36-63.

Forbes, A R 1923, *Place-names of Skye and Adjacent Islands*, Paisley: Gardner.

Foster, S 1996, *Picts, Gaels and Scots: Early Historic Scotland*, London: Batsford.

Fraser, I A 1974, 'The Place Names of Lewis: The Norse Evidence', *Northern Studies* 4, 11-21.

Fraser, I A 1978, 'Norse and Gaelic Coastal Terminology in the Western Isles', *Northern Studies* 11, 3-16.

Fraser, I A 1984, 'Some Further Thoughts on Scandinavian Place-Names in Lewis', *Northern Studies* 21, 34-41.

Fraser M D, V J Theobald, D R Davies, and J M Moorby 2009, 'Impact of Diet Selected by Cattle and Sheep Grazing Heathland Communities on Nutrient Supply and Faecal Micro-Flora Activity', *Agriculture, Ecosystems and Environment* 129, 367-77.

Gammeltoft, P 2006, 'Scandinavian Influence on Hebridean Island Names', in P Gammeltoft and B Jørgensen (eds), *Names through the Looking-Glass: Festschrift in Honour of Gillian Fellows-Jensen, July 5th 2006*. Copenhagen: Reitzel, 53-84.

Gammeltoft, P 2007, 'Scandinavian Naming-Systems in the Hebrides: A Way of Understanding How the Scandinavians were in Contact with Gaels and Picts?' in B Ballin Smith, S Taylor, and G Williams (eds), *West over Sea: Studies in Scandinavian Sea-Borne Expansion and Settlement before 1300*, Leiden: BRILL, 479-97.

Gilbertson, D, J Grattan, and J Schwenninger 1996, 'A Stratigraphic Survey of the Holocene Coastal Dune and Machair Sequences', in D Gilbertson, M Kent, and J Grattan (eds), *The Outer Hebrides: The Last 14,000 Years*, Sheffield: Sheffield Academic Press, 72-101.

Gloyne, R W 1968, 'The Structure of Wind and its Relevance to Forestry', *Forestry* 41 (sup.), 7-19.

Gold, J R 1980, *An Introduction to Behavioural Geography*. Oxford: Oxford University Press.

Grant, A E 2003, 'Scandinavian Place-Names in Northern Britain as Evidence for Language Contact and Interaction', unpublished PhD thesis, University of Glasgow.

Grattten, J 1998, 'The Response of Marginal Societies and Ecosystems in Britain to Icelandic Volcanic Eruptions', in C M Mills and G Coles (eds), *Life on the Edge: Human Settlement and Marginality*, Oxford: Oxbow, 13-30.

Gordon, J E 1993, 'North-West Coast of Lewis'. In J E Gordon and D G Sutherland (eds), *Quaternary of Scotland*. London: Chapman and Hall, 414-421.

Hall, A M 1995, 'Was All of Lewis Glaciated in the Late Devensian?', *Quaternary Newsletter* 76, 1-7.

Hastrup, K 1989. 'Saeters in Iceland, 900-1600', *Acta Borealia* 6:1, 72-85.

Henderson, G 1910, *The Norse Influence on Celtic Scotland*. Glasgow: James MacLehose.

Hishi, T, R Urakawa, N Tashiro, Y Maeda, and H Shibata 2014, 'Seasonality of Factors Controlling N Mineralization Rates among Slope Positions and Aspects in Cool-Temperate Deciduous Natural Forests and Larch Plantations', *Biology and Fertility of Soils* 50, 343-56.

Hitzler, E 1979, *Sel: Untersuchungen zur Geschichte des Isländischen Sennwesens Seit der Landnahmezeit*, Oslo: Universitetsforlaget.

Hofstetter, P, M Steiger Burgos, R Petermann, A Münger, J W Blum, P Thomet, H Menzi, S Kohler, and P Kunz 2011, 'Does Body Size of Dairy Cows, at Constant Ratio of Maintenance to Production Requirements, Affect Productivity in a Pasture-Based Production System?', *Journal of Animal Physiology and Animal Nutrition* 95:6, 717-29.

Hudson, G, W Towers, J S Bibby, and D J Henderson 1982, *Soil and Land Capability for Agriculture: Outer Hebrides*, Aberdeen: Macaulay Land Use Research Institute.

Hughes, J and B Huntely 1988, 'Upland Hay Meadows in Britain', in H H Birks, H J B Birks, P E Kaland, and D Moe (eds), *The Cultural Landscape: Past, Present and Future*, Cambridge: Cambridge University Press, 91-110.

Jakobsen, J 1936, *The Place-Names of Shetland*, London: Nutt.

James Hutton Institute 2016, 'Soils – Introduction', www.hutton.ac.uk/learning/exploringscotland/soils, accessed 20 January 2016.

Jennings, A and A Kruse 2005, 'An Ethnic Enigma – Norse, Pict and Gael in the Western Isles', in A Mortensen and S V Arge (eds), *Viking and Norse in the North Atlantic: Selected Papers from the Proceedings of the Fourteenth Viking Congress, Tórshavn, 19-30 July 2001*. Tórshavn: Føroya Fróðskaparfelag, 284-96.

Jockens, J 1995, *Women in Old Norse Society*, Ithaca: Cornell University Press.

Kent, M, R Weaver, D Gilbertson, P Wathern, and B Brayshay 1996, The Present-Day Machair Vegetation of the Southern Outer Hebrides, in D Gilbertson, M Kent, and J Grattan (eds), *The Outer Hebrides: The Last 14,000 Years*, Sheffield: Sheffield Academic Press, 133-45.

Kruse, A 2004, 'Norse Topographical Settlement Names on the Western Littoral of Scotland', in J Adams and K Holman (eds), *Scandinavia and Europe 800-1350: Contact, Conflict and Coexistence*, Turnhout: Brepols, 97-107.

Kruse, A 2005, 'Explorers, Raiders and Settlers: The Norse Impact upon Hebridean Place-Names', in P Gammeltoft, C Hough, and D Waugh (eds), *Cultural Contacts in the North Atlantic Region: The Evidence of Names*. Lerwick: NORNA, SPNS, and SNSBI, 141-56

Kruse, A 2007, 'Fashion, Limitation and Nostalgia: Scandinavian Place-Names Abroad', in *Images and Imaginations: Perspectives on Britain and Scandinavia*, A Kruse and P Graves (eds), Edinburgh: Lockharton, 3-33.

Larcher, W, C Kainmüller, and J Wagner 2010, Survival Types of High Mountain Plants under Extreme Temperatures, *Flora* 205, 3-18.

MacBain, A 1911, *An Etymological Dictionary of the Gaelic Language*, Stirling: Eneas Mackay.

MacBain, A 1922, *Place-Names of the Highlands and Islands of Scotland*, Stirling: Eneas Mackay.

MacLaren, A 1974. 'A Norse House on Drimore Machair, South Uist', *Glasgow Archaeological Journal* 3, 9-18.

Macniven, A 2006, 'The Norse in Islay: A Settlement Historical Case-Study for Medieval Scandinavian Activity in Western Maritime Scotland', unpublished PhD thesis, University of Edinburgh.

Magnus, B J 1986, 'Iron Age Exploitation of High Mountain Resources in Sogn', *Norwegian Archaeological Review* 19:1, 44-50.

Mahler, D 1991, 'Argisbrekka: New Evidence of Shielings in the Faroe Islands', *Acta Archaeologica* 61, 60-72.

Mahler, D 1995, 'Shielings and their Role in the Viking-Age Economy', in C E Batey, J Jesch, and C D Morris (eds), *The Viking Age in Caithness, Orkney and the North Atlantic*, Edinburgh: Edinburgh University Press, 487-505.

Mahler, D 2007, *Sæteren ved Argisbrekka. Økonomiske Forandringer på Færøerne i Vikingetid og Tidlig Middelalder*, Tórshavn: Fróðskaparsetur.

Marwick, H 1952, *Orkney Farm-Names*, Kirkwall: W R Mackintosh.

Matras, C 1956, 'Gammelfærosk Ærgi, n., og Dermed Beslaegtede Ord', *Namn och Bygd* 14, 51-67.

McNeill P G B and H L MacQueen 2000, *An Atlas of Scottish History to 1707*, Edinburgh: The Scottish Medievalists.

Megaw, E 1978, 'The Manx "Eary" and its Significance', in P Davey (ed), *Man and Environment in the Isle of Man*, Oxford: BAR, 327-46.

Met Office 2016, www.metoffice.gov.uk, accessed 20 January 2016.

Mulville, J 2005, 'The Machair – 2: Mammals', in N M Sharples (ed), *A Norse Farmstead in the Outer Hebrides: Excavations at Mound 3, Bornais, South Uist*, Oxford: Oxbow, 165-169.

Myrdal, J 2008. 'Women and Cows: Ownership and Work in Medieval Sweden', *Ethologia Scandinavica*, 38, 61-80.

Myers-Scotton, C 2002, *Contact linguistics: Bilingual Encounters and Grammatical Outcomes*, Oxford: Oxford University Press.

Nadal-Romero, E, K Petrlic, E Verachtert, E Bochet, and J Poesen 2014, 'Effects of Slope Angle and Aspect on Plant Cover and Species Richness in a Humid Mediterranean Badland', *Earth Surface Processes and Landforms* 39:13, 1705-16.

Nagy, L and G Grabherr 2009, *The Biology of Alpine Habitats*, Oxford: Oxford University Press.

Neighbour, T and C Burgess 1997, 'Traigh Bostadh (Uig Parish)', in R Turner (ed), *Discovery and Excavation in Scotland 1996*, Edinburgh: Council for Scottish Archaeology, 113-14.

Nicolaisen, W F H 1979-80, 'Early Scandinavian Naming in the Western and Northern Isles', *Northern Scotland* 3:2, 105-22.

Nicolaisen, W F H 2001, *Scottish Place-Names: Their Study and Significance*, Edinburgh: John Donald.

Nunn, P 2009, 'Geographical Influences on Settlement-Location Choices by Initial Colonizers: A Case Study of the Fiji Islands', *Geographical Research* 47:3, 306-19.

Odlin, T 1989, *Language Transfer: Cross-Linguistic Influence in Language Learning*. Cambridge: Cambridge University Press.

Oftadal, M 2009, *The Village Names of Lewis*, Laxay: Islands Book Trust.

Olson, D 1983, 'Norse Settlement in the Hebrides: An Interdisciplinary Study', unpublished Cand.Philol. thesis, University of Oslo.

Oram, R D 2000, *The Lordship of Galloway*, Edinburgh: John Donald.

Owen, N, M Kent, and P Dale 1996, 'The Machair Vegetation of the Outer Hebrides: A Review', in D Gilbertson, M Kent, and J Grattan (eds), *The Outer Hebrides: The Last 14,000 Years*, Sheffield: Sheffield Academic Press, 123-31.

Pankhurst, R J and J M Mullin (eds) 1991, *The Flora of the Outer Hebrides*, London: Natural History Museum.

Parker Pearson, M 2012, 'The Machair Survey', in M Parker Pearson (ed), *From Machair to Mountains: Archaeological Survey and Excavation in South Uist*, Oxford: Oxbow, 12-73.

Parker Pearson, M and H Smith 2012, 'Introduction', in M Parker Pearson (ed), *From Machair to Mountains: Archaeological Survey and Excavation in South Uist*, Oxford: Oxbow, 1-11.

Parker Pearson, M, H Smith, J Mulville, and M Brennand 2004, 'Cille Pheadair: The Life and Times of a Norse-Period Farmstead c. 1000-1300', in J Hines, A Lane, and M Redknap (eds), *Land, Sea and Home*, Leeds: Society for Medieval Archaeology, 235-54.

Peacock, J D 1984, *Quaternary Geology of the Outer Hebrides*. Norwich: HMSO.

Pearsall, W H 1961, 'Place-names as Clues to the Pursuit of Ecological History', *Namn och Bygd* 49, 72-89.

Pedersen, E A 1999, 'Transformations to Sedentary Farming in Eastern Norway: AD 100 or 1000 BC?', in C Fabech and J Ringtved (eds), *Settlement and Landscape: Proceedings of a conference in Århus, Denmark, May 4-7 1998*, Aarhus: Aarhus University Press, 45-52.

Plymale, A X, R E J Boemer, and T J Logan 1987, 'Relative Nitrogen Mineralization and Rimcation in Soils of Two Contrasting Hardwood Forests: Effects of Site Microclimate and Initial Soil Chemistry', *Forest Ecology and Management* 21, 21-36.

Prescott, C 1999, 'Long-Term Patterns of Non-Agrarian Exploitation in Southern Norwegian Highlands', in C Fabech and J Ringtved (eds), *Settlement and Landscape: Proceedings of a conference in Århus, Denmark, May 4-7 1998*, Aarhus: Aarhus University Press, 213-23.

Reinton, L 1969, *Til Seters: Norsk Seterbruk og Seterstell*, Oslo: Samlaget.

Roberts, B K 1982, *Rural Settlement: An Historical Perspective*, Norwich: Geo Books.

Sandnes, B 2006, 'Toponyms as Settlement Names-Of No Relevance in Settlement History?', in P Gammeltoft and B Jørgensen (eds), *Names through the Looking-Glass: Festschrift in Honour of Gillian Fellows-Jensen, July 5th 2006*. Copenhagen: Reitzel, 230-53.

Schulte-Thulin, B 1992, 'Notes on the Old and Middle Irish Loanwords in Old Norse', *NOWELE* 39, 53-84.

Schulte-Thulin, B 1996, 'Old Norse in lreland', in P Sture Ureland and I Clarkson (eds), *Language Contact across the North Atlantic*, Tübingen: Niemeyer Verlag, 83-113.

Scotland's Soils 2016, www.soils-scotland.gov.uk/data/scanned-soil-maps, accessed 20 January 2016.

Segertröm, U and M Emanuelsson 2002, 'Extensive Forest Grazing and Hay-Making on Mires: Vegetation Changes in South-Central Sweden Due to Land Use since Medieval Times', *Vegetation History and Archaeobotany* 11:3, 181-90.

Sharples, N 2005, *A Norse Farmstead in the Outer Hebrides: Excavations at Mound 3, Bornais, South Uist*, Oxford: Oxbow.

Sharples, N and R Smith 2009, 'Norse Settlement in the Western Isles', in A Woolf (ed), *Scandinavian Scotland: Twenty Years After*, St Andrews: The Committee for Dark Age Studies, 103-30.

Sigua, G C, S W Coleman, J Albano, and M Williams 2011, 'Spatial Distribution of Soil Phosphorus and Herbage Mass in Beef Cattle Pastures: Effects of Slope Aspect and Slope Position', *Nutrient Cycling in Agroecosystems* 89, 59-70.

Small, A 1968, 'The Historical Geography of the Norse Viking Colonization of the Scottish Highlands', *Norwegian Journal of Geography* 22:1, 1-16.

Stahl, A-B 1999, 'Place-Names of Barra in the Outer Hebrides', unpublished PhD thesis, University of Edinburgh.

Stahl, A-B 2000, *Norse in the Place-Names of Barra, Northern Studies* 35, 95-112.

Stewart, J 1987, *Shetland Place-Names*, Lerwick: Shetland Library and Museum.

Sveinbjarnadóttir, G 1991, 'Shielings in Iceland: An Archaeological and Historical Survey', *Acta Archaeologica* 61, 73-96.

Sæther, N H, K Bøe, and O Vangen 2006, 'Differences in Grazing Behaviour Between a High and a Moderate Yielding Norwegian Dairy Cattle Breed Grazing Semi-Natural Mountain Grasslands', *Acta Agriculturae Scandinavica, Section A - Animal Scienc*es 56, 91-98.

Thomason, S G 2001, *Language Contact: An Introduction*. Edinburgh: Edinburgh University Press.

Thomason, S G and T Kaufman 1991, *Language Contact, Creolization, and Genetic Linguistics*, Berkeley: University of California Press.

Thoms, J E 2003, 'Aspects of Economy and Environment of North-West Lewis in the First Millennium AD: The Non-Marine Faunal Evidence from Bostadh and Beirgh Considered within the Framework of North Atlantic Scotland', unpublished PhD thesis, University of Edinburgh.

Thorsteinsson, A 2008, 'Land Division, Land Rights, and Land Ownership in the Faroe Islands', in M Jones and K R Olwig (eds), *Nordic Landscapes: Region and Belonging on the Northern Edge of Europe*, Minneapolis: University of Minnesota Press, 77-105.

Watson, W J 1926, *The History of the Celtic Place-Names of Scotland*. Edinburgh: Blackwood.

Weaver, R, M Kent, D Gilbertson, P Wathem, and B Brayshay 1996, 'The Acidic and Upland Vegetation of the Southern Outer Hebrides', in D Gilbertson, M Kent, and J Grattan (eds), *The Outer Hebrides: The Last 14,000 Years*, Sheffield: Sheffield Academic Press, 147-62.

Weinreich, U 1968, *Languages in Contact: Findings and Problems*, Berlin: de Gruyter.

Whyte, I D 1985, 'Shielings and the Upland Pastoral Economy of the Lake District in Medieval and Early Modern Times', in J R Baldwin and I D Whyte (eds), *The Scandinavians in Cumbria*, Edinburgh: Scottish Society for Northern Studies, 103-18.

Wood, J J 1978, 'Optimal Location in Settlement Space: A Model for Describing Location Strategies', *American Antiquity* 43:2, 258-70.

Woolf, A 2007, *From Pictland to Alba, 789-1070*, Edinburgh: Edinburgh University Press.

Zimmermann, W H 1999, 'Why Was Cattle-Stalling Introduced in Prehistory? The Significance of Byre and Stable and of Outwintering', in C Fabech and J Ringtved (eds), *Settlement and Landscape: Proceedings of a conference in Århus, Denmark, May 4-7 1998*, Aarhus: Aarhus University Press, 301-18.

Øye, I 2003, 'Introduction', in I Holm, S Innselset and I Øye (eds), *'Utmark': The Outfield as Industry and Ideology in the Iron Age and the Middle Ages*. Bergen: University of Bergen, 9-20.

Øye, I 2004, 'Agricultural Conditions and Rural Societies c. 800-1350', in R Almås (ed), *Norwegian Agricultural History*, Trondheim: Tapir Academic Press, 79-140.

Øye, I 2005, 'Farming and Farming Systems in Norse societies of the North Atlantic', in A Mortensen and S V Arge (eds), *Viking and Norse in the North Atlantic: Selected Papers from the Proceedings of the Fourteenth Viking Congress, Tórshavn, 19-30 July 2001*. Tórshavn: Føroya Fróðskaparfelag, 359-70.

Øye, I 2009, 'Settlement Patterns and Field Systems in Medieval Norway', *Landscape History* 30:2, 37-54.

News Recording and Cultural Connections between Early Medieval Ireland and Northern Britain

Nicholas Evans

The Irish chronicles, surviving in Irish manuscripts from the late-eleventh to seventeenth centuries, are critical sources for understanding the early medieval history of Ireland and northern Britain. Often relating over ten events per year and involving hundreds of named people per century, they constitute a crucial resource for this period, unparalleled elsewhere in Western Europe. Apart from the *Iona Chronicle* source for the period from the late sixth century to AD 740, these texts were largely written in Ireland, but they also constitute our main evidence for Scottish events for the whole period up to 1100.[1] Since annalistic chronicles were the result of news travelling from the location of an event to chroniclers, they reflect, to some extent, existing networks of communications and social connections by which people travelled, bringing information with them.

Communications networks have been regarded as important, not just for cultural and social connections, but also as economic evidence, as goods travelled with people (an aspect studied on a wider European basis by Michael McCormick).[2] The archaeological evidence for Ireland and Britain has been studied, as have textual references, but the potential to utilise the patterns of recording in the Irish chronicles for determining interconnections has not been fully considered.[3] For the Irish chroniclers of the tenth and eleventh centuries (and potentially earlier), it is likely that the collection of news was not a matter of chance encounters with travellers, but a more organised affair, since there is evidence that chroniclers exchanged written notices of events.[4] Each chronicle, therefore, was not only a reflection of the principally

---

1   Bannerman 1974 [1968], 9-26; Evans 2010, esp. 112-13, 171-73, 208-13.
     Presumably, a copy of the *Iona Chronicle* ending in 740 was incorporated into the Irish chronicles, with later events dealing with Iona recorded as a result of subsequent connections, perhaps with chroniclers based on the island. Therefore, there is no reason to connect this development with any particular secular or ecclesiastical event.
2   McCormick 2001.
3   Bowen 1969; Wooding 1996; Campbell 2007; Edmonds 2009.
4   Evans, 2010, 231-33.

ecclesiastical authors' interests, but also of the nature of the webs of contacts through which they obtained their material. We can assume that there was a mutually reinforcing relationship between the connections which chroniclers maintained and what they decided to include, since the latter was itself determined partly by social relationships.

However, there is still the question of whether the record we have accurately reflects the contacts which existed, or primarily the degree of interest shown by chroniclers; were they including all or most of the news they were receiving, or were they more selective? In addition, how did chroniclers decide what to include? The record for northern Britain can be used as an effective case study for this inquiry, as well as for the wider issue of cultural connections between Britain and Ireland, as it constitutes a varied but manageable corpus of material. Although the low number of events involved does preclude the reconstruction of news networks, plausible explanations for the inclusion of particular events in the record may be proposed, and broader patterns in the evidence discerned.

In this study, northern Britain, roughly identified as the territory north of the River Humber in the Kingdom of Northumbria, will be the main focus, since Scotland – as we know it – did not exist as a unit in this period. In this region, close contacts with Ireland in the period up to 740 are readily apparent, since the *Iona Chronicle* includes many Irish events, as well as those concerning Dál Riata, the Picts, the northern Britons, and Anglo-Saxons – mainly of Northumbria and Mercia.[5] This is explained by the association of monasteries in both Britain and Ireland, headed by Iona.[6] However, after 740, the recording of events in Britain occurs at a much lower frequency.[7] This reduction makes it more

---

5   Bannerman 1974 [1968], 9-26.
6   Ibid., 9-10, 13-14, 19-25. For discussion of the terminology relating to Iona and associated establishments, such as *familia*, see Etchingham 1999, 90-93, 126-30, 172-77, 223-38. Apart from Lindisfarne in Northumbria (from 635 to 664) and mainly unidentified sites in northern Britain (like the subordinate monasteries at Mag Luinge on Tiree and on the unlocated island of Hinba), the continued significance of Iona for the Church in northern Britain after Columba's life is noted by Adomnán in his *Life of St Columba*, written c. 697 (see *Life of St Columba* for text and context), and by Bede in his *Ecclesiastical History of the English People*, completed in 731 (see Herbert 1988, 9-62, especially 33-34, 36; Fraser 2009, 237, 241, and for suggestions about Iona's role in Pictland, 256-62, 269-82). Iona's importance is also indicated by the reference to the expulsion of the *familia* of Iona by the king of the Picts in *AU* 717.4 (also *AT* 717.3, *CS* 717.2).
7   Bannerman 1974, 11, 25.

difficult to understand the nature of the connections between Ireland and northern Britain. However, when the corpus of chronicle material relating to northern Britain from 700 to 1100 is considered as a whole, it is possible to draw some conclusions. This was a period of significant change in both Ireland and Scotland, encompassing the impact of the Vikings, Scandinavian settlement and rule in the north and west, the end of the Pictish kingdom and language, the disappearance of Gaelic Dál Riata, and the emergence of the Gaelic Kingdom of Alba.[8] The Irish chronicle record could reflect these changes, or other developments of this era.

The Irish chronicles survive in manuscripts from the late-eleventh century onwards, the earliest being the *Annals of Inisfallen* (*AI*). However, the mid-fourteenth-century copy of the *Annals of Tigernach* (*AT*), the late-fifteenth-century 'H'-copy of the *Annals of Ulster* (*AU*), and the seventeenth-century *Chronicum Scotorum* (*CS*) preserve more events for northern Britain. As these texts have also been studied more comprehensively, they will be focused on in this study.[9] They are all interrelated, sharing a common ancestor for the early medieval Irish annals, which can be called the *Chronicle of Ireland*.[10] This chronicle itself was based on earlier texts. Up to c. 740, the *Iona Chronicle* represented one such source, although not necessarily the only one. Afterwards, the chronicle was maintained in Ireland, probably in Brega, the area to the north and west of Dublin.[11] Events from northern Britain were still reaching these Irish chroniclers, but the lines of transmission have only been tentatively discerned. For the decades of the eighth century after 740, it is likely that a chronicle from Iona and Pictish sources were utilised by annalists in Ireland, and Dauvit Broun has suggested that, in the late-ninth century, news about Pictland and Alba came from Dunkeld.[12]

---

8   For surveys, see Woolf 2007 and Fraser 2009 for Scotland, Ó Corráin 1972 and Charles-Edwards 2000 for Ireland, Downham 2007 for the Insular Vikings, Herbert 1988 and *Life of St Columba* for the Columban context, and Etchingham 1999 for the Church in Ireland.

9   Grabowski and Dumville 1984; Evans 2010. See also Mc Carthy 2008.

10 Hughes 1972, 101.

11 *The Chronicle of Ireland* 2006, 9-24; Hughes 1972, 133-35, for the view that the chronicle was kept in Armagh, but with Louth and Brega news derived from stewards of St. Patrick.

12 Broun 1997.

As the *Chronicle of Ireland* ended in 911, the subsequent section of *AU* is independent of the source underlying *AT* and *CS*. There is, however, solid evidence for the exchange of written notices of some events between chroniclers in Irish centres as late as 1060, and probably occasionally after that, which can account for a minority of the later record with common phraseology in different chronicles.[13] For their sections before 912, each chronicle contains a selection of items from the *Chronicle of Ireland*, the most comprehensive being *AU*, although the addition of extra material from other sources is also possible, especially in the case of *AT* and *CS*.[14] However, items from the common source can be identified when found in identical wording in *AU* and either *AT* or *CS*, or when an individual chronicle contains a unique item reflecting the phraseology, vocabulary, and subject matter focused on by the *Chronicle of Ireland*. It is therefore useful to consider all three texts individually and comparatively.

The first chronicle to be considered, *AU*, was, after the *Chronicle of Ireland,* kept in Brega or Conaille up to c. 938 by stewards of St Patrick, who were involved in the administration of the ecclesiastical centre of Armagh.[15] After this time, the evidence is less clear for some decades; it was probably kept somewhere in the Irish east midlands or in Ulster. By the last decade of the tenth century, it was clearly an Armagh source, and remained so until the mid-to-late-twelfth century, when it became a chronicle maintained by the clerics of Derry.[16] *AU* contains the most events relating to northern Britain, and has no lacunae which obscure trends over time; as such, I will mainly focus on this chronicle, using *AT* and *CS* as comparanda.

The corpus under consideration (see appendix) has been created on the basis of the following criteria:

1. The event took place in northern Britain.
2. If the location of an event is uncertain, an item is included if it involved people from or rulers of part of northern Britain.

---

13   Evans 2010, 67-72, 91-114. For an alternative view, see Mc Carthy 2008.
14   Evans 2010, 60-62, 189-224.
15   Hughes 1972, 133-34; Evans 2010, 21-24, 43-44.
16   Bannerman 1993, 36-42; Evans 2010, 44.

For the sake of analysis, this material has been divided into the following categories (see also Figure 1):

- Events taking place in northern Britain (labelled 'Northern Britain').
- Events possibly occurring in or involving people active in northern Britain ('Uncertain N. Britain').
- Events only involving Northumbrians ('Northumbrian only').
- Events definitely involving Scandinavians in northern Britain ('Scandinavians in N. Britain'), or without certainty ('Scandinavians Uncertain N. Britain').
- Events involving people travelling between Ireland and northern Britain ('Travel to/from N. Britain').
- Events concerning members of the Columban community who are not specifically linked to Iona, northern Britain, or Ireland (for instance, references to 'heirs of Columba' or the *familia* of Columba), for which the location of the event is not clear, and therefore could have taken place in either Ireland or Britain ('Columban Community').[17]
- Events concerning people with roles straddling the North Channel ('N.Britain & Ireland'), chiefly items relating to the people or kings of Dál Riata, which included the northern part of County Antrim.

In terms of interpretation, the transfer of the chronicle from Iona to Ireland (c. 740) means that there is no comparable evidence on

---

17 While it is likely that abbots of Iona remained the heirs (Latin *heres*, Gaelic *comarbaí*) of Columba - and therefore leaders of the wider Columban *familia* - beyond the ninth century, heirs of Patrick based in Armagh did also twice become heirs of Columba in the late ninth and tenth century (see 'Columba Community' items at *AU* 927.1, *CS* 927.1; *AU* 989.7; *AU* 998.2, *CS* 998.2). In the eleventh century, possibly in 1007, Kells in County Meath gained the coarbship from Iona (Clancy 2011), although links with Britain continued, as indicated by the drowning of Maicnia Ua hUchtáin, *fer léiginn* ('lector') of Kells, while bringing relics of Columba and Patrick from Alba (*AU* 1034.9). I have included eleventh-century items for heirs of Columba for Ferdomnach (*AU* 1008.1, *CS* 1008.1), Muiredach mac Críchán (*AU* 1011.1, also *fer léiginn* of Armagh), Máel Muire Ua hUchtáin (*AU* 1040.2, *CS* 1040.2), Robartach mac Ferdomnaig (*AU* 1057.8), Gilla Críst ua Maíl Doraid (*AU* 1062.2, *AT* 1062.3), and Domnall mac Robartaig (*AU* 1099.6), because they could have died in northern Britain – although an Irish location is more likely (see Herbert 1988, 88-97).

either side of that date, as the geographical focus of the chronicle alters so dramatically. While 701-740 has been included for the sake of comprehensiveness, we are not comparing like with like, so little value may be obtained from a quantitative analysis comparing, for instance, 701-720 and 781-800. However, in the period during which the chronicle was maintained and updated in Ireland (after 740), the results are potentially more significant, even if the annalists were writing in different centres there. If a new source became available to the chroniclers, this in itself would indicate contacts between Ireland and northern Britain. Although the number of events recorded in northern Britain after 740 is low – about one event per two years in *AU* – this still constitutes a substantial record, and with figures ranging from zero to nine per decade, there is scope for identifying significant patterns.

Nevertheless, as Colmán Etchingham and Roy Flechner have stressed, we have to be careful when using the chronicles as evidence for changes in the real world, because they could reflect the interests of the chroniclers rather than societal trends.[18] The original record would have undoubtedly been selective rather than comprehensive, and alterations may have been performed during the later history of the texts. In addition, Flechner has also suggested two further problems: that the chronicles, which predominantly focus on the deaths of people, are primarily records of absence rather than presence, and that the analysis of the annals in groups of years is arbitrary, producing false and varying results, depending on how the texts are divided.[19] Nevertheless, it should be stressed that the annals are neither records of absence or presence, but primarily records of events, with deaths presumably regarded as an important occurrence, marking a transition from this world to the next. It should be recognised that arbitrary groupings of annals can produce misleading results, although scholars like Etchingham have shown that their effective utilisation produces patterns not discernible by looking at the evidence year-by-year.[20] This is especially true if attention is paid to the finer detail and nature of the evidence. In addition, the representativeness of the record becomes less of a problem if the analysis is primarily focused on how reality was represented in the chronicle, as is the case here. However, the issue

---

18   Etchingham 1996; Flechner 2013, 429-32.
19   Flechner 2013, 429-32.
20   Etchingham 1996; Etchingham 2002.

of how to explain the patterns discerned in the text remains. In sum, we can fruitfully analyse the section from 741 onwards as evidence for the world-view of Irish chroniclers, as well as the degree and nature of contacts, even if we recognise that their works represent restricted and sometimes partisan reflections of society.

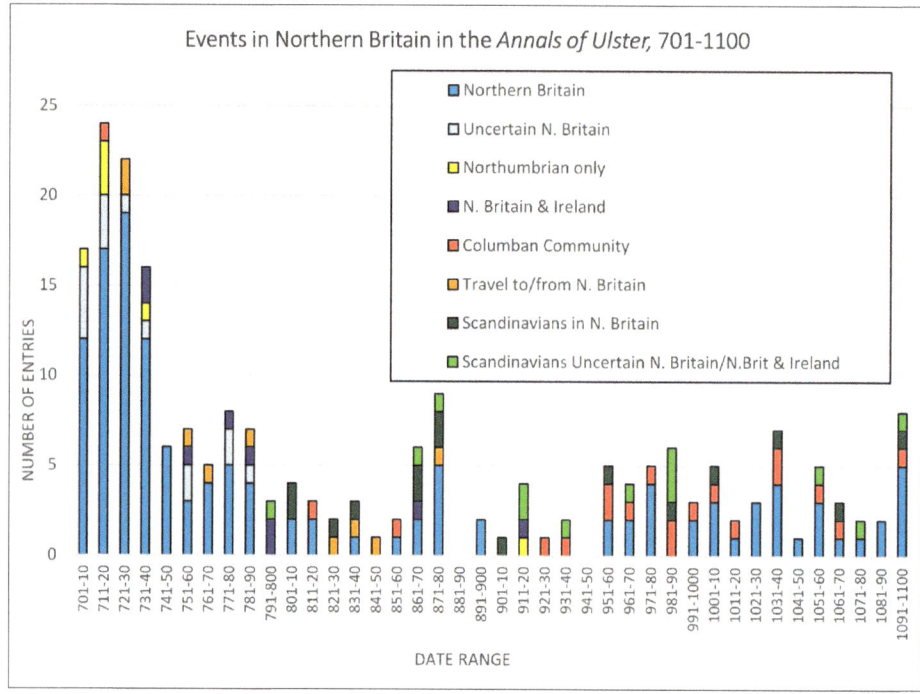

Figure 1: Events in northern Britain in the Annals of Ulster, 701-1100.

When the events for northern Britain in *AU* are analysed, changes over time can be discerned. The highest number of recorded events in northern Britain pertains, as expected, to the era of the *Iona Chronicle*, before 741, including many events not just in Gaelic Dál Riata, but also in Pictish, British, and Anglo-Saxon areas. After 740, when the text was composed in Ireland, there is a substantial fall in the record for northern Britain, although the overall number is generally still higher before 791 than in the following period before the mid-tenth century. After 790, the number is generally low, often fewer than three events per decade, with 861 to 880 representing a notable exception. We need to be careful not to place too much significance on individual figures, which can be affected not only by loss or addition during transmission, but also by the fact that the deaths of important people sometimes cluster or are lacking in particular periods. However, even when taking this into account, there does seem to be an overall pattern in *AU* of a reduction followed by an increase from the mid-tenth century onwards, which is long-term and as such less likely to be affected by such short-term factors.

The pattern in *AU* is, to some extent, also found in *AT* and *CS* (see Figure 2). Like *AU*, these had the *Chronicle of Ireland* as a major source before 912, but they also contain other material, mainly derived from Clonmacnoise (on the River Shannon) and Clonard (by the River Boyne in the midlands), places where their common source was situated.[21] As both *AT* and *CS* have large sections missing – 767-973 and 1003-17 from *AT* due to lost pages, and 723-803 from *CS* – both texts are only available for the years 701-722, 974-1003, and 1018 onwards. As a result, neither chronicle covers the period from part of 766 to part of 804. When both texts are available, it is likely that we have most of their common source, whilst only a partial picture is available outside this overlap. In general, the overall pattern in *CS* and *AT* is similar to *AU*: a high number up to 740, and a reduction after that. However, it is still higher during the immediate period after 740 than for 801-950, as is indicated by the high 751-60 figure when *AT* is available. This indicates that, if *AT* and *CS* had been available from 767 to 803, we would likely have seen the same general pattern as *AU* for those years. When *CS* becomes available again in 804, we find that it, like *AU*, contains very few events about northern Britain for the ninth and first half of the tenth century, apart from 861-880. Similarly, there is a greater degree of recording after the mid-tenth century, although the number fluctuates, particularly during the eleventh century.

For the period up to 911, the overall similarity to *AU* can be explained by a shared derivation from the *Chronicle of Ireland*, but *AU* and the common source for *AT* and *CS* were independent chronicles after this time. As such, they represent two texts displaying broadly the same pattern of interest. These commonalities are reflected in the relatively high proportion of events shared throughout the whole period, not just in the section covered by the *Chronicle of Ireland*, but also those found

---

21   Evans 2010, 67-90.

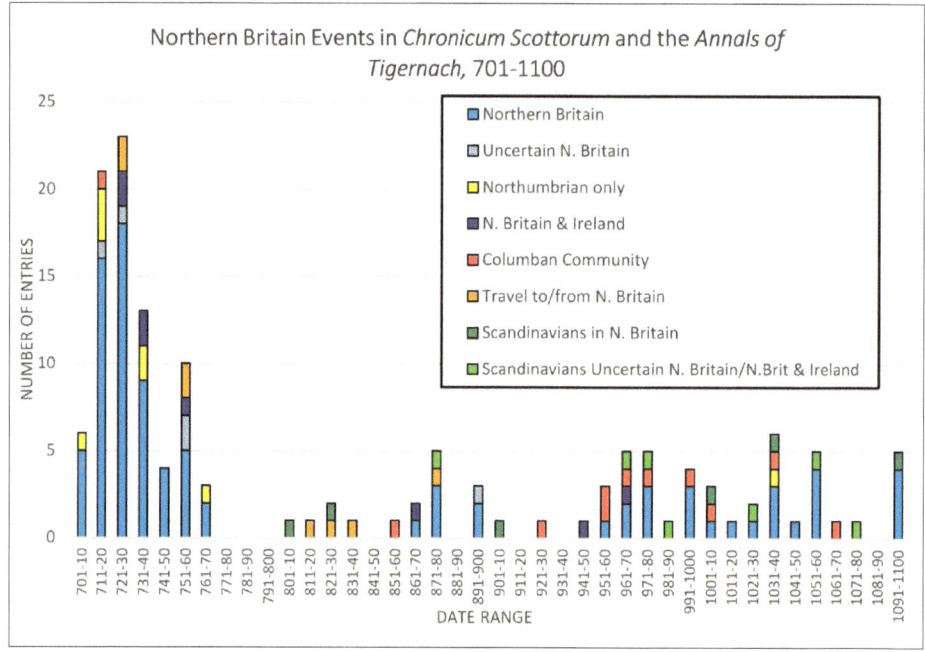

Figure 2: Events in northern Britain in *Chronicum Scottorum* and the *Annals of Tigernach*, 701-1100.

only in particular texts. Both *CS* and *AT* are the result of substantial later alterations. To simplify, *CS* retains ecclesiastical events but often omits secular ones (except for major kingdoms).[22] *AT,* on the other hand, is pretty comprehensive up to 766, but adds extra text from other sources, and from the tenth century tends to have a secular focus, omitting Church matters.[23] Each chronicle contains additions, although these are largely focused on the record for Ireland, rather than northern Britain, apart from perhaps a few items on Dál Riata and the Picts, derived from king-lists.[24] At least for the period before 800, most of the unique items concerning northern Britain in *AT* are likely to have been part of the *Chronicle of Ireland*. Similarly, while *AU* has many unique items for northern Britain before 912, it is likely that these have been lost during the transmission of *AT* and *CS*.[25]

---

22   Evans 2010, 65-66.
23   Ibid.
24   Ibid., 208-13.
25   Ibid., 201-4, 208.

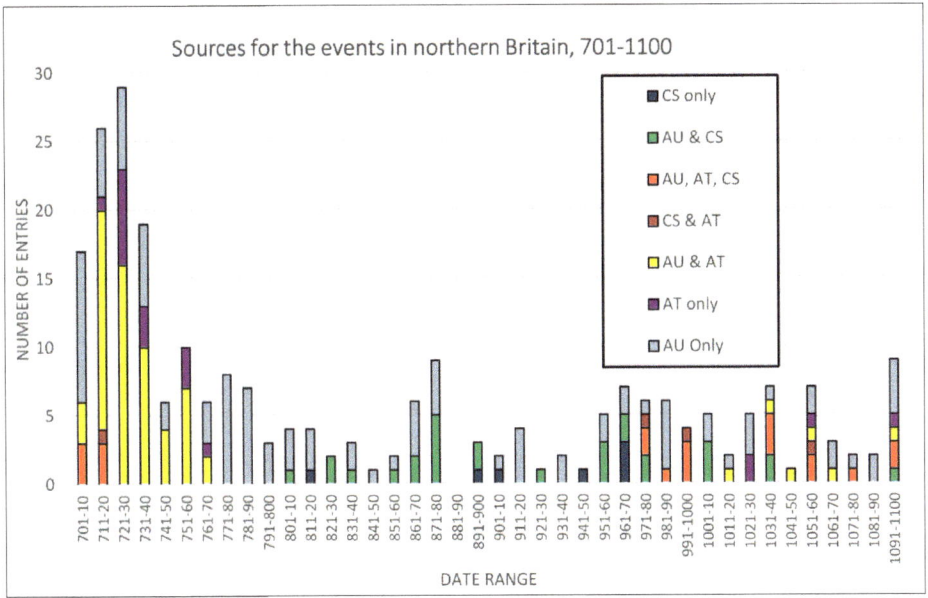

Figure 3: Sources for the events in northern Britain, 701-1100.

One issue is understanding the degree of omission in *CS* during the period from 804 to 973, for which *AT* is lacunose. Some idea of this can be gained by analysing which chronicles contain events in northern Britain (see Figure 3). From 701 to 722, *CS* lacks most of *AT*'s items for this region, only containing five items about Iona, and two conflicts relating to Dál Riata (one against the northern Britons). However, in the section from 974 to 1003, *CS* actually has more Scottish events than *AT*, including items unique to it, before again having fewer events during the eleventh century. From the high number of items unique to *AU* in 804-911, we might reasonably assume that many items had been omitted from *CS* in that section. However, it is unclear at which point between 912 and 974 *CS* increased its coverage of events in northern Britain, since *AT* cannot be used for comparison. Although this uncertainty, as well as the low overall number of events about northern Britain in these texts, should make us cautious, it would seem too much of a coincidence that *AU* and the combined *AT* and *CS* both exhibit an increase in the recording of affairs in northern Britain during the second half of the tenth century. The more frequent recording, reflected in eighteen events for northern Britain in *CS* from 951 to

1000 compared to three events in the previous fifty years, is significant, especially when we recognise that there is only a very slight increase in the overall number of events recorded in that source in the same period.[26] In sum, *AT* and *CS* confirm the overall trends found in *AU*, indicating that they are not the result of later changes.

An important further issue needs to be addressed before the significance of the discerned pattern may be argued. Colmán Etchingham, in his research on Viking activity in Ireland in the Irish chronicles, has stressed the importance of considering changing geographical and subject foci in the texts' contents before drawing conclusions.[27] Changes in chronicle interests and variations in the number of events recorded can affect the results of any quantitative analysis, so discerned patterns might not reflect actual changes, but simply altered chronicle practice. Considering first the overall number of chronicle items found in the text, the totals in *AU* for different periods can be seen in Figure 4. An item consists of one or more events verbally linked in the text by causation or a strong temporal or subject connection (so events merely connected by 'and' or 'then' are separately counted).

There are some similarities to the totals for northern Britain; after 740, the highest frequency is found in the late-eighth century, and there is a correspondingly greater number during the eleventh century compared to the tenth. In addition, a similarly low number is found during the period from 891 to 910 (54 for 891-900, and 44 for 901-910), with an average of only 4.9 items per annum. This may explain the appearance in *AU* of only four possible or certain events concerning northern Britain for that period. There are more substantial differences, however; the period with most items in *AU*, in which ten or more items are found per annum, spans from 731 to 840, although this includes a period in the early-ninth century during which the record for northern Britain is in significant decline. Moreover, the spike in items concerning northern Britain for 861-880 is not replicated in a high number of items in *AU* for the same period. Most significantly, there is a low number of items overall in *AU* from 961 to 1000, a time when there is a noticeable increase in the recording of events in northern Britain. Therefore, the overall number of items found in *AU* does not account for the changes

26   Totals of items are provided by Evans 2010, 70: AD 804-850, 219 items; 851-911, 267 items; 912-960, 220 items; 961-1010, 235 items.
27   Etchingham 1996; 2002. See also Flechner 2013.

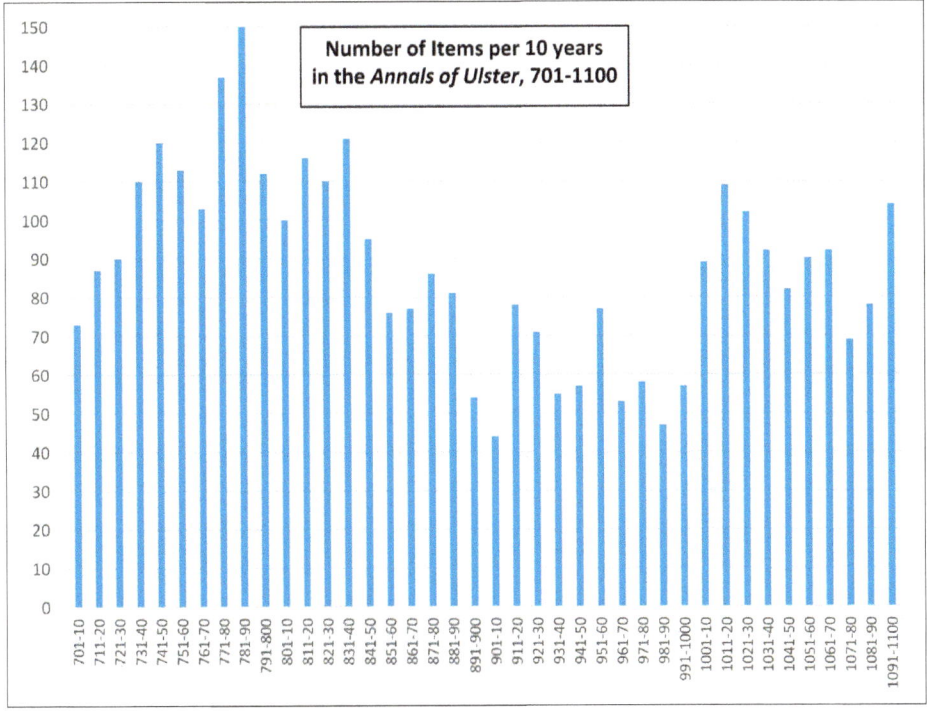

Figure 4: The number of items per 10 years in the *Annals of Ulster* (701-1100).

in the recording of events in northern Britain, except perhaps in the evidence for 891-910 and the eleventh century. What this comparison does in particular indicate is how anomalous the higher totals for northern Britain from 861-880 and 961-1000 are, and that the decline and subsequent increase in the record for the region does not closely correspond to the overall number of events recorded.

This fluctuation might, however, correspond with changes in the intensity of Viking activity. When the record for northern Britain is broken down into particular categories, it is noticeable that the period of sparse recording roughly corresponds to a period of significant Scandinavian activity in Ireland and northern Britain. According to Etchingham's analysis, the number of raids on ecclesiastical settlements and Scandinavian campaigns against or alongside Irish dynasts varied considerably, partly reflecting contrasting phases of Viking interaction with Irish polities and ecclesiastical establishments, as well as changing interests and regional foci of the Irish chroniclers.[28] Whilst Viking raids started in the 790s, the most intense period of Scandinavian activity in Ireland recorded in the Irish annals was from the 820s to the first half of the tenth century. They continued to be active, albeit to a lesser degree, until the end of his study period in 1015.[29] This corresponds broadly with the period when the recording of events in northern Britain is low, although the reduction for northern Britain starts during the period 790-820, when the Viking impact was not as extensive as later on.

This development might be explained by looking at Viking activity in Britain. When events involving Scandinavians in northern Britain are considered, these are initially recorded in the last decade of the eighth century, continuing right up to 1100 (see Figures 1 and 2). The record is sporadic, with two peaks in 861-880 and 981-1000, which do not correspond to high points of recorded Viking activity in Ireland, apart from 861-70.[30] Indeed, the *Chronicle of the Kings of Alba* contains a number of conflicts in northern Britain involving Scandinavians that are not found in the Irish chronicles, for instance, two or three events in the reign of Domnall, son of Constantine, King of Alba (889-900).[31] In the Irish chronicles, only four raids on churches are recorded – all targeting Iona – three of which occurred in the early ninth century (802, 806, and 825). It is highly unlikely that these constitute a representative sample, but they may indicate that Viking raids were more significant in western Scotland than in Ireland in the first decades of the ninth century.[32]

This Viking activity occurred before the great increase in activity in Ireland during the 820s. After 790, Scandinavians took over much of northern Scotland and the Hebrides, in what later became the Earldom of the Orkneys and Kingdom of the Isles. Meanwhile, in the south-west, a people called *Gallgoídil*, 'Foreigner-Gaels', settled. The exact dates of these conquests and settlements are uncertain.[33] Alex Woolf has stressed that Viking attacks were already substantial in the 790s, as is indicated by *AU* 794.7: 'The wasting of all the islands of Britain by the heathens'.[34] He has also suggested that Scandinavians may have controlled Dál

---

28 Etchingham 1996, 7-34, 55-57.
29 Ibid., 1996, 7-16; Etchingham 2002, 53-54, 56.
30 See Etchingham 1996, 51-53, 55; 2002, 55-56.
31 Anderson 1980, 251; Woolf 2007, 122-25.
32 Woolf 2007, 56.
33 Ibid., esp. 41-67, 275-311; Clancy 2008; Downham 2015.
34 Woolf 2007, 43-47.

Riata from 793 to 806, before, in the late 840s, conquering the southern Hebrides. This is based on a reference from the *Annals of St Bertin*, in which the Northmen take control of all the islands around Ireland in 847.[35] Although the view that the Scandinavians ruled Dál Riata from 793 to 806 is highly speculative, a scenario in which Vikings attacked the Hebrides and Argyll, whilst establishing bases there to raid elsewhere, is very plausible, especially since, as Woolf points out, the chroniclers at this point tended to focus on attacks on ecclesiastical foundations.[36] If not for major battles or attacks on clerical sites like Iona – which were more likely to be recorded – we probably would have no evidence for a Scandinavian presence in Dál Riata. It is possible, therefore, that Scandinavian activities were a major cause for the decline in the record for northern Britain during the late-eighth and early-ninth century, with attacks and settlement, particularly on the Hebrides and west coast of Scotland, reducing connections between Ireland and Scotland.

However, we should further investigate the evidence before coming to such a conclusion, since it could be argued that other factors might also contribute to this pattern. One obvious alternative is that the change is connected to the end of the kingdom of Dál Riata in Argyll, which was probably controlled by the Picts by 800. Indeed, the share in Britain of the kingship of Dál Riata ceases to be mentioned after 792, and, along with Argyll and the Hebrides (apart from Iona), the name is absent from the record until the later tenth century (see Figure 5).[37] The Irish share of the kingdom (in Antrim) is, however, occasionally mentioned during the following centuries.[38] The conquest of Dál Riata in Britain could have reduced the number of events of interest to the chroniclers, although Gaelic culture certainly survived Pictish rule; it even spread further into eastern Scotland in this period as part of the process through which Pictland became Gaelic Alba. Given the lack of comparative evidence for events in these regions, it is difficult to judge how many significant events took place in northern Britain in this period. Nevertheless, it would be expected that the settlement and conquest of much of Dál Riata – first by the Picts and subsequently by

---

35   Ibid., 55-64, 99-100.
36   Ibid., 57-58.
37   *AU* 792.4, 986.2, 989.4 (*CS* 989.2, *AT* 989.3).
38   The Irish Dál Riata continued to be mentioned, for instance in *CS* 914.3, *AU* 1013.10.

the Scandinavians – would have been considered newsworthy. For the Picts, a considerable record exists regarding their earlier conquest of Dál Riata in the 730s, which may have made the re-establishment of Pictish authority later on less dramatic as a result. A battle recorded in *AU* 789.11 (duplicated in 790.7) between Constantín, son of Uurguist, and Conall, son of Tadg, may have been related to this process; the latter is found in some Dál Riata king-lists, but the 789 item from *AU* depicts this as an internal Pictish affair. Similarly, having recorded the 'devastation of all the islands of Britain' in *AU* 794.7, the establishment of Scandinavian control on the western seaboard of Scotland may not have been so noteworthy. Smaller-scale events in northern Britain are not present in the Irish annals from about 740, as the secular record focused on the deaths of kings and a few other events involving them. Therefore, our inability to discern these processes in Dál Riata is not particularly striking.

What is noticeable, however, is that not only the record for Dál Riata declines during the early ninth century, but those for other kingdoms in northern Britain as well. There are two secular events involving northern Britons in 751-800: *AU* 780.1, on the burning of Dumbarton Rock, plus the death of the King of Dumbarton only found in *AT* 752.2 (not included in Figure 5), and one Northumbrian event at *AT* 764.12 about King Æthelwold Moll becoming a cleric. However, no secular events about Northumbrians or northern Britons exist from 801-850, and there are also fewer Pictish events in the same period. The exception for secular items is the 851-900 period, during which there are more frequent references to Britons, Picts, and the northern English. This is, however, primarily concentrated in 861-880, in the context of repeated attacks on these peoples by Scandinavians, so it only qualifies the picture of reduced recording. Corresponding to the general secular pattern is a decline in the recording of ecclesiastical affairs, with a fall in the number of clerical obituary notices, which, as a result, tend to focus on Iona. No longer are occasional references provided to clerics of Dál Riata, such as the abbots of Kingarth on Bute. These reductions in secular and ecclesiastical items do not correspond to any reduced general interest in these same subjects in the Irish chronicles, so they do seem to represent a significant development.[39] As the decline in

---

39   Etchingham 1996, 11-12, 15, 51.

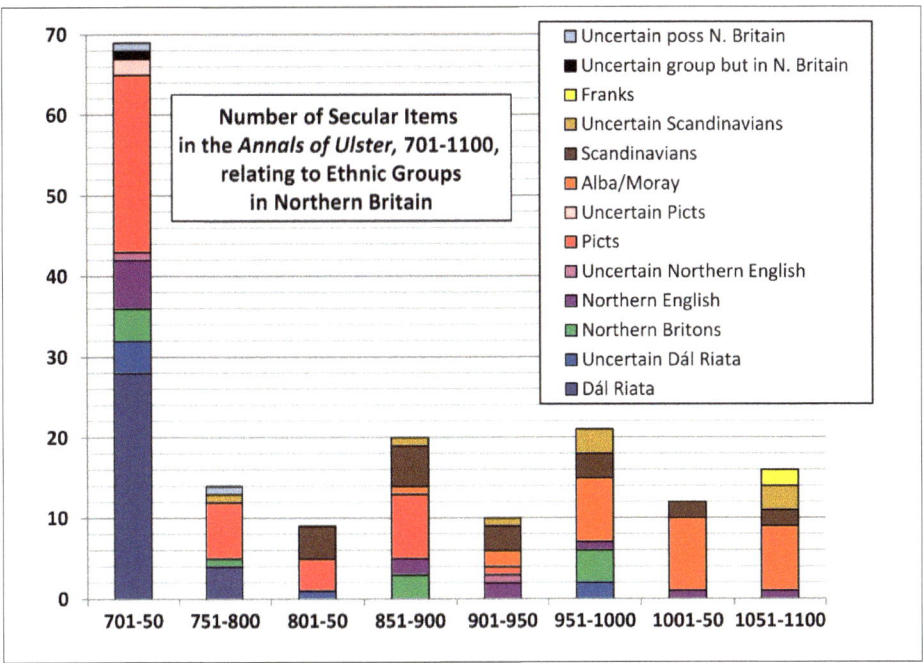

Figure 5: The number of secular items in the *Annals of Ulster* (701-1100) relating to ethnic groups in northern Britain.

recording is quite universal for northern Britain, the end of the kingship of Dál Riata in Britain cannot explain the reduction on its own (unless it also resulted in a decreased interest in northern Britain in general).

However, a lack of contacts cannot completely explain the pattern either, since news continued to reach Ireland from Iona after 800. That monastic centre continued to be the main ecclesiastical subject in northern Britain until 1100, although occasional references to Dunkeld, St Andrews, and bishops of Alba are also made.[40] From the mid-ninth century, the title *comarbae Coluim Chille* ('heir of Columba') often features, reflecting the increased use of saintly titles.[41] This,

---

40   Items are from *AU* unless stated. Iona events (in which the person is linked to Iona or the event took place there): 801.4; 802.9, 806.8 (*CS* 806.3), 815.6, 825.17 (*CS* 825.9), 865.2 (*CS* 865.2), 880.1 (*CS* 880.1), 891.1 (*CS* 891.1), *CS* 966.4, 978.1, *CS* 980.5 ('heir of Columba' in *AU* 980.3), *CS* 980.6 (*AT* 980.6), 986.3, 987.3, 1005.1 (*CS* 1005.1), 1025.1, 1070.6, 1099.6; Dunkeld events: 865.6 (for a cleric also called *prim-epscop*, 'head-bishop', of Fortriu), 873.8, 965.4, 1027.7, 1045.6 (*AT* 1045.10); St. Andrews events: *CS* 965.1; bishops of Alba: *CS* 1033.2, *CS* 1055.3 (*AT* 1055.5), 1093.2.

41   Bannerman 1993, 14-18; Etchingham 1999, 47-103, esp. 91-93, 99-103.

however, makes it difficult to be certain whether the person in question was based in northern Britain or in Ireland. This office holder was probably based at Iona before the end of the tenth century, and often at Kells during the eleventh, but in many instances it is nevertheless difficult to be sure where people associated with this community were situated when they died.[42] This is why such events have been placed in the separate 'Columban Community' category. In general, the events concerning Iona are not accompanied by other news related to western Scotland after 800, even though, presumably, it would have reached that monastery. There is one exception from 986 to 989, when *AU* records a number of events involving Iona, *Danair*, and the king of *Innse Gall* (the Scandinavian Hebrides) in Dál Riata (in this context probably in Britain rather than Ireland):

AU 986.2 Na Danair do thuidecht i n-airer Dail Riatai, .i. teora longa coro riagtha secht fichit diibh & coro renta olchena.

[The Danes arrived on the coast/in the territory of Dal Riata, that is, with three ships, and seven score of them were executed and others sold.]

AU 986.3 Í Coluim Cille do arcain do Danaraibh aidhchi Notlaic coro marbsat in apaidh & .xu. uiros do sruithibh na cille.

[Iona of Colum Cille was plundered by the Danes on Christmas night, and they killed the abbot and fifteen of the elders of the monastery.]

AU 987.3 Ár mor forsna Danaraibh ro oirg I coro marbtha tri .xx. it & tri cét diibh.

[A great slaughter of the Danes who plundered Iona, and three score and three hundred of them were slain.]

AU 989.4 (also **CS 989.2, AT 989.3**) Gofraidh m. Arailt, ri Innsi Gall, do marbad i n-Dal Riatai.

[Gothfrith son of Harald, king of *Innse Gall*, was killed in Dál Riata.]

---

42   Clancy 2011.

AU 989.7 Dub da Leithi, comarba Patraicc, do gabail comurbuis Coluim Cille a comurle fer n-Erenn & Alban.

[Dub dá Leithe, heir of Patrick, took the successorship of Colum Cille through the counsel of the men of Ireland and Alba.][43]

Given that the chronicle may already have been kept at Armagh by this time, it is likely that the close interest in events in and around Iona – concerning Scandinavians and Dál Riata – is connected to Dub dá Leithi's succession to leadership of the Columban confederacy, instigated by individuals in Britain as well as Ireland, and recorded at the end of the sequence in *AU* 989.7. During the abbacy of Mugrón (obit. 980), Iona had close connections with the king of Dublin, Amlaíb Cuarán, who notably went to die on that island after being defeated in 980.[44] It has been plausibly suggested that Amlaíb's strong support for the Columban *familia* led him to found the monasteries of Scrín Coluim Cille (Skreen, Co. Meath) and Sord Coluim Cille (Swords, Co. Dublin) in his Irish lands, and that he controlled at least some of the Hebrides.[45] It is therefore understandable that both Irish chroniclers from the Patrician *familia*, based in either Brega, Conaille, or Armagh (which kept the ancestor of *AU*), as well as the Clonard or Clonmacnoise chroniclers in the midlands of Ireland (who produced the ancestor of *AT* and *CS*), would have been interested in attacks conducted by other Scandinavians on Iona. In addition, Dublin's interest in the Hebrides and Argyll region, and the challenge to it by the sons of Harald of Limerick could have had significant ramifications for the political and ecclesiastical activities of Dublin and the Columban *familia* in Ireland.[46] Overall, the series of items in the 980s indicates that, whenever the desire existed to record events in Argyll and the Hebrides, this would happen, allowing us to infer that there was usually no such interest in this region in this period, despite the means being available.

A similar pattern can be found in the overall record of Scandinavian activity. As has previously been argued, it is very unlikely that the

---

43   All translations are based on the *AU* edition by Mac Airt and Mac Niocaill, with emendations by the author.
44   Clancy 2011, 90-91, 93-97.
45   Ibid., 90-91, 95.
46   Wadden 2016, 170-74.

account of their Scottish exploits is in any way complete. The chroniclers, based in Irish ecclesiastical establishments in the Midlands and later in Armagh, were living in close proximity to the Vikings, especially those of Dublin. Although they would have found them of particular interest, it is surprising how few Scandinavian events outside Ireland they recorded. This is perhaps best reflected by statements on the departure or arrival of particular leaders in Dublin, which lack their destination or origin (see for instance *AU* 893.4, 894.4, and perhaps 927.3). What we have for northern Britain are occasional events recorded from the 790s (see Figure 1), including a few periods during which chroniclers were particularly interested, as seems to have occurred in the 980s. Other decades of considerable interest were the 860s and 870s, when the Scandinavians of Dublin were involved in the conquest of much of Anglo-Saxon England, and repeatedly attacked the Picts and northern Britons. This interest is illustrated by items for 870 and 871:

> **AU 870.6** Obsesio Ailech Cluathe a Norddmannis, .i. Amlaiph & Imhar, duo reges Norddmannorum obsederunt arcem illum & distruxerunt in fine .iiii. mensium arcem & predauerunt.

> [The siege of Dumbarton by the Northmen, that is Amlaíb and Ímar, two kings of the Northmen, laid siege to the fortress and at the end of four months they destroyed the fortress and plundered.]

> **AU 871.2** (also **CS 871.2**) Amhlaiph & Ímar do thuidecht afrithisi du Ath Cliath a Albain dibh cetaibh long, & praeda maxima hominum Anglorum & Britonum & Pictorum deducta est secum ad Hiberniam in captiuitate.

> [Amlaíb and Ímar returned to Dublin from Britain with two hundred ships, bringing away with them in captivity to Ireland a great prey of Angles and Britons and Picts.][47]

After destroying Dumbarton Rock in 870, the Vikings returned to Dublin with many English, British, and Pictish captives during the following year. In terms of details and interest, the focus is on the

---

47   All translations are based on the *AU* edition by Mac Airt and Mac Niocaill, with emendations by the author.

Vikings, presumably because these campaigns, involving large numbers of people, could have had repercussions in Ireland, boosting the Dubliners' prestige and wealth. In contrast, no details are given for the peoples or leaders on the receiving end of this campaign.

The same overall pattern can be found in the period following the Vikings' return to Ireland in 914, which had a considerable impact on the following decades. The activities of these Scandinavians in northern Britain is occasionally described, betraying, again, a scant interest for those fighting against these attackers. One clear example is represented by the account of the Battle of the Tyne in *AU* 918.4, in which, unusually, the Viking leaders and their deployments are specified, but the identity of their enemies is not elaborated. 'Men of Alba' and maybe 'northern Saxons' are referred to as the Vikings' adversaries, but their leaders are not named. Another example is the account of the famous Battle of Brunanburh, which secured Æthelstan's conquest of northern England:

> **AU 937.6** Bellum ingens lacrimabile atque horribile inter Saxones atque Norddmannos crudeliter gestum est, in quo plurima milia Nordmannorum que non numerata sunt, ceciderunt, sed rex cum paucis euassit, .i. Amlaiph. Ex altera autem parte multitudo Saxonum cecidit. Adalstan autem, rex Saxonum, magna uictoria ditatus est.

> [A great, lamentable and horrible battle between the English and the Northmen was cruelly fought, in which several thousands of Northmen, who are uncounted, fell, but their king, that is Amlaíb, with a few escaped. A large number of English fell on the other side. Æthelstan, king of the English, however, enjoyed a great victory.][48]

This account of the Battle of Brunanburh names the English and Scandinavian leaders, but does not mention the presence of the men of Alba and their king, Constantine (or the more doubtfully present king of the northern Britons), whom we know were present from other sources.[49] Not only does this reflect the level of interest the chronicler

---

48   This translation is based on the *AU* edition by Mac Airt and Mac Niocaill, with emendations by the author.
49   Woolf 2007, 168-73.

had in particular subjects, but both here and in the aforementioned cases it indicates that the Scandinavians would have been the source of information, even if the annalists often depicted them negatively elsewhere.

These Scandinavian connections and the chroniclers' strong interest in their activities partly explains the spike in events taking place in northern Britain from 860 to 880. There are, however, events recorded for these decades which are not connected to the Scandinavians, such as the death of the *prim-epscop* ('head-bishop') of Fortriu and abbot of Dunkeld (*AU* 865.6), Pictish kings in *AU* 862.1 (also *CS* 862.1), 876.1 (*CS* 876.1), and 878.2, and the killing of the king of Strathclyde at the instigation of the Pictish king (*AU* 872.5, *CS* 872.4). The most likely explanation is that the activities of the Scandinavians simultaneously revived the Irish chroniclers' interest in the affairs of Pictland and the northern Britons. This is, perhaps, another indication that connections with the Picts were already in existence, but had previously only led to the recording of a few events.

It is unclear, however, why the increased record for northern Britain during the 860s and 870s is not replicated in the decades immediately after 914, when Vikings connected to the Scandinavian kingdom of York re-established themselves in Dublin and Waterford, and were active from Limerick. Why, for instance, were the activities of the Dublin Vikings in Northumbria, apart from the Battle of Brunanburh, not being recorded? An explanation may be that these events were not considered to be as directly relevant to the Irish situation as those in the 860s and 870s, when it may have been thought that a major reshaping of politics, creating a very powerful Scandinavian polity encompassing both Britain and Ireland, was possible. In contrast, the chroniclers producing the ancestors of *AU*, *AT*, and *CS* were more focused on Irish affairs than those active in the 861-880 period, and the conflicts between Scandinavians and the rising English kingdom of Wessex may not have seemed as immediately significant. As such, this is another demonstration of how the interests of the chroniclers, rather than their contacts, were primarily what is reflected by the record for northern Britain.

The evidence from secular and ecclesiastical records in both *AU* and the Clonmacnoise-Clonard chronicle (underlying *CS* and *AT*) indicates an overall increase in interest in northern Britain during the second half of the tenth century. There is a continuing record of events, involving Scandinavians, which concerns Iona and the Columban community more generally (see Figures 1 and 2, noting that most travel items in the ninth century concerned the movement of Columba's relics). Some of these events may have taken place in Ireland rather than northern Britain, but they have been included in the 'Columban Community' and 'Scandinavians uncertain N.Britain/N.Brit. & Ireland' categories, as evidence exists for their activities in northern Britain, or the action described may have taken place there. For example, in *AU* 1075.1, Gofraid mac Amlaíd is called king of Dublin, in *CS* 1075.3 and *AT* 1075.2 he is just called *rí Gall* ('king of the Foreigners'), and *AI* 1075.2 states that he died *re muir anall*, 'beyond the sea'. This probably means that he died somewhere in south-western Scotland or the north-western seaboard of English, although the issue is uncertain.[50] Similar examples are Gofraid mac Amlaíb (obit. *AU* 963.5, *CS* 963.1), active in Ireland but probably with Hebridean connections, and Ímar mac Arailt (Ivarr son of Harald), ruler of Dublin from 1038-1046, but perhaps also from 1052 to 1054 based on his title *rí Gall* in his obit at *AU* 1054.1.[51] He slaughtered members of the Ulaid at Raithlin Island off the Antrim coast in 1045, indicating that the Hebrides may have formed a base for him after 1046. Other events involved Scandinavian groups in both Britain and Ireland (*AU* 794.7, *AT* 1058.4), 'Irish' Vikings moving to or from Britain (*AU* 866.1, *AU* 871.2 (*CS* 871.2), *CS* 980.6 (*AT* 980.6)), conflicts involving the Irish and Vikings from Britain (*AU* 913.5, 918.4, 1098.2), those for which it is unclear where in Britain an event took place (*AU* 937.6, Battle of Brunanburh; *AT* 1030.11), or whether it took place in Britain or Ireland (*AU* 986.2 in Dál Riata, *AU* 987.3, 989.4 (*CS* 989.2, *AT* 989.3)). By not adhering to neat categories, these records often make our conclusions less certain, but they testify to the continued interaction between Ireland and northern Britain over the whole period.

On their own, however, references to Scandinavians, Iona, or vague references to the Columban community do not account for the increased number of events concerning northern Britain recorded from the 950s

---

50   Cf. Duffy 1992, 102; Clancy 2008. A similar case is *AU* 913.5, recording a battle between the Scandinavians and the Ulaid of Ireland on the 'Saxon coast', which Clancy (Ibid., 43-44) argues to be a probable reference to Galloway.

51   On Gofraid mac Amlaíb, see Etchingham 2001, 169-71; Downham 2007, 29, 48-49, 219-20, 253; Woolf 2007, 212-14. On Ímar mac Arailt, see Duffy 1992, 97-98; Etchingham 2001, 161-62.

onwards. The main difference from the preceding period (apart from the exceptional 861-880) is the increase in items about secular events and bishops of Alba. From the 950s onwards, there is a regular – if not frequent – record of battles, killings, and obituary notices for the kings of Alba, whilst the rulers of the Isles, south-west Scotland, and northern English (or those fighting against their northern neighbours) appear occasionally (see Figure 5).[52] In the second half of the tenth century, events involving the northern Britons feature on occasion, whilst the powerful rulers of Moray, bishops of Alba (especially in CS), and abbots of Dunkeld also appear during the eleventh century.[53] The cumulative picture is a modest, but wide-ranging increase in recording, the reasons for which are difficult to perceive.

This increase may have been partly facilitated by the transmission of written notices of events, since these occur quite frequently in both *AU* and *AT* or *CS*, sometimes using similar language.[54] For instance, for the accounts of the death of Máel Coluim III, his son Edward, and his wife Margaret (1093), the same wording is found not only in *AU*, *AT*, and *CS*, but also in the *Annals of Inisfallen* (*AI*), in a section of the manuscript contemporary to the event:

---

52   Items are from *AU* unless stated. Those involving fighting against Scandinavians are underlined. Secular events involving Alba: 952.1, <u>952.2</u>, 954.2 (*CS* 953.3), *CS* 962.2, 965.4, 967.1, 971.1 (*CS* 971.1), 977.4 (*CS* 977.2, *AT* 977.4), 995.1 (*CS* 995.1, *AT* 995.3), *CS* 997.1 (*AT* 997.1), 1005.5 (*CS* 1005.5), 1006.5, 1033.7, 1034.1 (*CS* 1034.1, *AT* 1034.1), 1040.5 (*CS* 1040.3, *AT* 1040.1), 1045.6 (*AT* 1045.10), 1054.6 (*AT* 1054.5), 1058.2 (*CS* 1058.1, *AT* 1058.1), 1058.6 (*CS* 1058.4, *AT* 1058.5), 1072.8, 1085.2, 1093.5 (x2) (*CS* 1093.1, *AT* 1093.4), 1094.7 (*CS* 1094.3), *AT* 1099.1. The Isles (not including those leaders also based in Ireland): 989.4 (*CS* 989.2, *AT* 989.3), 1005.1 (*CS* 1005.1). Rulers in south-western Scotland: 1034.10 (*AT* 1034.3), 1064.9 (Echmarcach, king of the Rhinns, presumably of Galloway, according to Marianus Scottus; see Duffy 1992, 97-99). Northern English (including battles between northern Britons, Alba, and the English): <u>952.2</u>, 1006.5, possibly *AT* <u>1030.11</u>, *CS* 1032.4 (*AT* 1032.4), 1054.6 (*AT* 1054.5).

53   Items are those in *AU* unless stated. Those involving fighting against Scandinavians are underlined. Northern Britons: <u>952.2</u>, 971.1 (*CS* 971.1), 975.2 (*CS* 975.4, *AT* 975.3), 997.5 (*CS* 997.2, *AT* 997.3), possibly *AT* <u>1030.11</u>. Dynasty of Moray (unless also king of Alba): 1020.6 (*AT* 1020.8), 1029.7 (*AT* 1029.5), 1032.2, 1033.7, 1085.1. Ecclesiastical events involving Alba: *CS* 965.1 (death on pilgrimage in St Andrews of Áed mac Máile Mithig, of the Síl nÁeda Sláine dynasty of Brega) 965.4 (death of abbot of Dunkeld in battle), 1027.7 (the burning of Dunkeld), *CS* 1033.2 (bishop of Alba), 1045.6 (*AT* 1045.10) (death of abbot of Dunkeld in battle), *CS* 1055.3 (*AT* 1055.5) (bishop of Alba), 1093.2 (bishop of Alba).

54   Evans 2010, 91-114.

AU 1093.5 Mael Coluim m. Donnchadha airdri Alban & Etbard a mc do marbadh do Francaibh [add. marg. H: .i. i n-Inber Alda i Saxanaibh.] A righan imorro .i. Margareta do ec dia cumaidh ria cenn nomaidhe.

[Malcolm son of Donnchad, great King of Alba, and Edward, his son, were killed by Franks (add. marg.H: that is, at the mouth/ confluence of the Aln among the English). His queen, moreover, that is Margaret, died of sorrow for him within nine days.]

AT 1093.4 (and **CS 1093.1**) Mael Colaim mac Donnchadha, rí Alban, occisus est o Frangcaib, & Edabard a mac, & Margarita, ben Mail Colaim, do ég da chumaidh.

[Malcolm son of Donnchad, King of Alba, was killed by the Franks, and Edward, his son, and Margaret, wife of Malcolm, died from sorrow for him.]

AI 1093.13 Mael Coluim mac Donnchada, rí Alban, & a mac do marbad do Rancaib a boegul chatha, & Margaréta, .i. a ben, do éc da chumaid.

[Malcolm son of Donnchad, King of Alba, and his son were killed by Franks in an unguarded moment in battle, and Margaret, that is, his wife, died of grief for him.][55]

This signifies that this phenomenon is probably a contemporary one, reflecting the existence of single written texts created either in Ireland or Alba, which were then distributed to different Irish chroniclers at Armagh, Clonmacnoise, and Munster (where *AI* was kept). However, the evidence would be overstretched by suggesting that all records for northern Britain (or Alba) would have originated in one particular location, or through one method of transmission, or that the existence of such written sources by themselves caused a higher rate of recording for northern Britain in this period.

The most plausible explanation is that Alba, the Isles, and south-west Scotland had become more relevant to the chroniclers. From the mid-tenth century, Alba increasingly expanded into the rich agricultural

---

55   Ibid., 112-13; *AI*, xxx-xxxi. All translations by the author.

territory of Lothian, enhancing the power and prestige of the ruling Gaelic dynasty, whilst *mormair* members of Alba's elite are recorded as taking part in conflicts in Ireland in *AT* 976.7 and the Battle of Clontarf in *AU* 1014.2 (*CS* 1014.2).[56] In turn, from the late-tenth century onwards, Irish leaders claimed and perhaps occasionally obtained control over parts of the Isles and western seaboard of Scotland.[57] Moreover, strong connections between the Isles (including Man) and Dublin are attested, with interaction in both directions, partly reflected in the biographies of those found in the Irish chronicles, but also in other sources.[58] It was also a period during which the Scandinavian elites in mainland Argyll and islands like Bute were adopting the Gaelic language.[59] The spread of Gaelic may also have been taking place in south-west Scotland, around the Firth of Forth, Galloway, and in the Kingdom of Strathclyde.[60] As a result, the increased prestige of these rulers, combined with the creation of a cultural and linguistic continuum from Ireland to the kingdom of Alba, made it more likely that events in northern Britain would have been recorded.

In conclusion, then, the Irish chronicle record for northern Britain, although undoubtedly the result of communications networks, was more dependent on what their writers considered to be relevant and important to include. This interest in itself was shaped by political and social realities, such as Armagh's involvement with the Columban *familia* in the late-tenth century, as well as the concerns of chroniclers based in Brega or Conaille about the potential power of the nearby Vikings of Dublin during their campaigns in northern Britain in the 860s and 870s. However, it was also shaped by the horizons of the world immediately relevant to chroniclers. Before 800, this meant that events in Dál Riata, Pictland, and, to a lesser degree, the lands of the northern Britons and Northumbrians, were recorded, but after that there was a decline. That change is unlikely to be straightforwardly attributable to the end of the kingdom of Dál Riata in Argyll, or to a particular source, since the record for the whole of northern Britain (except Iona) declined, despite sufficient connections remaining to maintain it, had the chroniclers

---

56   Woolf 2007, 193–5, 209–11, 234–40.
57   Wadden 2016.
58   Duffy 1992; Etchingham 2001; Downham 2007, 177-99.
59   Jennings and Kruse 2009, 89-99; Márkus 2012, 29-39.
60   Clancy 2008, 39-45.

been willing. The reduction can also plausibly be connected to the coming of the Vikings; first to the western seaboard of Scotland, and increasingly to attack Ireland from the 820s. Although the details of when and how Scandinavians became involved in western Scotland is difficult to determine, a period of substantial disruption and conquest at the end of the eighth and during the early-ninth century (before major settlement) is plausible. This conflict, as well as attacks on Ireland, did not sever contacts, but may have reduced the chroniclers' horizons, preserving their interest in events around the northern coastal regions of Antrim, yet no longer in those in the nearby, Scandinavian-dominated lands of Islay and Kintyre. It is also worth raising the possibility that an accompanying heightened sense of 'Irish' identity, reflected in the use of the terms *rí Érenn* ('king of Ireland') and *firu Érenn* ('men of Ireland') from the mid-ninth century onwards, itself perhaps a product of the Viking impact, may have been another contributing factor later on.[61] It may be suggested, given the date of such references, that the process was the other way around; the conquest and settlement of Gaelic Dál Riata by the Picts and Scandinavians may have made focusing on the island of Ireland more attractive, rather than directly causing a reduced interest in northern Britain's affairs earlier on.

What is clear from the surviving record, however, is that from the mid-tenth century, as the Gaelic language spread in western Scotland, rulers based in the Isles and Alba gained in power and sometimes became involved in Ireland. At the same time, northern Britain became increasingly relevant again to the Irish for political and cultural reasons, partly as a potential arena for expansion. Interest in northern Britain grew, so that this region again constituted a part – albeit a relatively minor one – of the world-view of the Irish chroniclers. Although the chroniclers in Ireland presumably knew much more than they recorded, the products of their labour provide us with important reflections on what they regarded to be significant events in this world.

APPENDIX

Categorised events relating to Northern Britain in the *Annals of Ulster*, *Annals of Tigernach*, and *Chronicum Scottorum*, 701-1100 (Items are from *AU* unless stated).

---

61   Herbert 2000, 62-66.

Northern Britain: 701.7, 701.8, 701.9, 704.1 (*CS* 704.1, *AT* 704.2), 704.2 (*CS* 704.2, *AT* 704.3), 705.4, 706.2 (*AT* 706.2), 707.9 (*AT* 707.5), 709.4, 710.1 (*CS* 710.1, *AT* 710.1), 710.4, 710.5, 711.3 (*AT* 711.3), 711.5 (*AT* 711.5), 712.1 (*AT* 712.1), 712.2, 712.5, 713.4 (*AT* 713.4), 713.5 (x2) (*AT* 713.5), 713.7 (*AT* 713.7), 714.2 (*AT* 714.2), *AT* 715.8, 716.2, 716.4 (*AT* 716.4), 717.1 (*CS* 717.1, *AT* 717.1), 717.4 (*CS* 717.2, *AT* 717.3), 717.5 (*CS* 717.3, *AT* 717.4), *CS* 718.3 (*AT* 718.6), 719.6 (*AT* 719.4), 719.7 (*AT* 719.5), 721.1 (*AT* 721.1), 722.1 (*AT* 722.1), 722.3 (*AT* 722.3), 722.6 (*AT* 722.8), 723.4 (*AT* 723.4), 724.1 (x2) (*AT* 724.1), *AT* 724.2 (x2), 725.3 (*AT* 725.3), 725.7 (x2), 726.1 (*AT* 726.1), *AT* 726.2, *AT* 726.4 (part), 726.3, 727.3, 728.4 (x2) (*AT* 728.4, *AT* 728.5), 729.1 (*AT* 729.1), *AT* 729.2, 729.2, 729.3 (*AT* 729.4), 730.4, 731.4, 731.6 (*AT* 731.5), *AT* 732.7, 733.2 (*AT* 733.2), 734.5 (*AT* 734.4), 734.6, 736.1 (x2) (*AT* 736.1), 736.2, 737.1 (*AT* 737.1), 737.2 (*AT* 737.2), 739.7 (*AT* 739.6), 740.3, 741.10, 747.5 (*AT* 747.6), 747.10 (*AT* 747.11), 749.7 (*AT* 749.7), 750.4 (*AT* 750.4), 750.11, 752.1 (*AT* 752.1), *AT* 752.2, 752.2 (*AT* 752.2), *AT* 752.3, 752.8 (*AT* 752.9), 761.4 (*AT* 761.3), 763.10 (*AT* 763.8), 767.5, 768.7, 772.5, 775.1, 776.6, 780.1, 780.5, 782.1 (x2), 789.11 (dupl. at 790.7), 790.1, 801.4, 807.3, 815.6, 820.3. 834.1, 858.2, 862.1 (*CS* 862.1), 865.6, 872.5 (*CS* 872.4), 873.8, 876.1 (*CS* 876.1), 878.2, 880.1 (*CS* 880.1), 891.1 (*CS* 891.1), 900.6 (*CS* 900.5), 952.1, 954.2 (*CS* 953.3), *CS* 962.2, 965.4, *CS* 966.4, 967.1, 971.1 (*CS* 971.1), 975.2 (*CS* 975.4, *AT* 975.3), 977.4 (*CS* 977.2, *AT* 977.4), 978.1, 995.1 (*CS* 995.1, *AT* 995.3), *CS* 997.1 (*AT* 997.1), 997.5 (*CS* 997.2, *AT* 997.3), 1005.1, 1005.5 (*CS* 1005.5), 1006.5, 1020.6 (*AT* 1020.8), 1025.1, 1027.7, 1029.7 (*AT* 1029.5), 1032.2, *CS* 1033.2, 1033.7, 1034.1 (*CS* 1034.1, *AT* 1034.1), 1040.5 (*CS* 1040.3, *AT* 1040.1), 1045.6 (*AT* 1045.10), 1054.6 (*AT* 1054.5), *CS* 1055.3 (*AT* 1055.5), 1058.2 (*CS* 1058.1, *AT* 1058.1), 1058.6 (*CS* 1058.4, *AT* 1058.5), 1070.6, 1072.8, 1085.1, 1085.2, 1093.2, 1093.5 (x2) (*CS* 1093.1, *AT* 1093.4), 1094.7 (*CS* 1094.3), *AT* 1099.1, 1099.6.

Uncertain N. Britain: 701.6, 703.5, 707.3, 708.3, 711.6, 712.4, 717.2 (*AT* 717.2), 727.4 (*AT* 727.4), 740.5, 757.4 (*AT* 757.4), 760.7 (*AT* 760.3), 776.10, 778.11, 781.3, *CS* 900.6.

Northumbrian Only (kings of England noted also): 704.3 (*AT* 704.4), 713.3 (*AT* 713.3), 716.1 (*AT* 716.1), 718.1 (*AT* 718.1), 731.3 (*AT* 731.3), *AT* 735.7, *AT* 764.12, 913.1, [939.6 K.Eng.], [975.1 K.Eng.], *CS* 1032.4 (*AT* 1032.4), [1035.1 K.Eng.], [1040.6 K.Eng.].

Scandinavians in N. Britain: 802.9, 806.8 (*CS* 806.3), 825.17 (*CS* 825.9), 839.9, 867.7, 870.6, 875.3, 875.4, 904.4, *CS* 904/5.6, 952.2, 986.3, 1005.1 (*CS* 1005.1), 1034.10 (*AT* 1034.3), 1064.9, 1095.11 (*AT* 1095.5).

Scandinavians Uncertain N. Britain (not clear where event took place – e.g. where ruler also involved in Ireland or Man – or where events involved Irish): 794.7, 866.1, 871.2 (*CS* 871.2), 913.5, 918.4, 937.6, 963.5 (*CS* 963.1), *CS* 980.6 (*AT* 980.6), 986.2, 987.3, 989.4 (*CS* 989.2, *AT* 989.3), *AT* 1030.11, 1054.1, *AT* 1058.4, 1075.1 (*CS* 1075.3, *AT* 1075.2), 1098.2.

N. Britain & Ireland: *AT* 726.4 (part), *AT* 726.9, 731.2 (*AT* 731.2), *AT* 733.5, 734.7, 757.9 (*AT* 757.9), 778.7, 781.3, 791.1, 792.4, 865.2 (*CS* 865.2), 913.1, *CS* 941.5, *CS* 965.1.

Travel to/from N. Britain: 727.5 (*AT* 727.5), 730.3 (*AT* 730.1), 754.3 (*AT* 754.4), *AT* 758.2, 766.6, 782.2, *CS* 818.4, 829.3 (*CS* 829.2), 831.1 (*CS* 831.1), 849.7, 878.9 (*CS* 878.9).

Columban Community: 716.5 (*AT* 716.4), 814.9, 854.3 (*CS* 854.2), 927.1 (*CS* 927.1), 938.1, 954.6 (*CS* 954.6), 959.2 (*CS* 959.2), 964.3 (*CS* 964.5), 980.3 (*CS* 980.5), 989.5, 989.7, 998.2 (*CS* 998.2), 1008.1 (*CS* 1008.1), 1011.1, 1034.9, 1040.2 (*CS* 1040.2), 1057.8, 1062.2 (*AT* 1062.3), 1098.9.

BIBLIOGRAPHY

PRIMARY SOURCES

Adomnán of Iona, Life of St Columba, Sharpe R (trans), 1995, London: Penguin.

Annals of Inisfallen (MS. Rawlinson B.503), Mac Airt S (ed and trans), 1951, Dublin: Dublin Institute for Advanced Studies.

Annals of Tigernach, Stokes W (ed and trans), 1993 [1896-97], 2 vols, Felinfach: Llanerch Publishers.

Annals of Ulster, Mac Airt S and Mac Niocaill G (eds and trans), 1983, Dublin: Dublin Institute for Advanced Studies.

Chronicum Scotorum: A Chronicle of Irish Affairs from the Earliest Times to A.D. 1135; With a Supplement Containing the Events from 1141 to 1150, Hennessy W M (ed and trans), 1866, London: Longmans, Green, Reader, and Dyer.

The Chronicle of Ireland, Charles-Edwards T M (trans), 2006, vol. i, Liverpool: Liverpool University Press.

Secondary Sources

Anderson, Marjorie O 1980, *Kings and Kingship in Early Scotland*, 2nd edn, Edinburgh: Scottish Academic Press.

Bannerman, John 1974 [1968], *Studies in the History of Dalriada*, Edinburgh: Scottish Academic Press, 9-26.

Bannerman, John 1993, 'Comarba Coluim Chille and the Relics of Columba', *The Innes Review* 44, 14-47.

Bowen, E J 1969, *Saints, Seaways and Settlements in the Celtic Lands*, Cardiff: University of Wales Press.

Broun, Dauvit 1997, 'Dunkeld and the Origin of Scottish Identity', *The Innes Review* 48, 112-24.

Campbell, Ewan 2007, *Continental and Mediterranean Imports to Atlantic Britain and Ireland, AD 400-800,* York: Council for British Archaeology.

Charles-Edwards, T M 2000, *Early Christian Ireland*, Cambridge: Cambridge University Press.

Clancy, Thomas Owen 2008, 'The Gall-Ghàideil and Galloway', *The Journal of the Scottish Name Studies* 2, 19-50.

Clancy, Thomas Owen 2011, 'Iona v. Kells: Succession, Jurisdiction and Politics in the Columban *Familia* in the Later Tenth Century', in Fiona Edmonds and Paul Russell (eds), *Tome: Studies in Medieval Celtic History and Law in Honour of Thomas Charles-Edwards*, Woodbridge: Boydell, 89-101.

Downham, Clare 2007, *Viking Kings of Britain and Ireland: The Dynasty of Ívarr to A.D. 1014*, Edinburgh: Dunedin Academic Press.

Downham, Clare 2015, 'The Break-Up of Dál Riata and the Rise of Gallgoídil', in H B Clarke and R Johnson (eds), *The Vikings in Ireland and Beyond: Before and After the Battle of Clontarf*, Dublin: Four Courts, 189-205.

Duffy, Seán 1992, 'Irishmen and Islesmen in the Kingdoms of Dublin and Man, 1052–1171', *Ériu* 43, 93-133.

Edmonds, Fiona 2009, 'The Practicalities of Communication between Northumbrian and Irish Churches, *c.* 635–735', in J Graham-Campbell and M Ryan (eds), *Anglo-Saxon/Irish Relations before the Vikings*, Oxford: Oxford University Press, 129-47.

Etchingham, Colmán 1996, *Viking Raids on Irish Church Settlements in the Ninth Century: A Reconsideration of the Annals*, Maynooth: Cardinal Press.

Etchingham, Colmán 1999, *Church Organisation in Ireland A.D. 650 to 1000*, Maynooth: Laigin Publications.

Etchingham, Colmán 2001, 'North Wales, Ireland and the Isles: The Insular Viking Zone', *Peritia* 15, 145-87.

Etchingham, Colmán 2002, 'Les Vikings dans les Sources Documentaires Irlandaises: Le Cas des Annales', in É Ridel (ed), *L'Héritage Maritime des Vikings en Europe de l'Ouest*, Caen: Presses Universitaires de Caen, 35-56.

Evans, Nicholas 2010, *The Present and the Past in Medieval Irish Chronicles*, Woodbridge: Boydell.

Flechner, Roy 2013, 'The Chronicle of Ireland: Then and Now', *Early Medieval Europe* 21:4, 422-54.

Fraser, James 2009, *From Caledonia to Pictland: Scotland to 795*, Edinburgh: Edinburgh University Press.

Grabowski, Kathryn and David Dumville 1984, *Chronicles and Annals of Mediaeval Ireland and Wales: The Clonmacnoise-Group Texts*, Woodbridge: Boydell.

Herbert, Máire 1988, *Iona, Kells and Derry: The History and Hagiography of the Monastic Familia of Columba*, Oxford: Clarendon Press.

Herbert, Máire 2000, '*Rí Éirenn*, *Rí Alban*, Kingship and Identity in the Ninth and Tenth Centuries', in Simon Taylor (ed), *Kings, Clerics and Chronicles in Scotland, 500-1297: Essays in Honour of Marjorie Ogilvie Anderson on the Occasion of her Ninetieth Birthday*, Dublin: Four Courts, 62-72.

Hughes, Kathleen 1972, *Early Christian Ireland: Introduction to the Sources*, London: Hodder and Stoughton.

Jennings, Andrew and Arne Kruse 2009, 'One Coast – Three Peoples: Names and Ethnicity in the Scottish West during the Early Viking Period', in Alex Woolf (ed), *Scandinavian Scotland – Twenty Years After*, St Andrews: Dark Age Studies Committee, 75-102.

Mc Carthy, Daniel P 2008, *The Irish Annals*: *Their Genesis, Evolution and History*, Dublin: Four Courts.

McCormick, Michael 2001, *Origins of the European Economy: Communications and Commerce, A.D. 300-900*, Cambridge: Cambridge University Press.

Márkus, Gilbert 2012, *The Place-Names of Bute*, Donington: Shaun Tyas.

Ó Corráin, Donnchadh 1972, *Ireland before the Normans*, Dublin: Gill and Macmillan.

Wadden, Patrick 2016, 'Dál Riata c. 1000: Genealogies and Irish Sea Politics', *The Scottish Historical Review* 95:2, 164-81.

Wooding, Jonathan 1996, *Communications and Commerce along the Western Sealanes AD 400-800*, Oxford: BAR.

Woolf, Alex 2007, *From Pictland to Alba 789-1070*, Edinburgh: Edinburgh University Press.

An Exploration of *Thing* Sites in the Islands on the Scottish West Coast

Alexandra Sanmark[1]

Viking and Norse *things* (ON *þing*, sing.), which functioned as both parliaments and courts, were held at outdoor assembly sites. *Thing* sites were widely distributed across Scandinavia as well as the Norse settlements in the west, showing the significance of the assembly institution and the practice of law to society at this time. If this institution had not served its purpose, the Norse settlers could have left it behind. Instead, both in Scandinavia and their new homes, the people of the Viking Age created an ever-shifting pattern of elaborate *thing* sites.[2]

This aspect of the Norse settlement in western Scotland has remained virtually unexplored, apart from brief discussions in overarching volumes, such as Barbara Crawford's *Scandinavian Scotland*.[3] Since 2012, however, a number of new potential *thing* place-names have been identified, all suggested to contain ON *þing*.[4] It is important to point out that *þing* is not the only element indicative of Norse assembly sites, and in this chapter two further suggested *thing* sites, identified on the basis of other types of place-names, are also discussed.[5] In this way, a total of eleven potential *thing* sites are found on the islands of the western seaboard of Scotland (Figure 1):

1. Eileann Thinngartsaigh, Harris
2. Tinwhill, Skye
3. Gruline, Mull
4. Grulin, Islay
5. Grulin, Eigg
6. *Edin, Bute
7. Finlaggan, Islay
8. Tiongal, Lewis
9. Cnoc nan Gall, Colonsay
10. Mannal, Tiree
11. Lagalgarve, Kintyre

---

1   I am grateful to the organisers of the SSNS conference in Northern Ireland for inviting me to present my research. I would also like thank the two anonymous reviewers for their useful comments.
2   For full details, see Sanmark forthcoming.
3   Crawford 1987, 206-10.
4   Macniven 2013; Whyte 2014; Márkus 2012.
5   Sanmark 2009, 231; Ahlberg 1946, 100.

Figure 1: Potential *thing* sites in the islands of western Scotland © Crown Copyright/database right 2011. An Ordnance Survey/EDINA supplied service. All rights reserved 2010. Map by Alex Sanmark and Tudor Skinner.

In addition, Govan on the Firth of Clyde will be brought into the discussion towards the end of this chapter, even though this site is located just outside the geographical scope of this study. Govan has been seen as a royal and administrative centre, which was redeveloped with the 'involvement' of the Norse.[6] This suggestion will be evaluated in the light of the findings and discussion of this chapter.

All sites will be evaluated in terms of features and characteristics, using archaeological evidence, written sources, and place-names, and placed in the context of recent research on *thing* sites.[7] Around half of the sites discussed in this chapter have been visited by the author, their location has been recorded with a GPS and pro forma, as well as 360-degree photography. The remaining sites have been examined through detailed map study. Recent research has shown that *thing* sites were located in carefully selected places, with specific features, the type and nature of which varied slightly between geographical areas. These different *thing*-site features served a purpose and were charged with symbolism and meaning, turning the sites into power statements in the landscape, signposted as places where important decisions were made – and obeyed.[8] The most important assembly features identified in Scandinavia can be summarised as follows:

- A location on the convergence of communication routes, often both land and water routes.
- A location by fords, isthmuses, or on islands.
- Large mounds.
- Prehistoric cemeteries.
- Linear stone or wooden monuments, forming processional routes and site boundaries.[9]

Using the knowledge of Scandinavian *thing* sites and the method described above, the viability of the potential assembly sites listed can be tested. This is particularly important in western Scotland, where no *thing* sites or *thing* meetings are referred to in written sources. This places an even higher degree of reliance on place-names, which are rarely recorded prior to the thirteenth century, and in many cases a

---

6   Owen and Driscoll 2011, esp. 343-44.
7   Sanmark forthcoming. ch. 1; 2009; 2013.
8   Sanmark forthcoming; 2009; 2013; Semple et al. forthcoming.
9   Sanmark forthcoming.

lot later. In addition, many of these place-names are rather difficult to interpret, having gone through a transition into Gaelic.[10]

HISTORICAL BACKGROUND

Viking raids are recorded in western Scotland from the early ninth century, whilst this area seems to have been under growing Norse domination from the middle of the century.[11] Over the next few hundred years, there were constant shifts between rulers and power centres, such as Dublin, the Isle of Man, and the Earldom of Orkney – and by extension the Kingdom of Norway. In the early period, the islands on the Scottish west coast are seen to have formed rather independent communities under the leadership of different chieftains, whose power was dependent on raiding and warfare.[12] During the tenth century, the Kingdom of the Isles developed, ruled by the *Gall-Ghàidheil*, the 'Foreign Gaels'; a term applied to the population of mixed Norse and Gaelic descent.[13] From the late eleventh century, the Kingdom of the Isles was joined with the Kingdom of Man. In the following century, further turbulence occurred with the rise of Somerled, also of Norse-Gaelic descent, who ruled until 1164, when he was killed in battle. After this date, the Isle of Man fell to the Manx kings, whilst the Isles were divided between his descendants, the MacSorleys, who ruled them until the Treaty of Perth in 1266, when Norway handed them over to Scotland.[14]

LAW AND ADMINISTRATIVE ORGANISATION

Although written sources on Norse law and assembly in western Scotland are almost non-existent, the place-name evidence shows that an administrative organisation was in place. No Norse laws from Scotland have survived, but just as for Orkney and Shetland, it seems likely that local versions of the Norwegian Law of the *Gulathing* were in place. This was indeed the case in the Faroe Islands and seemingly also in Iceland in the early tenth century.[15] Moreover, the use of local, Norse law, is supported by the wording of the Treaty of Perth, which

---

10   Gordon 1963, 90-91.
11   Crawford 1987, 40-42; Macniven 2013, 70, 79.
12   Crawford 1987, 26; Woolf 2007, 298-330.
13   McDonald 1997, 29-31; Crawford 1987, 47; Jennings and Kruse 2009.
14   McDonald 1997, 33-132; Griffiths 2010, 47, 159.
15   *Laws of Early Iceland*, 1.

states that the islands 'may be subject to the laws and customs of the kingdom of Scotland, and governed and judged according to these from this time henceforth'.[16]

The Norse assembly organisation was hierarchical, consisting of at least two tiers: local and top-level assemblies. A similar *thing* organisation for the islands on the Scottish west coast is implied by the *Annals of the Four Masters*. This source states that 'Lawmen of the Isles' existed in the tenth century.[17] Here, the term 'lawman' seems to have a wider meaning than usual, as these lawmen are said to have accompanied the Norse rulers on their expeditions. However, the *Annals'* statement may also indicate that some form of overarching administrative organisation for 'the Isles' existed.[18] As will be discussed below, the most likely candidate for a top-level assembly site is Finlaggan on Islay.[19] On the local level, the islands seem to have been at least partly divided into *herað* units, as was the case in many areas of Scandinavia.[20] This is suggested by place-name evidence; the Island of Harris (Gaelic *Na Hearadh*) and *Herries* in Islay are both seen to be derived from ON *herað,* and other such names are known from Orkney and Shetland. It is interesting to note that all these names refer to districts, although of different types.[21]

The Norse assembly organisation in Scotland was most likely a floating organisation, and the *herað* units may be of later date than some of the *thing* sites. Not all *thing* sites – those known and unknown today – were necessarily established at the same time and for the same reasons. In the early settlement period, a rather organic phase of *thing* site establishment can be envisaged, with assemblies set up by powerful individuals and families as a way of taking control – or attempting to take control – over a particular area. Some sites may therefore have been short-lived or temporary, whilst others may have remained in use for many hundreds of years.[22] This means that the eleven sites discussed here are not necessarily contemporary. It is also possible that some *thing* sites defined here as 'local' may, at times, have functioned as top-level sites.

---

16   McDonald 1997, 131; *Monumenta de Insula Manniae* iii, appendix.
17   These annals were compiled in the seventeenth century. Macniven 2013, 82.
18   Ibid.
19   Ibid.; Sanmark forthcoming, ch. 8.
20   Semple et al. forthcoming; Hafström 1961; 1962.
21   Macniven 2013, 80; 2015, 84; Stewart 1987, 130; Marwick 1952, 130-31.
22   Cf. Sanmark 2013, 96-98; Sanmark and Semple 2010.

In such a changeable political situation, it would have been particularly important for chieftains to acquire a site with the right attributes; one that sent out signals of power to the population as a whole. In the sections below, the attributes of the eleven potential *thing* sites on the western seaboard will be evaluated within the wider context of *thing* sites in other settlement areas and Scandinavia. The overriding trait of Norse assembly sites, identified across all areas, is their location on the convergence of important communication routes. It was essential for leaders to make sure that as many people as possible attended the assemblies, as their presence also implied their acceptance of the ruler and the law.[23] The two other key features of the assembly found in this study are a location near water and near mounds, both of which commonly occur at Norse assembly sites in other areas.[24] As shown towards the end of the chapter, two out of the eleven sites do not share any of these traits and are therefore unlikely to be assembly sites.

WATER LOCATION: ISLANDS, ISTHMUSES, AND LOCHS

In all Norse areas, there are close links between the large majority of *thing* sites and various forms of water, the types of which depend on the local topography. In northern Scotland, *thing* sites tend to be close to the sea, often on isthmuses or at the end of fjords. There are also examples of island *thing* sites.[25] Similar locations are found in the area currently under scrutiny.

There are two potential *thing* sites on isthmuses. The first is Edin on the Isle of Bute, recorded as *Atyngar* in 1319-1321 and preserved in the names Edinbeg and Edinmore.[26] *Atyngar* has been given two potential *thing* interpretations: either a derivation of ON *alþing* or of ON *eið* + *þing*. A third possible interpretation is simply 'rough face' (derived from *aodann garbh*).[27] Edinbeg and Edinmore are located in the middle of a low-lying isthmus, centrally situated on Bute where the St Colman Burn crosses this piece of land (Figure 2). This means

---

23   Sanmark forthcoming, ch. 5.
24   Ibid., ch. 4 and 5; 2013, 102-7.
25   Sanmark forthcoming, ch. 4 and 8; 2013, 102-4.
26   In 1475, this place-name was recorded as *Atyng'ar* and in 1577 as *Iding*. See Márkus 2012. Its interpretation as a *thing* site was initially suggested by Barbara Crawford.
27   Márkus 2012, 8; Andrew Jennings pers. comm. He added that *aodann* occurs rather frequently as a toponym, e.g. Edenmore, which is derived from *aodann mor*, 'big face'.

that, although the place-name is rather uncertain, the location at least is suggestive of a *thing* site. The second potential assembly site of this type is Gruline on the Isle of Mull, arguably derived from ON *grjót* and *þing,* in which *grjót* translates as '(rough) stones, stony ground', 'cleared and cultivated ground',[28] but 'chiefly with the notion of *rough stones* or *rubble* in a building, etc'.[29] This could be interpreted in the light of the many Scandinavian *thing* sites with names referring to cleared or non-agricultural land.[30] Gruline is situated on an isthmus between the sea and Loch Ba, more or less in the middle of the island (Figure 3).[31]

There are also a number of potential *thing* sites on small islands. Tiongal, on the west coast of the Isle of Lewis, is one such possible example. Its name is preserved in Cnoc an Tiongalairidh, where *Tiongalairidh* contains the genitive of either *þing-völlr* or *þing-vellir* and

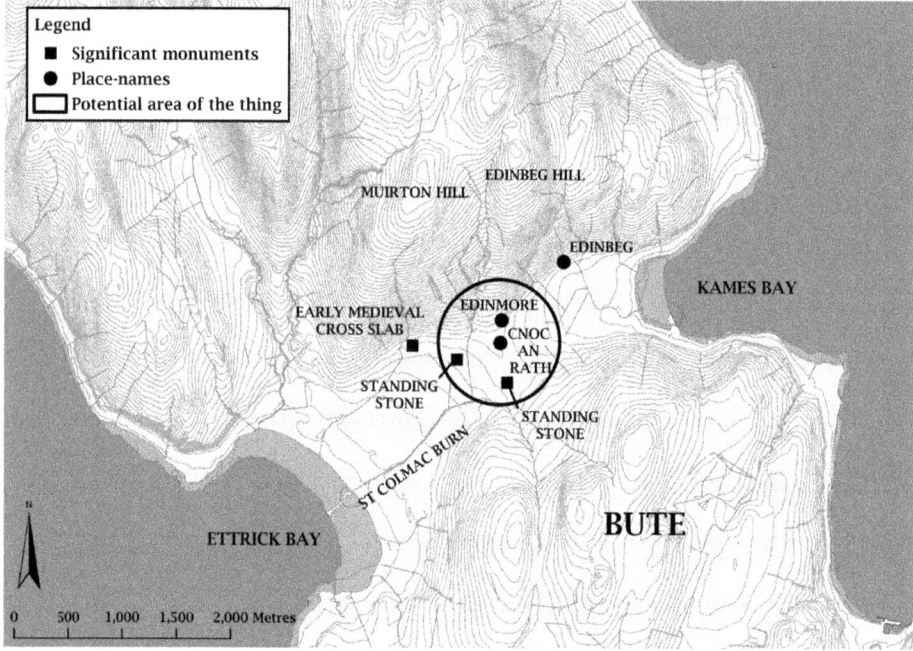

Figure 2: Edin on the Isle of Bute. © Crown Copyright/database right 2011. An Ordnance Survey/EDINA supplied service. All rights reserved 2010. Map by Alex Sanmark and Tudor Skinner.

---

28   Whyte 2014, 117, 119.
29   Cleasby and Vigfusson 1874, 216.
30   Semple and Sanmark 2013, 528-32.
31   Whyte 2014, 117, 119.

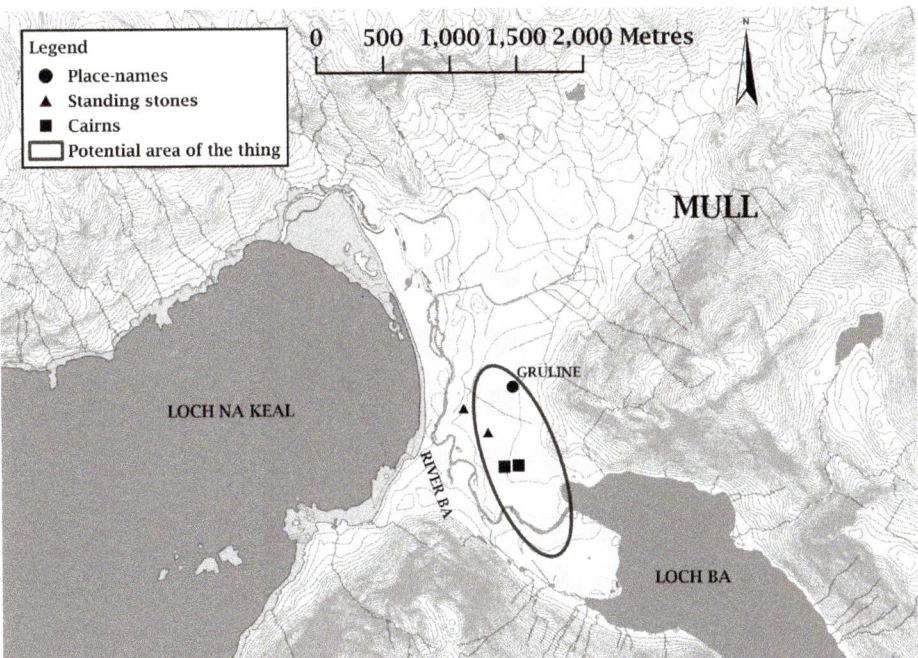

Figure 3: Gruline on the Isle of Mull. © Crown Copyright/database right 2011. An Ordnance Survey/EDINA supplied service. All rights reserved 2010. Map by Alex Sanmark and Tudor Skinner.

Figure 4: The possible *thing* site by Tiongalairidh and Loch a' Bhalie. Photograph by Fredrik Sundman.

Gaelic *áirge*, 'milking place/sheiling' (perhaps from the Scandinavian loanword *ærgi*), which is thus translated as 'the milking place of the *thing* field'. The full name Cnoc an Tiongalairidh refers to a hillock (*cnoc*) above Loch a' Bhalie (Figures 4 and 5).[32] As *Tiongalairidh* does not refer to the assembly itself, the actual meetings may have been held some distance away. A potential location is by the top of the loch, around 1 km away, where several small islands are found, one of which seems to be (at least partially) connected to the shore by a causeway. This loch is suitable as an assembly in terms of communication, being accessible from the sea and providing a sheltered harbour for boats. The reference to a milking place relating to the assembly is striking, representing one of the few occasions when such activities can be tied to *thing* sites. This supports the idea explored elsewhere that assemblies covered rather large areas, with different spaces assigned to different activities.[33]

Another example of an island *thing* site, albeit with different characteristics, is Eileann Thinngartsaigh ('Assembly-fence-island'), situated at the mouth Loch Claidh, a large sea loch in Harris (Figure 6).[34] This place-name is interesting, as it may refer to the 'sacred enclosure' (ON *vébǫnd*) described in written sources, such as *Egil's Saga*.[35] Enclosed *thing* sites have, moreover, been traced in Scandinavia.[36] The exact location of the assembly site has not been pinpointed, but the island is very small (only c. 500 by 200 m). A coastal location is unusual for an assembly site, but can be explained by the extremely rocky terrain in Harris, making travel on foot or horseback very difficult in comparison to most other areas of Scotland. In these circumstances, an assembly site in a sheltered position on the coast must have been ideal; there is also a good landing-place on the east side of the island.

In Islay, a number of potential *þing* names have been identified in the area around Loch Gorm, perhaps suggesting a rather large assembly area centred on the eastern end of the loch (Figure 7). These are Grulinmore, Grulinbeg, and Sunderland, although the uncertain nature of these interpretations must be stressed. Just like Gruline on Mull, the first two names are seen to derive from *grjót* and *þing*. A few hundred

---

32   Cox 1992, 139; 2002, 220.
33   Sanmark forthcoming, ch. 5.
34   I am grateful to Prof. Barbara Crawford for drawing my attention to this place-name.
35   Brink 2002, 87-91.
36   Sanmark forthcoming, ch. 4; 2015.

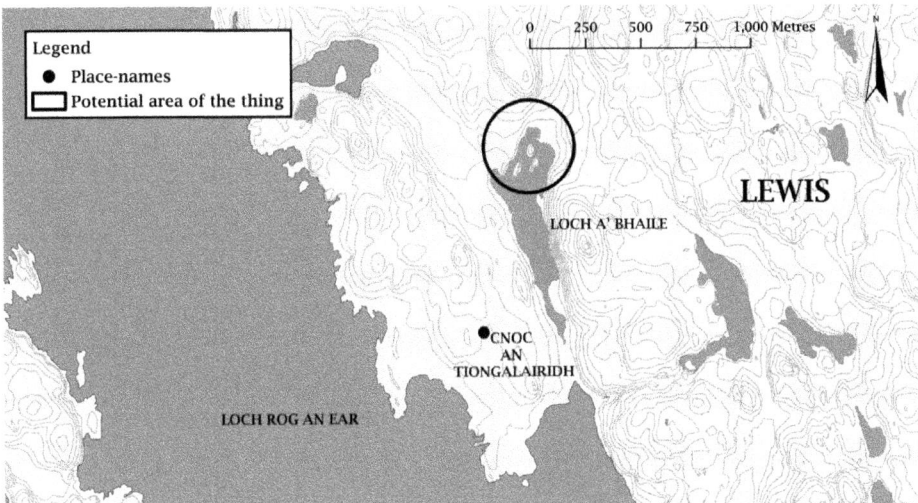

Figure 5: Tiongalairidh and Loch a' Bhalie, Lewis. © Crown Copyright/database right 2011. An Ordnance Survey/EDINA supplied service. All rights reserved 2010. Map by Alex Sanmark and Tudor Skinner.

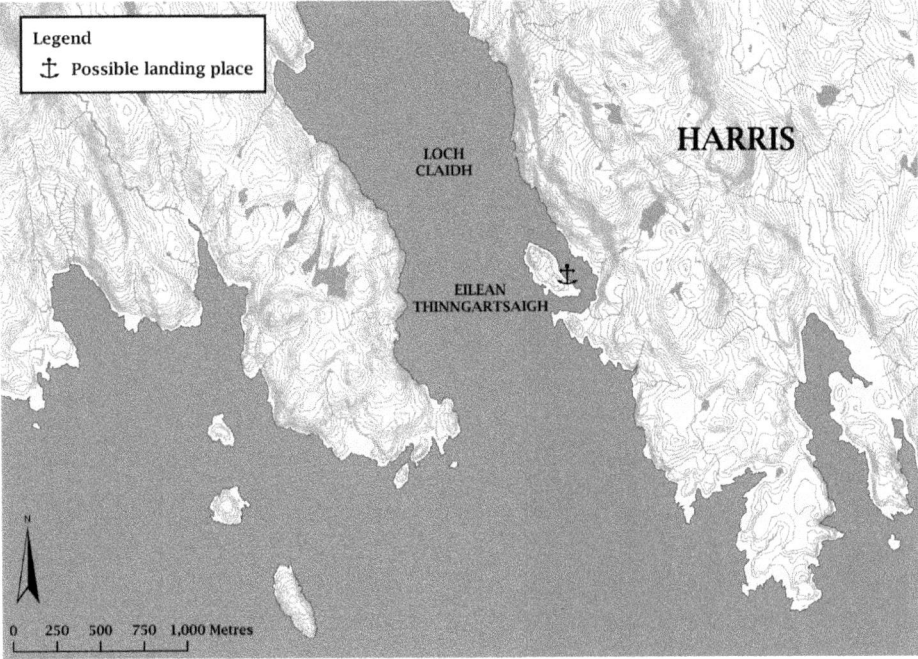

Figure 6: Eileann Thinngartsaigh in Loch Claidh, Harris. © Crown Copyright/ database right 2011. An Ordnance Survey/EDINA supplied service. All rights reserved 2010. Map by Alex Sanmark and Tudor Skinner.

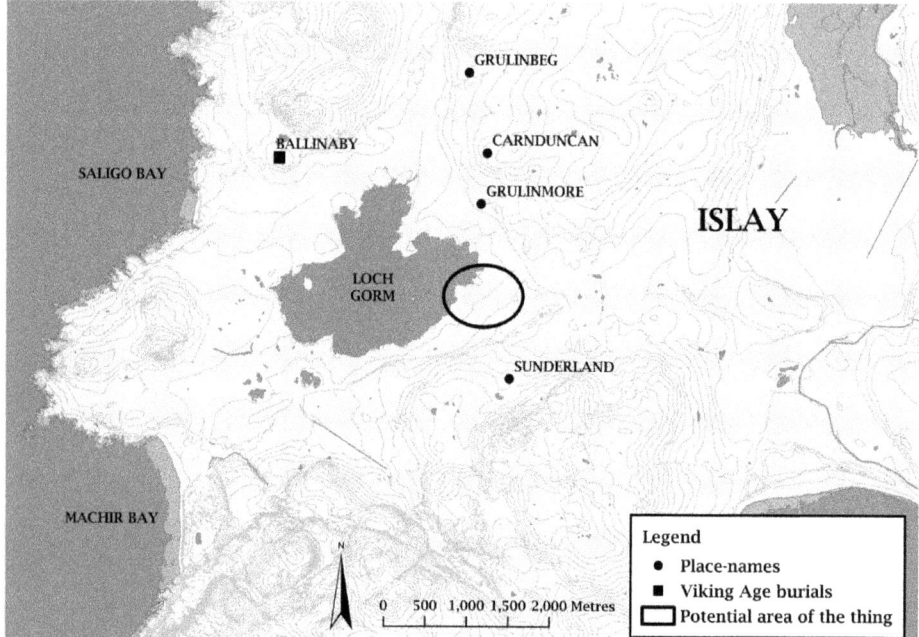

Figure 7: Potential *thing* sites around Loch Gorm. © Crown Copyright/database right 2011. An Ordnance Survey/EDINA supplied service. All rights reserved 2010. Map by Alex Sanmark and Tudor Skinner.

meters away lies Sunderland, which may incorporate ON *Sjóvarþing*, 'the assembly site by the lake', or ON *Sjúhundaraþing*, 'the assembly site of the seven hundreds'.[37]

Several foci for the potential *thing* site have been suggested. One is Carnduncan, a prehistoric cairn, located by a small watercourse, c. 1 km away from the loch. There is, however, another potential candidate for the focus of the *thing* site, which is perhaps more likely. Just below Sunderland farm, there is a large conical hillock with panoramic views of the loch. This feature clearly stands out in the landscape and slopes steeply down towards the shore (Figure 7).[38] Overall, Loch Gorm would have been suitable for a *thing* site, as there was a concentration of Norse settlements in this part of Islay. An immediate Norse presence is shown by the cemetery at Ballinaby, on the north side of the loch, which has been artefact-dated to the late-ninth and tenth centuries.[39]

---

37   Whyte 2014, 139-45; Macniven 2013, 81-82, 89.
38   Macniven 2013, 80-82.
39   Canmore ID 37407; Graham-Campbell and Batey 1998, 124-25.

In terms of communications, the loch is also relatively easy to access from the sea, where two beaches are suitable as landing places, from which an overland journey to the eastern end of the loch was only a few kilometres. Sunderland is also situated on an important land transit route across the island.[40]

Another potential *thing* site in Islay with similar traits is Finlaggan (in Loch Finlaggan), although no *þing* place-name has been identified (Figure 8). Finlaggan was the assembly and inauguration place of the MacDonalds, who emerged from the MacSorleys and traced their line back to Donald, son of Ranald, son of Somerled. Between 1336 and 1493, this clan ruled a large area, essentially recreating the Kingdom of Somerled, called the Lordship of the Isles; their ancestral link to the Kingdom of the Isles formed an important part of their powerbase. The MacDonalds were concerned with reinventing themselves as lords and created rituals of inauguration to show their power.[41] This can be traced both in the archaeology of Finlaggan and the late medieval assembly proceedings, described by Donald Monro, Dean of the Isles, in 1549 (i.e. only a generation after the Council had been abolished).[42]

Monro's text clearly shows the MacDonald claim to descent from Donald, stating that the Council members 'sat down into the Counsell-Ile, and decernit, decreitit and gave suits furth upon all debaitable matters *according to the Laws made be Renald McSomharkle* [Ranald McSorley] callit in his time King of the Occident Iles'.[43] It was common to provide laws with legitimacy by linking them to rulers further back in time, as seen, for example, in the thirteenth-century manuscripts of the Gulathing Law, in which some regulations are claimed to have been introduced by eleventh-century kings.[44] On this basis, it can be argued that Finlaggan was a Norse *thing* site, reused by the MacDonalds; similar site reuse has frequently been traced in Scandinavia.[45] This idea is similarly supported by other pieces of evidence: the area which was known as *Herries* in the early modern period was found here, in the central part of Kilmeny Parish, which was focused on Loch Finlaggan. Moreover, this part of Islay is dense with Norse place-names, and

40   Macniven 2013, 81.
41   McDonald 1997, 129; Caldwell 2014; forthcoming.
42   *Western Isles of Scotland*; O'Grady 2008, 17-19.
43   *Western Isles of Scotland*, 57. My emphasis.
44   Helle 2001, 17-20.
45   Crawford 1987, 208; Sanmark and Semple 2010; Brink 2004.

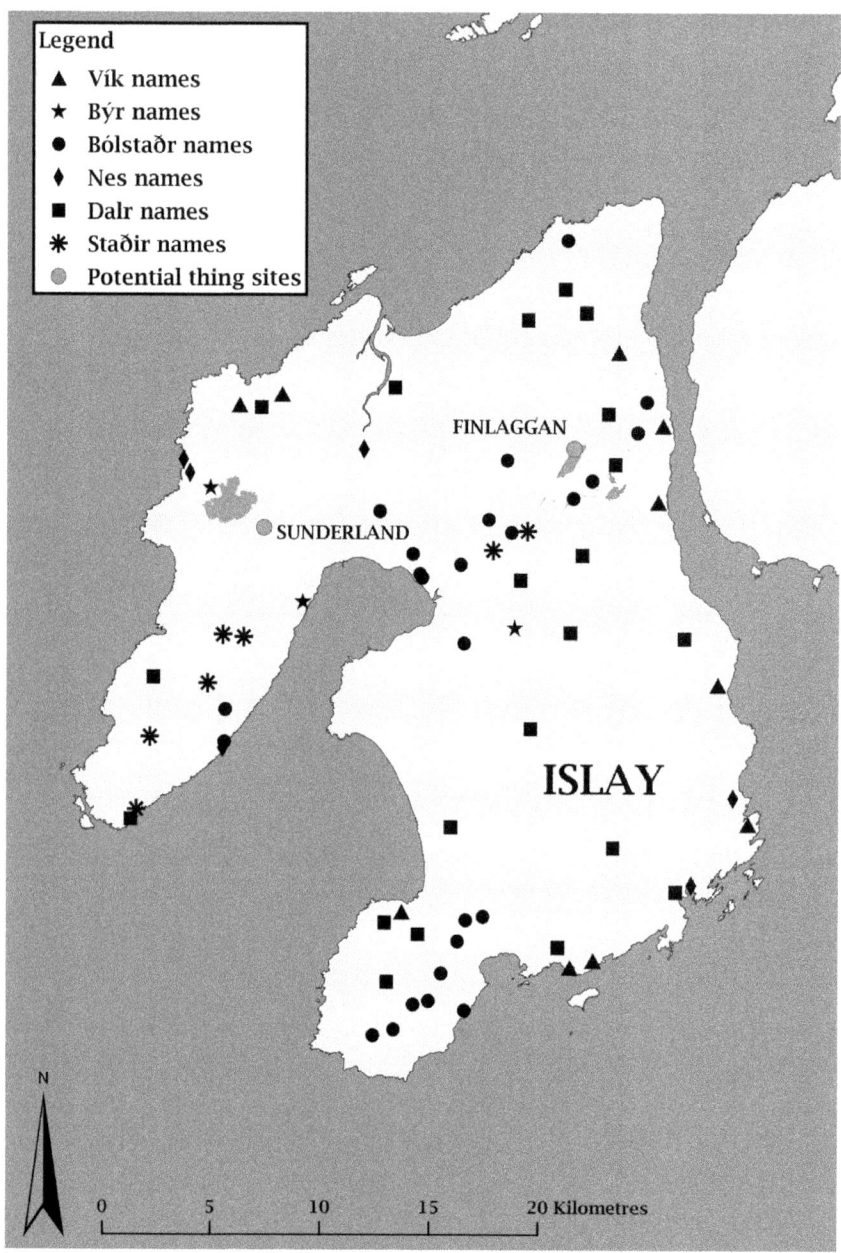

Figure 8: The potential *thing* sites at Finlaggan and by Sunderland in Islay, in relation to Norse place-names. © Crown Copyright/database right 2011. An Ordnance Survey/EDINA supplied service. All rights reserved 2010. Map by Alex Sanmark and Tudor Skinner.

has been argued to have been 'named and controlled by speakers of Old Norse' (Figure 8).[46] Alternatively, Finlaggan represented a hybrid assembly institution, consisting of both Norse and Gaelic elements, reflecting the population in this part of Scotland from the late Viking Age onwards.

Monro's account, other written sources, and local excavations show that the Finlaggan assembly meetings were held on two islands in the Loch: Eilean na Comhairle ('Council island') and Eilean Mòr ('Large island').[47] The two islands, connected by a causeway, have strikingly long biographies and were 'reinvented' on a number of occasions. The 'Council Island' was in use, although not continually, from around the first millennium AD, starting with a crannog, and followed by seventh-century structures and graves, possibly from a monastic centre. The next visible phase is a late-twelfth or thirteenth-century keep on top of which the fifteenth-century council chamber mentioned in documents was built.[48] Various phases of buildings are also seen on Eilean Mòr: in the thirteenth century, a large 'European-style' castle stood here, protected by a timber palisade. There was also a porch and a causeway that connected the island to the shore.[49] In the fifteenth and sixteenth centuries, these structures were replaced by various buildings, including a feasting hall. Rather than being permanently occupied, they were, in typical assembly fashion, only occasionally visited.[50] Finlaggan is derived from Gaelic *Port an Eilean* [*Fhindlagan*], 'Landing Place of the Island of St Findlug', to whom the chapel on Eilean Mòr is dedicated. This name is unlikely to be old, but the earlier name is unknown.[51]

The fifteenth-century council chamber on Eilean na Comhairle and the buildings on Eilean Mòr are dated to the period of the MacDonalds, whilst the keep on Eilean na Comhairle was erected by Somerled's descendants. This means that, on both islands, the McDonalds drew on their claimed ancestors. The keep is noticeably different from the usual building style of Somerled and his descendants, suggesting that this site represented something special to them.[52] Possible Norse links

---

46   Macniven 2013, 80-81, 86, figs. 2 and 4; 2015, 84.
47   *Western Isles of Scotland*; O'Grady 2008, 17-19; Caldwell 2003.
48   Caldwell 2010a; 2014; forthcoming.
49   Caldwell 2010b; forthcoming.
50   Caldwell 2014; forthcoming.
51   Macniven 2015, 263-64.
52   Caldwell 2014; forthcoming.

are seen in the name Eilean na Comhairle ('Council Island'), which is, in effect, the same name as 'Ting Holm' at Tingwall in Shetland. This may represent a parallel development, or perhaps a translation from Old Norse. The general layout of Finlaggan is, of course, also rather similar to Tingwall; both are located on causewayed islands in lochs, containing Iron Age settlement remains.[53]

It seems altogether plausible that Finlaggan was used as an assembly site over many hundreds of years. It was most likely a Norse assembly site focused on 'Council Island', perhaps the meeting site for the 'Lawmen of the Isles' from as early as the tenth century. It may also have been used for gatherings in the pre-Norse period. The absence of archaeological features between the eighth and the eleventh/twelfth centuries does not mean this was not an assembly. In fact, as these sites are often characterised by an absence of finds (e.g. Tingwall in Shetland), the opposite may be the case.[54] The intense building activity during the late-twelfth and early-thirteenth centuries may signal the rise of power after the separation from the Isle of Man in the middle of the twelfth century.[55] However, it should be noted that Finlaggan may have served as an assembly throughout the Norse period.

Mounds

Mounds are common features at Norse *thing* sites in Scotland and Scandinavia alike.[56] Gruline, on Mull, may be one such example (Figure 3). On the isthmus, there are two prehistoric cairns, which may have been the focus of the assemblies.[57] This may also be the case for the standing stones here, as such stones are known at Scandinavian *thing* sites.[58] Another possibility would be that *thing* meetings were held on the small island in the river, opposite the standing stones, although this seems less likely, as the course of the river is said to have been altered.[59] The potential assembly site around Loch Gorm may also have focused on a prehistoric mound, or more likely, on the mound-like hillock by the loch (Figure 7).

---

53 *Western Isles of Scotland*, 99; Crawford 1987, 208; Coolen and Mehler 2011; Caldwell 2003, 71; forthcoming.
54 Coolen and Mehler 2011.
55 Cf. Caldwell 2014; forthcoming.
56 Sanmark forthcoming, ch. 8 and 9.
57 Whyte 2014, 125.
58 Brink 2004, 309-12; Sanmark forthcoming, ch. 4.
59 Whyte 2014, 139-45.

It has been suggested that the large boulders forming a kerb around the cairns in Mull and by Loch Gorm constituted the sacred assembly enclosure (*vébǫnd*).[60] This interpretation seems rather unlikely, as kerbs are a rather frequently occurring feature on Neolithic and Bronze Age cairns. More importantly, they are far too small for assembly enclosures, which instead seem to have covered comparatively larger areas and a lot of people.[61]

In addition, Edin, on Bute, is potentially associated with a mound, Cnoc an Rath, surrounded by a ditch and bank and located in the middle of the isthmus with good views of the sea on both sides (Figure 2). A recent excavation of the mound yielded no results, as it had been severely disturbed in post-medieval times.[62] Just as on Mull, there are standing stones on the isthmus and there is also an early medieval cross slab, adjoining an undated chapel and burial ground.[63] It therefore seems clear that this has been an important area to Bute for several thousand years.

In Glen Hinnisdale, situated on the Trotternish peninsula on the Isle of Skye, a *thing* site is suggested by the place-name *Glen Tinwhill*, recorded in 1733 (Figure 9). Little is known about its location, but as is shown below, it is possible that it too was focused on a large mound. *Glen Tinwhill* may be derived from ON *þingvellir/þingvǫllr* and *dalr* and translated as '*thing* field' or '*thing* valley'.[64] The most likely focus of the assembly site is where the River Hinnisdal meets the modern road, which marks an important old routeway across the island. Two duns and a broch are found between the loch and the bridge, underneath which the river joins Loch Snizort. One of these mounds may have served as the focus of the gatherings.

The northern part of Skye has a concentration of Norse place-names, which provides some backing for a *thing* site here. The only certain Norse burial on Skye is found at Tote, at the southern end of the loch. A silver hoard has also been retrieved from the Storr Rock on the eastern side of Trotternish.[65] Slightly further south, at the very end of Loch Snizort, is Skeabost, which was the seat of the bishops of Sodor from

---

60   Ibid., 141.
61   Sanmark 2014, fig. 7; forthcoming, ch. 4.
62   Márkus 2012.
63   Canmore ID 40317.
64   Fellows-Jensen 1996, 23; Gordon 1963, 88-89: Crawford 1987, 208.
65   Graham-Campbell and Batey 1998, 77-79.

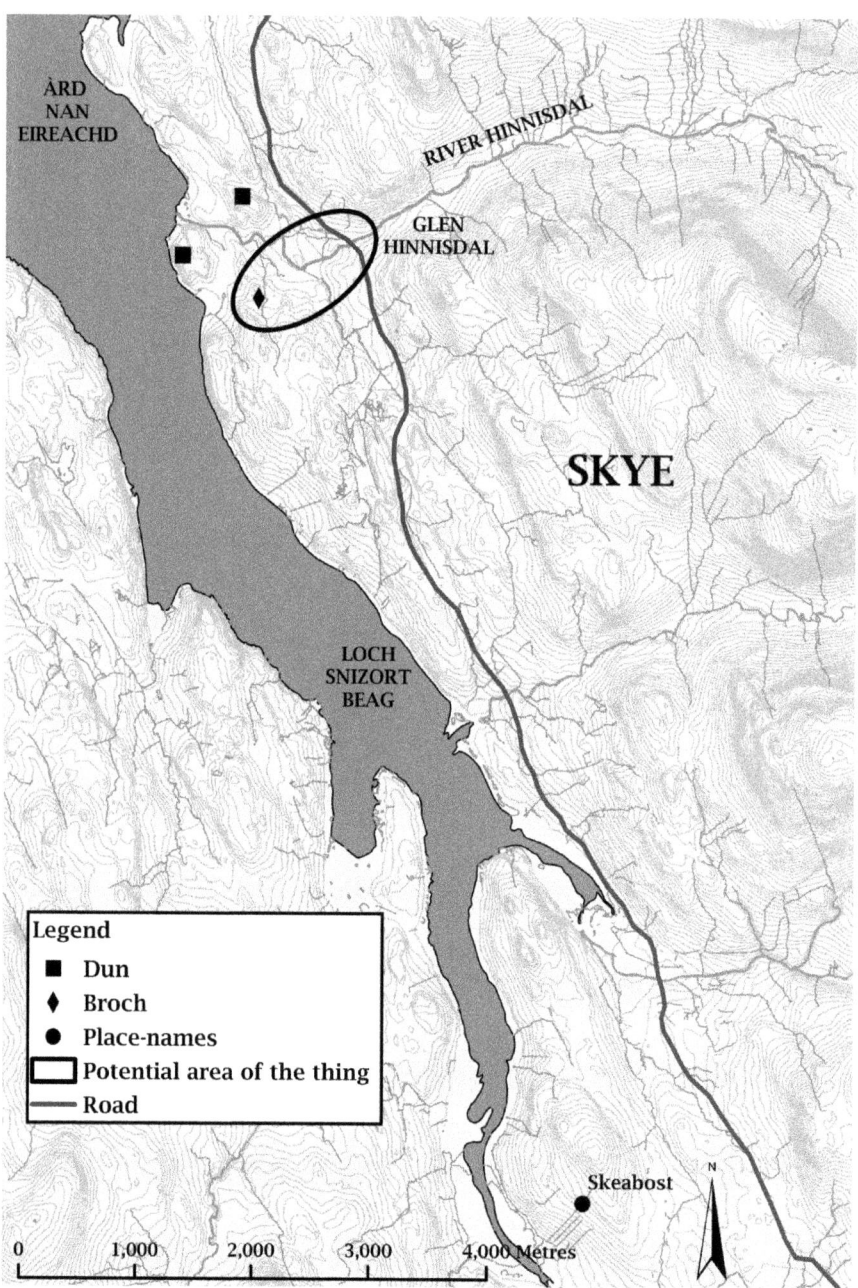

Figure 9: Glen Hinnisdale in the Isle of Skye. © Crown Copyright/database right 2011. An Ordnance Survey/EDINA supplied service. All rights reserved 2010. Map by Alex Sanmark and Tudor Skinner.

the late-fourteenth century, and the possible seat of the archdeacons of Sodor before this.[66] Moreover, in the vicinity of Skeabost, one of the few Pictish symbol stones in the Hebrides has been found.[67] The area around Loch Snizort has therefore clearly been a focus for a variety of elite expressions over a long period of time, which may support the suggestion that Tinwhill was a *thing* site. In connection to this, it should be mentioned that a Gaelic assembly site has been traced around 3 km to the northwest. This is a small headland, accessible via a thin strip of land, bearing the name Ard nan Eireachd ('Height of the Assemblies'). *Eireachd* (Old Irish *airecht*) is translated as 'assembly' or 'court' and seems to refer to a rather major assembly.[68] It is not known which of the two assemblies is the oldest, and this could therefore be an example of the Norse population taking over an earlier Gaelic assembly area or vice versa. So far, this is the only example from Scotland of a Norse and Gaelic/Pictish assembly having been located in close proximity to each other. Another possibility would be that this represents an example of bilingualism and language shift, and that this assembly site remained in use after the language had changed to Gaelic.

Cnoc nan Gall ('Hill of the Foreigners') on the west coast of Colonsay (Figure 10) is another potential *thing* site with a mound.[69] In Irish and Scottish Gaelic, the Norse often went by the term *Gaill/Gall*, which translates to 'gentiles' or 'foreigners', although it was not 'uniquely associated with a single ethnicity'.[70] It is therefore possible that Cnoc nan Gall refers to the Norse settlers, and perhaps even a *thing* site, although it should be noted that A.P. Morgan has suggested the name to be an antiquarian invention.[71] The location of Cnoc nan Gall is

---

66   Thomas 2014.
67   O'Grady 2008, 201-2.
68   Gavin Parsons pers. comm.; O'Grady 2008, 201-2; O'Grady 2014, 130; Crawford 1987, 208; Barrow 1992, 228, 241.
69   There are two further examples of Cnoc nan Gall place-names: the first is Cnoc Mòr nan Gall on Iona, which Morgan saw as a clear modern construction. The other one is Cnoc nan Gall on Ronay (located close to North Uist and Benbecula), which refers to a small rocky outcrop. This has also most likely been coined by antiquarians, and the location is not suggestive of an assembly. See Morgan 2013, 206-7.
70   Ibid.
71   Ibid.; Griffiths 2010, 36-37. Versions of Cnoch nan Gall are also found outside the Norse settlement of Wexford in Ireland. I am grateful to Prof. Liz Fitzpatrick for drawing my attention to these sites and their possible interpretation, and also to Dr Shane McLeod for reminding me of the existence of Cnoc nan Gall in Colonsay.

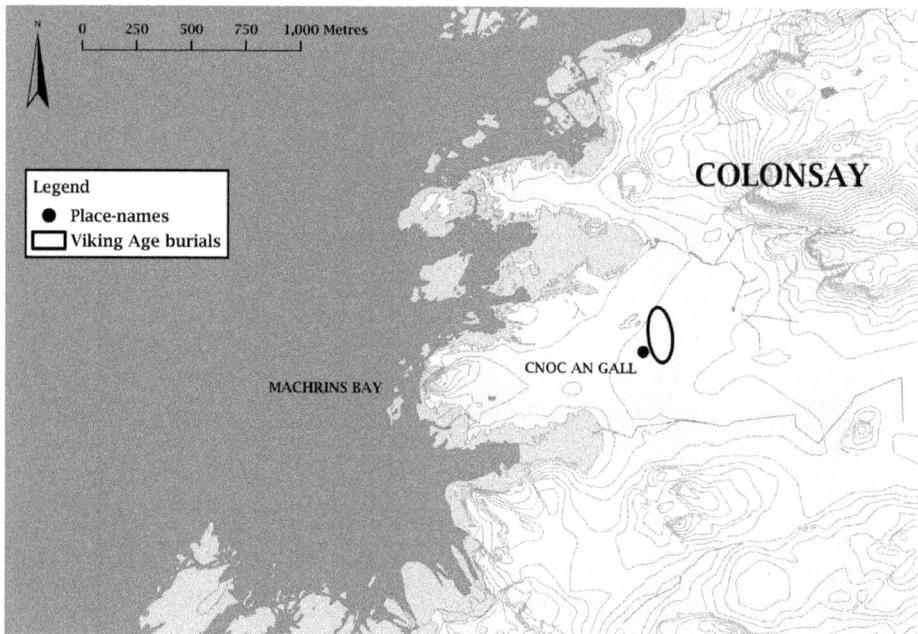

Figure 10: Cnoc nan Gall ('Hill of the Foreigners') in Colonsay. © Crown Copyright/database right 2011. An Ordnance Survey/EDINA supplied service. All rights reserved 2010. Map by Alex Sanmark and Tudor Skinner.

noteworthy, as a number of Viking burials are found here, together forming a cemetery (one of the few examples of a large collection of Norse graves from Viking-Age Scotland).[72] In Scandinavia, *thing* sites were commonly located in or by Iron Age cemeteries, which, in a sense, supports the idea of this being a place of assembly. This would, however, be the first such site identified in Scotland, as no correlation between Viking Age burials and *thing* sites has been found so far.[73] The location is suitable for an assembly, as Cnoc nan Gall is located very close to Machrins Bay, which must have been an appropriate landing place for ships and boats.

OTHER PROPOSED *THING* SITES

Three of the proposed *thing* sites, Grulin on the island of Eigg, Mannal on Tiree, and Lagalgarve in south-west Kintyre, must, with

---

72   Becket and Batey 2013. For a summary of the finds from Colonsay, see McLeod 2015.
73   Sanmark forthcoming, ch. 8 and 9.

regard to their archaeological and topographical profiles, be seen as rather unlikely assemblies. Grulin, just like Grulin on Skye and Gruline on Mull, is seen to be derived from *grjót* and *þing*.[74] This site does not, however, share any traits with other *thing* sites. Lacking any archaeological remains, it is located in an area of rough terrain that is very difficult to reach overland. Access by sea is also restricted, as it is situated above a rocky coastline with no suitable landing places. A more likely location for an assembly site on Eigg would be close to the sandy beaches in the central area of the island, where Viking Age burials are known (Figure 11).[75] This site is supposedly a striking natural amphitheatre and would therefore be suitable for assemblies.[76]

Mannal, on the south-west coast of Tiree, is thought to be derived from *mannavöllur* ('field of people') and suggested to refer to an assembly (Figure 12).[77] This site, however, has no visible assembly features and is also rather inaccessible, situated on a piece of land above a rocky coastline. In other parts of Tiree, there are several long, flat, good beaches, which would have been suitable as landing places, and where an assembly site would more plausibly have been located.

Lagalgarve, in south-west Kintyre, has been given a number of interpretations, such as 'the rough little hollow' and 'rough low field', or possibly 'law field' from ON *lagvǫllr*.[78] North and South Lagalgarve farms are located approximately 500 m apart, with no prehistoric or early historic archaeological remains recorded. There is a significant rise between the area around the farms and the rather rocky beach, thus making it difficult to spot and access from the sea. As such, the interpretation of Lagalgarve as an assembly site seems rather unlikely.

Finally, Govan, on the Firth of Clyde, has been identified as the royal and administrative centre of the Kingdom of Strathclyde in the tenth and eleventh centuries, and an assembly site developed under Norse influence. Judging by the place-name evidence, Govan was situated just outside the main areas of Scandinavian influence, although Strathclyde would have been a political melting pot of Britons, Gaels, Angles, Picts, and Norse during this period. In 870, Dumbarton Rock, the central

---

74   Whyte 2014, 145-47.
75   MacPherson 1878.
76   I am grateful to one of the anonymous reviewers, who pointed this out.
77   This suggestion was put forward by Dr Berit Sandnes, in Holliday 2016. I am grateful to Dr Andrew Jennings for drawing this to my attention.
78   Rixson 2010; Chinn 2016, 102; Jennings pers. comm.

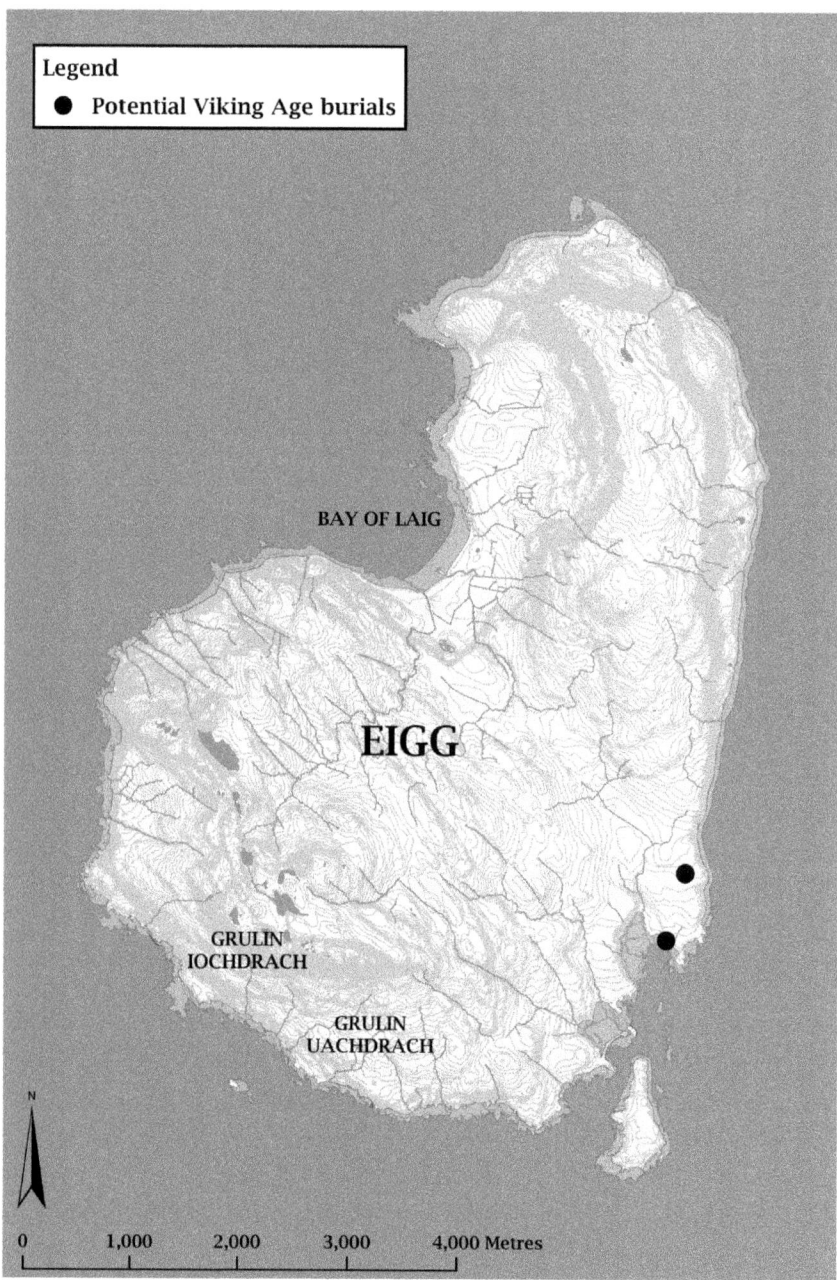

Figure 11: The Isle of Eigg with Grulin and potential Viking-Age burials. © Crown Copyright/database right 2011. An Ordnance Survey/EDINA supplied service. All rights reserved 2010. Map by Alex Sanmark and Tudor Skinner.

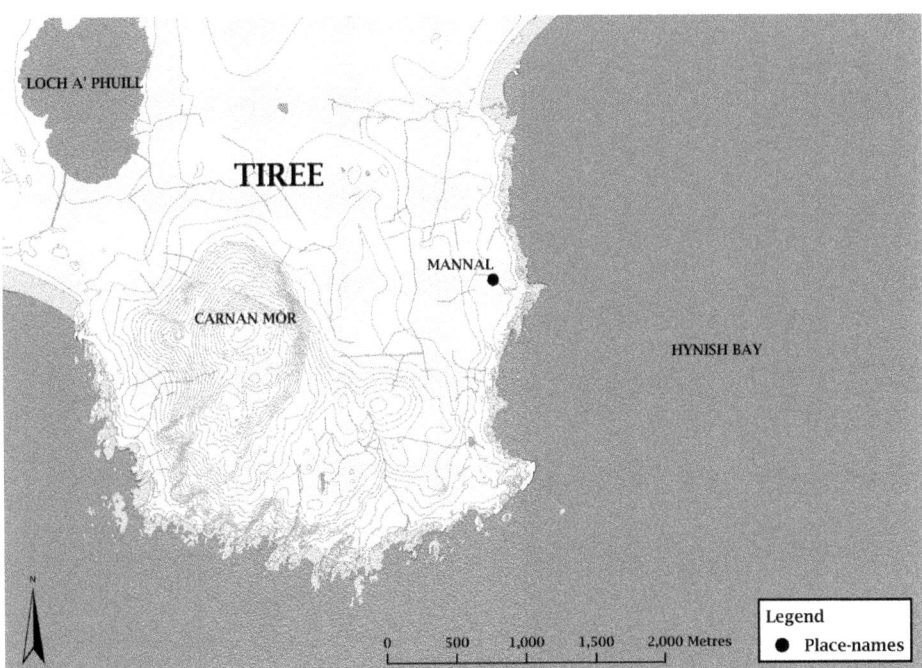

Figure 12: Mannal on the Isle of Tiree. © Crown Copyright/database right 2011. An Ordnance Survey/EDINA supplied service. All rights reserved 2010. Map by Alex Sanmark and Tudor Skinner.

stronghold of the Kingdom of Strathclyde, located on the Clyde, was sacked by Vikings. As a result, the kingdom's power base shifted to Govan in the tenth century. It is from this time that Norse influence has been suggested.[79]

Govan was positioned in a highly strategic location in the Firth of Clyde. It also has a very strong archaeological profile, with a sequence of churches stretching from the early historic period, an outstanding collection of stone sculpture (including hogbacks, dating between 900 and 1100), a large mound, as well as a possible 'processional route'. Norse influence has been seen in all of these elements.[80] The location is most convincing, as the Firth of Clyde seems to have been important to the Norse in this area for both commercial and political purposes. Together with the Firth of Forth, the Clyde formed a route through southern Scotland, which the Norse could well have utilised. Govan has

---

79   Owen and Driscoll 2011.
80   Ibid., 333-38.

two other locational traits that could suggest Norse influence; the Rivers Kelvin and Clyde meet here and there was also a fording point.[81]

The mound is known as Doomster Hill, which refers to the Doomster/ Dempster, a legal official known from post-medieval accounts. The mound had a stepped profile, which has been argued to be a feature of Norse assembly mounds around the Irish Sea.[82] Tynwald Hill, on the Isle of Man, is perhaps the most well-known example. This site has roots in prehistory, but even though the stepped mound profile predates the seventeenth century, this cannot be unquestionably attributed to the Norse. Another example of a stepped mound is Thingmount, in Little Langdale in Cumbria.[83] This site, however, seems an unlikely assembly, and its name, again, seems to have been coined by antiquarians.[84] At Tinwald in Dumfries, a geophysical survey revealed that the mound may had have a stepped profile, although this appearance could also be attributed to the later medieval motte construction.[85] Stepped mounds are not known from Scandinavia, and the question of whether they were a feature of Norse assembly places in the Irish Sea area must remain open until more detailed fieldwork has been carried out.

The processional route at Govan, which connects the church to the mound, has been seen as Norse, as it is similar to the one at Tynwald Hill. A calibrated radio-carbon date of AD 734-892 was used in support of this.[86] It has, however, been pointed out that this date comes from a 'repair', and the road itself may actually be earlier.[87] Although 'processional routes' of various types were a rather common feature at *thing* sites in Scandinavia, they are never found linking churches and mounds. Instead, this seems to be an aspect of early medieval assembly sites in Scotland, as, for example, at Bishop's Hill by Dunkeld Cathedral, as well as Moothill, located beside the Abbey of Scone.[88] The Norse nature of the Govan sculptural evidence is also debatable. Although hogbacks have traditionally been interpreted as Norse, this is currently under consideration, and they can therefore no longer be

81   Ibid., 338.
82   Ibid., 340; Darvill 2004, 228-30.
83   Owen and Driscoll 2011, 342-43; Darvill 2004, 228-30; Johnson 2012, 105-7, 111.
84   Wilson 2008, 125.
85   O'Grady et al. 2016, 202.
86   Owen and Driscoll 2011, 333-38.
87   O'Grady et al. 2016, 201.
88   O'Grady 2014, 114, 116-17, 119-22, 123-25.

accepted wholesale as Norse.[89] In sum, the evidence does not support the suggestion that Govan was designed by a Norse group among the rulers of Strathclyde. Indeed, this site is more in line with assembly-site design in Scotland and the Isle of Man than any Norse influence. A more detailed study of assembly sites in Scotland and Ireland may, in due course, produce a more nuanced view.

CONCLUDING REMARKS

This chapter has provided the first overview of all potential *thing* sites in the islands on the western seaboard of Scotland. The almost complete absence of written sources on *thing* sites has created a particularly high reliance on place-name evidence in this area of Scotland. As has been shown, place-names alone are not enough to identify assembly sites, and the interdisciplinary methodology applied here therefore represents an important step forward. Moreover, this evaluation would not have been possible without knowledge of a large number of *thing* sites in the Viking homelands and other areas of Norse settlement. It is hoped that this chapter can inspire further interdisciplinary research into the assembly sites of Scotland, and indeed further afield.

BIBLIOGRAPHY

PRIMARY SOURCES

Laws of Early Iceland: Grágás I, Dennis A, Foote P, and Perkins R (trans), 1980, Winnipeg: University of Manitoba Press.

Monro's Western Isles of Scotland and Genealogies of the Clans 1549, Munro R W (ed), 1961, Edinburgh: Oliver & Boyd.

Monumenta de Insula Manniae, or a Collection of National Documents Relating to the Isle of Man, Oliver J R (ed), 1860-62, 3 vols, Douglas: The Manx Society.

SECONDARY SOURCES

Ahlberg, O 1946, 'Tingsplatser i Södermanland och Närke före Tillkomsten av 1734 års Lagar', *Rig* 29, 96-125.

Barrow, G W S 1992, *Scotland and its Neighbours in the Middle Ages*. London: Hambledon Press.

Becket, A and C E Batey 2013, 'A Stranger in the Dunes? Rescue Excavation of a Viking Age burial at Cnoc nan Gall, Colonsay', *Proceedings of the Society of Antiquaries of Scotland* 143, 303-18.

---

89   O'Grady et al. 2016; Williams 2015; Victoria Whitworth pers. comm.

Brink, S 2002, 'Law and Legal Customs in Viking Age Scandinavia', in J Jesch (ed), *Scandinavians from the Vendel Period to the Tenth Century: An Ethnographic Perspective*, Woodbridge: Boydell, 87-127.

Brink, S 2004, 'Mytologiska Rum och Rskatologiska Föreställningar i det Vikingatida Norden', in A Andrén, K Jennbert, and C Raudvere (eds), *Ordning mot Kaos: Studier av Nordisk Förkristen Kosmologi*, Lund: Nordic Academic Press, 291-316.

Caldwell, D H 2003, 'Finlaggan, Islay – Stones and Inauguration Ceremonies', in R Welander, D J Breeze, and T O Clancy (eds), *The Stone of Destiny: Artefact and Icon*, Exeter: Short Run Press, 61-75.

Caldwell, D H 2010a, *Finlaggan Report 7: Eilean na Comhairle*, Edinburgh: National Museums Scotland. http://repository.nms.ac.uk/214/2/Finlaggan_report_1_-_introduction_and_background.pdf, accessed 27 February 2016.

Caldwell, D H 2010b, *Finlaggan Report 3: Eilean Mor Excavations*, Edinburgh: National Museums Scotland. http://repository.nms.ac.uk/214/2/Finlaggan_report_1_-_introduction_and_background.pdf, accessed 27 February 2016.

Caldwell, D H 2014, 'Finlaggan, Islay – A Place for Inaugurating Kings', Lecture, Royal Scone Conference. https://www.youtube.com/watch?v=VlU2sUsj6eM, accessed 27 February 2016.

Caldwell, D H forthcoming, 'Finlaggan, Islay: A Medieval Centre of Power', Royal Scone Project Publication.

Canmore, https://canmore.org.uk, accessed 14 September 2016.

Chinn, F 2016, 'Why did the Norse Settle in Kintyre? What Was the Nature of their Settlement and Relationships with the Gaels?', unpublished MLitt dissertation, University of the Highlands and Islands.

Cleasby, R and G Vigfusson 1874, *An Icelandic-English Dictionary*, Oxford: Oxford University Press.

Cox, R A V 1992, 'The Norse Element in Scottish Gaelic', *Études Celtiques* 29, 137-45.

Cox, R A V 2002, *The Gaelic Place-names of Carloway, Isle of Lewis: Their Structure and Significance*, Dublin: Dublin Institute for Advanced Studies.

Crawford, B E 1987, *Scandinavian Scotland*, Leicester: Leicester University Press

Darvill, T 2004, 'Tynwald Hill and the 'Things' of Power', in A Pantos and S J Semple (eds), *Assembly Places and Practices in Medieval Europe,* Dublin: Four Courts, 217-32.

Fellows-Jensen, G 1996, 'Tingwall: The Significance of the Name', in D Waugh (ed), *Shetland's Northern Links*, Edinburgh: Scottish Society for Northern Studies, 16-29.

Graham-Campbell, J and C Batey 1998, *Vikings in Scotland: An Archaeological Survey*, Edinburgh: Edinburgh University Press.

Gordon, B 1963, 'Some Norse Place-Names in Trotternish, Isle of Skye', *Scottish Gaelic Studies* 10, 82-112.

Griffiths, D 2010, *Vikings of the Irish Sea: Conflict and Assimilation AD 790-1050*, Stroud: History Press.

Hafström, G 1961, 'Herred', in I Andersson and J Granlund (eds), *Kulturhistoriskt Lexikon för Nordisk Medeltid från Vikingatid till Reformationstid, vol. 6*, Malmö: Allhem, cols. 491-92.

Hafström, G 1962, 'Hundare', in I Andersson and J Granlund (eds), *Kulturhistoriskt Lexikon för Nordisk Medeltid från Vikingatid till Reformationstid, vol. 7*, Malmö: Allhem, cols. 74-78.

Helle, K 2001, *Gulatinget og Gulatingslova*, Leikanger: Skald.

Holliday, J 2016, *Tiree Place-Names: Manal or Mannal*, http://www.tireeplacenames.org/mannal/manal, accessed 3 November 2016.

Jennings, A and A Kruse 2009, 'One Coast – Three Peoples: Names and Ethnicity in the Scottish West during the Early Viking Period', in Alex Woolf (ed), *Scandinavian Scotland – Twenty Years After*, St Andrews: Dark Age Studies Committee, 75-102.

Johnson, A 2012, 'Tynwald – Ancient Site, Modern Institution – Isle of Man', in O Owen (ed), *Things in the Viking World,* Lerwick: Shetland Amenity Trust, 104-17.

MacPherson, N 1878, 'Notes on the Antiquities from the Island of Eigg', *Proceedings of the Society of Antiquaries of Scotland* 12, 586-92

Macniven, A 2013, 'Borgs, Boats and the Beginnings of Islay's Medieval Parish Network', *Northern Studies* 45, 68-99.

Macniven, A 2015, *The Vikings in Islay.* Edinburgh: John Donald.

Marwick, H 1952, *Orkney Farm-Names*, Kirkwall: W.R. Mackintosh.

Márkus, G 2012, *The Place-Names of Bute*, Donington: Shaun Tyas.

McDonald, R A 1997, *The Kingdom of the Isles: Scotland's Western Seaboard c.1100-c.1336,* East Linton: Tuckwell Press.

McLeod, S 2015, *Viking Burials in Scotland*, https://vikingfuneralscapes.wordpress.com/inner-hebrides/, accessed 30 March 2016.

Morgan, A P 2013, 'Ethnonyms in the Place-Names of Scotland and the Border Counties of England', unpublished PhD thesis, University of St Andrews, http://hdl.handle.net/10023/4164, accessed 26 August 2016.

O'Grady, O 2008, 'The Setting and Practice of Open-Air Judicial Assemblies in Medieval Scotland: A Multidisciplinary Study', unpublished PhD thesis, University of Glasgow, http://theses.gla.ac.uk/506, accessed 2 March 2016.

O'Grady, O 2014, 'Judicial Assembly Sites in Scotland: Archaeological and Place-Name Evidence of the Scottish Court Hill', *Medieval Archaeology* 58, 104-35.

O'Grady, O, D MacDonald, and S MacDonald 2016, 'Re-Evaluating the Scottish Thing: Exploring A Late Norse Period and Medieval Assembly Mound at Dingwall', *Journal of the North Atlantic* sp. vol. 8.

Owen O A and S T Driscoll 2011, 'Norse Influence at Govan on the Firth of Clyde, Scotland', in S Sigmundsson, *Viking Settlements & Viking Society*, Reykjavik: University of Iceland Press, 333-46.

Rixson, D 2010, 'The Shadow of "Onomastic Graffiti"', *The Journal of Scottish Name Studies* 4, 131-58.

Sanmark, A 2009, 'Assembly Organisation and State Formation: A Case Study of Assembly Sites in Viking and Medieval Södermanland, Sweden', *Medieval Archaeology* 53, 205-41.

Sanmark, A 2013, 'Patterns of Assembly: Norse Thing Sites in Shetland', *Journal of the North Atlantic* sp. vol. 5, 96-110.

Sanmark, A 2014, 'Women at the Thing', in N Coleman and N L Løkka (eds), *Kvinner i Vikingtid*, Oslo: Scandinavian Academic Press, 85-100.

Sanmark, A 2015, 'At the Assembly: A Study of Ritual Space', in W Jezierski, L Hermanson, H J Orning, and T Småberg, *Power of Practice: Rituals and Politics in Northern Europe c. 650-1350*, Turnhout: Brepols, 79-112.

Sanmark, A forthcoming, *Viking Law and Order*. Edinburgh: Edinburgh University Press.

Sanmark, A and S Semple 2010, '"Something Old, Something New": The Topography of Assembly in Europe with Reference to Recent Field Results from Sweden', in H Lewis and S J Semple (eds), *Perspectives in Landscape Archaeology: Papers Presented at Oxford 2003-5*, Oxford: BAR, 107-19.

Semple, S J and A Sanmark 2013, 'Assembly in North West Europe: Collective Concerns for Early Societies?', *European Journal of Archaeology* 16:3, 518-52.

Semple, S J, A Sanmark, N Mehler, and F Iversen forthcoming, *Negotiating the North: Meeting Places in the Middle Ages,* London: Taylor and Francis.

Stewart, J 1987, *Shetland Place-Names*, Lerwick: Shetland Library and Museum.

Thomas, S 2014, 'From Cathedral of the Isles to Obscurity - The Archaeology and History of Skeabost Island, Snizort', *Proceedings of the Society of Antiquaries of Scotland* 144, 245-64.

Whyte, A C 2014, 'Gruline, Mull, and Other Inner Hebridean Things', *The Journal of Scottish Name Studies* 8, 115-52.

Williams, H 2015, 'Hogbacks: The Materiality of Solid Spaces', in H Williams, J Kirton, and M Gondek (eds), *Early Medieval Stone Monuments: Materiality, Biography, Landscape*, Woodbridge: Boydell, 241-68.

Wilson, D M 2008, *Vikings in the Isle of Man*, Aarhus: Aarhus University Press.

Woolf, A 2007, *From Pictland to Alba, 789-1070*, Edinburgh: Edinburgh University Press.

Beyond
the Inner Seas

The Norway to Be: *Laithlind* and Avaldsnes

Arne Kruse[1]

Laithlind in the Irish annals

The forms *Laithlind*, *Laithlinn*, and *Lothlind* feature in Irish sources during the ninth century AD, and appear to be the name of a location from which the king of the Vikings originates. The claim pursued in this chapter is that the sovereignty in question is likely to be a strong kingdom in pre-unified Norway. It aims to locate this particular polity, to discuss a potential semantic content of the early name forms, and to suggest a motive behind their designation.

The forms *Laithlinn* or *Laithlind* appear three times in the Irish annals. Their initial occurrence is found in the *Annals of Uster* (*AU*), as we are told that a deputy of 'the King of Laithlinn' takes part in a mighty battle south-west of Dublin in 848:

> **AU 848.5** Bellum re nOlcobur, ri Muman, & re Lorggan m. Cellaig co Laighniu for gennti ecc Sciaith Nechtain in quo ceciderunt Tomrair erell, tanise righ Laithlinne, & da cet dec imbi
>
> [Ólchobor, king of Mumu, and Lorcán son of Cellach, with the Laigin, won a battle against the heathens at Sciath Nechtain, in which fell the jarl Tomrair, tanist of the king of Laithlinn, and two hundred about him.][2]

Although this *Tomrair erell* (Old Norse *Þórir jarl*) was an ostensibly important chieftain, this reference represents the only occasion we hear about him. The title 'King of Laithlinn' reappears five years later, however:

---

1   This work represents a much edited version of a longer article in Norwegian in *Namn og Nemne* (Kruse 2015). The principal subject matter of the former article – not included here – constitutes a discussion on what the skaldic poems say about King Harald Fairhair's possible interest in Ireland/Scotland and his struggle with the Danes, which is likely to be reflected by the Viking in-fighting in Ireland.

2   Unless stated otherwise, the Old Irish texts and corresponding English translations are all taken from CELT (https://www.ucc.ie/celt). The usual substitution of *Laitlinn/Laithlind* with *Lochlann* is <u>not</u> followed here.

AU 853.2 Amhlaim m. righ Laithlinde do tuidhecht a nErinn coro giallsat Gaill Erenn dó & cis o Goidhelaib

[Amlaib, son of the king of Laithlind, came to Ireland, and the foreigners of Ireland submitted to him, and he took tribute from the Irish.]

Amlaib (ON *Áleifr*, later *Óláfr*) evidently has or assumes command of the 'foreigners' in Ireland, which also had to be achieved a few years before; in 849 (*AU* 849.6), we hear that 'the king of the foreigners' (*rígh Gall*) came with 140 ships to submit the Vikings in Ireland. As no names are chronicled here, it is impossible to know whether this refers to the same King of *Laithlind*. Nevertheless, a king's son by the name Amlaib does appear in *The Fragmentary Annals* (*FA*):[3]

FA 239 Isin mbliadain-si bhéos .i. in sexto anni regni Maoil Seaclainn, tainig Amhlaoibh Conung .i. mac rígh Lochlainne i nEirinn & tug leis erfhuagra cíosa & canadh n-imdha ó a athair & a fagbhail-sidhe go h-obann. Tainig dno Iomhar an brathair ba sóo 'na deaghaidh-sidhe do thobhach na ccios ceadna

[Also in this year, i.e. the sixth year of the reign of Máel Sechlainn, Amlaib Conung, son of the king of Lochlainn, came to Ireland, and he brought with him a proclamation from his father of many tributes and taxes, and he departed suddenly. Then his younger brother Imar came after him to levy the same tribute.]

From what we know about Máel Sechnaill from other sources, Amlaib Conung[4] (ON *Óláfr konungr*) and Imar (ON *Ívarr*) are likely to

---

3   The *FA* is a non-contemporary compilation of earlier sources and, thus, as a
     source it is not nearly as valuable as the contemporary *AU*. In this case, we notice
     that the presumably original *Laithlinn* has been substituted with *Lochlann*, which
     is not otherwise attested in contemporary sources before the eleventh century.
     The entry, however, could be regarded as an example of the type of annal entry
     that Peter Hunter Blair terms 'embellished annals'. See Blair 1939.

4   Note that the form *Conung* is different from the Old Irish personal name
     Conaing, which is likely to be a pre-umlaut borrowing from Old English into
     Irish, i.e. before AD 700 (Greene 1976, 78; 1978, 119). The implication is that the
     Irish scribe writing *Conung* does not see the word as a name but most probably
     as the title that it is. The same applies to the title *erell* or *iarla* from Old Norse
     jarl (Greene 1976, 78).

have accomplished this in 852 or 853. As such, these must be the same events that are referred to in the *AU* for the year 853. Furthermore, the son of the same 'Óláfr of Dublin' is likely to be the one taking part in the battle at Cell Ua nDaigri in 868, as described in the *Annals of the Four Masters*:

> **M866.10** Dos-fail dar Findabhair fhind,
> fiallach grinn dond dar laith linn luind,
> As ar chédaibh rimhthear Goill,
> do cath fri righ n-Etair n-uill.
>
> [There comes over fair Findabair
> a keen host from fierce Laithlind –
> the Foreigners are counted in hundreds –
> to do battle against the king of great Étar.][5]

The final ninth-century Irish source to be mentioned here is perhaps the most often cited, providing us with a glimpse of a scribe's personal experience of this unsafe century. Found in the margins of a copy of Priscian's *Institutiones Grammaticae* (see Figure 1), this Old Irish poem is usually dated to the mid-ninth century:[6]

> Is acher in gaíth in-nocht
> fu-fúasna fairggæ findf[.]olt;
> ní ágor réimm mora minn
> dond láechraid lainn úa Lothlind
>
> [The wind is sharp tonight
> he throws up the white mane on the sea;
> I have no worries that the wild warriors from Lothlind
> shall lay their course over a calm sea.]

We notice that the form *Lothlind* is different from the previous annal entries with *Laithlinn/Laithlind*. We shall see that the form *Lothlind* is given much attention in the many attempts to explain the name complex.

---

5 Translation from O'Corrain 2001.
6 O'Corrain 1998, 302-3.

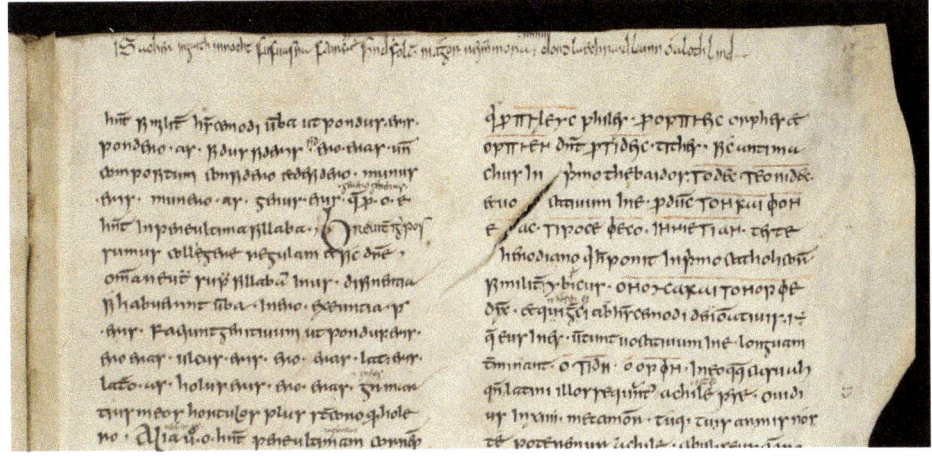

Figure 1: Marginal note in Priscian's *Institutiones Grammaticae,* Stiftsbibliothek St Gallen, Cod. Sang. 904, 112. With permission from Stiftsbibliothek St Gallen.

RESEARCH HISTORY

The numerous authors who have written about the name complex *Laithlind/Laithlinn/Lothlind* may be placed into two categories: those who claim that the name denotes a Scandinavian location, and those who rather see a British/Irish denotation. Unsurprisingly, most early Scandinavian and German Celticists adhere to the first category, Heinrich Zimmer being the first.[7] He claimed that the name in the Irish sources signified the Danish island of *Lolland,* a theory that Alexander Bugge proved unlikely.[8] Carl J. S. Marstrander, later supported by Alf Sommerfelt, initially suggested that *Lochlann* had an origin in the area name *Rogaland* in the south-west of Norway, whilst the former author, upon reflection of the earlier forms, came to doubt this etymology.[9]

Egon Wamers is the most recent to propose that the Irish name forms may be traced to a specific Scandinavian name.[10] He suggested that the first element of the name might be *Hlaðir,* now *Lade,* near Trondheim – a well-attested seat of power in the early Viking Age.[11] There are, however, linguistic issues with Wamers' proposition; in the suggested transition *Hlaðir > Laith-,* one of the two syllables is syncopated in

7   Zimmer 1891.
8   Bugge 1900, nos. 4-6.
9   Marstrander 1911, 250-51; 1915, 56-57; Sommerfelt 1950.
10   Wamers 1997; 1998, 66.
11   For the name *Hlaðir,* see Stemshaug 2010, 108-9.

the Irish form, and a monophthong becomes a diphthong – if it is the case that the written <ai> represents a diphthong, as is argued here. Colman Etchingham supports Wamers' proposal and suggests that the second syllable in *Hlaðir* is dropped in compositions.[12] This, however, does not seem to be the case. Although *Hlaðir/Lade* is not attested in compounds with -*land* in any of the medieval or modern name forms, the second syllable of the farm name remains present in other compositions, cf. *Hlaðajarl* (m.), 'earl of Laðir', and the modern name *Ladehammaren*. Etchingham also suggests that the Irish *linn*, 'pool, sea', may serve as the basis for the second element, and as such refers to the Trondheimsfjord. In this case, it would have been the Irish who were the name-givers, implying their familiarity with the area. There is no evidence to sustain a claim that the Irish (clerics, nobles?) knew Norwegian local geography in such detail by the middle of the ninth century, at a time when they had just started to record the names of the leaders of the marauding incomers. In addition, should *Laithlind* represent a Norwegian place-name compounded with an Irish generic element, it will be a typological exception to the degree that one struggles to find similar compounds in Irish sources.

David Greene, proposing that 'it is at least possible that the original *Lothlind* was [...] perhaps in Gaelic-speaking Man or Western Scotland', has suggested a Celtic word *loth/lath*, 'marsh', as the origin to the first element in *Lothlind*.[13] In spite of his own uncertainty, his proposal has won the support of Anders Ahlqvist.[14] Most scholars, including Ahlqvist, believe that the element -*lind* or -*linn* derives from Germanic -*land*. If Greene is right, the name will be a hybrid creation, this time with a Germanic generic and Celtic specific. The rarity of such constructions is probably why Greene himself suggested that we might have to instead accept Irish *linn*, 'pool', referring to the estuaries in which Vikings often camped.[15] We shall return to this proposal shortly.

In 1998, Donnchadh Ó Corráin, who has discussed this name on several occasions, proposed a much-quoted etymology for the form *Lothlind*.[16] He believed it to have originated from ON *loð* ('hairy' or,

---

12   Etchingham 2010, 83; 2014.
13   Greene 1976, 76-77.
14   Ahlqvist 2005, 19-27.
15   Greene 1978, 119-23.
16   Ó Corráin 1998.

more specifically, 'covered with long grass'), which would have turned into **loth* in Irish, and which he believes refers to the good grassy land the Vikings found in Orkney and the north-east of Scotland.[17] Accentuating Greene's proposal, Ó Corráin argues that *Lothlind/Laithlind* does not refer to Norway or any part of Norway, but instead designates 'Viking Scotland', a kingdom the Vikings had established on the Scottish islands, which was used as a foundation for further expansion southwards into the Irish Sea.

Although the source material is scarce, it is reasonable to assume that Shetland, Orkney, the Hebrides, and the Scottish coastal strip to the north and west were colonised before Man and Ireland. Nevertheless, Greene and Ó Corráin's hypothesis falters in the assumption that there would have been a political organisation in these areas since 'the main thrust of the ninth-century Viking attack on Ireland (c. 825-850) was mounted from Scotland'.[18] There is no archaeological or historic evidence to support any Norse 'maritime centre' in the north or west of Scotland as early as this.[19] A review of the Norse graves in the area shows that these mostly emerge between 850 and 950, and only in exceptional cases before this – an indication that any large-scale settlement only took place after c. 850.[20] The first sign of what can be perceived as a political initiative is the Vikings' apparent control over the Gaelic-Pictish kingdom of Dál Riata around the mid-ninth century.[21] The Irish monks reporting on these events, however, never imply that *Laithlind* equals Dál Riata. They, on the contrary, state that Gallgoídil warriors – possibly with a base in Viking-controlled Dál Riata – were in conflict with the Dublin dynasty. In summing up his criticism of Ó Corrain's hypothesis, Etchingham bluntly states: 'Only the eye of faith can locate the *Laithlinn* of the sources in Scotland'.[22]

There is also a pragmatic objection to Ó Corráin's hypothesis. By presuming a Scottish place of origin for the aggression towards Ireland, Ó Corráin removes from Old Irish a term for the provenance of a people that terrorised and suppressed large parts of Ireland during

---

17   As a metaphoric adjective referring to rich grassland, it is found in *Fornmanna sögur* ii, 278: 'á grasi þóat loðit væri'.
18   Ó Corráin 1998, 297.
19   Etchingham 2007.
20   Graham-Campbell and Batey 1998, 152-53.
21   Jennings and Kruse 2009; Downham 2015.
22   Etchingham 2010, 83.

the ninth century.[23] It is simply not enough to claim that the Vikings in Ireland had stronger contacts with the western colonies than those with Norway directly. The archaeological material – which we shall return to shortly – convincingly demonstrates a strong and direct link between Norway and Ireland during the ninth century.

Within the Irish poem known in English as *The March Roll of the Men of Leinster*, the titular men warn against *forlunn echtrann*, 'hordes of foreigners', who arrive *dar glasa in mara móir*, 'over the big blue ocean'.[24] If the proposed tenth-century origin of the poem is accurate, it seems that, at any case, there existed an impression for the foreigners (i.e. Vikings) at that time to have come from somewhere further away than just the opposite side of the North Channel.

In contrast to the non-committal style of the Irish annalists, the scribe who penned the poem containing *Lothlind* provides the modern reader with a glimpse of genuine human emotion, and it is understandable that this text is so frequently used to illustrate exactly this; the terror and anguish the Vikings produced, perhaps especially among the relatively well-informed but also vulnerable clerics.[25] It is, however, another matter when the form *Lothlind* has played a pivotal role in the scholarship around the name complexe, and it may be justified to ask if the linguistic importance of *Lothlind* is warranted. As in other cases when a name is recorded in various written forms, the etymologist will have to choose what form or forms appear the most reliable or trustworthy. In this case, *Laith-* is the more recurrent, with *Loth-* only occuring once. Apart from the uncertainty about when and where the poem containing *Lothlind* is written[26], the text itself is difficult to contextualise. Unlike the annalistic entries with *Laithlind*, the unknown

---

23   See also Greene 1976, 77.
24   *The March Roll of the Men of Leinster*, 122.
25   There is a slight possibility that the form *Lothlind* is influenced by the name
      Lotharingia or *Lotharii regnum,* one of the successor kingdoms to the
      Carolingian Empire, carved out by the Treaty of Verdun in 843 and named after
      Emperor Lothar II in 855. The unknown monk glossing Priscian's *Institutiones
      Grammaticae* would have been part of a monastic network which included
      clerical and political institutions inside of this Frankish kingdom. Could it be that
      the poet monk is actually referring to Vikings menacing the coast of the Low
      Countries, i.e the littoral of *Lotharingia*, or 'Lothar's land', and that his expressed
      fear is that the wild warriors who raided that land would now find their way
      across the sea to where he is?
26   Ó Neill 2000.

poet provides the name *Lothlind* in isolation; no further information is supplied in the form of place names or personal names. In addition, we may assume that the poet is not writing his text as a record of events – meant for future references and where one would expect a degree of accuracy – but rather as an outburst of personal anguish, expressed in a verse which is perhaps only meant for himself. Of the four ninth-century entries discussed above, the poem containing *Lothlind* is the odd one out, both linguistically and contextually. As we have seen, a majority of scholars have actually focused their efforts on the form *Loth-* and, in light of the relative anomaly of the source, it can be argued that the form *Loth-* has been given an exaggerated importance in the research history of the name complex. The most important consequence, however, is that scholars have assumed that the variation *Loth-/Laith-* is indicative of a monophthong, and it has been taken for granted that the written <ai> follows the Old Irish orthographic habit where the <i> indicates that the preceding consonant is 'slender', i.e. that it has a palatal quality. The complicating factor is that the diphthong /ai/, which 'should' be written <aí>, is in practice very often written without an accent, such as in the examples from *AU* when the Norse name *Áleifr* (Proto-Scandinavian **AnulaißaR*) is rendered *Amlaim* or *Amlaib*. If we adjust the importance of *Loth-* to the anomaly that it is, we simply cannot know for sure if the form *Laith-* contains a monophthong or a dipthong. An etymology based on a monophthong has – in spite of much scholarly attention – not produced an irrefutably satisfying proposal, and other options deserve to be tested. In the following, therefore, our main focus will be on the annalistic forms where the first element is *Laith-*, and the <ai> in both *Amlaib* and in *Laitlind* will be treated as the Irish scribes' attempts at representing the Common Scandinavian diphthong /ai/.

Laithlind and Lochlann

Until relatively recently, it has been mostly taken for granted that the name *Laithlind/Laithlinn/Lothlind* is the equivalent of *Lochlann*, which in Modern Irish and Scottish Gaelic depicts 'Norway' and has done so since at least 1102, when Magnús berfœttr was referred to as *rí Lochlainni.*[27] It has been assumed that folk etymology has gradually converted the name to *Lochlann*, where the first element, 'fjord, lake', aptly reflects a characteristic feature of the Norwegian coastline.[28]

Several scholars have recently pointed out that it is not obvious for *Laithlind* to be an early form of later *Lochlann*. In fact, there are good phonological and historical reasons for claiming that the forms are independent creations. Colman Etchingham accentuates the semantic content:

> *Laithlinn* is hardly an earlier form of *Lochla(i)nn* ('Norway'). Why should we assume they were the same? After all, the words are different, even if the latter replaces the former in linguistically modernised annals (*AFM* and *FA*). They occur in annals of distinct periods.[29]

John MacInnes points to the early, mythical use of *Lochlann*:

> Lochlann, translated 'Norway' above, and in many contexts in modern Gaelic meaning just that, is in earlier, medieval Gaelic a fabulous land which later came to be associated with the Vikings and their homeland.[30]

Máire Ní Mhaonaigh discusses this in more detail, demonstrating that *Lochlann* had an early literary life as a mythological name of the home country of the Vikings. In such stories, they are portrayed as almost invincible warriors, who are still defeated by clever Irish heroes.[31] The name *Berbhe* has a similar duality, acting as both the Irish name of the present-day town of Bergen and the name of a mythical and nebulous town in folk tradition. Ní Mhaonaigh believes that, rather than folk traditions having created *Lochlann* from *Laithlind*, the early literary mythical name *Lochlann* would have assimilated the similar sounding

---

27 *AU* 1102.7. In the eleventh century, the linguistically modernised annals, such as the *Fragmentary Annals*, are using *Lochla(i)nn* with the meaning 'Norway'. In 1058, the *Annals of Tigernach* make use of the name in reference to the son of Haraldr harðráði.
28 See, for example, Greene 1976, 77.
29 Etchingham 2010, 82.
30 MacInnes 2006, 190.
31 Ní Mhaonaigh 2006.

Lathlinn and *Lothlind* prior to taking over the particular meaning of 'Norway':

> One could in fact argue that it was this term [*Lathlind*] which applied originally to an actual historical place whence Viking raiders came – wherever it might have been – and that Lochlann was from the beginning a created imaginative location.[32]

It is probable that the name *Lochla(i)nn* would have assimilated *Laithlind* at a time when *Laithlind* had ceased to exist – as a political entity and, therefore, as a name used by the Vikings residing in Ireland – because it had been included within the larger realm that became 'Norway' in English.

The element *-lann* in *Lochlann* has the expected vowel for a potential origin from Germanic *-land*, whereas the equivalent element in *Laithlind/Laithlinn/Lothlind* possesses an unexpected vowel for that same origin, and Etchingham, therefore, finds it unlikely that *-lind* derives from *-land*.[33] A possible explanation for the fronted vowel /i/ is that the Irish would have often been exposed to the Scandinavian ending *-lendingr*, the mutated form designating a person from a particular area, as in ON *Íslendingr*, 'person from Iceland', or *Hallendingr*, 'person from Halland', and also the derived adjective, *íslenzkr*, etc. Even though the inhabitant variation or the adjective is not found in any documented Irish form,[34] it may be assumed that frequently used *-lendingr* and *-lenzkr* would have helped to weaken the impression of the back phoneme /a/ in *-land*, paving the way for a fronted vowel in the Irish records.

The transition *-land* to *-lind* or *-linn*, 'pool, lake, sea, ocean' or 'drink, liquid, brew, ale, beer, intoxicating drink', need not merely be morphophonologically driven but may also be semantically motivated.[35]

---

32   Ibid., 36.
33   Etchingham 2010, 83.
34   We do not often see the inhabitant form of names in annalistic or legal documents. A survey of eighty-one medieval documents concerning Iceland in *Diplomatarium Norvegicum* did not produce a single find of the inhabitant form *íslendingr*, and only one of *íslenzkr*. This is in contrast to the relatively frequent use of these forms in the epic Icelandic sagas.
35   Both meanings are used, for example, in the glosses of Priscian's *Institutiones Grammaticae* (*eDIL*, s.v.1 *linn* and s.v.2 *linn*).

David Greene's claim that *Lothlann* may have carried the meaning of 'pool of mud' is interesting, although not quite for the reason he imagined (i.e. as a purely Irish composite creation).[36] What instead warrants interest is that Green's suggested semantic meaning could have added an associative aspect to the name *Laithlind*. When the Vikings started overwintering in Ireland, they established a type of camp the Irish often refer to as *longphort*, 'ship-place', which would typically be located some distance up a navigable river at a confluence, allowing two sides of the camp to be protected by water.[37] This is archaeologically documented as the origin of Dublin, Old Irish *Duiblinn*, 'dark pool', and other *longphuirt* (pl.) are similarly situated.[38] In addition to *Duiblinn*, *linn* is frequently used in connection with Viking bases, including *Linn Duachaill* in Annagassan, where a *longphort* has been archaeologically identified on the confluence of two rivers:[39]

> **AU 842.8:** Longas Nordmannorum for Boinn, for Linn Roiss. Longas Nordmannorum oc Linn Sailech la Ultu.

> [A naval force of the Norsemen was on the Bóinn at Linn Rois. There was also a naval force of the Norsemen at Linn Sailech in Ulaid.]

> **AU 842.9**: Moran m. Indrechtaigh, abbas Clochar M. nDaimeni, du ergabail do Gallaibh Linne, & a éc leo iarum.

> [Mórán, son of Indrehtach, abbot of Clochar Mac nDaiméni, was taken prisoner by the foreigners of Linn and he later died on their hands.][40]

> **AU 842.10:** Comman, abbas Linne Duachail, do guin & loscadh o genntibh & Goidhelaibh.

> [Comán, abbot of Linn Duachaill, was fatally wounded and burned by heathens and Irish.]

---

36 Greene 1976, 77.
37 Griffiths 2010, 31.
38 Simpson 2010.
39 Wallace 2008.
40 The 'Gallaibh Lindae' is again referred to in *AU* 852.2.

The use of *Laithlind* in the Irish sources does not provide us with the impression that the name is an original Irish compound, but rather that it is an Irish phonological and possibly semantic adaptation of a name that was originally introduced by the Vikings themselves. The use of the name is related to a royal title, which on one occasion survives directly from Scandinavian in the form of *Amhlaoibh Conung* (ON *Óláfr konung*).[41] It is unlikely that the Vikings would have adopted an Irish place name and given their chieftain a royal title based on the Irish name. The impression is given that the royal title is – quite unsurprisingly – linked to their place of provenance, which we hear they are traveling to and from and in which they have affairs to tend to. Even Colmán Etchingham admits the possibility for the name *Laithlind* to be Scandinavian, and, by extension, its potential to hold valuable information:

> Could it be that the contemporary Irish annals afford a glimpse of ninth-century Scandinavian history that is more reliable than the Icelandic sagas, albeit one that is fleeting, tantalizing and capable only of tentative interpretation?[42]

The historian Mary Valante argues that *Laithlind* must be localised to a still Danish-controlled Vestfold by the Oslofjord, principally based on rich finds of Insular material at the trading centre Kaupang.[43] The archaeologist David Griffiths opposes this view by noting:

> In the opinion of this author and numerous others, the most likely location is the south-west coast of Norway, around the powerful Iron Age chiefdom centres of Avaldsnes on Karmøy, and Jaeren south of modern Stavanger – the area with Norway's densest concentration of insular material from ninth- and tenth-century graves.[44]

The following supports Griffith's preferred location for *Laithlind*. Griffith does not discuss the matter any further, and his archaeological

41   *FA* § 239.
42   Etchingham 2010, 84.
43   Valante 2008, 68-69.
44   Griffiths 2010, 36-37.

assertion will need to be reinforced with evidence. A subsequent proposal for the interpretation of the name *Laithlind* will be put forward, linking the name to the south-west coast of Norway.

THE ARCHAEOLOGY

Archaeological evidence suggests that the south-west of Norway is an exceptionally relevant area in this context, exhibiting a remarkably consistent concentration of finds. By far the greatest amount of imported Roman artefacts in Norway is found here. At Avaldsnes on the island Karmøy, a chieftain with a massive golden neck ring and silver shield boss was found to have been buried in the mound Flagghaugen in the third century. A recent investigation has unearthed a continuous set of buildings at Avaldsnes for AD 200-500, all of which exhibit an aristocratic character and are likely to have economic roots beyond mere local resources.[45] Although no buildings are manifest to prove a continued aristocratic presence after 500, the burial mounds confirm this nonetheless. Between the Oslofjord and Trøndelag, there is only one large burial mound from the eighth century: Storhaug, 'Large Mound', at Avaldsnes. The elites buried in this mound and in Grønhaug, another mound containing a ship from the second half of the eighth century, were furnished with grave goods featuring evidence of cultural contacts with the Frankish realm.[46]

On the other, southern side of the wide Boknafjord, near the farms close to today's Stavanger, major buildings dating to AD 500-800 have been identified.[47] Here, at Gausel, a female burial from the first half of the ninth century has been found, characterised by Egil Bakka as the richest and most high-ranking female grave in Norway after Oseberg.[48] The burial included high-quality domestically produced artefacts, as well as Irish or Scottish objects such as metal finials from a sarcophagus, possibly associated with Iona.[49] In the area surrounding Stavanger, there are more finds of Insular metalwork than anywhere else on the Continent (Figure 2), and there are forty-three of such ninth-century finds in wider Rogaland overall.[50]

---

45   Skre 2012.
46   Opedal 1998; 2005.
47   Børsheim and Soltvedt 2002.
48   Bakka 1993.
49   Kruse 2013.
50   Børsheim 1997.

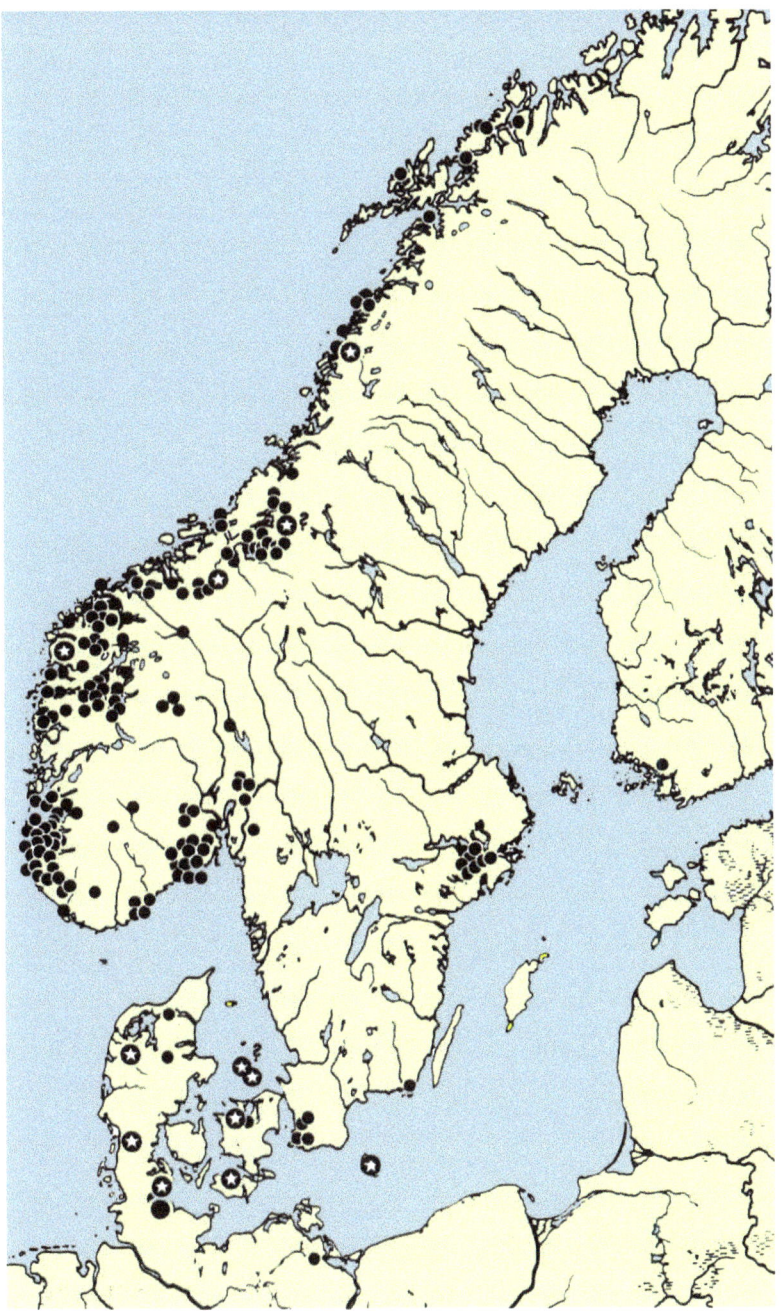

Figure 2: The distribution of Viking Age Insular artefacts in Scandinavia. After Wamers 1997, with permission.

Heading north along the coast to the region of Hordaland, however, surprisingly few Insular objects are evident in Viking Age graves from the ninth century compared to more northern and southern areas (see Figure 2).[51] How, then, does this correspond to the historical record, in which people from this area feature among the first identified Vikings?[52] Modern archaeologists have interpreted this pattern of distribution as a likely indicator of a concentration of power and increased social stratification, in which local farmers have lost their independence.[53] This may also account for the dramatic drop in Insular grave goods in the second half of the ninth century in Jæren, the fertile area south of Stavanger, the very same district where the intensity of Insular objects was highest a generation before.[54] By the end of the ninth century, a centralised power structure seem to have arrived in the south of Rogaland as well.[55]

This shift is concurrent to what Ann Zanette Tsigaridas Glørstad has observed concerning Celtic and Celtic-inspired penannular brooches in Norwegian graves.[56] Before c. 850, this type of brooch was nearly always evident alongside other Insular artefacts in female graves. Subsequently, however, these are mainly found in prestigious male graves, concentrated around south-west Norway and Vestfold. The early brooches used by men were locally-produced copies or derivatives of Irish originals, made of iron or bronze and glazed with silver or pewter. Glørstad interprets this change as the arrival of a new type of power structure, whose background is an ideological influence from Ireland, where such brooches were used to express hierarchy and to reinforce political alliances. She also defines the homemade brooches worn by

51 See also the table in Iversen 2007, 157.
52 Around AD 900, a number of manuscripts of the *Anglo-saxon Chronicle* were supplemented with local traditions from Northumbria. One such addition is for the year 787 [=789], when 'þréo scipu Norðmanna of Hæreðalande' are noted to have arrived at Portland in Dorset (*English Historical Documents*, 180.). This late addition only demonstrates that *Horðaland* was known in the north of England towards the end of the ninth century. See also Woolf 2007, 64, 100.
53 Skre 1998, 247ff.; Iversen 1999; 2004.
54 Although Sola and Madla, just south of Stavanger, have divulged twenty-two Insular grave objects from the ninth century, only two appear after AD 900. See Myhre 1980, Solberg 2003, 286-87.
55 I have argued elsewhere (Kruse 2015, 73-74) that the skaldic poem *Haraldskvæði* – the closest that one gets to a contemporary Old Norse source – alludes to Jæren being under the control of Haraldr hárfagri <u>before</u> the battle of Hafrsfjǫrðr, Jæren.
56 Glørstad 2010; 2012.

Figure 3: Penannular brooch from a single find near Avaldsnes, Karmøy. Made of bronze, it is likely to have been produced in Norway, and closely mirrors Irish and Scottish silver thistle brooches. According to Glørstad 2010, 255-56, the brooch is of a type associated with high-status male burials from c. 850 to 950, with a large concentration in Rogaland and Vestfold. Image from the Museum of Archaeology, University of Stavanger (S331a), with permission.

men as symbols of authority, linked to the instigation of a central power structure in Norway.[57]

Ships were found in both the Storhaug and Grønhaug mounds at Avaldsnes, estimated to be 22-24 m and c. 15 m long, respectively. Dendrochronology has dated the ships to c. 770 and c. 780, whilst the Storhaug ship seems to have been entombed in 779.[58] Because of their relatively weak keel structures, it has been assumed that the ships were propelled by oar rather than sail, although no doubt exists that ships of this size were able to cross open seas. The first large dedicated sailing ship discovered in Scandinavia is the famous Oseberg

---

57   Glørstad 2010, 254-79.
58   Bonde and Stylegar 2009.

ship, buried in 834 in Vestfold. The dendrochronological investigation of the ship concluded that it was built in 820. Surprisingly, it was not manufactured in the local Oslofjord region but rather in the south-west of Norway.[59] This provides the region with a unique continuity of large, seagoing ships at the very beginning of the Viking Age. Moreover, the provenance of the Oseberg ship is interesting, as Vestfold and the south-west of Norway both stand out as centres of power, which Glørstad has also pointed to.[60]

AVALDSNES AS A CENTRE

The island name Karmøya (ON *Kǫrmt*, genitive *Karmtar*), a dental derivation related to the Old Norse noun *karmr* (m.), 'chest protection', carries the meaning 'that which protects (from the ocean)'.[61] Avaldsnes is located on Karmøya at the narrowest passage of the sound separating the island from the mainland, and it is difficult to overestimate the importance of this position, which is the starting point of the *Leið*, the all-important sailing course northwards along the coast of Norway. There can hardly be any doubt that this setting represents the economic foundation for Avaldsnes, centre of the most powerful pre-unification kingdom on the west coast of Norway.[62]

Around the southern tip of Norway, between Lista and Stavanger, no islands exist to provide shelter for ships. This is a common coastal stretch, similar to those found across Europe (e.g. along the Atlantic coast of France or the North Sea coast of England). Northwards from Karmøya, however, the *Leið* embarks on its long way along the Norwegian coast. The *Leið*, in Modern Norwegian *Leia,* names the sailing course, the aquatic highway northwards from Avaldsnes. At this point, it is possible to venture inshore along a series of islands protecting travellers from the predominant westerly weather. A transport network along the *Leið* north to Trøndelag and the north of Norway would have certainly existed as early as the Migration Period.[63] Bjørn Myhre has linked the emerging west Norwegian elite to a control over the northward

---

59   Ibid.
60   Vestfold was probably under Danish authority well into the ninth century, although Glørstad 2012 and Bonde and Stylegar 2009 have argued its transfer into the jurisdiction of Avaldsnes during this period.
61   Rygh et al. 1897-1936, vol. x, 378.
62   Skre 2014.
63   Solberg 2003, 108ff.

AUGVALDSNÆS KIRKE OG RUINER.

Figure 4: 'Augvaldsnæs [Avaldsnes] Church and Ruins', illustration from Wergmann 1833-1836. National Library of Norway (public domain). The church, now restored, was constructed by King Hákon Hákonarson around 1250, on the site of an older wooden church, assumed to have been built by King Oláf Tryggvason.

transport of goods along the *Leið*, as well as from the inner parts of the country out to the coast.[64] To govern the entrance to this protected sea-course meant to take charge of northern commodity flows along the coast of Norway, as well as goods coming from the north and west of Norway (e.g. fur, hide, and soap stone). In addition, Avaldsnes was also situated on a junction of communication lines between the interior of south-western Norway and the coast, granting it access to trade and the transport of iron, antlers, hides, etc.

Its position at a crossroads of crucial communication lines is an explanation for the remarkable continuity in Avaldsnes' history as a

---

64   Myhre 1993, 56-58.

Figure 5: After Opedal 1998, 138, illustrating what Opedal interprets as manor farms under Avaldsnes in the eighth century. See also Opedal 2005, 130-34; 2010. For an analysis of Avaldsnes as a central place, see Reiersen 2009. Map data © Norwegian Mapping Authority/Kartverket.

central place of power. After the battle of Hafrsfjord, Harald Fairhair decided to make this his main seat of residence and, according to tradition, this is where he chose to be interred. Avaldsnes remained a major residence for Norwegian royalty for 500 years. To the early Norwegian royals, control of western Norway, knitted together by communication lines which started and ended at Avaldsnes, was a first priority.

The extent of the chiefdom around Avaldsnes at Harald's time is indicated in Snorri's *Heimskringla* (see Figure 6).[65] Knut Helle regards this list among the most reliable parts of an otherwise untrustworthy prose tradition after Harald:

> En er Haraldr konungr tók að eldast þá settist hann oftlega að stórbúum er hann átti á Hörðalandi, á Alreksstöðum eða Sæheimi eða Fitjum, og á Rogalandi, að Útsteini og á Ögvaldsnesi í Körmt.[66]

> [And when King Harald started to grow old he often stayed at the large farms he owned in Hordaland at Alreksstad or Seim or Fitjar, and in Rogaland at Utstein and at Avaldsnes in Karmøya.][67]

These farms are, apart from Utstein to the south, located along the *Leið*, as if to underline the importance of this communication line to the kingdom. The farms Etne and Halsnøy are also likely to have been central places, strategically located along the *Leið* and rich in gravemounds. Arnfrid Opedal points to several other similarly-positioned farms, rich in finds from the eighth century (see Figure 5).[68] Common features of these strategically located farms are artefacts of Frankish origin, as well as the occurrence of large boathouses. No such farms are located north of Sunnhordland and south of the Boknafjord.

Frode Iversen, having investigated Seim, Alrekstad and Fitjar, concludes that the medieval farms are unusually large.[69] He identifies them as part of a network demarking an ambulant Iron Age kingdom, whose king controlled the coastal landscape by frequently changing residence between farms.

---

65   *Heimskringla*, ch. 39.
66   Helle 1993, 149f.
67   My translation, with modern place names.
68   Opedal 1998, 109-40; 2005, fig. 11.
69   Iversen 2004; 2007.

Figure 6: Harald's farms according to *Heimskringla*. The *Leið* is highlighted. Map data © Norwegian Mapping Authority/Kartverket.

Avaldsnes will have been severely affected by Frankish developments in the second half of the eighth century. Because of northward Carolingian aggression into Saxony and Frisia, the normal routes of contact and trade across the North Sea region would have been seriously disrupted. This would have undermined an economic fundament for Avaldsnes – the control of the transport along the *Leið* – as the customary and amicable supply of goods, ordinarily distributed along the lines of aristocratic power, is very likely to have dried up. Consequently, this provided the rulers of a powerful kingdom in the west of Scandinavia with an excellent incentive to explore alternative supply routes. There is hardly any better candidate than the kingdom encompassing Avaldsnes as a likely starting point for the Viking *adventus*.

THE NAMING MOTIVE

We do not know the name of this Iron Age, pre-unification kingdom, which is likely to have been unrivalled in size and organisation across the west of Norway. Its name does not appear in any runic inscription, skaldic poem, or saga, and neither are its vestiges evident in any modern place name. The extent of the kingdom, as suggested by Iversen[70] and Opedal,[71] comprises present-day northern *Rogaland* and southern *Hordaland*, i.e. parts of old landscape names denoting the extent of the *rygir* and *hǫrðar* people.[72] Rather than being based on tribal units, however, it seems that the kingdom around Avaldsnes was politically organised around an ambulant chieftain.[73]

Although the name *Laithlind* cannot be attached to the south-western Norwegian kingdom through the use of documentary evidence, a good reason for this parity nevertheless exists. I will argue that the name *Laithlind* corresponds to a Common Scandinavian **Laiþland* and a later Old Norse **Leiðland*, and that the name refers to the *Leið*, the protected northward coastal route that starts at Avaldsnes.

From the earlier discussion around the Irish form *Laithlind* it is reasonable to claim that we are dealing with a compound name with two elements, the first of which, the specific *Laith-*, would have been

---

70   Iversen 2004.
71   Opedal 2005.
72   Mentioned as 'Rugi' and 'Arochi' by sixth-century author Jordanes (*Iordanis Romana et Getica*, 60), and the latter is possibly the 'Harudes' noted by Julius Caesar in 52 BC (*Bellum Gallicum*, 35).
73   Iversen 2007.

Leið- in Old Norse. This 'classic' ON form will – with an expected voicing of the dental fricative and a raised diphthong – have developed from Common Scandinavian *Laiþ-*.[74] This represents the language stage spoken by the Vikings who arrived in Ireland at the beginning of the ninth century. The Irish written form of the Scandinavian dental fricative is as expected[75] and, as argued earlier, the diphthong /ai/ is recorded with the digraph <ai>, a usual practice for Irish scribes, as in *Amlaib* (Proto-Scandinavian **AnulaißaR*, Old Norse *Áleifr*, later *Óláfr*). This corresponds to the representation of the diphthong in near-contemporary West Norwegian runic inscriptions, for example, **stAin** ('stone') in the well-known inscription on the stone from Eggja, Sogndal.[76]

An interesting legal and administrative use of the noun *leið* is the Icelandic 'local assembly in the summer or in the autumn a few weeks after the end of the Althing, for the announcement of its decisions and judgement'.[77] In Iceland, the term is found in names like Leiðöllur in Skaftafellssýsla and Leiðarhólmur in Dalasýsla.[78]

A legal-administrative meaning of *leið* is certainly relevant when discussing the possible name of a kingdom, and it may well be that this connotation of the word could have played an associative role in a name like **Leiðland*. Our focus, however, will be on the principal meanings of Old Norse *leið* (f.), which are

- 'that which leads, a lode',
- 'way, road',
- 'the course on the sea'[79]

This focus is justified by the geographical and historic importance that the *Leið* has had for Avaldsnes as a centre of power.

---

74 According to Einar Haugen, the term 'Proto-Scandinavian' refers to the period up to AD 550, 'Common Scandinavian' to AD 550-1050, followed by 'Old West Scandinavian' (= Old Norse) and 'Old East Scandinavian'. See Haugen 1976, 89-93.
75 Ó Corráin 1998, § 13.
76 *Norges indskrifter med de ældre runer*, NiæR 55. This inscription represents a transitional phase between Proto-Scandinavian and Common Scandinavian. Among the runes in the Older Futhark there are novelties like the oral **A**-rune which is used alongside the old **a**-rune, now representing /ã/.
77 Lárusson 1963, 341. My translation.
78 Cleasby, Vigfusson, and Craigie 1957, 380.
79 Ibid.

The Germanic **laiðō-* produced the cognate Old English *lād*, Middle Low German *leide*, Old Norse *leið,* Old Swedish *lēþ* and Old Danish *lēth*, all with the main meaning 'road' or 'journey', developed from the Germanic strong verb *léiþan-*, 'go'.[80] In Middle English, *lode* means 'water-course', cognate in Old Scots with *lade*, 'mill-race'.[81] In Old Norse, *leið* forms compounds with *-ar-*; *leiðarsteinn*, 'lodestone, magnet', *leiðarstjarna*, 'lodestar', *leiðarsund*, 'sound where one's vessel is taken through'; or without a genitive morph; *leiðvísi* (f.), 'knowing the right course', *leiðsagari* (m.), 'guide, pilot', *leiðsagnarmaðr* (m.), 'pilot'.[82]

In Flateyjarbók, a difference exists between *innleið* and *útleið*, a distinction which is still made along the Norwegian coast when there is a choice between an inner and outer route along the course.[83] The latter is also referred to as the *djúpleið*, 'the deep course', which can be quicker, broader, and deeper, but also more exposed and dangerous than the inner route.

Parts of the main course are named with *-lei(d)* used as a generic, like *Kobbaleida* (first element ON *kobbi* (m.), 'seal'), the sound between Sotra and Tyssøy in Hordaland. In Modern Norwegian, *Leia* (f. def. sing.) can be used in local contexts as a name for a sailing course between islands and skerries leading to a settlement or harbour.[84] Outside of local usage, however, and all along the west coast, the simplex definite form *Leia* will consistently refer to the important main sailing course. Many compound names exist with *Lei-* as a specific, such as *Leiskjeret*, *Leiholmen*, *Leiøya*, and *Leisundet*,[85] all of which indicate a relationship to the main course or a local sailing route.

The name *Leidland* is found as a farm name on one occasion, on Eigerøya, some 60 km south-east of Stavanger. According to Oluf Rygh, the farm name has an origin in Old Norse *leirr* (m.), 'clay', which is likely, considering the exceptional amounts and quality of clay this location has provided for the production of porcelain.[86] This particular

---

80   Nielsen, 1989, 257; Bjorvand and Lindeman 2007, 640.
81   *Dictionary of the Scots Language.*
82   Fritzner 1867. My translation.
83   *Flateyjarbók* ii, 308.
84   The usual pronounciation of the indef. form of the appellative is /lei/. In some dialects in the north-west of Vestlandet, the dental stop /d/ reflects the older dental fricative /ð/, such as in the name *Leiaflua*, /leidaflu'da/. Slyngstad 1951, 33.
85   Referring, respectively, to a skerry, islet, island, and a sound.
86   Rygh et al. 1897-1936, vol. x, 80.

farm name is one of many holding the generic *-land*, which shows a remarkably dense concentration to the south-west of Norway. Out of the approximate 2,000 names of habitation with *-land* in Norway, 80% are found between Telemark and Hordaland. In certain settlements in this area, the majority of the old farm names carry the generic *-land*. The element seems to have been employed during two periods of agrarian expansion – c. AD 200-500 and c. AD 650-1000. As a habitational generic, it is productive during the Viking expansion, with c. 80 such names in Iceland, c. 75 in Shetland, and c. 35 in Orkney, as well as more sparsely on the mainland of Scotland, the north-west of England, and the Isle of Man. In Norway, the lack of specifics indicative of Christian culture is seen as proof of the habitative generic *-land* going out of fashion around the year 1000.[87]

In the late-ninth-century accounts of both Ohthere and Wulfstan, we can observe that *land* is both used as an appellative and as a generic in compound names. On his journey from Hedeby to Truso, Wulfstan uses *land* to indicate a territory ruled over by a king:

> Þonne æfter Burgendalande wæron us þas land, þa synd hatene ærest Blecingaeg, and Meore, and Eowland, and Gotland on bæcbord; and þas land hyrað to Sweon.

> [Then after Bornholm we had on our port side the lands which are called Blekinge, Möre, Öland and Gotland, and these lands belong to the Swedes.][88]

We note that Bornholm is thus mentioned, and that Wulfstan claims that the *svear* as a people will have had some sort of superiority over the 'lands' of Blekinge, Möre, Öland, and Gotland.

A similar frequency in the use of *-land* for large areas, either geographically defined or settled by a people or a kingdom, is also evident in Old Norse tradition.[89] A suitable example is Níkulás Bergsson's lesson in geography for the benefit of pilgrims, *Leiðarvísir og borgarskipan*, produced around 1157.[90] Here, the generic *-land* is

---

87 Sandnes and Stemshaug 1997; Særheim 2001.
88 From *Two Voyagers at the Court of King Alfred*. See also Bately and Englert 2007.
89 See also Brink 2008.
90 *Leiðarvísir og borgarskipan*, 395-415.

almost systematically used to indicate a kingdom or land area, e.g. '[...] Jórsalaland, er þeir kalla Sýrland'.[91] Closer to home, Níkulás lists areas surrounding Norway:

> Gautland er fyrir austan Gautelfi, en þar næst Svíþjóð, þá næst Helsíngaland, þá Finnland; þá er talið til móts við Garðaríki, sem fyrr er (sagt). En öðrumegin hjá Gautlandi er Danmerk.
>
> Næst Danmerk er Svíþjóð en minne, þar er Eyland; þá er Gotland; þá Helsíngaland; þá Vermaland; þá Kvenlönd ij, ok eru þau norðr frá Bjarmalandi. Af Bjarmalandi gánga lönd óbygð of norðr ætt, unz við tekr Grænland.[92]
>
> [Götaland is to the east of Götaälv, and next to that is Svíþjóð (the land of the Svear), next is Hälsingland, then Finland; this, it is said, meets the realm of Garðaríki (the Kievan Rus) as said before. And on the other side of Götaland is Denmark.
>
> Next to Denmark is lesser Svíþjóð (Småland?), there is Öland; then Gotland; then Hälsingland, then Värmland, then two Kvenlands, and they are to the north of Bjarmaland. North from Bjarmaland the land stretches unsettled by Norse people until it meets Greenland.][93]

The generic *-land* is the most productive element for large land areas in both the old and the modern Scandinavian languages.[94] Compounds with peoples or tribes serve as one of its principal group, as seen in Níkulás Bergsson's lists: *Götaland, Hälsingland, Gotland, Värmland, Finland, Kvenland,* and *Bjarmaland.* Current Norwegian area names are *Hordaland, Rogaland, Hadeland,* and *Hålogaland.* The productivity of this type of name-creation during the Viking Age is witnessed by names like *Skotland, Íraland,* and *Péttland.* During the Viking Age, however, *-land* is also used in area names with elements other than the names of peoples and tribes. In reference to the Abbasid Caliphate, *Serkland* indicates how its people are dressed, whilst *Blámannaland,* the Old

---

91   Ibid., 414.
92   Ibid., 405.
93   My translation, with modern names.
94   Særheim 2001, 26.

Norse name for Africa, refers to the skin colour of its inhabitants.[95] Moreover, we find *-land* as part of geographically descriptive area names, such as *Uppland* and *Småland* in Sweden. This usage is also common during the Viking Age; from *Ísland* and the newly discovered *Grœnland*, the Scandinavians travelled to *Markland, Helluland*, and *Vínland*.[96]

When referring to its inhabitants, the meaning of *-land* is clearly 'nation, kingdom', although it may also have developed as a secondary meaning in names like *Uppland* and *Småland*. In the names of some large islands, like *Gotland, Lolland*, and *Sjælland*, it is uncertain if *-land* was originally employed to designate 'island' or 'land area'.[97]

As an appellative, *land* carries the general meaning 'land, surface not covered by water'. This meaning is evident in the English noun *island*, from Indo-European **akwa-*, 'water', and Germanic **aujo*, 'something on the water' + *land*. This is probably the origin of the name of the large Swedish island Öland. Other Swedish names like *Svartsjölandet* and *Mörttjärnlandet* similarly employ *-land* in its definition 'land as opposed to water, beach area'.[98] In Norway, *-land* has sometimes been added to old island names, like *Hareidlandet* and *Gomalandet,* whilst it is also frequently used in coastal names signifying '(main)land (as opposed to water)'.[99] The latter usage is still alive as an appellative. Personally, I know this usage from Nordmøre in Norway, where fishermen mark fishing grounds by orienting themselves with landmarks 'oppi landet' [up on the land], or in this case 'oppi smølalandet' [up on the land of the island Smøla]. It is a usual naming pattern all over Norway to name a stretch of land along a section of the coast, a fjord, a lake, or a river, with the generic *-land*, for example *Monsåslandet* (Romsdal) and *Tysselandet* (Sogn), where the named stretch of land is limited to a headland or a settlement. However, in the examples *Strandalandet, Haugalandet*, and *Lyselandet*, all from Rogaland, the generic *-land* denotes a larger area along the sea, including several settlements.[100] A similar practise is documented from the west coast of Sweden, for example *Vettekullalandet* and *Maralandet*, Blekinge.[101] Such usage of *-land* allows an appellative

95   ON *serk* (m.) means 'sark, shirt', and *blá* (adj.) can mean both 'blue' and 'black'.
96   The specifics respectively mean 'ice', 'green', 'forest', 'flat stone', and 'wine'.
97   Sandnes and Stemshaug 1997, 279-82.
98   Wahlberg 2003, 185, 387. My translation.
99   Sandnes and Stemshaug 1997, 279. My translation.
100 Særheim 2001, 31-32.
101 Ohlsson 1939, 165.

leiland(et) to be straightforwardly understood by people along the coast of Scandinavia as 'the land along the *Leið*'.

THE MISSING EVIDENCE

It is evident that *Leiðland* would have been an exceptionally suitable name for a coastal kingdom which was relating to the *Leið* in two ways: the control of the *Leið* as the main route of transport and a network of major farms along the *Leið*. Although the motive for this designation is obvious, there is, of course, a serious flaw in the argument that *Leiðland* would be located in Avaldsnes and south-west Norway; namely, that such a name is not documented in any Scandinavian source. It is, however, reasonable to advance the question whether one should expect a name of this kind to exist in medieval Scandinavian texts or in the form of a modern place-name. Apart from some well-defined geographical names with long histories, such as Sogn, Møre, and some area names based on old tribal names, such as Rogaland and Hordaland, we do not know the names of the small kingdoms which are likely to have existed along the coast of pre-unified Norway.

Around 500, Jordanes, historian of the Goths, listed some of Norway's tribal names, most of which are recognisable in modern area names: *Grannii* (Grenland), *Augandzi* (Agder), *Taetel* (possibly Telemark), *Arochi* (Hordaland), *Rugi* (Rogaland), and *Ranii* (possibly Romsdalen).[102] In his list, he also includes *Eunixi*, which is presently not recognisable and thus serves as a reminder that such names can vanish. This is better documented in countries with longer written histories than Norway, such as the British Isles. The main reason for us to know the names of the kingdoms Dál Riata and Fortriu (in what is today Scotland) is that they were recorded in the unusually early Irish written tradition.[103] Both Dál Riata and Fortriu ceased to exist in the second half of the ninth century, becoming parts of the larger Scotland or Alba. The names of the Celtic and subsequent Anglian kingdoms Bernicia and Deira disappeared as they were united into Northumbria, although both were relatively well-documented in contemporary Welsh and English sources. The documentation for subdivisions of larger kingdoms are much poorer, but they are sometimes mirrored in modern place names. For example,

---

102 Svennung 1967.
103 The inhabitants of *Fortriu* are first mentioned in the fourth century in Latin as *Verturiones* (Woolf 2007, 188).

the *Anglo-Saxon Chronicle* informs us that the kingdom 'Hwicce' was established in 577, after the Battle of Deorham, and became a sub-kingdom of Mercia after the Battle of Cirencester in 628. The name of the kingdom is thought to be reflected in the modern place names Wychwood and Whichford,[104] but the name of the kingdom cannot be deducted from the modern names alone. If the written sources had not emerged from the British Isles as early, we would not have known the names of many of the pre-unification kingdoms of Scotland and England.

The name 'Norway', too, is for a long time only documented in English sources, perhaps already Latinised as *Nortuagia* in the Durham *Liber Vitae* as early as c. 840, and then indisputably recorded by Alfred of Wessex, who quotes *Norðweg* after Ohthere visited his court just before 900.[105] Around 965, the name first occurs in Scandinavian as **nuruiak** on the Danish Jelling Stone. In Norway itself, its initial appearance dates to 1034, when the name **i nuriki** was carved on the Kuli Stone. As such, we may observe that the name existed without any other documentation than an English source for two to three generations.

A scenario is feasible in which the name **Leiðland* disappears as the larger, unified *Norway* is created towards the end of the ninth century, in a fashion similar to what we have seen in the examples from Britain when Dál Riata and Fortriu, as well as Bernicia and Deira, disappeared into Scotland and Northumbria, respectively. Semantically, the name 'Norway' may carry two meanings. Based on the neighbouring English name and German *Norwegen*, it is very likely that the generic is 'way, road, course'. The most common interpretation of the specific is 'north', creating a meaning of 'the way to the north', which could hardly be anything different than the *Leið*, the coastal route northwards, as seen from the south. A second interpretation is based on the adjective *nór*, 'narrow', for which the name then becomes 'the narrow way'. If this is the case, it must likewise denote the *Leið* or the narrow beginning of the *Leið*, i.e. Karmsundet by Avaldsnes. Both **Leiðland* and **Norðveg/*Nórveg* could have existed as compound appellatives long before they became specific names of politically defined areas, expedited by historical developments. Both as an appellative and a name, 'Norway' is a semantic parallel to **Leiðland*, and in both cases based on the economic infrastructure for a political unit: the *Leið*.

---

104   Mills 2011.
105   Johnsen 1968.

BIBLIOGRAPHY

PRIMARY SOURCES

Annals of the Four Masters, Corpus of Electronic Texts, University College Cork, http://www.ucc.ie/celt/published/T100005A/index.html, accessed 3 June 2014.

Annals of Ulster, Corpus of Electronic Texts, University College Cork, http://www.ucc.ie/celt/published/T100001A/index.html, accessed 20 December 2014.

Bellum Gallicum, Klotz A (ed), 1952, vol. i, Leipzig: Teubner.

Diplomatarium Norvegicum, University of Oslo, http://www.dokpro.uio.no/dipl_norv/om_dn.html, accessed October 2016.

English Historical Documents I: c. 500-1042, Whitelock D (ed), 1979, London: Eyre Methuen.

Flateyjarbók: En samling af norske konge-sagaer med indskudte mindre fortællinger om begivenheder i og udenfor norge samt annaler, Vigfusson G and Unger, C R (eds), 1860-68, 3 vols, Christiania: Malling.

Fornmanna sögur, eptir gömlum handritum, Egilsson S (ed), 1826, vol. ii., Copenhagen: Kongelige Nordiske Oldskriftselskab.

Fragmentary Annals of Ireland, Corpus of Electronic Texts, University College Cork, http://www.ucc.ie/celt/online/G100017.html, accessed 3 June 2016.

Heimskringla, Aðalbjarnarson A (ed), 1941, Íslenzk Fornrit XXVI, Reykjavík: Hið Íslenzka Fornritafélag.

Iordanis Romana et Getica, Mommsen T (ed), 1882, MGH AA 5.1, Berlin: Weidmann, 53-138.

Leiðarvísir og borgarskipan, in *Antiquités Russes d'après les Monuments Historiques des Islandais et des Anciens Scandinaves*, Rafn C C (ed), 1852, vol. ii, Copenhagen : Imprimerie des Frères Berling, 395-415.

Norges indskrifter med de ældre runer, Bugge S and Olsen M (eds), 1891-1924, 4 vols, Christiania: A.W. Brøhhers Bogtrykkeri.

Prisciani Grammatica, Stiftsbibliothek St Gallen, Cod. Sang. 904, http://www.e-codices.unifr.ch/en/csg/0904/21, accessed 25 August 2016.

The March Roll of the Men of Leinster, *Ériu* 6, Meyer K (trans), 1912, 121-24.

Two Voyagers at the Court of King Alfred, Lund N (ed) and Fell C E (trans), 1984, York: William Sessions.

SECONDARY SOURCES

Ahlqvist, A 2005, 'Is acher in gaith ... úa Lothlind', in L E Jones and J F Nagy (eds), *Heroic Poets and Poetic Heroes in Celtic Tradition: A Festschrift for Patrick K. Ford*, Dublin: Four Courts, 19-27.

Bakka, E 1993, 'Gauselfunnet og bakgrunnen for det', *Arkeologiske skrifter* 7, 248-304.

Bately, J and A Englert (eds) 2007, *Ohthere's Voyages: A Late 9ᵗʰ-Century Account of Voyages along the Coasts of Norway and Denmark and its Cultural Context*, Roskilde: Viking Ship Museum.

Blair, P H 1939, 'Olaf the White and the Three Fragments of Irish Annals', *Viking: Tidsskrift for norrøn arkeologi* 3, 1-35.

Bjorvand, H and F O Lindeman 2007, *Våre arveord: Etymologisk ordbok*, Oslo: Novus.

Bonde, N and F A Stylegar 2009, 'Fra Avaldsnes til Oseberg: Dendrokronologiske undersøkelser av skipsgravene fra Storhaug og Grønhaug', *Viking: Tidsskrift for norrøn arkeologi* 72, 149-68.

Brink, S 2008, 'People and *Land* in Early Scandinavia', in I H Garipzanov, P Geary, and P Urbańczyk (eds), *Franks, Northmen, and Slavs: Identities and State Formation in Early Medieval Europe*, Turnhout: Brepols, 87-112.

Bugge, A 1900, *Contributions to the History of the Norsemen in Ireland*, Christiania: Dybwad.

Børsheim, R L 1997, 'Nye undersøkelser av Gauseldronningens grav', *Frá haug ok heiðni* 4, 3-9.

Børsheim, R L and E-C Soltvedt 2002, *Gausel: Utgravingene 1997-2000*, Stavanger: Arkeologisk Museum.

Cleasby, R, G Vigfusson, and W Craigie 1957, *Icelandic-English Dictionary*, Oxford: Clarendon Press.

Downham, C 2015, 'The Break-Up of Dál Riata and the Rise of Gallgoídil', in H B Clarke and R Johnson (eds), *The Vikings in Ireland and Beyond: Before and after the Battle of Clontarf*, Dublin: Four Courts, 189-205.

DSL - Dictionary of the Scots Language, University of Glasgow, http://www.dsl.ac.uk, accessed 2 November 2016.

eDIL - Electronic Dictionary of the Irish Language, Royal Irish Academy, http://www.dil.ie, accessed 2 June 2016.

Etchingham, C 2007, 'The Location of Historical *Laithlinn/Lochla(i)nn*: Scotland or Scandinavia?', in Mícheál Ó Flaithearta (ed), *Proceedings of the Seventh Symposium of Societas Celtologica Nordica*, Uppsala: Uppsala Universitet, 11-31.

Etchingham, C 2010, '*Laithlinn*, "Fair Foreigners" and "Dark Foreigners": The Identity and Provenance of Vikings in Ninth-Century Ireland', in J Sheehan and D Ó Corráin (eds), *The Viking Age: Ireland and the West – Proceedings of the Fifteenth Viking Congress, Cork, 2005*, Dublin: Four Courts, 80-88.

Etchingham, C 2014, 'Names for the Vikings in Irish Annals', in J V Sigurðsson and T Bolton (eds), *Norse Relationships in the Irish Sea in the Middle Ages 800-1200*. Leiden: BRILL, 23-38.

Fritzner, J 1867, *Ordbog over det gamle norske Sprog*, Christiania: Feilberg & Landmarks Forlag.

Glørstad, A Z T 2010, 'Ringspennen og kappen: kulturelle møter, politiske symboler og sentraliseringsprosesser i Norge ca. 800-950', PhD thesis, University of Oslo.

Glørstad, A Z T 2012, 'Sign of the Times? The Transfer and Transformation of Penannular Brooches in Viking-Age Norway', *Norwegian Archaeological Review* 45:1, 30-51.

Graham-Campbell, J and C E Batey 1998, *Vikings in Scotland: An Archaeological Survey*, Edinburgh: Edinburgh University Press.

Greene, D 1976, 'The Influence of Scandinavian on Irish' in B Almqvist and D Greene (eds), *Proceedings of the Seventh Viking Congress*, Dundalk: Dundalgan Press, 75-82.

Greene, D 1978, 'The Evidence of Language and Place-Names in Ireland', in T Andersson and K Sandred, *The Vikings: Proceedings of the Symposium of the Faculty of Arts of Uppsala University, June 6-9, 1977*, Stockholm: Almqvist & Wiksell, 119-23.

Griffiths, D 2010, *Vikings of the Irish Sea: Conflict and Assimilation AD 790-1050*, Stroud: History Press.

Haugen, E 1976, *The Scandinavian Languages: An Introduction to their History*, London: Faber and Faber.

Helle, K 1993, 'Rikssamlingen etter Harald Hårfagre', in M S Vea (ed), *Rikssamlingen og Harald Hårfagre,* Kopervik: Karmøy, 147-61.

Iversen, F 1999, *Var middelalderens lendmannsgårder kjerner i eldre godssamlinger: En analyse av romlig organisering av graver og eiendomsstruktur i Hordaland og Sogn og Fjordane,* Bergen: Universitetet i Bergen.

Iversen, F 2004, 'Eiendom, makt og statsdannelse: Kongsgårder og gods i Hordaland i yngre jernalder og middelalder', unpublished Dr.Art. thesis, University of Bergen.

Iversen, F 2007, 'Könige an der Küste und Bauern im Binnenland: Regionale Unterschiede in Westnorwegen in der Jüngeren Eisenzeit (800-1050 n. Chr.)', in T Iversen, J R Myking, and G Thoma (eds), *Bauern zwischen Herrschaft und Genossenschaft – Peasant relations to Lords and Government: Scandinavia and the Alpine Region 1000-1750*. Trondheim: Tapir, 149-65.

Jennings, A and A Kruse 2009, 'From Dál Riata to the *Gall-Ghàidheil*', *Viking and Medieval Scandinavia* 5, 123-49.

Johnsen, A O 1968, 'Er Nortuagia den eldste fremmede navneform for Norge?', *Historisk tidsskrift* 47, 219-21.

Kruse, A 2013, 'Columba and Jonah – A Motif in the Dispersed Art of Iona', *Northern Studies* 45, 1-26.

Kruse, A 2015, 'Laithlind', *Namn og Nemne* 32:3, 49-86.

Lárusson, M M 1963, 'Leið', in A Karker et al. (eds), *Kulturhistorisk leksikon for nordisk middelalder*, vol. 8, Copenhagen: Rosenkilde og Bagger.

MacInnes, J 2006, *Dùthchas nan Gàidheal: Selected Essays of John MacInnes*, Edinburgh: Birlinn.

Marstrander, C J S 1911, 'Lochlainn', *Ériu* 5, 250-51.

Marstrander, C J S 1915, *Bidrag til det norske sprogs historie i Irland*, Christiania: Dybwad.

Mills, A D 2011, *A Dictionary of British Place Names*, Oxford: Oxford University Press.

Myhre, B 1980, 'Sola og Madla i førhistorisk tid', in S I Langhelle (ed), *Soga om Sola og Madla*, Sola: Sola Kommune.

Myhre, B 1993, 'Rogaland forut for Hafrsfjord-slaget', in M S Vea (ed), *Rikssamlingen og Harald Hårfagre*, Kopervik: Karmøy, 41-64.

Nielsen, N Å 1989, *Dansk etymologisk ordbog*, Copenhagen: Gyldendal.

Ní Mhaonaigh, M 2006, 'Literary Lochlann' in W McLeod, J E Fraser, and A Gunderloch (eds), *Cànan & Cultar (Language and Culture): Rannsachadh na Gàidhlig 3*, Edinburgh: Dunedin, 25-37.

Ó Corráin, D 1998, 'The Vikings in Scotland and Ireland in the Ninth Century', *Peritia* 12, 296-339.

Ó Neill, P 2000, 'Irish Observance of the Three Lents and the Date of the St. Gall Priscian (MS 904)', *Ériu* 51, 159-80.

Ohlsson, B 1939, *Blekingekusten mellan Mörrums- och Ronnebyån. Namnhistorisk undersökning,* Uppsala: Lundequistska Bokhandeln.

Opedal, A 1998, *De glemte skipsgravene: Makt og myter på Avaldsnes*. Stavanger: Arkeologisk Museum.

Opedal, A 2005, *Kongens død i et førstatlig rike*, Oslo: Universitetet i Oslo.

Opedal, A 2010, *Kongemakt og kongerike: Gravritualer og Avaldsnes-områdets politiske rolle 600-1000*, Oslo: Universitetet i Oslo.

Reiersen, H 2009, 'The Central Place of the Avaldsens Area, SW Norway: An Analysis of Elites and Central Functions along Karmsund, 200 BC - AD 1000', unpublished MA thesis, University of Bergen.

Rygh, O et al. 1897-1936, *Norske Gaardnavne*, 19 vols, Christiania: Cammermeyer.

Sandnes, J, and O Stemshaug (eds) 1997, *Norsk stadnamnleksikon*, Oslo: Norske Samlaget.

Simpson, L 2010, 'Pre-Viking and Early Viking Age Dublin: Some Research Questions' in S Duffy (ed), *Medieval Dublin X*, 49-92.

Skre, D 1998, *Herredømmet: Bosetning og besittelse på Romerike 200-1350 e.Kr.*, Oslo: Universitetsforlaget.

Skre, D 2012, 'Utgravningene på Avaldsnes avsluttet!', *Frá haug ok heiðni* 4.

Skre, D 2014, 'Norðvegr - Norway: From Sailing Route to Kingdom', *European Review* 22:1, 34-44.

Slyngstad, A 1951, *Skjergardsnamn frå Sunnmøre*, Oslo: Norske Samlaget.

Solberg, B 2003, *Jernalderen i Norge ca. 500 f.Kr.-1030 e.Kr.*, Oslo: Cappelen.

Sommerfelt, A 1950, 'The Norsemen in Present Day Donegal Tradition', *Journal of Celtic Studies* 1:2, 232-38.

Stemshaug, O 2010, '*Lø* – gard, lagerplass og hamn', *Namn och bygd* 98, 101-10.

Svennung, J 1967, *Jordanes und Scandia: Kritisch-Exegetische Studien*, Uppsala: Almqvist & Wiksell.

Særheim, I 2001, *Namn og gard: Studium av busetnadsnamn på –land*, Stavanger: Høgskolen i Stavanger.

Valante, M A 2008, *The Vikings in Ireland: Settlement, Trade and Urbanization*, Dublin: Four Courts.

Vigfusson, G and R Cleasby 1874, *An Icelandic-English Dictionary Based on the MS. Collections of the Late Richard Cleasby*, Oxford: Clarendon Press.

Wahlberg, M (ed) 2003, *Svenskt ortnamnsleksikon*, Uppsala: Språk- och Folkminnesinstitutet.

Wallace, P 2008, 'Archaeological Evidence for the Different Expressions of Scandinavian Settlement in Ireland, 840-1100', in S Brink (ed), *The Viking World*, London: Routledge, 434-38.

Wamers, E 1997, 'Insulære importfunn i vikingtidens Skandinavia og spekulasjoner om Norges samling,' in J F Krøger (ed), *Rikssamlingen: høvdingmakt og kongemakt.* Stavanger: Dreyer, 8-21.

Wamers, E 1998, 'Insular Finds in Viking Age Scandinavia and the State Formation of Norway', in H B Clarke, M. Ní Mhaonaigh, and R. Ó Floinn (eds), *Ireland and Scandinavia in the Early Viking Age,* Dublin: Four Courts, 37-72.

Wergmann, P F 1833-1836, *Norsk Prospect-Samling*, Christiania: P F Wergmann.

Woolf, A 2007, *From Pictland to Alba: 789-1070*, Edinburgh: Edinburgh University Press.

Zimmer, H 1891, 'Keltische Beiträge III: Weitere Nordgermanische Einflüsse in der Ältesten Überlieferung der Irischen Heldensage', *Zeitschrift fur Deutches Alterthum und Deutsche Litteratur* 35, 1-176.

HAMMERHEAD CROSSES OF THE VIKING AGE

JAMIE BARNES[1]

INTRODUCTION

This chapter will present a reconsideration of Viking Age hammerhead crosses and suggest a possible interpretation of their role in the landscapes of the British Isles. As such, its aims are threefold: to consider the definition of the hammerhead cross, to provide a corpus of twenty-three such crosses, and to propose a suggested function of the hammerhead cross. In order to achieve this, a case study on the Kilmorie Cross is presented, and an argument made for hammerhead crosses to represent syncretic sculptures, the products of hybrid practice. This is expressed through the idea of common difference, which is primarily explored by an analysis of the cross of Christ and the hammer of Thor. The approach of this chapter is entirely archaeological, largely looking beyond the art historical work already undertaken on many hammerhead crosses.[2] At this juncture, it should be noted that this research is ongoing and therefore subject to change.[3] It is hoped that this will reinvigorate discussions of hammerhead crosses in Viking Age scholarship.

BACKGROUND

In the early twentieth century, William Gershom Collingwood, in his influential *Northumbrian Crosses of the Pre-Norman Age,* christened a certain form of pre-Norman carved stone, found only on the British Isles, as 'hammer-head'.[4] The hammerhead nomenclature seemingly relates explicitly to the form of the cross-head, although this is ultimately ill-defined and as such its use has become problematic.

---

1   The author wishes to acknowledge the generous financial assistance from The Catherine Mackichan Trust in support of certain fieldwork components of this research and to thank Dr Colleen Batey for her guidance. The author is grateful to Caroline Paterson, Linda Hodgson, and Adam Parsons for their open discussions on the Workington carved stones, and to Ross Trench-Jellicoe for the numerous helpful discussions on the Kilmorie Cross and the Canticle of Habakkuk. The author also wishes to thank the two reviewers and the editorial team for their helpful comments.
2   See Bailey 1996a for an example of such work.
3   This chapter will be expanded upon in the author's current doctoral research project.
4   Collingwood 1927, 90.

Earlier on, the hammerhead cross form had been encountered by John Stuart, as well as John Romilly Allen and Joseph Anderson,[5] although they did not explicitly consider the hammerhead cross forms, such as those detailed on a drawing of the Kilmorie Cross (Figure 1). In considering this carved stone, Allen and Anderson classified its cross form as ECMS Type No. 101A (Figure 2),[6] which, as a Latin cross form, differs from the 'hammer-head' cross subsequently defined by Collingwood. The latter type is perhaps more closely associated with the Greek cross form (Figure 3), but often features an added lower arm of the same width as its upper counterpart (Figure 4).[7] However, this is not universally the case, and the diversity of these features will be the focus of the following discussion.

Collingwood's classification provides both the inspiration and fundamental starting point for this chapter. He suggested that the 'hammer-head' may have 'evolved out of the coffin type',[8] or what the *Corpus of Anglo-Saxon Stone Sculpture* would refer to as a cross with oblong-block type arms, of AS Type A3 or – more likely – Type A10.[9] This form can be seen on cross-head fragments from Carlisle.[10] The use of 'hammerhead' as a nomenclature, therefore, needs to be reconsidered and redefined.

It was not until the 1980s that this form of Viking Age carved stone was granted further attention by Bailey, as he elaborated on the hammerhead cross in reference to Collingwood's work.[11] This small yet revealing discussion, in which the author presents a fully articulated evolution of the hammerhead form, represents the most significant consideration of hammerhead crosses since Collingwood's work. Despite indicating that his predecessor's suggestions had merit, he highlights that the origin of the hammerhead cross is not clear.[12] It is noticeable that the hammerhead cross form depicted most prominently

---

5   Stuart 1856-1867, vol. 2, 34-35, plate 70; Allen and Anderson 1993 [1903], vol. 2, part III, 482-83, fig. 514.

6   'ECMS Types' refer to those described in *Early Christian Monuments of Scotland* by Allen and Anderson 1993 [1903], vol. 2, part III, 482-83, fig. 514.

7   Bailey 1980, 182-83.

8   Collingwood 1927, 90.

9   The 'AS Type' refers to the types described in the *Corpus of Anglo-Saxon Stone Sculpture* by Cramp 1984, xvi, fig. 2.

10   See Carlisle 2 and 3 in Bailey and Cramp 1988, 85-87.

11   Bailey 1980, 182-3; 1988a, 31.

12   Bailey 1988a, 31.

Figure 1: Nineteenth-century illustration of the Kilmorie Cross (Stuart 1856-1867, Plate 70).

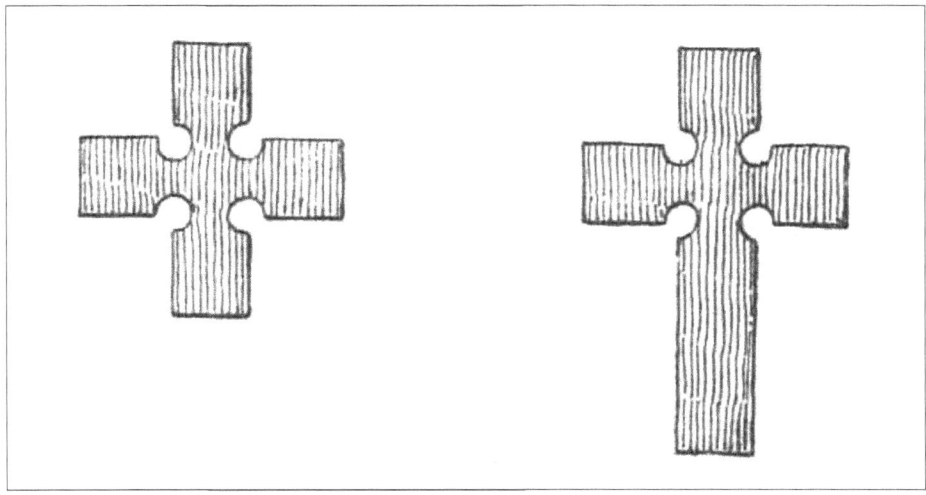

Figure 2: ECMS Type No. 101 (left) and Type No. 101A (right) cross forms (Allen and Anderson 1993 [1903], vol. 1, 51.

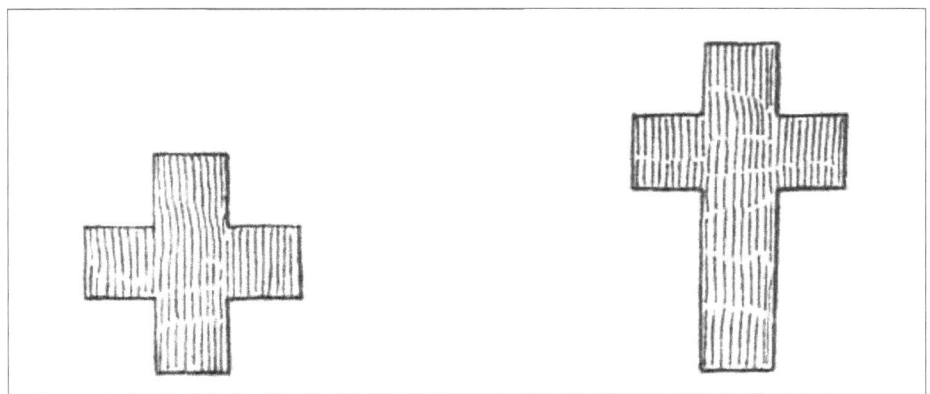

Figure 3: Greek (left) and Latin (right) cross forms (Allen and Anderson 1993 [1903], vol. 1, 46).

in the *Corpus* (AS Type A5) differs from those found elsewhere in the same series (Figures 5 and 4, respectively), which present more marked similarities to the type found in Bailey's seminal work.[13] Ultimately, had it not been for the work of Richard Bailey and Rosemary Cramp, both independently and collectively, such idiosyncratic forms would remain obscured by more distinctive sculptural forms, such as the hogback.[14]

---

13   Bailey 1980, 182, fig. 46; 1988a, 29, fig. 6a.
14   For examples of this considerable body of published work, see Cramp 1978; Bailey 1980; Cramp 1984; Bailey and Cramp 1988.

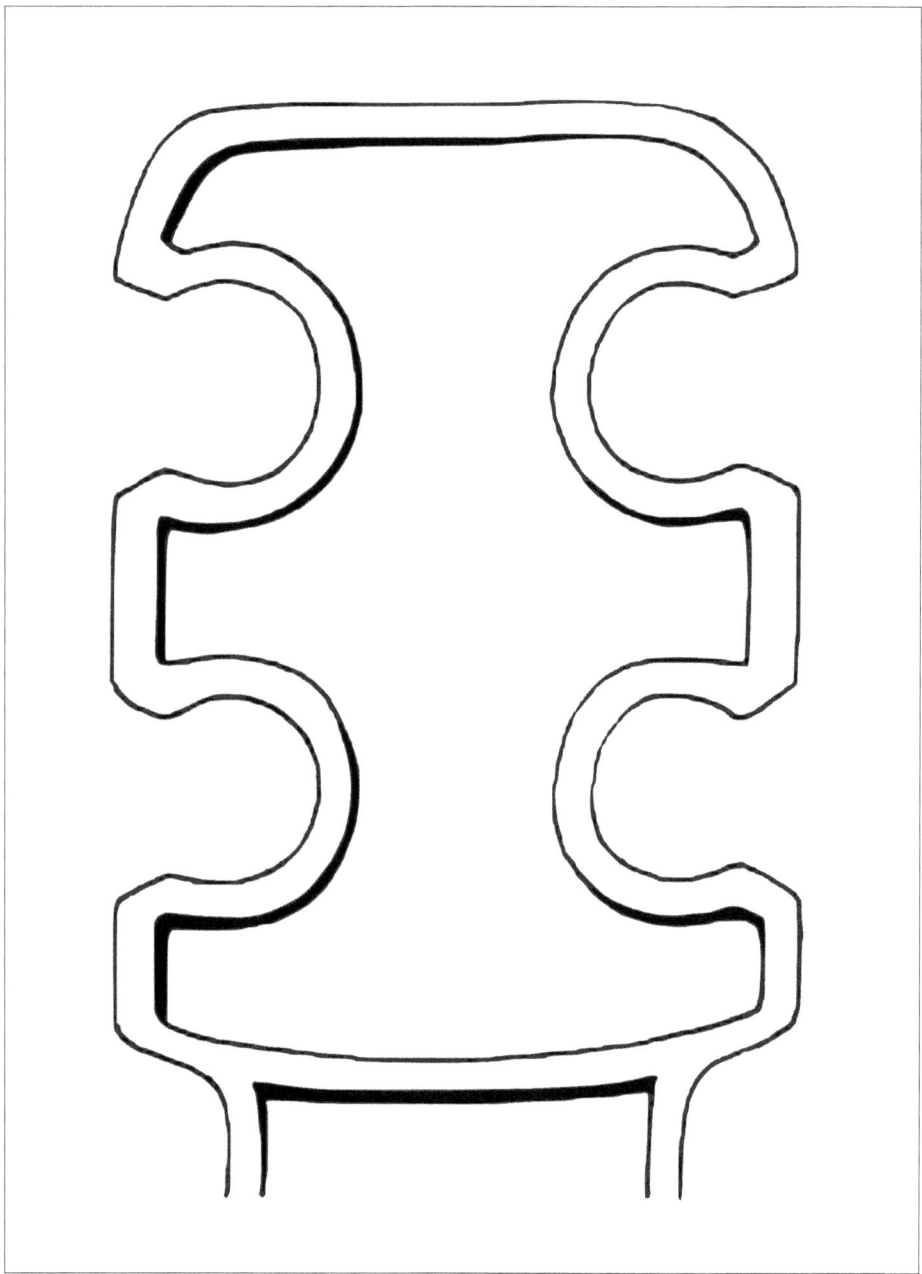

Figure 4: Illustration of the hammerhead cross form, in which the cross may be indicative of the evolved AS Type A10 (Copyright Corpus of Anglo-Saxon Stone Sculpture; drawing by Yvonne Beadnell).

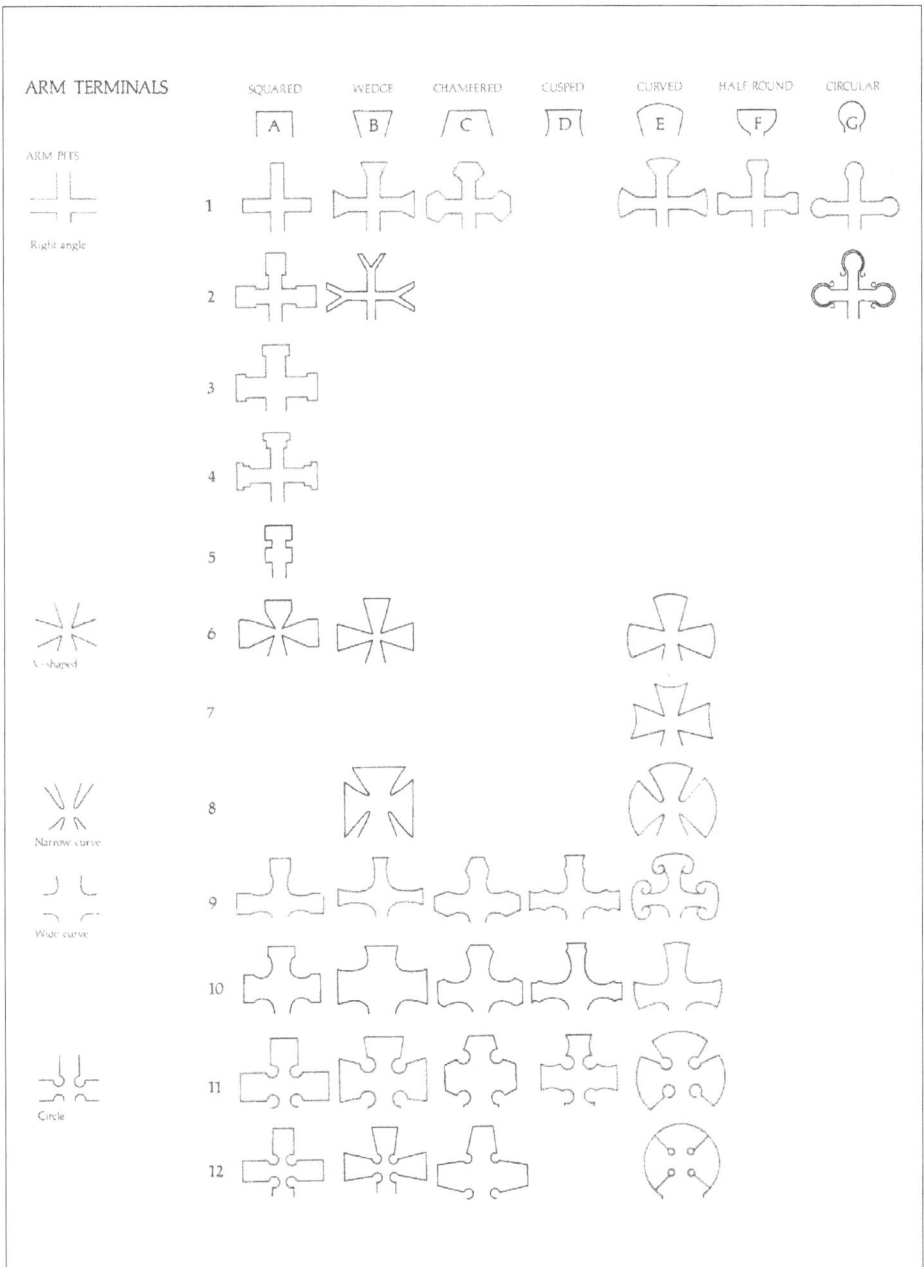

Figure 5: Schematic of cross shapes and arm types, in which the hammerhead cross is A5 (Copyright Corpus of Anglo-Saxon Stone Sculpture; drawing by Yvonne Beadnell).

NATURE OF THE PROBLEM

This brief, illustrated discussion serves to highlight the problem of defining the form of a hammerhead cross. Would a cross, for example, be considered to feature a hammerhead form when only 'the end of the upper arm is broadened to the width of the transverse arms' (matching AS Type A5, see Figure 5), or would it need to have both upper and lower arms expanded to the width of the transverse arms, conforming to the *Corpus*' other illustration (see Figure 4)?[15] The latter view seems to be held by B. J. N. Edwards.[16] However, this may also denote the ringed hammerhead cross form, as seen at Addingham (Figure 6), or the pseudo-ringed hammerhead cross found on the figurative face of the Kilmorie Cross (Figure 1). At this stage, it must be noted that Bailey, prior to the publication of the *Corpus* series, stated that 'the upper (and often lower) arm [of the hammerhead cross form] is expanded so that it is the same width as the entire span of the lateral arms'.[17] This statement is perhaps the best working definition of the hammerhead cross form.

Apart from the oft-cited Kilmorie Cross from Galloway (Scotland), the publications which have thus far dealt with hammerhead crosses have focused mainly on English examples, with Scottish outliers brought in as comparanda.[18] For example, in the *Corpus*, some Scottish hammerhead crosses are highlighted in reference to the hammerhead cross at Addingham in Cumbria.[19] From an archaeological perspective, however, this material has not yet been fully considered and discussed. As a consequence, this chapter will consider all proposed and supposed hammerhead crosses from the British Isles, and thus will not be delimited by the modern cultural and political boundary of the Scotland-England border.

RECONSIDERING THE HAMMERHEAD CROSS

In reconsidering the hammerhead cross, the difference between those akin to AS Type A5 and those akin to a form that appears to have

---

15   Bailey 1988a, 29, fig. 6a, 31.
16   Edwards 1998, 92.
17   Bailey 1980, 182-83.
18   The Kilmorie Cross is discussed extensively by Richard Bailey in his Whithorn Lecture. See Bailey 1996a.
19   Bailey and Cramp 1988, 45.

evolved from AS Type A10 or similar must be deliberated. Are they the same? Furthermore, the addition of a lower arm to AS Type A5 must also be considered, as it often provides symmetry to the cross shape, but also again tends to indicate a type evolved from AS Type A10. It may therefore be suggested that a cross is a hammerhead when it is either AS Type A5, A10 with upper and lower arms – the latter being optional – expanded to a similar width as its transverse arms, or a ringed version of the supposedly evolved AS Type A10. These details should also be considered in the context of the form of the carved stone, be it a free-armed cross, a cross-slab, or a recumbent, for example.

This is not an exact classification of the hammerhead cross. Rather, it has revealed that many forms may be included. This variety is demonstrated when the Kilmorie, Addingham, and Middlesmoor hammerhead crosses are jointly considered (Figures 1, 6, and 10). These appear to be completely different in both form and hammerhead cross shape, yet they are all referred to as hammerhead crosses, a potentially oversimplified terminology.

With this in mind, it may be worth considering that differences may exist between what is meant by a hammerhead cross, a hammer-headed cross, and a cross with hammer-headed cross-arm terminals. The variability of the cross-heads within this terminology are best exemplified around Galloway, where the influence of the Whithorn School of carvers can be seen. These sculptures have been studied extensively by Derek Craig, who uses a broader definition of the hammer-headed form.[20] In order to highlight the perceived problems and allow for a reconsideration of the hammerhead cross, a preliminary corpus of material is presented in the discussion below, which should be read in conjunction with the Appendix.

HAMMERHEAD CROSSES

This section will present a summary of every Viking Age carved stone that has been, or could be, referred to as hammerhead, hammer-head, or hammer-headed, with a brief discussion on the significant points of each example. Although dating this type of material is notoriously difficult, the *Corpus* series declares that the hammerhead crosses in England are all of the tenth to eleventh centuries. This is provided on

---

20   Craig 1992.

an art historical basis, and it is supposed that the Scottish and Welsh material is of a similar date range. Collingwood's 'hammer-head' crosses will be presented first, followed by the remainder of the proposed corpus. All sites included in the discussion have been mapped in Figure 18.

COLLINGWOOD IDENTIFICATIONS

Collingwood has categorised seven crosses as being of a definite 'hammer-head' form.[21] Although other instances are present in his publication, demonstrated by their illustrations in his section on 'hammer-head' crosses, these are of indiscernible fragments.[22] For England, he presents six such crosses, as well as one for Scotland, the latter perhaps being the most significant in the corpus. One of the foremost examples of a hammerhead cross can be found at Addingham in Cumbria (Figure 6).[23] This ringed hammerhead cross, found standing within the churchyard, is situated in the Eden Valley, a route-way connecting Cumbria and Yorkshire during the Viking Age, and an area rich in Scandinavian place-names.[24] Further examples of this form of hammerhead cross, featuring expanded upper and lower arms but lacking a ring, can be found on the cross-slabs at Kilmorie, Kilmory Knap, and Gargrave, as well on the recumbent cross-slab at Heysham. There are incised St Andrew's crosses found at each end of Addingham's transverse arms, a style of ornamentation popular in the Solway region during the Viking Age.[25]

At Brigham in Cumbria, a free-armed hammerhead cross may be found, although its only remnants consist of two conjoining fragments of a cross-head (Figure 7).[26] These are located within the church, as are a hogback fragment and several other notable pieces of Anglian and Anglo-Scandinavian carved stone.[27] In addition, this piece has an incised Latin cross on its face, similar to that found on the hammerhead

---

21 Collingwood 1927, 90-93.
22 Ibid., 93, fig. 116.
23 Bailey and Cramp 1988, 45-46, illus. 1-4.
24 See Higham 1985, 46-47; Fellows-Jensen 1985.
25 For a discussion on the significance and spread of small incised crosses as a form of ornament on Viking Age carved stones, particularly in the Solway region, see Bailey and Cramp 1988, 45.
26 Ibid., 77, illus. 148-51.
27 Ibid., 74-9, 163.

Figure 6: Addingham, Cumbria (photo by author).

Figure 7: Brigham, Cumbria (photo by author).

cross at Middlesmoor. However, the former has terminals on the arms of its incised cross, which may depict additional hammerheads. The Brigham cross may serve to highlight an issue with Collingwood's original identification, as its minimally expanded upper arm does not really conform to the suggested form of a hammerhead cross.

A fine example of a free-armed hammerhead cross can be found at Carlisle in Cumbria (Figure 8), although it only survives as a fragmentary cross-head. As such, it cannot be determined whether this cross originally featured a lower arm.[28] It is acknowledged elsewhere that the cruciform ornament carved on the cross-head is one 'favoured by the spiral-scroll school', a style prevalent in Viking Age Cumbria.[29] A

---

28   Ibid., 87, illus. 214-17.
29   Ibid., 87; Bailey 1988b, 33-38.

Figure 8: Carlisle, Cumbria (photo by author).

close parallel to Carlisle, both in form and cruciform ornament, may be found in the newly discovered probable hammerhead cross-fragment from Workington.[30] Similarly from Cumbria, and also surviving as a fragmentary cross-head, is another free-armed hammerhead type cross from Dearham.[31] This cross perhaps best illustrates Collingwood's suggestion that hammerhead crosses evolved out of the AS Type A3 or A10 cross form (see above). In considering its form and fragmentary nature, the Dearham cross is not a definite hammerhead cross, despite being included in the corpus.

30   See McCarthy and Paterson 2014, 131-33, fig. 8.7.
31   Bailey and Cramp 1988, 95-96, illus. 263.

Figure 9: Gargrave, Yorkshire (photo by author).

A finely executed hammerhead cross is found at Gargrave in Yorkshire (Figure 9).[32] This form of cross-slab and hammerhead appears to be a

---

32   Coatsworth 2008, 155-56, illus. 278-81.

Figure 10: Middlesmoor, Yorkshire (photo by author).

rare find in the county, although a close parallel may be identified at Heysham in Lancashire. There are, however, three other hammerhead crosses from Yorkshire, located at Fountains Abbey, Hartlington, and Middlesmoor. This final example (Figure 10) is found in a prominent landscape location at the head of the Nidderdale, appearing isolated yet potentially significant.[33] It is a near-complete free-armed cross, with a rather similar hammerhead to that of Gargrave, although the latter has wedge-shaped arms, the lower of which is expanded. The cross face has an incised Latin cross, similar to that found on the hammerhead cross from Brigham. As this cross on the Middlesmoor piece is the only such example known to the east of the Pennines, it ultimately reflects a Cumbrian (or Solway) style in Yorkshire.[34] Overall, it may be suggested that the examples from Yorkshire, particularly those from Gargrave and Middlesmoor (with their ornamental characteristics of the spiral-scroll school), are local Anglian reflexes of those found in the Solway region – the supposed hammerhead heartland.[35] As previously stated, perhaps the most significant hammerhead cross identified by Collingwood is a cross-slab from Kilmorie in Galloway, which will be discussed as a case study below.[36]

SUBSEQUENT IDENTIFICATIONS

The following sixteen crosses have all been noted to display hammerhead features in one form or another. Returning to Cumbria, one of the most recent hammerhead cross discoveries is Workington (Figure 11).[37] This fragmentary cross-head of a free-armed cross was found during an archaeological intervention, following a fire that largely destroyed St Michael's Church in 1994.[38] This example is akin to the Carlisle hammerhead cross, although it has a much narrower upper arm. Similar to Carlisle, it displays the cruciform ornament associated with the spiral-scroll school. There is also an example from Bromfield in Cumbria, which appears to be similar to Carlisle and Workington, although its exact type cannot be ascertained due to deterioration, and thus it is

---

33   Ibid., 212-13, illus. 538-40.
34   Bailey and Cramp 1988, 45.
35   See Coatsworth 2008, 156, 213.
36   Stuart 1856-1867, vol. 2, 34-35, plate 70; Allen and Anderson 1993 [1903], vol. 2, part III, 482-83, fig. 514; Collingwood 1927, 91-92; Bailey 1996a.
37   McCarthy and Paterson 2014, 131-33, fig. 8.7.
38   Ibid., 127.

Figure 11: Workington, Cumbria (photo by author).

not included in the corpus.[39] In considering these factors, it might be suggested that examples such as Carlisle and Workington are perhaps only probable hammerhead crosses, fitting somewhere in between AS Types A10 and A5. The final example from Cumbria comes from Walton, where only the fragmentary cross-head of a free-armed cross remains.[40] Unlike crosses like Brigham and Workington, its upper arm is expanded to the full width of its lateral arms. Significantly, the sides of these arms contain incised St Andrew's crosses, which also occur on the lateral

---

39   Bailey and Cramp 1988, 80, illus. 172.
40   Ibid., 153, illus. 573-6.

Figure 12: Heysham, Lancashire (photo by author).

arms of the cross from Addingham, further highlighting the use of such incised ornamentation in the Solway region during the Viking Age.

The only example from Lancashire is found on the coast at Heysham (Figure 12), where one of the finest examples of a hogback can also be found.[41] The Heysham example is perhaps the only known truly recumbent hammerhead cross. It is probably emulating a free-armed analogue, and, in addition, has an equal-armed cross carved in relief on the centre of its cross-head. Parallels to this hammerhead cross form may be found at Addingham – which is ringed – and at Kilmorie and Kilmory Knap. The cross ultimately reflects the Cumbrian (or Solway) style in Lancashire during the Viking Age. The three final examples from England are all fairly recent discoveries; the first is found in Milnrow, Greater Manchester.[42] This is a small fragment, which, despite having been discovered in 1987, has avoided the attention of the Portable Antiquities Scheme until 2009.[43] It appears to be a fragment of a disc-headed cross, whose cross-arm remains suggest that it may be of a hammerhead form. This supposed hammerhead cross form, prevalent

---

41   Bailey 2010, 201-5, illus. 526.
42   Richard Bailey alludes to a 'hammer-head' fragment from Milnrow [Rochdale] in the *Corpus*. Bailey 2010, 205n1, 238n1. For further information on Milnrow, see Bailey et al. 2012, 260-68.
43   Ibid., 260.

in the Solway region, 'adds further evidence to the case for a northward cultural orientation of the region lying to the north of the Mersey' during the Viking Age.[44] Another intriguing hammerhead cross fragment was discovered in 1995 at Fountains Abbey in Yorkshire (Figure 13).[45] Such an incomplete example confuses the hammerhead classification, as it could be referred to as a fragmented example of a pseudo-ringed or ringed hammerhead cross, or a hammerhead cross with only an expanded upper arm. Nevertheless, should this cross have had a curved lower arm (expanded to the same width as the upper one), it is likely to have been created out of the transition between its cross-head and cross-shaft, as can be seen on the examples from Maesmynys and, perhaps, Llanbadarn Fawr, both from Wales. The Hartlington Cross is the final example from Yorkshire (Figure 14).[46] It was discovered in 2005, although it was not published in the *Corpus* due to the timing of its discovery. Through its decoration, which appears to be Hiberno-Norse influenced, this fragmentary cross-head demonstrates stylistic connections with the Solway region. In addition, its find spot is close to St Wilfrid's Church in Burnsall, which notably houses several hogbacks and other Viking Age crosses. It may be suggested that one of the crosses from Burnsall references Thor's hammer in its cross-arms. It is, however, more likely that this example is a reflex of the Scandinavian ring-head.[47]

The two Welsh examples are perhaps the most visually distinctive of the corpus, as they are both very large. Both are pillar-crosses; Llanbadarn Fawr features a hammerhead-type cross-head, and Maesmynys exhibits a pseudo-ringed hammerhead cross type.[48] The former is the taller of the two and only appears to have an expanded upper arm, whereas the latter is more complex in its hammerhead form. Both are noted by Bailey as being a 'variant form' of hammerhead cross, and perhaps reflect a local preference for an Anglo-Scandinavian form of carving.[49] The form of hammerhead cross found at Maesmynys becomes even more significant when compared to the grave-cover from Spennithorne in Northern Yorkshire, with its almost 'hammer-head' upper arm.[50]

---

44   Ibid., 264.
45   Coatsworth 2008, 152, illus. 256-59.
46   Yorkshire Post 2010a; 2010b.
47   See Burnsall 7 in Coatsworth 2008, 111, illus. 105-8.
48   Edwards 2007, 135-39; Redknap and Lewis 2007, 227-30.
49   Bailey 2010, 205.
50   See Spennithorne 2 in Lang 2001, 198, illus. 745.

Figure 13: Fountains Abbey, Yorkshire (photo by author).

In Scotland, there are several additions to Collingwood's original corpus of hammerhead crosses. The most northerly example is found at Kilmory Knap, Argyll.[51] It is a fine hammerhead cross with expanded

---

51   RCAHMS 1992, 163, fig. C (2).

Figure 14: Hartlington, Yorkshire (photo by author).

upper and lower arms carved on a cross-slab. As it is located on the west coast of Scotland, which was a pivotal location on the route between the *Norðreyjar* and *Suðreyjar*, this example potentially demonstrates a cultural connection between Argyll – in the former Gaelic Kingdom of Dál Riata – and the Solway region during the Viking Age. In South Ayrshire, a suggested hammerhead cross was discovered at Shallochwreck, also on the west coast of Scotland.[52] This example looks noticeably different from the majority of the corpus, and as such could probably be classified as a hammerhead cross variant. The cross shape is not necessarily a hammerhead, although the terminals of the arms are expanded to form hammerheads. A similar decoration is found at Brigham, in the Latin cross incised on its cross-head. Another analogue is found at Whithorn in Galloway (Figure 15), although this example has a different expanded upper arm to its lateral arms.[53] In 1997, Derek Craig stated that 'this is the only hammer-headed cross-slab known from Whithorn'.[54] However, he previously noted that two other pieces of carved stone from Whithorn might also be fragments of hammerhead crosses, although these two examples are different in form, and both exhibit a similar curved hammerhead-shaped upper arm to that found on the example from Kirkmadrine.[55] Craig also appropriately describes a runic-inscribed fragment from Whithorn as having a 'hammer-headed cross', although I would not necessarily classify any of these three additional Whithorn examples as hammerhead crosses.[56]

At the significant chapel site of Kirkmadrine in Galloway, known for its Early Christian carved stones, a fairly complex hammerhead cross fragment is located.[57] It has a curved hammer-headed upper arm on one face, whilst the back of the slab is carved, incorporating a wedge-shaped cross superimposed on a rough saltire cross, with two small, seemingly conjoining crosses below.[58] Interestingly, however, the terminals of the arms of these two small crosses are hammerhead-shaped, much like the lateral arms of the Whithorn example. It has also been noted that another piece from Kirkmadrine appears to have a rectangular hammer-headed cross.[59] At High Auchenlarie in Galloway,

---

52   Foster 1958, 9-11.
53   Craig 1997, 434-36, fig. 10.107(7).
54   Ibid., 435.
55   See Whithorn 33 and 34 in Craig 1992, vol. 3, 363-66 and vol. 4, plates 188c, 189a-b.
56   See Whithorn 6 in Ibid., vol. 3, 302-10 and vol. 4, plate 175a-e.
57   See Kirkmadrine 5 in Ibid., vol. 3, 137-38 and vol. 4, plate 136a-b.
58   Ibid.
59   Ibid., vol. 3, 135-36 and vol. 4, plate 137a.

Figure 15: Whithorn, Galloway (photo by author).

there is a pillar stone with a crude hammerhead cross carved upon it.[60] It is part of a pair of pillar stones, possibly originally associated with a cairn, although they may have served as boundary markers.[61] They do not relate to any other carved stone found in this area and are probably reused prehistoric standing stones.[62] The next two examples, both from Galloway, are particularly similar in their hammerhead cross form, although different overall. The first, from Boghouse (Figure 16), is a wedge-shaped pillar stone carved with an excellent example of a

---

60   Ibid., vol. 2, 312-15 and vol. 4, plate 83a.
61   Ibid., vol. 1, 188, for a more detailed discussion on this.
62   Ibid.

Figure 16: Boghouse, Galloway (photo by author).

Figure 17: Glenluce, Galloway (photo by author).

hammerhead cross, whose upper arm is expanded, suggesting it could be classified as AS Type A5.[63] Its obverse face is also carved, but with a Whithorn-type cross-head.

The Barhobble example exists as two separately discovered conjoining fragments.[64] It is carved on a cross-slab, although its

---

63   Anderson 1927, 116-18.
64   Cormack 1995, 62-63.

hammerhead cross form is much the same as that found at Boghouse. The potential significance of the site of Barhobble in the eleventh century is discussed elsewhere, and it should be noted that a cross fragment from nearby House of Elrig (suggested below) may have also come from there.[65] The final positive example comes from Glenluce (Figure 17), also in Galloway.[66] Although fragmentary, this is a crisp example of a hammerhead cross. It appears to be a hybrid of – or intermediary between – the Whithorn School type and a hammerhead cross. As such, it is particularly significant at this location, perhaps representing a Whithorn School reaction to a Solway tradition that was predominant in Cumbria during the Viking Age.

Finally, Derek Craig suggests that a runic cross-slab from St Ninian's Cave is hammer-headed, and that fragments of crosses from Glasserton, House of Elrig, and a second from St Ninian's Cave (all from Galloway) may also have hammer-headed crosses carved on them.[67] This small list of possible fragments demonstrates the potential for the corpus to be increased beyond the twenty-three considered here.

The Kilmorie Cross

Perhaps the best example of a Viking Age hammerhead cross is the Kilmorie Cross from Galloway in Scotland (Figure 1).[68] For several reasons, this stone makes a good focus for a theoretical discussion, most notably due to the apparent co-existence of pagan and Christian iconographies in its many intricate carvings. It primarily demonstrates a cultural connection between Northern England and Galloway through its display of zoomorphic Anglian scrolls and plaits on one of its faces.[69] This alone attests to the importance of considering contemporary carved stones on either side of the Border. Originally, this very face would have been polychrome with a possible inserted jewel or precious glass fragment in its cross centre, and may also once have had an inscription.

---

65   Cormack 1995.
66   Anderson 1935, 141-42.
67   St Ninian's Cave 1 in Craig 1992, vol. 3, 239-43 and vol. 4, plate 161a-c; Glasserton
      1 in Ibid., vol. 3, 70-71 and vol. 4, plate 129a; House of Elrig in Ibid., vol. 3, 87-88
      and vol. 4, plate 122b; 'St Ninian's Cave' 18 in Ibid., vol. 3, 272-72 and vol. 4, plate
      168c-d.
68   Stuart 1856-1867, vol. 2, 34-35, plate 70; Allen and Anderson 1993 [1903], vol. 2,
      part III, 482-83 and fig. 514; Bailey 1996a.
69   Collingwood 1927, 92; Bailey 1996a.

Figure 18: Distribution of the hammerhead cross corpus (map by author, Ordnance Survey data © Crown copyright/database right 2016).

Hence, it must have been extremely visible in the landscape. Bailey has described this cross as having a parochial ambition, or more explicitly, an awareness of its surroundings.[70] This is an apt description, as, upon fuller inspection, a figural scene of a non-Christian mythological character may be seen on one of its faces.

This carved stone is now almost unique in its discovery in this region, and perhaps it was similarly rare at the time of its creation. This begs the question of what the function of this type of sculpture would have been, particularly regarding its prominent landscape location on the west shore of Loch Ryan, near the North Channel, representing a specific interface between the Irish Sea, Solway Firth, and Firth of Clyde.

There is a substantial repertoire of iconographies and ideologies represented on the Kilmorie Cross. On one face, there is a hammerhead cross, perhaps an evolved form of AS Type A10, filled with Anglian interlace. Below this, a scene – although difficult to interpret – seems to depict two intertwining drinking horns at first glance.[71] This, however, may also be a reference to a scene described in the Old Latin version of the Canticle of Habakkuk. Habakkuk 3:2 reads 'In medio duorum animalium innotesceris' [In the midst of two animals you will be recognised].[72] This was likely sung every Friday morning – the significance of which was emphasised by Bede – and is suggested to have been 'intimately associated with Good Friday liturgy'.[73] A similar scene, although more easily discernible and preceding the Kilmorie Cross, may be found on a doorjamb from Monkwearmouth, where it appears to represent 'the concept of the recognition of Christ between two beasts'.[74] If the scene on the Kilmorie Cross is a reference to the Canticle of Habakkuk, it should, therefore, be considered in conjunction with both the Crucifixion themes and pagan mythology also apparent on this cross-slab.

Below the supposed Habakkuk motif on the Kilmorie Cross are three serpents, two of which are intertwined. The cross-head is separated from it by the aforementioned inscription panel. The predominant

---

70   Bailey 1996a.
71   See Cormack 1995, 51.
72   Ó Carragáin 1986, 384.
73   Ibid., 383-85.
74   Bailey 1996b, 38.

feature of this face is, of course, the hammerhead cross with its central hollow. Bailey suggests that, on this face, the cross is created by vines emanating from a chalice in its lower arm, which is indicative of Eucharistic imagery.[75] As such, this face is best understood as being Christian. Nevertheless, if it is accepted that the cross of Christ shares common difference with Thor's hammer motifs, it may not be as unambiguous as this. In considering the theoretical concept of common difference, a term borrowed from Richard Wilk,[76] this allows for an approach where the principal accent is placed on difference, rather than similarity. This will be expanded below.

The other face is far more ambiguous, displaying a crucified Christ set amongst a hammerhead cross, as well as a mythological figure below. Perhaps the pagan god Thor is embodied in this hammerhead cross, sharing common difference with the predominant idea of the crucified Christ being embodied in this form of cross-head. An example of this may also be seen in a silver pendant from Foss in Iceland.[77] This artefact may represent both a stylised Thor's hammer and a Christian crucifix, including an incised equal armed cross. It also displays a beast-headed terminal, which should also be considered in the context of the end-beasts found on hogbacks, themselves neither overtly Christian nor pagan. This is not an isolated manifestation of syncretic religious practice in portable antiquities. For example, a soapstone mould from Trendgaarden in Denmark perhaps also indicates religious syncretism.[78] This artefact was able to produce both a Christian cross and hammer of Thor simultaneously. In such objects, there appears to have been a recognition and consumption of differing ideologies.

In addition to the supposed pagan imagery mentioned above, the figure below the supposed different hammerhead cross may seem to represent the pagan story of Wayland the Smith, depicting a blacksmith with his tongs and anvil to one side. Two birds also appear on the other side, with an indecipherable carving below – although the latter is not represented on Stuart's drawing (Figure 1). The suggested Wayland scene may also be interpreted as a representation of the pagan Norse hero Sigurd, the son of a smith who slew the dragon Fafnir

---

75   Bailey 1996a.
76   Wilk 2004, 91.
77   See Graham-Campbell 1980, 156, plate 526.
78   Ibid., 128, plate 429.

and then killed his father Regin (as described in *The Lay of Fafnir*).[79] The inclusion of the two birds and the indecipherable carving are rather problematic. Putting this caveat aside, however, the following interpretation is suggested: the Christ figure in the hammerhead, which itself is supposedly imbued with connotations of Thor, is arising through a rebirth out of the legend of Sigurd, which details the destruction of evil with his famous sword, Gram. This may be an allegory for Christ now being accepted into the pagan pantheon upon the conversion of Viking Age settlers, thereby indicating the presence of a new and syncretic identity. The application of the common difference framework to this face allows for such an interpretation.

In summary, the figural face is ostensibly analogous to the themes of life, death, and rebirth apparent on the opposing face, where the Eucharistic symbolism suggests the entering of Heaven with an awaiting banquet.[80] Notably, this Eucharistic symbolism surmounts the supposed reference to a scene described in the Canticle of Habakkuk. In this, the two intertwining beasts are bookended from above by the death and rebirth themes of Christ in the cross, and from below by the serpents, which may represent the struggles of Hell or supposed release of the Devil therefrom during the Final Judgement.[81] This is of course just a possible interpretation of the varied and at times confusing iconography apparent on this hammerhead cross.[82] However, if accepted, the apparent juxtaposition of Christian motifs with pagan Norse hero imagery is particularly difficult to dismiss. This interpretation of the Kilmorie Cross recognises that religious syncretism occurred during the Viking Age, resulting in the creation of accordingly syncretic carved stones. It should also be acknowledged that such syncretic carved stones would have allowed for religious syncretism to occur; this was not necessarily a one-way process. Hence, these stones are a product of hybrid practice, which is defined here as the outcome of interacting cultures and ideas, predominantly in colonial environments.[83] I would argue that this hybrid practice can be used as a framework to better understand and extract identities from material culture. Perhaps the

---

79   Craig 1991, 51; *Poetic Edda*, 157-64.
80   Bailey 1996a.
81   For a discussion on Hell and serpents, see Bailey 1980, 140-42.
82   For a discussion on the Kilmorie Cross and its links with the wider world of Christian symbolism and exegesis, see Bailey 1996a.
83   See Dommelen 2005 for a further exploration of this theoretical framework.

most notable example of a manifestation of such hybrid practice can be seen in the Gosforth Cross from Cumbria.[84]

In considering this interpretation of the Kilmorie Cross, the carved stone would have been accessible to both pagans and Christians alike, as well as to those of a new syncretic identity. The supposed Canticle of Habakkuk reference also gives this cross a potential liturgical significance. Furthermore, if the Kilmorie Cross was indeed a polychrome statement, much like the painted Jelling Stone from Denmark, it must have been a significant attribute to its landscape.[85] Questions should therefore be asked as to whether this form and type of evidently syncretic and thus differently carved stone was erected for funerary or other purposes.

HAMMERHEAD CROSSES AND HYBRID PRACTICE

The prevalence of hammerhead crosses in the landscapes of South West Scotland and Cumbria – surrounding the Solway basin (like the Hiberno-Norse areas of Yorkshire) – is hard to avoid when the evidence is considered *en masse*. The connections between them and their landscapes have yet to be fully discussed within current scholarship. This chapter aims to initiate that discussion. The juxtaposition of pagan and Christian iconographies and art, as well as hybrid practice, appears to be a conscious and deliberate effort.[86] This must also be treated as a back-and-forth process of negotiation, and not merely a conversion of one ideology to another.

Although William Cormack notably described the practices of mingling beliefs and ideologies in Galloway as ambivalent, this is not necessarily the case.[87] It may be argued that hybrid practice moves beyond mere ambivalence, particularly where common difference is as explicit as it appears on the Kilmorie Cross. Moreover, it may be argued that William Cormack's view ultimately underplays the free will of the peoples present in the Solway region during the Viking Age. Hybrid practice, which is an outcome of negotiation and manifest in the creation of hammerhead crosses, is therefore a conscious strategy

---

84   Bailey 1980, 125-31.
85   See Graham-Campbell 2013, 15, for a painted replica of the Jelling Stone.
86   In considering this idea, Bailey discusses the 'chameleon-like way in which Scandinavian settlers adopted and adapted to the indigenous behaviour patterns of the peoples amongst whom they found themselves'. See Bailey 1996b, 84.
87   Cormack 1995, 51.

deployed to create and manage a third space, resulting in different and syncretic identities.[88] This third space may be a neutral zone of reciprocity in which each active party is mutually respected, able to trade, and, more importantly, able to take part in forthright negotiation. This is a particularly important element to consider in a period of religious conversion. In a zone of cultural interaction – such as the Solway region – this negotiation is imperative for a productive existence within the culturally rich milieu of the Viking Age.

The creation of different or syncretic carved stones, including hammerhead crosses, might therefore be a product of negotiation and consumption. Strikingly, the majority of these crosses are to be found in the Solway region. This raises the question of why this development occurred here. Perhaps it may be attributed to the area's integral bond to the Irish Sea region during the Viking Age, a landscape and seascape facilitating the interaction of numerous cultures through contact and exchange. As such, the erection of syncretic carved stones in these locations may have been the result of more than mere ambivalence, allowing hammerhead crosses to serve a functional purpose in the landscape, other than funerary.

HAMMERHEAD CROSSES AND BEACH MARKETS

In outlining a functional purpose of hammerhead crosses, I propose a potential landscape link between them and various beach markets. Such locations would have been influential in facilitating the trade of goods and wealth during the Viking Age, particularly in Scotland, where no significant Viking Age towns are known to have existed. The significance of Whithorn in Galloway should not be underestimated within the context of such towns, as archaeological evidence suggests that it would have been a thriving commercial settlement during this period.[89] Although perhaps not comparable to York or Dublin, it should be regarded as a significant nodal point within a much larger trading network of beach markets and towns, all centred on the Irish Sea region.

The hammerhead crosses found along the coasts of the Irish Sea and its surrounding waterways are perhaps indicative of a negotiated space in the landscape, and as such could be closely associated with potential beach market sites. Ultimately, they should be considered to signify a

---

88   See Bhabha 1990.
89   See Hill 1997.

space created for mutual, secure exchanges, as well as the negotiation and consumption of contrasting religious ideas. The hammerhead cross may perhaps serve as a symbol of this theoretical space, and not necessarily be a direct locator of such activity. Nevertheless, the proximity to waterways of each hammerhead cross should be considered when evaluating its potential relationship to the landscape.

The supposed affiliation between carved stones and trading sites is, however, not a new idea. David Stocker discussed this potential relationship in reference to tenth-century Lincolnshire and Yorkshire, whilst this link was later also discussed by David Griffiths concerning the beach market site of Meols in the Wirral.[90] Nevertheless, the proximity of hammerhead crosses to waterways has not been expressly considered until now, despite the potential of this commonly apparent relationship to identify points of access in the landscape. The majority of these crosses are found in low-lying locations, close to either a coastline, riverine route, or overland route-way. Unfortunately, it is often difficult to ascertain the original location of carved stones. Many early medieval stones appear to have been moved into churches, although I would argue that, due to their size, they are not likely to have been moved far from their original context. Whilst considering this, a possibility exists to archaeologically determine a functional relationship between the find spots of the artefacts associated with beach markets and the supposed original locations of hammerhead crosses.[91]

Regrettably, beach markets have proven to be elusive trade nodes on the British Isles. Considering the situation in Galloway, Luce Bay may be a perfect candidate. This bay has numerous hammerhead crosses in its general vicinity – the closest being those found at Kirkmadrine, Glenluce, Barhobble, and Boghouse. The Rhins of Galloway appears to have a spread of hammerhead crosses across it, predominantly situated close to Loch Ryan and Luce Bay. This location in Galloway has also produced numerous finds of copper-alloy artefacts, including a ringed pin, finger ring, padlock, and stick pins, as well as thirteen mixed-material stycas.[92] At Piltanton Burn, close to Luce Bay, a silver ingot was also recently discovered.[93] The significance of the recent Viking hoard

---

90   Stocker 2000; Griffiths 2014, 40-45.
91   See Stocker 2000, 207, for a similar discussion of this theory.
92   Graham-Campbell 1995, 87; Barnes 2014.
93   Hunter 2003, 50.

found by a metal detectorist in Galloway should also be considered.[94] Overall, the sheltered nature of Luce Bay, as well as its direct connection to the Irish Sea, must have made it an ideal portage point. With the important site of Whithorn to its south-east, Luce Bay was an ideal place for a beach market.

CONCLUSION

This chapter has brought together an expanded corpus of hammerhead crosses; through their re-examination, it aims to highlight the potential for generating further research into a possible landscape relationship between hammerhead crosses and beach markets. Primarily through a consideration of the apparent common difference between the cross of Christ and hammer of Thor, it has been argued that hammerhead crosses appear to be syncretic. These carved stones are the products of hybrid practice, and are neither explicitly Christian nor pagan. It should also be pointed out that the hammerhead cross definition is far more complex than initially presented by Collingwood, as well as acknowledged that the work of Bailey is fundamental for beginning to understand the development and distribution of these crosses.

In closing, this research does not – and cannot – serve as a comprehensive study of hammerhead crosses. Instead, it is designed to present an overview of the associated research currently being undertaken. It is ultimately hoped that this interim presentation and reconsideration of hammerhead crosses will highlight the significance of this often overlooked Viking Age carved stone type, and that it should be considered to be a product of negotiation and consumption within a landscape strewn with the fragments of old, new, and otherwise contrasting religions.

APPENDIX: CATALOGUE

Borrowing from the *Corpus*' recording framework, carved stones are described by their name/location, National Grid Reference, last known current location, form, hammerhead form, AS Type, and *Corpus* number, if relevant. As these carved stones are generally well-recorded elsewhere, they will be limitedly described here, with only the noteworthy points presented. This catalogue is listed alphabetically and should be read in conjunction with the 'Hammerhead Crosses' section above.

---

94   Pringle 2016.

Addingham (Cumbria, England)
NGR: NY574383.
Current Location: Churchyard, St Michael's Church, Addingham.
Form: Cross-head, part of cross-shaft.
Hammerhead form: Ringed hammerhead cross with both upper and lower arms expanded to the width of its transverse arms, all connected in the ring. Seems to be a variant of AS Type A5, as lower arm is present.
AS Type: Cross shape – A5; Arm type – Lateral B10.
Corpus Number: Addingham 1.

Barhobble (Galloway, Scotland)
NGR: NX310494.
Current Location: Whithorn Trust.
Form: Incomplete, broken, cross-slab.
Hammerhead form: Hammerhead cross carved on a cross-slab, where its curved upper arm is expanded to the same width as its lateral arms.
AS Type: n/a, although possibly a variant of A5 and the top of its upper arm is curved and its lateral arms appear to be B10.
Corpus Number: n/a.

Boghouse (Galloway, Scotland)
NGR: NX345463.
Current Location: Whithorn Museum.
Form: Wedge-shaped pillar stone.
Hammerhead form: Latin cross face – Hammerhead cross carved on a rude pillar, where its curved upper arm is expanded to the same width as its lateral arms; Obverse face – Whithorn type cross with four bosses.
AS Type: n/a, although possibly a variant of A5. The top of its upper arm is curved and its lateral arms appear to be B10.
Corpus Number: n/a.

Brigham (Cumbria, England)
NGR: NY085309, which is *contra* to the grid reference given in the *Corpus*.
Current Location: Inside St Bridget's Church, Brigham.
Form: Part of cross-head, broken.
Hammerhead form: Free-armed hammerhead cross with its upper arm almost expanded to the width of its lateral arms.
AS Type: Cross shape – A5; Arm type – Upper A6, lateral B10.
Corpus Number: Brigham 6.

Carlisle (Cumbria, England)
NGR: NY399559, which is *contra* to the grid reference given in the *Corpus*.
Current Location: Inside Carlisle Cathedral, Carlisle.
Form: Part of cross-head.
Hammerhead form: Free-armed hammerhead cross with an upper arm expanded to the width of its lateral arms.
AS Type: Cross shape – A5; Arm type – B6.
Corpus Number: Carlisle 4.

Dearham (Cumbria, England)
NGR: NY072365.
Current Location: Inside St Mungo's Church, Dearham.
Form: Part of cross-head.
Hammerhead form: Free-armed hammerhead cross, although it appears to have a cross-head form of somewhere between AS Type A5 and A10, as the upper arm does not extend to the full width of the lateral arms.
AS Type: Cross shape – A5; Arm type – A10.
Corpus Number: Dearham 3.

Fountains Abbey (North Yorkshire [formerly West Riding of Yorkshire], England)
NGR: SE272682 (supposed original location).
Current Location: Helmsley Archaeology Storage (EH88100869).
Form: Part of cross-head.
Hammerhead form: At first sight, this appears as a pseudo-ringed hammerhead cross, although this is uncertain, being broken and therefore without a lower arm. The upper arms are expanded to the same width as its lateral arms.
AS Type: Cross shape – E12. This is questionable, however, as this example is referred to as a hammerhead form; Arm type – None provided, although its lateral arms may be referred to as a variant of B10 and E12.
Corpus Number: Fountains Abbey 1.

Gargrave (North Yorkshire [formerly West Riding of Yorkshire], England)
NGR: SD932539.
Current Location: Inside St Andrew's Church, Gargrave.
Form: Part of cross-shaft.
Hammerhead form: Hammerhead cross carved on a cross-slab, where its upper and lower arms are expanded to the same width as its transverse arms. It seems to be a variant of AS Type A5, as a lower arm is present.
AS Type: Cross shape – A5; Arm type – E10.
Corpus Number: Gargrave 1.

Glenluce (Galloway, Scotland)

NGR: NX184586.

Current Location: Glenluce Abbey Museum.

Form: Incomplete cross-slab.

Hammerhead form: Hammerhead cross carved on a cross slab, where its upper arm is expanded to more or less the same width as its transverse arms. Although broken, it may have had a similar lower arm. The armpits of the cross are circular and almost closed, tying it to the Whithorn School.

AS Type: n/a, although it may be described as somewhere between A5 and A10.

Corpus Number: n/a.

Hartlington (North Yorkshire [formerly West Riding of Yorkshire], England)

NGR: SE039610, approximately, as find spot not published.

Current Location: Inside St Wilfrid's Church, Burnsall.

Form: Part of cross-head.

Hammerhead form: Free-armed hammerhead cross whose upper arm does not extend to the full width of the lateral arms. The presence of a lower arm is indeterminate.

AS Type: n/a, although it appears to have a cross-head form similar to A5.

Corpus Number: n/a.

Heysham (Lancashire, England)

NGR: SD411617.

Current Location: Churchyard, St Peter's Church, Heysham.

Form: Recumbent cross-slab.

Hammerhead form: Hammerhead cross carved on a recumbent cross-slab, where its upper and lower arms are expanded to the same width as its transverse arms. It seems to be a variant of AS Type A5, as a lower arm is present.

AS Type: Cross shape – A5; Arm type – None provided, although its lateral arms appear to be B10.

Corpus Number: Heysham 8.

High Auchenlarie (Galloway, Scotland)

NGR: NX536534.

Current Location: Displayed west of Kirkdale House (NX514532).

Form: Pillar Stone.

Hammerhead form: Hammerhead cross carved on a rude pillar, where its upper and lower arms are expanded to the same width as its transverse arms.

AS Type: n/a, although possibly a variant of A5, as a lower arm is also present, and the lateral arms may be described as either A10 or B11.

Corpus Number: n/a.

Kilmorie (Galloway, Scotland)
NGR: NX033658.
Current Location: Churchyard, Kirkcolm Church, Kirkcolm.
Form: Cross-slab.
Hammerhead form: Figural face – Pseudo-ringed hammerhead cross;
Obverse face – Like the Dearham hammerhead cross, this face may display a
hammerhead cross representative of the suggested evolution of AS Type A10
to A5, as the upper and lower arms do not extend to the full width of the
transverse arms. Nevertheless, Bailey suggests that this form is 'intermediate
between the fully-developed class and heads of the Carlisle/Lancaster type'.[95]
AS Type: n/a, but see above.
Corpus Number: n/a.

Kilmory Knap (Argyll, Scotland)
NGR: NR702751.
Current Location: Inside Kilmory Knap chapel, Kilmory.
Form: Incomplete cross-slab.
Hammerhead form: Hammerhead cross carved on a cross slab, where its
upper and lower arms are expanded to the same width as its transverse arms.
AS Type: n/a, although possibly a variant of A5, as a lower arm is also present.
Corpus Number: n/a.

Kirkmadrine (Galloway, Scotland)
NGR: NX080483.
Current Location: Built into the exterior wall of the chapel at Kirkmadrine.
Form: Incomplete cross-slab.
Hammerhead form: Hammerhead cross carved on a cross slab, where its
upper arm is expanded to almost the same width as its lateral arms. The
obverse contains two small crosses with hammerhead-shaped cross-arm
terminals.
AS Type: n/a, although possibly a variant of A5, but with a curved upper arm
and lateral arms of type B10.
Corpus Number: n/a.

Llanbadarn Fawr (Ceredigion, Wales)
NGR: SN599809.
Current Location: Inside St Padarn's Church, Llanbadarn Fawr.
Form: Pillar-cross, with 'hammer-head'.
Hammerhead form: It appears as a variant of a hammerhead cross, as it is a
pillar-cross with a hammerhead type cross-head, featuring a curved upper

---

95   Bailey 1988a, 31.

arm and very thick lateral arms. It may also be described as a pseudo-ringed hammerhead cross if a lower arm is imagined.

AS Type: n/a, although possibly a variant of A5 with a curved upper arm and lateral arms similar to B10.

Corpus Number: n/a, although it is catalogued as CD4 in the Welsh corpus.[96]

Maesmynys (Powys, Wales)
NGR: SO013475.
Current Location: Brecknock Museum, Brecon.
Form: Pillar-cross, with 'hammer-head'.
Hammerhead form: It appears as a pseudo-ringed hammerhead cross due to the way in which the cross-shaft connects to the cross-head, implying a lower arm symmetrically opposing the upper arm. This is particularly so on the cross face (A) with a visible ring and four hollows present, whereas the obverse cross face (C) has hollows with bosses.
AS Type: n/a, although possibly a variant of A5 with a curved upper arm and B10 lateral arms, and thus similar to the form described for Llanbadarn Fawr.
Corpus Number: n/a, although catalogued as B39 in the Welsh corpus.[97]

Middlesmoor (North Yorkshire [formerly West Riding of Yorkshire], England)
NGR: SE092741.
Current Location: Inside St Chad's Church, Middlesmoor.
Form: Incomplete, broken, free-armed cross and cross-shaft.
Hammerhead form: Free-armed hammerhead cross with an upper arm expanded to that of its lateral arms.
AS Type: Cross shape– A5; Arm type – Upper arm seems to be 'an exaggerated form of AS Type A10', although the lateral arms are similar to A1.[98]
Corpus Number: Middlesmoor 1.

Milnrow (Greater Manchester, England)
NGR: Unknown, but possibly close to SD933131.
Current Location: Unknown.
Form: Part of cross-head.
Hammerhead form: Possibly a hammerhead cross form carved on a disc-headed cross, although this is admittedly a difficult fragment to classify.[99]
AS Type: n/a, although the lateral arms may be B10, and so the fragment

---

96   Edwards 2007, 135-39.
97   Redknap and Lewis 2007, 227-30.
98   Coatsworth 2008, 213.
99   Bailey et al. 2012, 264.

could be a badly damaged piece of a ringed hammerhead cross. This is, however, tentative.

Corpus Number: n/a.

Shallochwreck (South Ayrshire, Scotland)

NGR: NX069773

Current Location: Hunterian Museum Collections, Glasgow (GLAHM C.1961.41).

Form: Incomplete, broken, cross-slab.

Hammerhead form: Latin cross carved on a cross-slab whose terminals of the upper and lateral arms are each expanded to the form of a hammerhead.

AS Type: n/a.

Corpus Number: n/a.

Walton (Cumbria, England)

NGR: NY522645.

Current Location: Not located, however, last known location was at St Mary's Church, Walton.

Form: Part of cross-head.

Hammerhead form: Free-armed hammerhead cross with its upper arm expanded to the width of its lateral arms.

AS Type: The *Corpus* states E10, although this may be erroneous, as this cross is more akin to A5 with possible A10 upper arms.

Corpus Number: Walton 1.

Whithorn (Galloway, Scotland)

NGR: NX444403.

Current Location: Whithorn Trust.

Form: Incomplete cross-slab.

Hammerhead form: Hammerhead cross carved on a cross slab, where its upper arm is expanded to almost the same width as its transverse arms.

AS Type: n/a, although it seems to be a slender variant of A5, but with lateral arms similar to B6.

Corpus Number: n/a.

Workington (Cumbria, England)

NGR: NX997289.

Current Location: Inside St Michael's Church, Workington.

Form: Part of cross-head.

Hammerhead form: Free-armed hammerhead cross with its upper arm expanded almost to the width of its lateral arms.

AS Type: n/a, although the cross-head appears to be somewhere between A5 and A10, whilst the lateral arms appear to be either B6 or B10.

Corpus Number: n/a.

BIBLIOGRAPHY

PRIMARY SOURCES

Poetic Edda, Larrington C (trans), 2008, Oxford: Oxford University Press.

SECONDARY SOURCES

Allen, J R and J Anderson 1993 [1903], *The Early Christian Monuments of Scotland*, 2 vols, Balgavies: The Pinkfoot Press.

Anderson, R S G 1927, 'Crosses and Rock Sculptures Recently Discovered in Wigtownshire', *Proceedings of the Society of Antiquaries of Scotland* 61, 115-22.

Anderson, R S G 1935, 'Sculptured Stones of Old Luce church, Wigtownshire', *Proceedings of the Society of Antiquaries of Scotland* 70, 139-45.

Bailey, R N 1980, *Viking Age Sculpture in Northern England*, London: Collins.

Bailey, R N 1988a, 'Viking-Period Forms', in R N Bailey and R Cramp, *Corpus of Anglo-Saxon Stone Sculpture. Volume 2: Cumberland, Westmoreland and Lancashire North-of-the-Sands*, Oxford: Oxford University Press, 29-32.

Bailey, R N 1988b, 'Schools of Viking-Period Sculpture', in R N Bailey and R Cramp, *Corpus of Anglo-Saxon Stone Sculpture. Volume 2: Cumberland, Westmoreland and Lancashire North-of-the-Sands*, Oxford: Oxford University Press, 33-40.

Bailey, R N 1996a, *Ambiguous Birds and Beasts: Three Sculptural Puzzles in South-West Scotland*, Whithorn: Friends of the Whithorn Trust.

Bailey, R N 1996b, *England's Earliest Sculptors*, Toronto: Pontifical Institute of Mediaeval Studies.

Bailey, R N 2010, *Corpus of Anglo-Saxon Stone Sculpture. Volume 9: Cheshire and Lancashire*, Oxford: Oxford University Press.

Bailey, R N and R Cramp 1988, *Corpus of Anglo-Saxon Stone Sculpture. Volume 2: Cumberland, Westmoreland and Lancashire North-of-the-Sands*, Oxford: Oxford University Press.

Bailey, R N, V Oakden, and E Okasha 2012, 'Notes', *Medieval Archaeology* 56:1, 260-300.

Barnes, J 2014, 'The Vikings in Western Scotland: From the Firth of Clyde to the Solway Firth', unpublished MLitt dissertation, University of Glasgow.

Bhabha, H K 1990, 'The Third Space', in J Rutherford (ed), *Identity: Community, Culture, Difference*, London: Lawrence and Wishart, 207-21.

Coatsworth, E 2008, *Corpus of Anglo-Saxon Stone Sculpture. Volume 8: Western Yorkshire*, Oxford: Oxford University Press.

Collingwood, W G 1927, *Northumbrian Crosses of the Pre-Norman Age*, London: Faber and Gwyer.

Cormack, W F 1995, 'Barhobble, Mochrum - Excavation of a Forgotten Church Site in Galloway', *Transactions of the Dumfriesshire and Galloway Natural History and Antiquarian Society* 70, 5-106.

Craig, D J 1991, 'Pre-Norman Sculpture in Galloway: Some Territorial Implications', in R D Oram and G P Stell (eds), *Galloway: Land and Lordship*, Edinburgh: Scottish Society for Northern Studies, 63-75.

Craig, D J 1992, 'The Distribution of Pre-Norman Sculpture in South-West Scotland: Provenance, Ornament and Regional Groups', 4 vols, unpublished PhD thesis, Durham University.

Craig, D J 1997, 'The Sculptured Stones', in P H Hill, *Whithorn and St Ninian: The Excavation of a Monastic Town, 1984-91,* Stroud: Sutton, 433-41.

Cramp, R 1978, 'The Anglian Tradition in the Ninth Century', in J Lang (ed), *Anglo-Saxon and Viking Age Sculpture and Its Context*, Oxford: British Archaeological Reports.

Cramp, R 1984, *Corpus of Anglo-Saxon Stone Sculpture in England. Volume 1: County Durham and Northumberland,* Oxford: Oxford University Press.

Dommelen, P van 2005, 'Colonial Interactions and Hybrid Practices: Phoenician and Carthaginian Settlement in the Ancient Mediterranean' in G J Stein (ed), *The Archaeology of Colonial Encounters: Comparative Perspectives*, Santa Fe: School of American Research Press; Oxford: James Currey, 109-41.

Edwards, B J N 1998, *Vikings in North-West England: The Artefacts*, Lancaster: Centre for North-West Regional Studies.

Edwards, N 2007, *A Corpus of Early Medieval Inscribed Stones and Stone Sculpture in Wales. Vol. 2: South-West Wales*, Cardiff: University of Wales Press.

Fellows-Jensen, G 1985, 'Scandinavian Settlement in Cumbria and Dumfriesshire: The Place-Name Evidence', in J R Baldwin and I D Whyte (eds), *The Scandinavians in Cumbria*, Edinburgh: Scottish Society for Northern Studies, 65-82.

Foster, J 1958, 'The Ballantrae Cross', *Ayrshire Archaeology and Natural History Collection* 6, 9-11.

Graham-Campbell, J 1980, *Viking Artefacts: A Select Catalogue,* London: British Museum Publications.

Graham-Campbell, J 1995, *The Viking-Age Gold and Silver of Scotland (AD 850-1100),* Edinburgh: NMS.

Graham-Campbell, J 2013, *Viking Art,* London: Thames and Hudson.

Griffiths, D 2014, 'A Brief History and Archaeology of Viking Activity in North-West England', in S E Harding, D Griffiths, and E Royles (eds), *In Search of Vikings: Interdisciplinary Approaches to the Scandinavian Heritage of North-West England*, Boca Raton: CRC Press, 33-49.

Higham, N 1985, 'The Scandinavians in North Cumbria: Raids and Settlement in the Later Ninth to Mid-Tenth Centuries', in J R Baldwin and I D Whyte (eds), *The Scandinavians in Cumbria*, Edinburgh: Scottish Society for Northern Studies, 37-51.

Hill, P H 1997, *Whithorn and St Ninian: The Excavation of a Monastic Town, 1984-91*, Stroud: Sutton.

Hunter, F 2003, 'Piltanton Burn (Old Luce parish), Viking Ingot', *Discovery Excavation Scotland* 4, 50.

Lang, J T 2001, *Corpus of Anglo-Saxon Stone Sculpture. Volume 6: Northern Yorkshire*, Oxford: Oxford University Press.

McCarthy, M and C Paterson 2014, 'A Viking-Age Site at Workington, Cumbria: Interim Statement', in S E Harding, D Griffiths, and E Royles (eds), *In Search of Vikings: Interdisciplinary Approaches to the Scandinavian Heritage of North-West England*, Boca Raton: CRC Press, 127-36.

Ó Carragáin, E 1986, 'Christ over the Beasts and the Agnus Dei: Two Multivalent Panels on the Ruthwell and Bewcastle Crosses', in P E Szarmach and V D Oggins (eds), *Sources of Anglo-Saxon Culture*, Kalamazoo: Medieval Institute Publications, 377-403.

Pringle, H 2016, 'Pictures: An Elite Viking's Prized Possessions', National Geographic, http://news.nationalgeographic.com/2016/03/160323-vikings-galloway-hoard-treasure-scotland-archaeology/, accessed 27 October 2016.

RCAHMS 1992, *Argyll: An Inventory of the Monuments, Volume 7: Mid Argyll and Cowal, Medieval and Later Monuments*, Edinburgh: The Royal Commission on the Ancient and Historical Monuments of Scotland.

Redknap, M and J M Lewis 2007, *A Corpus of Early Medieval Inscribed Stones and Stone Sculpture in Wales. Vol. 1: Breconshire, Glamorgan, Monmouthshire, Radnorshire and Geographically Contiguous Areas of Herefordshire and Shropshire*, Cardiff: University of Wales Press.

Stocker, D 2000, 'Monuments and Merchants: Irregularities in the Distribution of Stone Sculpture in Lincolnshire and Yorkshire in the Tenth Century', In D M Hadley and J D Richards (eds), *Cultures in Contact: Scandinavian Settlement in England in the Ninth and Tenth Centuries*, Turnhout: Brepols, 179–212.

Stuart, J 1856-1867, *Sculptured Stones of Scotland*, 2 vols, Aberdeen: Spalding Club.

Wilk, R 2004, 'Miss Universe, the Olmec and the Valley of Oaxaca' *Journal of Social Archaeology* 4:1, 81-98.

Yorkshire Post 2010a, 'Stone cross find could point way to Viking burial ground in the Dales', http://www.yorkshirepost.co.uk/news/stone-cross-find-could-point-way-to-viking-burial-ground-in-the-dales-1-2558780, accessed 27 October 2016.

Yorkshire Post 2010b, 'Vikings return to Dales for weekend celebration', http://www.yorkshirepost.co.uk/news/vikings-return-to-dales-for-weekend-celebration-1-2587899, accessed 27 October 2016.

Late Medieval Vikings:
The MacDonald Raids on Orkney c. 1461

Ian Peter Grohse[1]

The late medieval community of Orkney was a far cry from the ninth-century Viking stronghold from which it originated. Portrayed in high medieval sagas as a society imbued with the mores of militancy and fed off the spoils of foreign conquest and plunder, the Orcadian community had settled into peaceful retirement by the fourteenth and fifteenth centuries, cultivating a decidedly more pacific lifestyle predicated upon law and landholding.[2] Perhaps as a result, the late medieval period has at times been marginalised from scholarship on the pre-modern history of the Northern Isles.[3] Vikings, although always in high demand by students and scholars of the medieval North, were few and far between in the twilight of the Norse power in the west.[4]

Somewhat ironically, the last impulses of the Viking legacy in northern Britain came not from Orkney, but from the Hebrides. Although the Western Isles' formal ties to the Norwegian motherland and the Norse realm were severed when Norway ceded its dominion to Scotland in 1266, social and political organisation along Scotland's western seaboards in the late Middle Ages preserved elements of a Viking past long after they were obscured in other parts of northern

---

1   The following is based on a paper delivered for *From Gall to Gael and Gallowglas,* SSNS' residential conference organised on Islay between 12 and 15 April 2012. Parts were adapted and included in my contribution to Petre 2015, 612-15. I would like to extend my thanks to James for cooperation in that piece, and in encouraging work on this chapter.

2   For Viking Orkney, see e.g. Crawford 1987; Beuermann 2011. For pacification, see Grohse 2013; 2014a.

3   Clouston 1932, for example, devotes 214 pages to Orkney between the ninth and fourteenth centuries, and just forty-six to the late medieval period.

4   Particularly in British scholarship, studies dealing with Norse-Scottish relations rarely look beyond Norway's relinquishment of the Western Isles in 1266, an event that marked a 'Norwegian sunset' and 'Scottish dawn' in Scottish historiography (Cowan 1990). Research by Barbara E. Crawford (e.g. Crawford 2013) and William P.L. Thomson (Thomson 2008a) are notable exceptions. To apply an open definition, 'a Viking was a sea-borne raider, and to go a-viking was to undertake sea-borne raiding' (Somerville and McDonald 2013, 1). Crucially, a Viking was not a raider by profession, but rather augmented his standard means of income by way of conquest and plunder (Ibid.).

Europe.[5] Despite their ethnic and linguistic distance from the Norse world, the Gaelic-speaking Lords of the Isles continued to expand their political and socio-economic influence through seaborne raiding,[6] a tradition that Norwegians and Orcadians once upheld with great pride, yet had essentially abandoned in the late-thirteenth century.[7] Andrew Jennings has recently shed light on this phenomenon in his study of the Northern Isles in the sixteenth century, when 'latter-day Vikings' from the west sought to extend Hebridean lordship over Orkney and Shetland.[8]

Looking further back, we find Hebridean raiders earning notoriety in the Northern Isles a century or two earlier. This is witnessed most spectacularly in the fifteenth century, when Orkney fell subject to recurrent, large-scale attacks originating along Scotland's western seaboards. The most devastating of these assaults by so-called 'Wild-Scots' occurred in or around 1461, when John MacDonald, Earl of Ross and Lord of the Isles, commissioned raids on the militarily hapless inhabitants of the Northern Isles.[9] Once raiders, the Orcadians had become the raided. The attacks are recorded in vivid detail in two letters from the burgesses, baillies, and bishop of Orkney. The first, addressed to Christian I, King of Denmark, Sweden, and Norway by his officials in Kirkwall on February 29, 1461, reports how MacDonald, the country's 'old great enemy' (*antiquo inimicus*) had long striven to destroy the country through arson, plunder, and the general destruction of the inhabitants.[10] Their only hope, the writers claimed, was their noble prince, William Sinclair, Earl of Orkney, who took up their 'deadly conflict' (*letali conflictu*) against MacDonald.[11] The second, purportedly compiled by Thomas Tulloch, Bishop of Orkney, echoes and elaborates

---

5 There is ample research on Norse activities in the Irish Sea and the Western Isles. See e.g. Ó Corráin 1997; McDonald 1998; Forte, Oram and Pedersen 2005, 81-117, 217-64; Beuermann 2007; Sigurðsson and Bolton 2014; Macniven 2014.

6 For a general overview of the lordship, see Bannerman 1977; Grant 1988; Macdougall 2000; Kingston 2004; Oram 2014.

7 Grohse 2013; 2014a.

8 Jennings 2013.

9 For previous discussions, see e.g. Thomson 2008a, 196-97; Boardman 2006, 175-76; Grohse 2014b, 174-76; Petre 2015, 612-15.

10 *DN* v, no. 827. The letter is dated *vltimo Februarii* 1460. However, Barbara E. Crawford suggests the author was adhering to the Scottish, rather than Norwegian calendar, concluding that it refers to the close of February 1461 (Crawford 1969, 41; Petre 2015, 614; cf. *REO*, xxii).

11 *DN* v, no. 827.

on the former.[12] He reports that MacDonald employed his 'men of Sudor, Ireland, and the Scottish wildlands' (*hominibus Sodorensibus Ybernensibus et Scotis siluestribus*) to invade Orkney and visit its inhabitants 'with all manner of cruelty' (*omnimoda crudelitate*).[13]

Both accounts underscore that the attacks were not isolated incidents. MacDonald and his men had striven to destroy the Orcadians, attacking and plundering the beleaguered population from 'year to year and day to day' (*anno in annum et indies*).[14] Despite describing in detail the MacDonald raids, the letters do not relate when or why the attacks began. The following examines the Hebridean raids in a broader context of foreign violence in late medieval Orkney. It aims to identify the perpetrators and explain their motives for aggression, and gauge the victims' capacity for coping with that aggression. Whilst the struggle was undoubtedly more complex than a mere revival of Viking Age animosities, it almost certainly reflects the preservation of Viking Age mores in the west.

MacDonald Raids on Orkney – Personal Feud and Political Struggle

The letters from 1461 describe the attacks as expressions of MacDonald's personal depravity, but are unspecific as to why he singled out the Northern Isles as a target for his aggression. A seventeenth-century MacDonald family history claims that the conflict was instigated by a personal feud between Alexander MacDonald, John's father and predecessor as Earl of Ross and Lord of the Isles, and William Sinclair, Earl of Orkney and Caithness.[15] It recounts how the two men met at James II's court and challenged one another to a gentlemen's wager over who could host the finest breakfast feast the following morning. In spite of his attempt to rig the bet, and much to his chagrin, Sinclair was

---

12   Ibid., no. 836.
13   Ibid. Clouston translates *Scotis siluestribus* as 'Scottish caterans' in *REO*, no. xxiii. 'Ketherans', the English form of the Gaelic *ceatharn*, were those Highland and Island militants 'involved in raids and the imposition of "unjust" exactions' (Boardman 2012, 233-34). According to the Lowland chronicler Walter Bower, 'among the Highland Scots and Wild Scots, there are caterans, which we call ketherans' (*ac etiam inter Scotos transalpinos et silvestres quos catervanos seo ketheranos vocamus*). *Scotichronicon*, 48-49; MacGregor 2007, 23.
14   *DN* v, no. 827.
15   *History*, 36-37.

outdone by MacDonald's venison spread.[16] Outraged, Sinclair asked MacDonald whether he imagined he could equal Sinclair in power and authority. McDonald replied that even his son could outmatch Sinclair and, to prove the point, would be dispatched to harass the Orkney earl's lands just as soon as they departed the king's court. Agreeing to the challenge, the two went their separate ways, presumably to make arrangements for what would become a bloody interfamilial feud. The account goes on to describe the manner in which MacDonald's son, Austin (also known as Hugh MacDonald of Sleat), together with all the 'young heritors of land', steered their galleys toward Orkney, soundly trumping the comparatively weak Orcadian opposition.[17] Having claimed victory, the war party ravaged Orkney, for it was 'the only reward they had for their pains and fatigue'.[18]

This McDonald account is captivating, but unfortunately from a dubious source. Composed by family genealogist Hugh MacDonald over a century after the events occurred, it displays features of bias one expects to find in early-modern clan histories, including its categorical celebration of clan patrons and the degradation of their enemies.[19] Sinclair is portrayed as a cheat and braggart and common Orcadians as 'no great warriors, whatever their gentry'.[20] The most unconvincing aspect is its erroneous assertion that a retainer, Murdo MacCotter, singlehandedly slew the Orkney earl.[21] In fact, Sinclair lived well into his seventies, and, according to the letters from 1461, was not in Orkney at the time of the attacks, but at court with young King James III in Scotland.[22] It is also noteworthy that Alexander MacDonald, and not one of his sons, is portrayed as Sinclair's principal adversary. It is unclear as to which of MacDonald's sons he intended to pit against Sinclair

---

16 Lachlane MacLean supposedly prepared MacDonald's winning breakfast (Ibid., 36), and was later granted the Isle of Tirie (Ibid., 37), seemingly in remuneration. For MacLean as 'vassals of the lords of the Isles', see e.g. MacLean 1899, 39-55.

17 *History*, 37.

18 Ibid.

19 Petre points out that MacDonald's account intended to substantiate the claim of his particular branch of the MacDonald line (Glann Ùisdean) as rightful heritors of the lordship of the Isles and contested estates (Petre 2015, 604). For the source's provenance, see MacGregor 2002, 212; Cameron 2014, 148.

20 *History*, 37.

21 Ibid. MacCotter supposedly belonged to MacLeod of Harris' retinue and later became MacLean's standard-bearer (Ibid.), seemingly in recognition of his service.

22 *DN* v, nos. 827, 836.

when he first proposed the feud. Was it his presumed successor to the earldom and lordship, John, or his illegitimate son and the purported leader of the Orkney raid, Hugh MacDonald of Sleat? The letters from 1461 make no mention of Alexander or Hugh, mentioning only John MacDonald and his unnamed warriors.[23]

Although replete with narrative liberties, couched within the source are select details that will be readdressed below. We can, however, conclude it implausible that such extensive and long-term violence arose from a boastful dispute over breakfast-hosting talents. More structural, practical explanations have to be considered. One possibility is that MacDonald was reviving unmet political aspirations in the Norse island province. As Earl of Ross, MacDonald's attacks may have functioned as leverage in his campaign of encroachment in the north, reinvigorating a political campaign first championed by William III in the mid-fourteenth century.[24] However, without any indication that MacDonald staked claim to land, title, or office in the Norse isles, it seems improbable that the fifteen-century raids sought to revive Ross' fourteenth-century aspirations.

It is plausible that the raids were, as the MacDonald family history purports, by-products of a distinctly inner-Scottish struggle. However, personal pride was likely a secondary matter in the MacDonald-Sinclair feud, which almost certainly entailed matters of land, title, and influence in Scottish politics. Like his father, John MacDonald maintained an uneasy, and at times openly hostile, relationship with the Stewart kingship of Scotland, a stance in opposition to that taken by Sinclair.[25] Whilst MacDonald's alliance with the Earls of Douglas and Crawford in the 1450s positioned him as the most formidable adversary to royal authority in the north of the kingdom, Sinclair proved himself a stanch

---

23 Ibid., no. 827.
24 William III of Ross sought a foothold in Caithness and then Orkney through the promotion of his then-protégés, the Sinclairs of Rosslyn, in the mid-fourteenth century, although these plans failed to materialise (Crawford 2013, 319-20).
25 See e.g. *ALI*, lxiv–lxx; Nicholson 2014. The fifteenth-century Lords of the Isles 'to all intents and purposes, [ruled] autonomously over what was arguably the most successful regional lordship to have been created in late medieval Britain and Ireland' (Petre 2015, 601). See also Boardman 2013, 152. Cf. Bannerman 1977, 214-15, which argues that the lords were not geared toward 'establishing a separatist state in the west'.

supporter of the Stewart house.[26] His grant of the earldom of Caithness in 1455 further anchored royal power at the northern fringes of the kingdom.[27] Hugh MacDonald, the illegitimate half-brother of the earl and supposed commander of the amphibious raid, had aspirations to land and power in Sinclair's Scottish patrimony and may have been responsible for inciting the MacDonald-Sinclair feud.[28] Both of the Orkney letters report that Sinclair was using these Scottish lands as a staging point for his struggle with MacDonald, with the baillies and burgesses explaining that the earl was 'wisely engaged in his earldom of Caithness and elsewhere in putting a stop to malicious and savage attacks of these cruel enemies' (*in comitatu suo Cathtanie et alibi inimicorum crudelium maliciosis et seuissimis propositis sagaciter obuiando*).[29] The letters also make clear that Sinclair was attending to his duties as guardian of the future James III during his 'tender years' (*teneris annis*) of minority, a post which MacDonald had aspired to but failed to secure.[30]

From this background, it is not difficult to understand MacDonald's reason for these actions against Orkney. Although Sinclair was not on the isles at the time, MacDonald must have envisioned a scenario in which devastation of Sinclair's lands to the north, and the resulting petitions for peace by the native inhabitants, would incapacitate the Orkney earl or otherwise compel him to relinquish his aspirations to power in northern Scotland.[31] For all its embellishments, the claim made by MacDonald's seventeenth-century historian, that the devastation in Orkney could be traced back to the political posturing of rival magnates within Scotland, seems to have some credence.

HEBRIDEAN RAIDING IN ORKNEY – A LEGACY OF VIOLENCE

For all their finite strategic value, MacDonald's amphibious attacks reflected a longer tradition of foreign aggression toward Orkney in the

---

26   For the alliance between Douglas and Crawford, and a review of pertinent scholarship, see Petre 2015, 609-12. For Sinclair and the Stewart kings, see e.g. Crawford 2013, 356-65; Macdougall 2009, 41-42.
27   Crawford 2013, 358-59.
28   Boardman 2006, 176, 197n39.
29   *DN* v, no. 827.
30   *DN* v, no. 836. On Sinclair and James III's minority see Boardman 2006, 174-79; Macdougall 2009, 40-41.
31   Boardman 2006, 176. MacDonald raids also facilitated an aimed alliance with Yorkist England (Petre 2015, 627).

later Middle Ages. In 1312, Robert I, King of Scots, and Hákon V, King of Norway, settled damages relating to attacks in and around Orkney by unnamed 'malefactors of Scotland', a group of rogues of whom the Scottish king claimed no prior knowledge.[32] The early-fifteenth-century *Genealogy of Orkney's Earls*, compiled by Bishop Thomas Tulloch, relates that Henry I, Earl of Orkney, was 'for the defence of the country slain there cruelly by his enemies' (*pro defencione patrie mihi crudeliter ab inimiciciis peremptus est*).[33] Historians have posited that the incursion, likely occurring sometime around 1400, was led by misguided English fishermen seeking retribution for attacks by Scottish pirates.[34] Another excerpt from that document recounts how the isles long suffered the 'hostilities and wars of certain rivals and enemies' (*hostilitatis tempore et guerrarum emulorum inimicorumque nonnullorum*)[35] and that the 'principal and special house of mansion of the lord earls' had often been reduced to nothing as the whole country was laid waste by rivals and enemies.[36] While the adversaries cannot be conclusively identified, the bishop's description suggests that they included foreigners.

One source that suggests that Hebridean aggression in Orkney long predated the MacDonald raids is the so-called *Complaint of the People of Orkney*, a catalogue of grievances against their governor, David Menzies of Weem, and his mismanagement of public office.[37] One complaint concerned Menzies' depraved indifference to attacks by certain 'Wild-Scots' (*Willeschotta*) on the island of Ronaldsay. The men of the island claimed that 'the Wild-Scots came in such numbers to them and did them great injury to their goods, meat, and drink and much other mischief' (*the Willeschotta komo swa marghe thil them oc giordo them stoor skada oppa there gotz maat oc dryk oc mykit annat fortreet*).[38]

Who were these marauders? As a proper noun, the term 'Wild-Scots' pertained not to just unruly interlopers with Scottish origins, but to a finite variety of Scots with supposedly identifiably uncultivated

---

32   *DN* ii, no. 114.
33   *DN* xx, no. 833.
34   Thomson 2008a, 170.
35   *DN* xx, no. 833.
36   Ibid.
37   *DN* ii, no. 691.
38   Ibid.

characteristics.[39] The Norse term corresponds to the phraseology used by English and Lowland Scots authors to describe the people of the Highlands, Western Isles, and Ireland.[40] The thirteen-century Bartholomeus Anglicus described what he saw as inherent differences between the 'wild men' (*silvestres*) to the north, the Scots and Irish, and their more civilised counterparts in England.[41] The concept of a natural dichotomy between the cultivated, law-abiding, Germanic-speaking Lowlanders and the barbaric, larcenous, Gaelic-speaking people of the Highlands and Scotland's western seaboard islands was elaborated famously by John of Fordun. He described the latter as 'a wild and untamed race, primitive and independent, given to rapine and the easy life' (*ferina gens est et indomita, rudis et immorigerata, raptu capax, otium diligens, ingenio docilis et callida*).[42] By the early-fifteenth century, 'Wild Scot' had become the term used in discriminatory discourse about Highlanders and Hebrideans, as is witnessed in the works of, for example, Walter Bower (*Scotos transalpinos et silvestres quos catervanos seo ketheranos*),[43] John Major (*Scoti Silvestres et insulani Scoti*),[44] and Andrew of Wyntoun (*wyld, wykkyd Heland-men*).[45] Orkney's social and linguistic ties to Scotland in the fifteenth century appear to have been forged primarily with the Lowlands, and numerous sources demonstrate Orcadians' adoption of the 'Teutonic' Scots tongue that Fordun associated with civilised Scotland. Accustomed to cultural prejudices of the Lowlands, the men of Ronaldsay appear to have invoked an established stereotype of Highland Scots when describing their attackers.

Bishop Thomas used similar terminology in 1461 when he reported that MacDonald's force included 'men from Sudor, Ireland, and the Scottish wildlands' (*Sodorensibus Ybernensibus et Scotis siluestribus*).[46] The 'Scottish wildland', from which the latter group originated, was presumably the same peripheral region of northern and western

---

39   Previously, the description was not regarded as a proper noun, but as an adjective for certain Scots from Caithness (Imsen 2012, 20). I argued against this in Grohse 2014b, 174-76.
40   Nicholson 1968; MacGregor 2007; Broun 2007; Boardman 2007.
41   MacGregor 2007, 22-23.
42   *Chronica*, 42.
43   *Scotichronicon*, 48-49.
44   *Historia*, 13.
45   *Orygynale Cronykil*, 55.
46   *DN* v, no. 836.

Scotland which Fordun and other Lowland commentators associated with the wild Gaels. Given the parallel phraseology between the different fourteenth and fifteenth-century sources, there is little doubt that the Wild-Scots of the 1420s were of the same stock as the *Scoto transalpinos et silvestres* described in Lowland sources and the *hominibus Scotis sylvestribus* who re-emerged in Orkney around 1460.

The bishop's mention of MacDonalds' 'men from Ireland' (*hominibus Ybernensibus*) illustrates the impressive scope of his lordship at the time.[47] MacDonald's connection to Ulster built upon centuries of acculturation and political interaction across the Irish Sea, bonds which were manifest in the MacDonalds' lordship over the glens of Antrim.[48] The other named participants, the 'men from the Sudors' (*hominibus Sodorensibus*), likely originated from the inner-Hebridean caput of MacDonald's island lordship.[49] It is tempting to identify the Hebrideans with those mentioned in Hugh MacDonald's family history, including Hugh MacDonald of Sleat and William MacLeod of Harris.[50] A charter from June 28, 1449, brings the two figures' interrelations into close focus when it shows MacDonald granting Sleat in Skye to his *frater carnilis*, Hugh, a transfer to which MacLeod (*Willielmus Macleod de Glenelg*) bore witness.[51] Beyond filial associations, enfeoffment of this kind, both here and in further subdelegations of land, must have underpinned the cultivation of MacDonald's forces, a point which may find expression in the seventeenth-century claim that the Orkney raids were conducted largely by 'young heritors of land'.[52]

Taken together, the evidence is strong that the Hebridean raids on Orkney around 1460 were rooted in a tradition of aggression stemming from within the Lordship of the Isles. Hostilities may have elevated to a new level under John MacDonald, but he was not the first of his ilk to

---

47   Ibid.
48   On MacDonald and Ireland, see Kingston 2004; Petre 2015, 606, 608. The MacDonald family history underscores the connection to Antrim in Ulster, claiming 'he had as strong a country as any in Ireland, to protect him from the pursuit of his enemies, the seven proportions of the glens being his property; at the same time he was much more beloved in Ireland than the king of Scots, for generally those Irish were not very obedient to the Crown of England, [and] cared very little for that of Scotland [...]' (*History*, 44).
49   Caldwell 2008.
50   *History*, 37.
51   Burke 1838, 477.
52   *History*, 37.

lead an amphibious assault on the Northern Isles. MacDonald's actions cannot be explained as merely expressions of a personal feud or even as a specific political struggle between himself (or his kinsmen) and the Sinclair earl of Orkney in the mid-fifteenth century.

Accusations of plunder are common throughout the Orcadian reports. The men of Ronaldsay's claim that Wild-Scots 'did them great injury to their goods, meat, and drink' (*stoor skada oppa there gotz maat oc dryk oc mykit annat fortreet*)[53] is echoed in the bishop's accusation that MacDonald's forces 'carried away with them goods, animals, utensils, jewels, money, and everything they could for their own use, leaving little or nothing except the burnt soil of the earth, empty and useless' (*depopularunt catalla animalia vtensilia jocalia nummisma et generaliter omnia bona depredarunt secum ad propria deferentes nichil vel parum reliquerunt nisi solum terre combustum vacuum et inane*).[54] Even in the flattering MacDonald family history, the attackers are said to have 'ravaged the country' and 'loaded their galleys', excusing their piracy as a just reward for their exhaustion.[55] The burgesses and baillies of Kirkwall claimed that MacDonald's raiders also attacked Shetland.[56] Although Shetland was not part of Sinclair's grant from the Norwegian king, the conditions of his installation charter as earl from 1434 stipulated that he was to protect those islands.[57] Whether MacDonald knew of this arrangement appears to have been of no consequence for his raiders looking for spoils of war.

In each of the fifteenth-century accounts, the people of Orkney are portrayed as beleaguered victims. The burgesses and baillies call them 'poverty-stricken' (*pauperculis*),[58] and the bishop excuses himself from visiting royal court because of his 'extreme, prevalent poverty' (*nimia vigens paupertas*).[59] Although perhaps embellished to inspire sympathy from the Norwegian king, such claims reflect what was a true economic stagnation in late medieval Orkney.[60] The *Complaint* from the 1420s reports that 'the country was plagued that grain would not grow' (*landit*

---

53   *DN* ii, no. 691.
54   *DN* v, no. 836.
55   *History*, 37.
56   *DN* v, no. 827.
57   *NgL* 2r, i, no. 74.
58   *DN* v, no. 827.
59   Ibid., no. 836.
60   Grohse 2014c, 313.

war plagat thet kornit wæxte eke),[61] and modern studies of cadastral surveys from the late-fifteenth century reveal the wasting of large swaths of land.[62] While MacDonald's raids certainly did not cause the Orcadian recession, they no doubt increased the suffering associated with them. Beyond poverty, Orkney was militarily ill-equipped to resist the amphibious attacks. While the MacDonald family history may exaggerate the Orcadians' incompetence in combat, theirs was a far less militarised society than that of their western adversaries.[63] Of the native members of the knightly class, few appear to have wielded any physical authority in practice as witnessed, for instance, in the rapid and forceful suppression of the Orcadians by their corrupt governor, David Menzies of Weem, and his small band of foreign retainers in the 1420s.[64]

This is in stark contrast to the militant milieu from which the raiders emerged. The Lordship of the Isles was, in the fifteenth-century, a 'tremendous military and naval might, being able to muster highly mobile forces, which could number several thousands of men, and keep them in the field for considerable periods'.[65] The so-called *Roll-Call of the Isles*, compiled roughly a century after the attacks in question, provides a rough impression of the scale of forces amassable from the Hebrides alone.[66] While the 6,990 men available from the Hebrides, including 2,300 elite mercenary 'gallowglasses', probably exceed the number available to MacDonald in the fifteenth century, his forces would have been substantial.[67] In 1437, Alexander MacDonald is reported to have commanded an island contingent of 3,000 men.[68] Within the maritime environs of western and northern Scotland, the lords depended on an amphibious style of warfare, using galleys, including the *luing* and *birlinn*, which 'were little different from the craft in which Vikings had operated'.[69] If the scale and technology of Highland and Island forces threatened political and military instability within the Scottish kingdom,

---

61 *DN* ii, no. 691.
62 Thomson 2008b, 101-17.
63 Grohse 2014b. Military features in late medieval Orkney served the purposes of social structuring more than practical defence, particular with regard to the peasant population and landed aristocracy.
64 Ibid., 179.
65 Petre 2015, 617. See also Kingston 2004, 172-201; Boardman 2012.
66 Skene 1880, 428-40.
67 Kingston 2004, 184.
68 *History*, 45.
69 Kingston 2004, 188. See also MacInnes 1972; Rixson 1995.

the perceived 'militarism' of their societies engendered in contemporary observers a sense of fear and disdain for the 'caterans', a pejorative label with strongly military connotations.[70]

What recourse, if any, did the Orcadians have to stop these attacks? It is interesting that the letters from 1460 and 1461 are not petitions for help from their king, Christian I. In each case, the writers show great faith in the abilities of their earl to quell the assaults. The burgesses and baillies claim that 'for our defence in the aforementioned, he [Sinclair] has laid out himself and his in our deadly struggle to his no small suffering and loss, bearing the expenses, labours, and dangers of war, principally for the sake of the honour of your [Christian I's] excellence' (*ob nostri defensionem a premissis de nostro letali conflictu finali detrimento apparente compaciens signanter propter vestre excellencie honorem ad guerras expensas labores et pericula*). They add that the Orcadians would have already been utterly destroyed by the sword, had it not been for 'his presence and defence' (*presencia et defensione*).[71] Bishop Thomas echoed these sentiments, elaborating that he was confident in Sinclair's ability to halt MacDonald 'by way of treaty or otherwise' (*per concordiam uel cessas(s)ent alias*).[72]

The faith placed in Sinclair by Orkney's administrators is remarkable given his apparent absence from the isles during the MacDonald raids. By Orcadian standards, he was indeed a formidable martial leader. His strength was promoted by the Norwegian king's grant of the earldom, which stipulated his obligation to serve the crown when called upon and engross his own retinue for the defence of Orkney and Shetland.[73] To do this, he was permitted to command Kirkwall Castle and enlist his 'kinsmen, friends and servants' (*propinquorum amicorum et seruitorum*) from beyond the border in Scotland in defence of the isles.[74] The question is whether this theoretical strength was employed for the practical defence of the Norse province. In fact, Sinclair's military exploits were more prolific in mainland Scotland than they ever were in Orkney. In 1455, Sinclair was entrusted by James II to accompany 'the great bumbard', perhaps the famous Mons Meg, in the siege on the

---

70   Boardman 2012, 233-34.
71   *DN* v, no. 827.
72   Ibid., no. 836.
73   *NgL* 2r, no. 74.
74   Ibid.

Douglas stronghold of Threave.[75] As capable a martial leader as he may have been, Sinclair is not known to have demonstrated his prowess north of the Pentland Firth, and is not in fact recorded as being present in the isles after 1439, suggesting that he essentially left the civilians of the isles unshielded from the raids of his formidable adversaries.[76]

CONCLUSION

The preceding aimed to shed light on a legacy of Hebridean seaborne aggression in and around the Northern Isles in the late Middle Ages. MacDonald's raids in Orkney have previously been treated as part of the burgeoning political struggle between the Stewart crown's adherents and adversaries. Although not opposed to these views, the preceding sought to demonstrate that the expression of that rivalry in Orkney in and around 1461 was predicated upon a more endemic tradition of Hebridean hostility. For decades, perhaps centuries, so-called 'Wild-Scots' from the Highlands and islands along Scotland's western seaboards sailed to Orkney with piratical aims. Whilst personal feuds and underlying political agendas presumably heightened the tenor of hostility, the raids – from the perspective of the Orcadians who suffered under them – were essentially acts of plunder carried out by a malicious and untamed society to the west.

The raiders along Orkney's shores were borne of a highly militarised Hebridean society. Recruiting from their far-flung power base, which stretched from Ross to the Glens of Northern Ireland, the MacDonald Lords of the Isles preserved their autonomy and enhanced their power by commanding grand fleets and scores of combatants driven by the prospect of spoils. The emergence of these amphibious warriors upon the western horizons must have struck fear into the hearts of Orkney's inhabitants, who appear to have long since lost touch with the fighting spirit of their Viking forebears. Their only recourse, it seems, lay with their earl, William Sinclair, a functionary who devoted less energy to the isles' defence than he invested in pursuing his own, self-serving agendas on the Scottish mainland.

---

75   Thomson 2008a, 194.
76   Grohse 2014b, 78. The weakness of Norse frontier defences lay in the endowment of earls 'with almost exclusive power to orchestrate defense', thus predisposing 'the frontier communities to the strengths and weakness of a handful of fallible individuals'.

Returning to the points raised at the outset of this chapter, the reader might ask whether the term 'Viking' serves any function – save sensationalism – for the study of northern Britain in the late medieval period. Andrew Jennings, for one, is willing to employ it to the describe MacDonald's raids on Orkney, the contemporary reports of which read much like a 'monastic account of a Viking raid 500 years earlier'.[77] Indeed, if we divorce ourselves from the historiographic construct that is the 'Viking Age', we can appreciate fundamental commonalities between the seaborne exploits of Norsemen of the early medieval period and those of their Gaelic successors of Western Scotland in the late Middle Ages. For central medieval observers, the concept was largely void of ethnolinguistic connotations, but pertained principally to a lifestyle of maritime adventure in which seaborne raids created opportunities to enhance the raiders' prestige, enrich them materially, and compel compliance from their victims. The nature of the fifteenth-century raids on Orkney, which featured pillage and plunder, and the sudden amphibious retreat of the perpetrators, gives the impression that 'Wild Scots' from the west had, for lack of a contemporary phrase, gone 'a-viking'. For Orkney, a community once founded upon the exploits of famous raiders, many of whom sought fortune in the Hebrides and Northern Ireland in the early and central Middle Ages, the destructive raids on their own turf of the late medieval period were a bitter twist of fate.

BIBLIOGRAPHY

PRIMARY SOURCES

Acts of the Lords of the Isles, 1336-1493, Munro J and Munro R (eds), 1986, Edinburgh: Scottish History Society.
Chronica Gentis Scotorum, Skene W (ed), 1871, vol. i, Edinburgh: Edmonston and Douglas.
Diplomatarium Norwegicum, Lange C et al. (eds), 1849-1995, 21 vols, Christiania and Oslo.
Historia Majoris Britanniae, tam Angliae quam Scotiae, 1740, Edinburgh.
History of the MacDonalds. MacPhail J (ed), in *Highland Papers*, 1914, vol. i, Edinburgh: Scottish History Society.

---

77   Jennings 2013, 36.

q*Norges gamle Love. Anden Række 1388-1604*, Taranger A et al. (eds), 1904-1995, Christiania and Oslo.

The Orygynale Cronykil of Scotland, Laing D (ed), 1879, vol. iii, Edinburgh: William Patterson.

Records of the Earldom of Orkney, 1299-1614, Clouston J S (ed), 1914, Edinburgh: Scottish History Society.

Scotichronicon, MacQueen, J, MacQueen W, and Watt D (eds), 1993, vol. i, Aberdeen: Aberdeen University Press.

SECONDARY SOURCES

Bannerman, J 1977, 'The Lordship of the Isles', in J Brown (ed), *Scottish Society in the 15th Century*, New York: St Martin's, 209-40.

Beuermann, I 2007, *Masters of the Narrow Sea: Forgotten Challenges to Norwegian Rule in Man and the Isles, 1079-1266*, Oslo: Universitetet i Oslo.

Beuermann, I 2011, 'Jarla Sǫgur Orkneyja: Status and Power of the Earls of Orkney According to their Sagas' in G Steinsland, J V Sigurðsson, J Rekdal, and I Beuermann (eds), *Ideology and Power in the Viking and Middle Ages: Scandinavia, Iceland, Ireland, Orkney and the Faeroes*, Leiden: Brill, 109-62.

Boardman, S 2006, *The Campbells 1250-1513*, Edinburgh: Birlinn.

Boardman, S 2007, 'The Gaelic World in the Early Stewart Court', in D Broun and M MacGregor (eds), *Mìorun Mòr nan Gall, 'The Great Ill-Will of the Lowlander'? Lowland Perceptions of the Highlands, Medieval and Modern*, Glasgow: Centre for Scottish and Celtic Studies, 83-109.

Boardman, S 2012, 'Highland Scots and Anglo-Scottish Warfare, c.1300-1513', in A King and D Simpkin (eds), *England and Scotland at War, c.1296-c.1513*, Leiden: Brill, 231-53.

Boardman, S 2013, 'The Lost World: Post-Medieval Accounts of the Lordship of the Isles', in S Duffy and S Foran (eds), *The English Isles: Cultural Transmission and Political Conflict in Britain and Ireland, 1100–1500*, Dublin: Four Courts, 151–74.

Broun, D 2007, 'Attitudes of Gall to Gaedhel in Scotland before John of Fordun', in D Broun and M MacGregor (eds), *Mìorun Mòr nan Gall, 'The Great Ill-Will of the Lowlander'? Lowland Perceptions of the Highlands, Medieval and Modern*. Glasgow: Centre for Scottish and Celtic Studies, 49-82.

Burke, J 1838, *A Genealogical and Heraldic History of the Landed Gentry*, London: Henry Colburn.

Caldwell, D 2008, *Islay: The Land of the Lordship*, Edinburgh: Birlinn.

Cameron, S 2014, '"Contumaciously Absent"? The Lords of the Isles and the Scottish Crown', in R Oram (ed), *Lordship of the Isles*, Leiden: Brill, 146-75.

Clouston, J S 1932, *A History of Orkney*, Kirkwall: WR Mackintosh.

Cowan, E 1990, 'Norwegian Sunset – Scottish Dawn: Hakon IV and Alexander III', N Reid (ed), *Scotland in the Reign of Alexander III*, Edinburgh: John Donald, 103-31.

Crawford, B 1969, 'The pawning of Orkney and Shetland: a reconsideration of the events of 1460-9', *Scottish Historical Review* 48, 35-53.

Crawford, B 1987, *Scandinavian Scotland*, Leicester: Leicester University Press.

Crawford, B 2013. *The Northern Earldoms: Orkney and Caithness from AD 870 to 1470*, Edinburgh: Birlinn.

Forte, A, R Oram, and F Pedersen 2005, *Viking Empires*, Cambridge: Cambridge University Press.

Grant, A 1988, 'Scotland's "Celtic Fringe" in the Late Middle Ages: The MacDonald Lords of the Isles and the Kingdom of Scotland', in R Davis (ed), *The British Isles 1100-1500: Comparisons, Contrasts and Connections*, Edinburgh: John Donald, 118-41.

Grohse, I 2013, 'From Asset in War to Asset in Diplomacy: Orkney in the Medieval Realm of Norway', *Island Studies Journal* 8:2, 255-68.

Grohse, I 2014a, 'Medieval Maritime Diplomacy: The Case of Norwegian-Scottish Relations ca. 1266-1468/69', *International Journal of Maritime History* 26:3, 512-28.

Grohse, I 2014b, 'Defending Country and Realm: Military Features of the Norse-Scottish Frontier', in S Imsen (ed), *Rex Insularum. The King of Norway and His Tributary Lands as a Political System c.1260-1450*, Bergen: Fagbokforlaget, 163-80.

Grohse, I 2014c, 'Orknøyene og Norgesveldet: Økonomisk eller politisk avhengighet?', *Heimen* 51, 307-18.

Imsen, S 2012, 'The Country of Orkney and the Complaints against David Menzies', *New Orkney Antiquarian Journal* 6, 9-33.

Jennings, A 2013, 'Latter-day Vikings: Gaels in the Northern Isles in the 16th Century', *Across the Sólundarhaf: Connections between Scotland and the Nordic World. Selected Papers from the Inaugural St. Magnus Conference 2011. Journal of the North Atlantic* 4 (spec. vol.), 35-42.

Kingston, S 2004, *Ulster and the Isles in the Fifteenth Century. The Lordship of the Clann Domhmaill of Antrim*, Dublin: Four Courts.

McDonald, R 1998, *The Kingdom of the Isles: Scotland's Western Seaboard c.1100-c.1336*, East Linton: Tuckwell.

Macdougall, N 2000, 'Achilles' Heel? The Earldom of Ross, the Lordship of the Isles, and the Stewart kings, 1449–1507', in E Cowan and R A McDonald (eds), *Alba: Celtic Scotland in the Middle Ages*, East Linton: Tuckwell, 248–75.

Macdougall, N 2009, *James III*, Edinburgh: John Donald.

MacGregor, M 2002, 'The Genealogical Histories of Gaelic Scotland', in A Fox and D Woolf (eds), *The Spoken Word: Oral Culture in Britain, 1500-1850*, Manchester: Manchester University Press, 196-239.

MacGregor, M 2007, 'Gaelic Barbarity and Scottish Identity in the Later Middle Ages', in D Broun and M MacGregor (eds), *Mìorun Mòr nan Gall, 'The Great Ill-Will of the Lowlander'? Lowland Perceptions of the Highlands, Medieval and Modern*. Glasgow: Centre for Scottish and Celtic Studies, 7-48.

MacInnes, J 1972, 'West Highland Sea Power in the Middle Ages', *Transactions of the Gaelic Society of Inverness* 48, 518-56.

MacLean, J 1899, *A History of the Clan MacLean: From Its First Settlement at Duard Castle, in the Isles of Mull, to the Present Period*, Cincinnati: R. Clark.

Macniven, A 2014, *The Vikings in Islay: The Place of Names in Hebridean Settlement History*, Edinburgh: Birlinn.

Nicholson, L 2014, 'From the River Farrar to the Loire Valley: The MacDonald Lord of the Isles, the Scottish Crown, and International Diplomacy, 1428-1438', in R Oram (ed), *Lordship of the Isles*, Leiden: Brill, 88–100.

Nicholson, R 1968, 'Domesticated Scots and Wild Scots: the relationship between Lowlanders and Highlanders in medieval Scotland', in *Proceedings of the First Colloquium on Scottish Studies* (University of Guelph), Guelph, 1–16.

Ó Corráin, D 1997, 'Ireland, Wales, Man and the Hebrides', in P Sawyer (ed), *The Oxford Illustrated History of the Vikings*, Oxford: Oxford University Press, 83-109.

Oram, R (ed) 2014, *Lordship of the Isles*, Leiden: Brill.

Petre, J 2015, 'Donald Balloch, the "Treaty of Ardtornish-Westminster" and the MacDonald raids of 1461-3', *Historical Research* 88, 599-628.

Rixson, D 1995, *The West Highland Galley*, Edinburgh: Birlinn.

Sigurðsson, J V and T Bolton (eds) 2014, *Celtic-Norse Relationships in the Irish Sea in the Middle Ages 800-1200*, Leiden: Brill.

Skene, W 1880, *Celtic Scotland: A History of Ancient Alban*, vol. iii, Edinburgh: David Douglas.

Somerville, A and R A McDonald (eds) 2013, *The Viking Age: A Reader*, Toronto: University of Toronto Press.

Thomson, W 2008a, *The New History of Orkney*, Edinburgh: Birlinn.

Thomson, W 2008b, *Orkney Land and People*, Kirkwall: The Orcadian Limited.